Global Economic Prospects

A World Bank Group
Flagship Report

JUNE 2021

Global
Economic
Prospects

 **WORLD BANK GROUP**

Summary of Contents

Contents

Acknowledgments

This World Bank Group Flagship Report is a product of the Prospects Group in the Equitable Growth, Finance and Institutions (EFI) Vice Presidency. The project was managed by M. Ayhan Kose and Franziska Ohnsorge.

Global and regional surveillance work was coordinated by Carlos Arteta. The report was prepared by a team that included John Baffes, Justin-Damien Guénette, Jongrim Ha, Osamu Inami, Alain Kabundi, Sergiy Kasyanenko, Sinem Kilic Celik, Gene Kindberg-Hanlon, Patrick Kirby, Peter Nagle, Cedric Okou, Lucia Quaglietti, Franz Ulrich Ruch, Naotaka Sugawara, Ekaterine Vashakmadze, Dana Vorisek, Collette Wheeler, and Takefumi Yamazaki.

Research assistance was provided by Damien Boucher, Dhruv Devesh Gandhi, Hrisyana Doytchinova, Arika Kayastha, Maria Hazel Macadangdang, Muneeb Ahmad Naseem, Julia Roseman Norfleet, Vasiliki Papagianni, Lorëz Qehaja, Shijie Shi, Kaltrina Temaj, Anh Van Le, Jingran Wang, Xinyue Wang, Jinxin Wu, and Juncheng Zhou. Modeling and data work were provided by Rajesh Kumar Danda and Shijie Shi.

Online products were produced by Graeme Littler. Alejandra Viveros managed communications and media outreach with a team that included Mark Felsenthal, Mikael Reventar, and extensive support from the World Bank's media and digital communications staffs. Graeme Littler provided editorial support, with contributions from Adriana Maximiliano.

The print publication was produced by Adriana Maximiliano, in collaboration with Luiz Almeida, Andrew Charles Berghauser, Cindy A. Fisher, Michael Harrup, Maria Hazel Macadangdang, and Jewel McFadden.

Regional projections and write-ups were produced in coordination with country teams, country directors, and the offices of the regional chief economists.

Many reviewers provided extensive advice and comments. The analysis also benefited from comments and suggestions by staff members from World Bank Group country teams and other World Bank Group Vice Presidencies as well as Executive Directors in their discussion of the report on June 1, 2021. However, both forecasts and analysis are those of the World Bank Group staff and should not be attributed to Executive Directors or their national authorities.

Foreword

Following last year's collapse, the global economy is experiencing an exceptionally strong but uneven recovery. While advanced economies are rebounding, many of the world's poorest countries are being left behind, and much remains to be done to reverse the pandemic's staggering human and economic costs. Moreover, the recovery is not assured: the possibility remains that additional COVID-19 waves, further vaccination delays, mounting debt levels, or rising inflationary pressures deliver setbacks.

The near-term resumption of growth cannot make up for the misery that the pandemic has inflicted on the poorest and its disproportionate impact on vulnerable groups, including women, school-age children, and informal and unskilled workers, which has widened inequality. As this edition of the *Global Economic Prospects* highlights, the uneven recovery underscores the need for a forceful policy effort to address multiple near- and long-term challenges. This policy response requires speedy action from governments, the private sector, and the international community.

First and foremost, expanding vaccine distribution and deployment, especially to developing countries, is a precondition to economic recovery. This requires overcoming obstacles in procuring and distributing vaccines including by redirecting excess vaccine supplies from some advanced economies to developing countries that have delivery programs in place. This also entails expanding vaccines production, lifting trade restrictions on vaccine inputs, and improving the transparency of vaccine orders, options and delivery schedules.

Attention to debt is another critical task. The last decade saw the largest, fastest, and most broad-based increase in debt levels around the world. The pandemic, which spurred an unprecedented buildup in government debt in many economies, amplified this trend. These developments highlight the importance of careful use of debt-financed spending. In particular, capital needs to

be allowed to flow for productive uses, especially in countries that have implemented large-scale fiscal support. Effective domestic revenue mobilization and robust medium-term fiscal frameworks are essential to widen fiscal space, foster policy credibility, and bolster debt sustainability. Improved debt management and debt transparency are critical components of sound governance.

These challenges are particularly important for low-income countries, half of whom faced debt distress or were at high risk of it even before the pandemic struck. The resources required to service debt—due to high interest rates and elevated debt levels divert funds from investment in health, nutrition, education, and other critical development needs. It will take continued global cooperation—including greater participation by the private sector—to provide debt relief to the poorest countries and fund the investments needed to foster and sustain longer-term growth.

The pandemic not only reversed gains in global poverty reduction for the first time in a generation but also deepened the challenges of food insecurity and rising food prices for many millions of people. This is particularly prevalent among the poorest countries and populations, where higher prices of food can devastate discretionary incomes. As the report highlights, attempts to lower food price inflation through distortionary, opaque price subsidies or protectionist policies could prove to be self-defeating and ultimately lead to higher costs. Instead, measures to scale up social safety net programs would be more helpful. International support to improve logistics and climate resilience of local food supply could also help with longer-term food security.

The post-pandemic recovery presents policy makers with a unique opportunity to steer countries onto a path of green, resilient, and inclusive development. To achieve this, climate and development policies need to be integrated, and incentives aligned to achieve both climate and development goals. Smart climate action includes investing in low carbon and renewable energy sources, improving diagnostics to identify priority areas for greenhouse gas emissions reduction and climate resilience, and prioritizing climate spending to achieve maximum impact. Private investment will be needed to meet green investment needs. An effective and transparent regulatory environment, including an adequate carbon tax policy, are of paramount importance.

For these and other policy objectives, fostering data transparency is essential to guarantee a more efficient allocation of resources. In the context of trade, this is exemplified by the need to enhance information flows among participants of global value chains. Another important avenue to bolster trade is to reduce the costs of cross-border trading. These costs currently double the price of traded goods over domestic goods and far exceed the costs of tariffs alone, and they are particularly high in many developing economies. Measures to lower trade costs include simplifying burdensome border procedures, improving transport infrastructure and governance, enabling greater competition in shipping, logistics, and wholesale and retail trade, lowering trade barriers, and ensuring greater transparency and predictability of trade policy. As the report explores in detail, such actions could help trade—long a key driver of development—become a solid engine of growth again.

How national governments, the private sector, and international institutions respond to the challenges of poverty, inequality, and climate change as we emerge from a crisis that has affected us all will be defining choices of our age. We need to act forcefully to address these challenges and be able to pursue green, resilient, and inclusive development.

David Malpass
President
World Bank Group

Executive Summary

The world economy is experiencing an exceptionally strong but highly uneven recovery. Global growth is set to reach 5.6 percent in 2021—its strongest post-recession pace in 80 years—in part underpinned by steady but highly unequal vaccine access. Growth is concentrated in a few major economies, with most emerging market and developing economies (EMDEs) lagging behind: while about 90 percent of advanced economies are expected to regain their pre-pandemic per capita income levels by 2022, only about one-third of EMDEs are expected to do so. In low-income countries, the effects of the pandemic are reversing earlier gains in poverty reduction and compounding food insecurity and other long-standing challenges. The global outlook remains highly uncertain, with major risks around the path of the pandemic and the possibility of financial stress amid large debt loads. Controlling the pandemic at the global level will require more equitable vaccine distribution, especially for low-income countries. In addition to the necessary efforts to pursue widespread vaccination, policy makers face a difficult balancing act as they seek to nurture the recovery through efficiently allocated fiscal support while safeguarding price stability and fiscal sustainability. Policy makers can also help entrench a lasting recovery by undertaking growth enhancing reforms and steering their economies onto a green, resilient, and inclusive development path. Prominently among the necessary policies are efforts to lower trade costs so that trade can once again become a robust engine of growth.

Global outlook. The global economy is set to expand 5.6 percent in 2021—its strongest post-recession pace in 80 years. This recovery is uneven and largely reflects sharp rebounds in some major economies—most notably the United States, owing to substantial fiscal support—amid highly unequal vaccine access. In many emerging market and developing economies (EMDEs), elevated COVID-19 caseloads, obstacles to vaccination, and a partial withdrawal of macroeconomic support are offsetting some of the benefits of strengthening external demand and elevated commodity prices. By 2022, global output will remain about 2 percent below pre-pandemic projections, and per capita income losses incurred last year will not be fully unwound in about two-thirds of EMDEs. The global outlook remains subject to significant downside risks, which include the possibility of large COVID-19 waves in the context of new virus variants and financial stress amid high EMDE debt levels. Controlling the pandemic at the global level will require more equitable vaccine distribution, especially for low-income countries. The legacies of the pandemic exacerbate the challenges facing policy makers as they balance the need to support the recovery while safeguarding price stability and fiscal sustainability. As the recovery becomes more entrenched,

policy makers also need to continue efforts toward promoting growth-enhancing reforms and steering their economies onto a green, resilient, and inclusive development path.

Regional Prospects. The recovery in all EMDE regions is expected to be insufficient to reverse the damage from the pandemic. By 2022, output in all regions is expected to remain below pre-pandemic projections, weighed down by the ongoing pandemic and its legacies, which include higher debt loads and damage to many of the drivers of potential output. The recovery in small, tourism-dependent economies is expected to be particularly weak as some travel restrictions will remain in place until the pandemic is brought under control. The pace of vaccine rollout varies across countries, with low-income countries lagging considerably. The recovery is expected to be strongest in East Asia and the Pacific, primarily due to strength in China. In South Asia, India's recovery is being hampered by the largest outbreak of any country since the beginning of the pandemic. In the Middle East and North Africa and Latin America and the Caribbean, the pace of growth in 2021 is expected to be less than the magnitude of the contraction in 2020, while the tepid recovery in Sub-Saharan Africa will make little progress in reversing the increase in extreme poverty caused by the pandemic. In most regions, risks to the outlook are tilted to the downside. All regions remain vulnerable to renewed outbreaks of COVID-19, which could feature variant strains of the virus; financial stress amplified by elevated debt levels; deeper-than-expected scarring from the pandemic; and rising social unrest, potentially triggered by rising food prices.

This edition of *Global Economic Prospects* also includes analytical chapters on policy options for reducing trade costs, so that trade can once again become an engine of growth, and on prospects for inflation as an exceptionally fast global rebound is associated with growing price pressures.

High Trade Costs: Causes and Remedies. As the global economy rebounds from the COVID-19-induced global recession, the accompanying strength in global trade offers an opportunity to jumpstart the recovery in EMDEs. Lowering cross-border trade costs could help revive trade growth. Trade costs are high: on average, they double the cost of internationally traded goods over domestic goods. Tariffs account for only one-fourteenth of average trade costs; the bulk of trade costs are incurred in shipping and logistics as well as cumbersome trade procedures and processes at and behind the border. Despite a decline since 1995, trade costs remain almost one-half higher in EMDEs than in advanced economies; about one-third of the gap may be accounted for by higher shipping and logistics costs and another one-third by trade policy. A comprehensive reform package to lower trade costs would include trade facilitation measures; deeper trade liberalization; efforts to streamline trade processes and clearance requirements; better transport infrastructure; more competition in domestic logistics, retail, and wholesale trade; and less corruption. Some of these measures could yield large dividends: Among the worst-performing EMDEs, a hypothetical reform package to improve logistics performance, maritime connectivity, and border processes to those of the best-performing EMDEs is estimated to halve trade costs.

Emerging Inflation Pressures: Cause for Alarm? After declining in the first half of 2020, global inflation has rebounded quickly on recovering activity. While global inflation is likely to continue rising in the remainder of this year, inflation is expected to remain within target bands in most inflation-targeting countries. Among EMDEs where recent price pressures may raise inflation above their target ranges, they may not warrant a monetary policy response—provided they are temporary and inflation expectations remain well-anchored. However, higher inflation may complicate the policy choices of EMDEs that are in danger of persistently breaching their inflation targets while also relying on expansionary policies to ensure a durable recovery. Measures to strengthen central bank credibility can help anchor inflation expectations in these economies. Unless risks from record-high debt are addressed, EMDEs remain vulnerable to financial market stress should investor risk sentiment deteriorate as a result of actual or perceived inflation pressures in advanced economies. Low-income countries are likely to experience rising aggregate and food price inflation in the remainder of this year, exacerbating food insecurity and threating to increase poverty. Attempts to control food prices through price subsidies in many countries, or the re-emergence of protectionist policies could drive global prices higher and prove to be self-defeating.

Abbreviations

AE	advanced economy
CA	Central Asia
CAPB	cyclically-adjusted primary balance
CE	Central Europe
CEMAC	Central African Economic and Monetary Union
CEPR	Center for Economic and Policy Research
CFA	Financial Community of Africa
CPI	consumer price index
EAP	East Asia and Pacific
ECA	Europe and Central Asia
ECB	European Central Bank
EE	Eastern Europe
EMBI	Emerging Market Bond Index
EMDE	emerging market and developing economy
EU	European Union
FAO	Food and Agriculture Organization of the United Nations
FAVAR	factor-augmented vector autoregression
FDI	foreign direct investment
FSIN	Food Security Information Network
G7	Group of Seven: Canada, France, Germany, Italy, Japan, the United Kingdom, and the United States
GCC	Gulf Cooperation Council
GDP	gross domestic product
GEP	Global Economic Prospects
GFC	global financial crisis
GNFS	goods and nonfactor services
GRID	green, resilient, and inclusive development
IDA	International Development Association
ILO	International Labour Organization
IMF	International Monetary Fund
LAC	Latin America and the Caribbean
LIC	low-income country
MNA/MENA	Middle East and North Africa
MIC	middle-income country
NBER	National Bureau of Economic Research
OECD	Organisation for Economic Co-operation and Development
OPEC	Organization of the Petroleum Exporting Countries
OPEC+	OPEC and Azerbaijan, Bahrain, Brunei Darussalam, Kazakhstan, Malaysia, Mexico, Oman, Russian Federation, Sudan, and South Sudan
PMI	Purchasing Managers' Index
PPP	purchasing power parity
RHS	right-hand scale

RTA	regional trade agreement
SAR	South Asia
SCC	South Caucasus
SDG	Sustainable Development Goal
SSA	Sub-Saharan Africa
TFP	total factor productivity
UN	United Nations
UNCTAD	United Nations Conference on Trade and Development
WAEMU	West African Economic and Monetary Union
WBK	Western Balkans
WFP	World Food Programme

CHAPTER 1

GLOBAL OUTLOOK

The global economy is set to expand 5.6 percent in 2021—its strongest post-recession pace in 80 years. This recovery is uneven and largely reflects sharp rebounds in some major economies—most notably the United States, owing to substantial fiscal support—amid highly unequal vaccine access. In many emerging market and developing economies (EMDEs), elevated COVID-19 caseloads, obstacles to vaccination, and a partial withdrawal of macroeconomic support are offsetting some of the benefits of strengthening external demand and elevated commodity prices. By 2022, global output will remain about 2 percent below pre-pandemic projections, and per capita income losses incurred last year will not be fully unwound in about two-thirds of EMDEs. The global outlook remains subject to significant downside risks, which include the possibility of large COVID-19 waves in the context of new virus variants and financial stress amid high EMDE debt levels. Controlling the pandemic at the global level will require more equitable vaccine distribution, especially for low-income countries. The legacies of the pandemic exacerbate the challenges facing policy makers as they balance the need to support the recovery while safeguarding price stability and fiscal sustainability. As the recovery becomes more entrenched, policy makers also need to continue efforts toward promoting growth-enhancing reforms and steering their economies onto a green, resilient, and inclusive development path.

Summary

Following a 3.5 percent contraction caused by the COVID-19 pandemic in 2020, global economic activity has gained significant momentum; however, it remains well below pre-pandemic projections (figure 1.1.A). Moreover, the recovery is uneven, passing over many poorer countries, and there is considerable uncertainty about its durability.

The ongoing pandemic continues to shape the path for global economic activity, with severe outbreaks continuing to weigh on growth in many countries. The most recent wave of COVID-19 is now centered in some emerging market and developing economies (EMDEs), where more transmissible and virulent strains are spreading and where vaccine access remains limited (figure 1.1.B). Vaccination remains especially feeble in low-income countries (LICs). In contrast, advanced economies have generally seen substantial vaccination progress, which has helped limit the spread of COVID-19.

Amid continued vaccination, economic activity is firming across major advanced economies—most notably in the United States, where the recovery is being powered by substantial fiscal support.

Growth in China remains solid but has moderated as authorities have shifted their focus from buttressing activity to reducing financial stability risks. Many other countries, primarily EMDEs, are experiencing subdued pickups alongside surges of COVID-19 cases, even if recent waves of infections appear to be less disruptive to economic activity than previous ones. Recoveries in fragile and conflict-affected LICs are particularly weak, as the pandemic has exacerbated underlying challenges. Whereas global manufacturing activity has firmed, with industrial production surpassing its pre-pandemic level, services activity—especially travel and tourism—remains soft.

Global financial conditions have tightened somewhat, partly reflecting a rise in U.S. bond yields amid increased inflation pressures. Nevertheless, they remain generally supportive, reflecting continued extraordinary policy accommodation by major central banks. Commodity prices have increased markedly, owing to the improving global outlook as well as commodity-specific supply factors. The recovery in global activity and in commodity prices is contributing to an increase in inflation, especially in some EMDEs that have experienced currency depreciation.

Against this backdrop, global output growth is projected to strengthen to 5.6 percent in 2021—its strongest post-recession pace in 80 years (figure 1.1.C). The recovery is underpinned by steady but highly uneven global vaccination and the associated gradual relaxation of pandemic-control

Note: This chapter was prepared by Carlos Arteta, Justin-Damien Guénette, Patrick Kirby, and Collette Wheeler, with contributions from Lucia Quaglietti, Sergiy Kasyanenko, Gene Kindberg-Hanlon, Peter Nagle, Cedric Okou, and Ekaterine Vashakmadze.

TABLE 1.1 Real GDP[1]

(Percent change from previous year)

Percentage point differences from January 2021 projections

	2018	2019	2020e	2021f	2022f	2023f	2021f	2022f
World	**3.2**	**2.5**	**-3.5**	**5.6**	**4.3**	**3.1**	**1.5**	**0.5**
Advanced economies	**2.3**	**1.6**	**-4.7**	**5.4**	**4.0**	**2.2**	**2.1**	**0.5**
United States	3.0	2.2	-3.5	6.8	4.2	2.3	3.3	0.9
Euro area	1.9	1.3	-6.6	4.2	4.4	2.4	0.6	0.4
Japan	0.6	0.0	-4.7	2.9	2.6	1.0	0.4	0.3
Emerging market and developing economies	**4.6**	**3.8**	**-1.7**	**6.0**	**4.7**	**4.4**	**0.8**	**0.4**
East Asia and Pacific	6.5	5.8	1.2	7.7	5.3	5.2	0.3	0.1
China	6.8	6.0	2.3	8.5	5.4	5.3	0.6	0.2
Indonesia	5.2	5.0	-2.1	4.4	5.0	5.1	0.0	0.2
Thailand	4.2	2.3	-6.1	2.2	5.1	4.3	-1.8	0.4
Europe and Central Asia	3.5	2.7	-2.1	3.9	3.9	3.5	0.6	0.1
Russian Federation	2.8	2.0	-3.0	3.2	3.2	2.3	0.6	0.2
Turkey	3.0	0.9	1.8	5.0	4.5	4.5	0.5	-0.5
Poland	5.4	4.7	-2.7	3.8	4.5	3.9	0.3	0.2
Latin America and the Caribbean	1.8	0.9	-6.5	5.2	2.9	2.5	1.4	0.1
Brazil	1.8	1.4	-4.1	4.5	2.5	2.3	1.5	0.0
Mexico	2.2	-0.2	-8.3	5.0	3.0	2.0	1.3	0.4
Argentina	-2.6	-2.1	-9.9	6.4	1.7	1.9	1.5	-0.2
Middle East and North Africa	0.6	0.6	-3.9	2.4	3.5	3.2	0.3	0.3
Saudi Arabia	2.4	0.3	-4.1	2.4	3.3	3.2	0.4	1.1
Iran, Islamic Rep. [3]	-6.0	-6.8	1.7	2.1	2.2	2.3	0.6	0.5
Egypt, Arab Rep. [2]	5.3	5.6	3.6	2.3	4.5	5.5	-0.4	-1.3
South Asia	6.4	4.4	-5.4	6.8	6.8	5.2	3.6	3.0
India [3]	6.5	4.0	-7.3	8.3	7.5	6.5	2.9	2.3
Pakistan [2]	5.5	2.1	-0.5	1.3	2.0	3.4	0.8	0.0
Bangladesh [2]	7.9	8.2	2.4	3.6	5.1	6.2	2.0	1.7
Sub-Saharan Africa	2.7	2.5	-2.4	2.8	3.3	3.8	0.0	-0.2
Nigeria	1.9	2.2	-1.8	1.8	2.1	2.4	0.7	0.3
South Africa	0.8	0.2	-7.0	3.5	2.1	1.5	0.2	0.4
Angola	-2.0	-0.6	-5.2	0.5	3.3	3.5	-0.4	-0.2
Memorandum items:								
Real GDP[1]								
High-income countries	2.3	1.6	-4.7	5.3	4.0	2.2	2.1	0.5
Developing countries	4.7	3.9	-1.4	6.3	4.8	4.5	0.8	0.4
EMDEs excluding China	3.2	2.4	-4.3	4.4	4.2	3.7	1.0	0.6
Commodity-exporting EMDEs	2.0	1.8	-4.0	3.6	3.3	3.1	0.6	0.0
Commodity-importing EMDEs	6.0	4.9	-0.6	7.3	5.4	5.0	1.0	0.6
Commodity-importing EMDEs excluding China	4.9	3.2	-4.7	5.4	5.3	4.5	1.6	1.2
Low-income countries	4.7	4.3	0.7	2.9	4.7	5.6	-0.5	-0.7
BRICS	5.8	4.9	-0.3	7.5	5.2	4.7	1.1	0.6
World (PPP weights) [4]	3.6	2.8	-3.2	5.7	4.5	3.5	1.4	0.6
World trade volume [5]	**4.2**	**1.2**	**-8.3**	**8.3**	**6.3**	**4.4**	**3.3**	**1.2**
Commodity prices [6]								
Oil price	29.4	-10.2	-32.8	50.3	0.0	0.9	42.2	-13.6
Non-energy commodity price index	1.7	-4.2	3.0	22.5	-2.5	-2.7	20.1	-3.8

Source: World Bank.

1. Headline aggregate growth rates are calculated using GDP weights at average 2010-19 prices and market exchange rates. The aggregate growth rates may differ from the previously published numbers that were calculated using GDP weights at average 2010 prices and market exchange rates.

2. GDP growth rates are on a fiscal year basis. Aggregates that include these countries are calculated using data compiled on a calendar year basis. Pakistan's growth rates are based on GDP at factor cost. The column labeled 2019 refers to FY2018/19.

3. GDP growth rates are on a fiscal year basis. Aggregates that include these countries are calculated using data compiled on a calendar year basis. The column labeled 2018 refers to FY2018/19.

4. World growth rates are calculated using average 2010-19 purchasing power parity (PPP) weights, which attribute a greater share of global GDP to emerging market and developing economies (EMDEs) than market exchange rates.

5. World trade volume of goods and nonfactor services.

6. Oil price is the simple average of Brent, Dubai, and West Texas Intermediate prices. The non-energy index is the weighted average of 39 commodity prices (7 metals, 5 fertilizers, 27 agricultural commodities). For additional details, please see https://www.worldbank.org/commodities.

Note: e = estimate; f = forecast. World Bank forecasts are frequently updated based on new information. Consequently, projections presented here may differ from those contained in other World Bank documents, even if basic assessments of countries' prospects do not differ at any given date. Country classifications and lists of EMDEs are presented in table 1.2. BRICS include: Brazil, the Russian Federation, India, China, and South Africa. Due to lack of reliable data of adequate quality, the World Bank is currently not publishing economic output, income, or growth data for Turkmenistan and República Bolivariana de Venezuela. Turkmenistan and República Bolivariana de Venezuela are excluded from cross-country macroeconomic aggregates.

measures in many countries, as well as rising confidence. A substantial share of this rebound is due to major economies, with many EMDEs lagging behind (figure 1.1.D). The United States and China are each expected to contribute over one-quarter of global growth in 2021, with the U.S. contribution nearly triple its 2015-19 average. Vaccination progress is a key determinant of near-term forecast revisions (figure 1.1.E). Despite the strong pickup, the level of global GDP in 2021 is expected to be 3.2 percent below pre-pandemic projections.

The recovery is envisioned to continue into 2022, with global growth moderating to 4.3 percent. Still, by 2022, global GDP is expected to remain 1.8 percent below pre-pandemic projections. Compared to recoveries from previous global recessions, the current cycle is notably uneven, with per capita GDP in many EMDEs remaining below pre-pandemic peaks for an extended period (figure 1.1.F).

In advanced economies, the rebound is expected to accelerate in the second half of 2021 as a broader set of economies pursue widespread vaccination and gradually reopen, with growth forecast to reach 5.4 percent this year—its fastest pace in nearly five decades. Growth is projected to moderate to 4 percent in 2022, partly as fiscal support in the United States begins to recede absent additional legislation.

Aggregate EMDE growth is forecast to reach 6 percent in 2021, as the effects of the pandemic gradually wane and as EMDEs benefit from elevated commodity prices and improving external demand. Nevertheless, the strength of the rebound this year mainly reflects robust pickups in a few large economies. In many other EMDEs, recoveries are expected to be dampened by elevated COVID-19 caseloads and obstacles to vaccine procurement and uptake, as well as by a partial withdrawal of monetary and, especially, fiscal support (figure 1.2.A). Aggregate EMDE growth is projected to moderate to 4.7 percent next year, owing to the continued unwinding of fiscal support and subdued investment, leaving EMDE output 4.1 percent below pre-pandemic projections in 2022. Among LICs, growth is

FIGURE 1.1 Global prospects

Global output is rebounding but remains below pre-pandemic projections, with more subdued recoveries in poorer countries. Vaccination has helped limit the spread of the virus, but progress is highly unequal and concentrated in advanced economies. Compared to previous global recoveries, the current cycle is strong but uneven, and primarily reflects rebounds in some major economies. With the pandemic and limited vaccination in many emerging market and developing economies (EMDEs) contributing to downward revisions to growth, per capita income in a majority of EMDEs is expected to remain below pre-pandemic peaks for an extended period.

A. Deviation of output from pre-pandemic projections

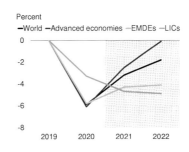

B. Distribution of COVID-19 cases and vaccine doses from mid-April to mid-May

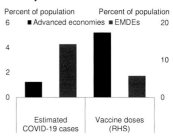

C. Global recoveries after recessions

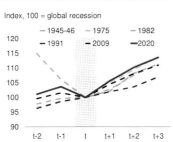

D. Contributions to global growth

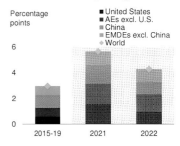

E. Forecast revisions to global growth in 2021, by vaccination progress

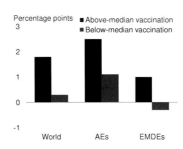

F. Share of EMDEs exceeding pre-global-recession peaks in per capita output after 2 years

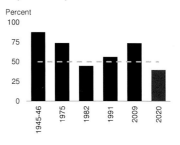

Sources: Bolt et al. (2018); Kose, Sugawara, and Terrones (2020); Our World in Data (database); World Bank.
Note: AEs = advanced economies; EMDEs = emerging market and developing economies; LICs = low-income countries. Unless otherwise denoted, aggregates are calculated using real U.S. dollar GDP weights at average 2010-19 prices and market exchange rates.
A. Figure shows percent deviation between the levels of June 2021 and January 2020 baseline World Bank projections. Shaded area indicates forecasts.
B. Figure shows the one-month accumulation of COVID-19 cases in AEs and EMDEs over April 17-May 17, 2021, as estimated by the Institute for Health Metrics and Evaluation (IHME), and vaccinations as a share of the population. Sample includes 36 advanced economies and 120 EMDEs.
C. Lines show global recessions, with "t" as their final year. Data for 2021-23 used in the "2020" episode are forecasts.
D. Figure shows contributions to global growth forecast for 2021 and 2022 compared to average contributions to growth in 2015-2019 period. Shaded area indicates forecasts.
E. GDP-weighted forecast revisions for all countries above and below each aggregate's median share of population that has received at least one COVID-19 vaccine dose as of June 1, 2021. Sample includes 36 advanced economies and 132 EMDEs.
F. Data for 2021-22 used in the "2020" episode are baseline forecasts.

FIGURE 1.2 Global risks and policy challenges

In many emerging market and developing economies (EMDEs), the recovery will be constrained by elevated COVID-19 caseloads, obstacles to vaccination, and a partial withdrawal of macroeconomic support. In many EMDEs, the pandemic has slowed or reversed progress at per capita income catch-up with advanced economies. Inflation is expected to exceed targets in about half of inflation-targeting EMDEs, which could trigger monetary tightening and potentially result in financial stress. Bolstering a green, resilient, and inclusive recovery will necessitate the efficient use of historic increases in debt, the promotion of investments in education and environmental sustainability, and the reduction of trade costs.

A. Fiscal and monetary policy stance in 2021

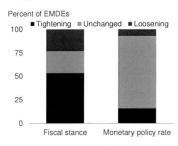

B. Per capita income growth relative to advanced economies

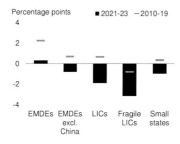

C. Forecast for EMDE inflation

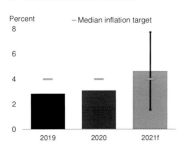

D. Inefficiencies in public spending

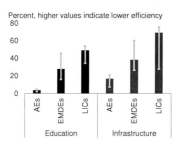

E. Global greenhouse gas emissions

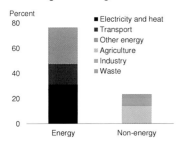

F. Trade costs and tariff rates

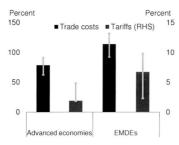

Sources: Comtrade (database); Consensus Economics; ESCAP-World Bank Trade Cost Database; Haver Analytics; International Monetary Fund; World Bank; World Resources Institute.
Note: AEs = advanced economies; EMDEs = emerging market and developing economies; LICs = low-income countries; Fragile LICs = fragile and conflict-affected LICs.
A. The threshold for fiscal loosening/tightening is a fiscal impulse of +/- 0.5 percentage point of potential GDP. Fiscal impulse is the negative change in the cyclically-adjusted primary balance from the previous year. Monetary policy stance shows whether countries have had net policy rate hikes/cuts this year. Sample includes 30 EMDEs for fiscal balance and 70 EMDEs for monetary policy rate.
B. Relative per capita income growth is computed as a difference in per capita GDP growth between respective EMDE groups and advanced economies. For more information on "Small states," see: https://www.worldbank.org/en/country/smallstates/overview.
C. Based on median inflation in 125 EMDEs and inflation target in 30 inflation-targeting EMDEs. 2021 EMDE inflation forecast described in chapter 4. Vertical line indicates 16-84 confidence bands.
D. Figure shows median efficiency gap: The difference between a country's spending efficiency and that of best performers. Yellow whiskers show interquartile ranges. Sample includes 34 advanced economies, 139 EMDEs, and 24 LICs. See figure 1.23.E notes for more detail.
E.F. Data are for 2018.
F. Blue bars show average trade costs expressed as ad valorem (tariff) equivalent of the value of traded goods. Red bars show average tariffs for all products. Trade costs aggregated using bilateral country export shares. Yellow whiskers show interquartile ranges.

expected to pick up to an average of 3.8 percent in 2021-22—well below the average pace of 5.1 percent in the 2010-19 period, and leaving the 2022 level of output 4.9 percent below pre-pandemic projections.

Notwithstanding these projected recoveries, the pandemic has had a devastating effect on per capita income growth, poverty, and inequality, which will linger for a protracted period. Although per capita income growth in EMDEs is projected to be 4.9 percent this year, it will be essentially zero in LICs. As a result, per capita income catch-up with advanced economies could slow or even reverse in many poorer countries (figure 1.2.B). Moreover, per capita income losses incurred in 2020 will not be fully unwound by 2022 in about two-thirds of EMDEs, including 75 percent of fragile and conflict-affected LICs. By the end of this year, it is expected that about 100 million people across EMDEs will have fallen back into extreme poverty. The pandemic's impact on poverty could reverberate for a prolonged period due to its scarring effects on long-term growth prospects. The pandemic has also exacerbated inequality as it has disproportionately affected vulnerable groups—including women, children, and unskilled and informal workers.

Moreover, the global outlook is clouded by uncertainty and subject to various risks (box 1.1). The continued spread of COVID-19 shows that repeated outbreaks are still possible, especially in light of the emergence of new variants that are more virulent, deadly, and resistant to vaccines. Elevated debt levels make the financial system vulnerable to a sudden increase in interest rates, which could stem from a rise in risk aversion, inflation, or expectations of faster monetary tightening. A spike in bankruptcies could damage the banking system, restrict the flow of credit, and trigger credit crunches.

The near- and longer-term consequences of the COVID-19 crisis pose enormous policy challenges. The immediate priority continues to be pandemic control, including overcoming obstacles in procuring and distributing vaccines. International cooperation is needed to help ensure timely and equitable vaccine distribution—

particularly in LICs, where inoculation continues to be very slow. As the pandemic is brought under control, policy actions will also be needed to address its adverse legacies, which will require balancing competing priorities.

In many economies, central banks will need to carefully weigh the continued weakness of domestic demand against near-term inflation pressures. Model-based forecasts and inflation expectations point to an increase in inflation in 2021 that will exceed target ranges in about one-half of inflation-targeting EMDEs (chapter 4; figure 1.2.C). Although this may not warrant an aggressive policy response, additional inflation pressure across EMDEs may risk de-anchoring inflation expectations and could trigger monetary tightening despite subdued recoveries, which in some cases could also result in financial stress.

Similarly, many EMDEs will need to be careful to avoid a premature withdrawal of fiscal support, while still keeping a steady eye on medium-term debt sustainability. Given the historic increase in sovereign debt, it will be essential to improve the efficiency of public spending (figure 1.2.D). Strengthening domestic revenue mobilization and medium-term fiscal frameworks can help widen fiscal space and bolster policy credibility. Global cooperation, including private sector participation, is needed to provide debt relief to the world's poorest countries and fund the investments needed to boost growth and lower greenhouse gas emissions (figure 1.2.E).

Notwithstanding the expected near-term recovery, EMDE output is likely to remain below its pre-pandemic trend for a prolonged period, as many fundamental drivers of growth have been scarred by the pandemic. A comprehensive set of policies will be required to promote a strong recovery that mitigates inequality and enhances environmental sustainability, ultimately putting economies on a path of green, resilient, and inclusive development (GRID). For example, labor market reforms and improved social safety nets can bolster labor productivity by facilitating the movement of labor toward high-growth sectors while protecting vulnerable groups. Productivity can also be boosted by efforts to increase access to digital

connectivity and reduce trade costs, which are particularly elevated in EMDEs (figure 1.2.F). Increasing investments in learning infrastructure and education will also be required to boost human capital and arrest recent declines in associated budgets, while expanding green investment can enhance climate resilience.

Global context

COVID-19 continues to spread, particularly in many emerging market and developing economies (EMDEs) amid unequal vaccine deployment. Although world trade is benefiting from the global recovery, it is being constrained by supply bottlenecks and travel restrictions. Financial conditions, while still benign, have tightened somewhat as global yields have risen due in part to higher inflation expectations. Almost all commodity prices have been boosted by the global recovery, with some prices further lifted by supply factors.

Pandemic developments

The pandemic continues to exact a heavy toll, particularly across EMDEs (figure 1.3.A). Since COVID-19 started to spread, it has infected at least 160 million people and caused more than 3 million deaths. Hundreds of thousands of new cases are being reported every day, and the number of unreported cases is estimated to be substantial, particularly in South Asia (figure 1.3.B; Bhattacharyya et al. 2020). Global outbreaks of the virus have come in several waves, each cresting at a higher daily infection rate than the one before. Recent outbreaks have disproportionately affected India and, to a lesser extent, some other large EMDEs such as Brazil.

Vaccination campaigns are gathering pace in many advanced economies and a number of EMDEs, with about 9 percent of the global population having received at least one vaccine dose. Nevertheless, this average conceals enormous regional and income disparities—especially the paltry rate of vaccination in the poorest countries. Countries that have administered vaccines to a greater share of their population are seeing a far slower accumulation of caseloads than the sizable share of EMDEs that have so far administered

FIGURE 1.3 Pandemic developments

The pandemic has continued to spread worldwide, and particularly in emerging market and developing economies (EMDEs). The number of confirmed cases is lower than the estimated number of actual cases, particularly in South Asia. Countries where vaccination campaigns are proceeding quickly have generally seen new cases of COVID-19 fall to a low level. These are mostly advanced economies, as most EMDEs have so far administered only a limited number of shots, and low-income countries have scarcely begun.

A. Evolution of the pandemic

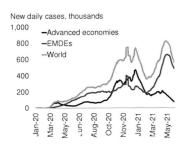

B. Confirmed versus estimated COVID-19 cases

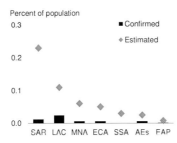

C. Daily new COVID-19 cases, by vaccination progress

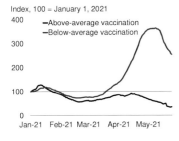

D. Distribution of new COVID-19 cases and vaccine doses from mid-April to mid-May

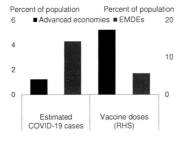

Sources: Johns Hopkins University (database); Our World in Data (database); World Bank.
Note: AEs = advanced economies; EMDEs = emerging market and developing economies; EAP = East Asia and Pacific, ECA = Europe and Central Asia, LAC = Latin America and the Caribbean, MNA = Middle East and North Africa, SAR = South Asia, SSA = Sub-Saharan Africa.
A. Figure shows the seven-day moving average of daily new COVID-19 cases. Sample includes 36 advanced economies and 147 EMDEs. Last observation is May 25, 2021.
B. Bars represent the new COVID-19 confirmed cases, whereas the diamonds represent the COVID-19 cases as estimated by the Institute for Health Metrics and Evaluation (IHME). Data retrieved on May 26, 2021. Last observation available taken for both confirmed and estimated cases. Sample includes 36 advanced economies, 7 EAP, 23 ECA, 26 LAC, 19 MNA, 7 SAR, and 41 SSA economies.
C. Figure shows the seven-day moving average of daily new COVID-19 cases per million people for 36 advanced economies and 147 EMDEs above and below the global average vaccination rate. Last observation is May 25, 2021.
D. Figure shows the one-month accumulation of COVID-19 cases in AEs and EMDEs over April 17-May 17, 2021, as estimated by the Institute for Health Metrics and Evaluation (IHME), and vaccinations as a share of the population. Sample size includes 36 advanced economies and 120 EMDEs.

shots to only a small proportion (figure 1.3.C-D). Coverage in poorer countries remains extremely limited, but the COVAX initiative and the potential temporary waiving of intellectual property protections for COVID-19 vaccines may contribute to global distribution becoming more equitable over time.

New variants that were originally identified in Brazil, India, South Africa, and the United Kingdom are now circulating globally. There is evidence that these new strains may spread more easily and cause more severe disease (Davies et al. 2021). Some of the strains also appear to be resistant to the immune responses triggered by a previous infection or by the current set of vaccines (Wang et al. 2021). All countries remain vulnerable to renewed outbreaks so long as the virus continues to circulate in some areas amid unequal global vaccine coverage (Çakmaklı et al. 2021).

Despite continued waves of infection, the impact of the virus and associated lockdown measures on economic activity appears to be diminishing in most countries. Over time, firms and households have adjusted their behavior to mitigate disruptions and shift activity to less-affected sectors (ECB 2021). In addition, compliance with lockdown measures appears to have waned somewhat over time (Goldstein, Yeyati, and Sartorio 2021).

Global trade

Global trade has continued to rebound; however, the strength of global trade growth is set to be dampened by shifting activity from manufacturing to the low-trade-intensity domestic services sector in countries where COVID-19 caseloads have been declining. The recovery in global trade started earlier and has been stronger than that of other components of global output, as the pandemic's impact on activities requiring face-to-face contact initially encouraged a rotation in demand toward the consumption of durable goods, which have a high trade intensity (figure 1.4.A).

Manufacturing trade is currently being constrained by supply bottlenecks and strains in global value chains, which were temporarily exacerbated by the blockage of the Suez Canal in March (Ferrantino et al. 2021). Companies have experienced a sharp rise in freight rates and localized shortages of shipping containers (figure 1.4.B). In order to increase resilience and mitigate logistical problems, companies have increased their use of digital technologies and diversified suppliers and production sites (Saurav et al. 2020).

BOX 1.1 What is next? Growth scenarios beyond 2021

Global growth is set to reach 5.6 percent in 2021—the strongest post-recession pace in 80 years. Nonetheless, the recovery is expected to be highly uneven, and there is substantial uncertainty about the strength and durability of this anticipated upturn beyond 2021. This box explores two alternative scenarios. In a "Faltering Recovery" scenario, the global economy slows in response to the possibility of recurring local COVID-19 outbreaks, mounting inflationary pressures, and a sharp tightening of global financial conditions during the next two years. In contrast, in a "Sustained Expansion" scenario, vaccine-driven COVID-19 containment, re-opening, and ambitious reforms catalyze an even stronger response of private activity and potential output, with positive global spillovers. These scenarios illustrate that the current signs of recovery may be fleeting and underscore the need for policy makers in emerging market and developing economies (EMDEs) to take advantage of present opportunities to put in place growth-enhancing reforms.

Introduction

Global economic activity is accelerating as the world emerges from the deepest global recession since World War II (World Bank 2020a). Barring a protracted global resurgence of COVID-19, the baseline outlook described in the main text envisages the strongest global recovery from any of the five global recession in the past 80 years. However, the recovery is remarkably uneven across countries, as it largely reflects sharp rebounds in some major economies, with poorer countries lagging behind. In addition, there is substantial uncertainty around the baseline growth trajectory, especially beyond 2021. The recovery in global activity may not last, as explored in a "**Faltering Recovery**" scenario. In this case, growth would slow starting in 2022 as recurring COVID-19 flareups would weigh on risk sentiment, while mounting inflation pressures amid elevated macroeconomic vulnerabilities would trigger a sharp tightening of global financial conditions (Reinhart and Reinhart 2020). Alternatively, in a "**Sustained Expansion**" scenario, the rebound could broaden and become self-sustaining, anchored by improved confidence, an accelerated pace of technological change, and a renewed push for reforms that boost longer-term productivity in EMDEs (World Bank 2021a; Kose and Ohnsorge 2021). The global implications of these scenarios are assessed using a large-scale global semi-structural projection model. [a]

Baseline scenario

In the baseline scenario, global output is set to bounce back strongly, expanding 5.6 percent this year—the fastest post-recession pace in 80 years—following a 3.5 percent contraction in 2020. Advanced economies are expected to grow 5.4 percent in 2021, with substantial fiscal support and faster-than-expected vaccinations in the United States adding fuel to the rebound. Growth in EMDEs is also projected to strengthen, reaching 6 percent in 2021 on the back of improving external demand and elevated commodity prices. This baseline outlook is predicated on the assumption that widespread vaccination allows advanced economies to achieve effective containment of the pandemic by the end of the year, while many major EMDEs are envisaged to substantially reduce local transmission rates. In contrast, slow progress of vaccination campaigns would allow COVID-19 to disrupt activity to varying degrees in many other EMDEs, including low-income countries.

The surge in growth envisaged for 2021 reflects, to varying degrees, the combination of ongoing macroeconomic policy support and the release of pent-up demand associated with the easing of the pandemic. In response to the COVID-19 shock, central banks have eased monetary policy forcefully, by cutting policy rates and in many cases committing to keeping them low for an extended period, as well as rolling out unconventional policies (figure B1.1.1.A-B). Fiscal authorities also announced a series of large-scale support packages across advanced economies and, to a lesser extent, EMDEs (figure B1.1.1.C). More-over, the pandemic and associated lockdown measures forced households to reduce spending on services involving personal contact, leading to a sizable accumulation of personal savings, particularly in advanced economies (figure B1.1.1.D).

Although financial conditions remain benign, they have tightened somewhat as firming activity raises the prospect of stronger inflation and a faster withdrawal of supportive monetary policies. The ebbing of the pandemic is also revealing heightened macroeconomic vulnerabilities in many EMDEs—in particular, high debt burdens and sizable current account and fiscal deficits—leaving many

---

Note: This box was prepared by Justin-Damien Guénette, with contributions from Alain Kabundi and Takefumi Yamazaki.

a. The scenarios were constructed using the Oxford Economics Global Economy Model (Oxford Economics 2020), which includes 81 individual country blocks (35 advanced economies and 46 EMDEs), most of which are available at a quarterly frequency, with behavioral equations governing domestic economic activity, monetary and fiscal policy, global trade, and commodity prices.

BOX 1.1 What is next? Growth scenarios beyond 2021 (*continued*)

FIGURE B1.1.1 Policy support and vulnerabilities

Global economic activity is experiencing an uneven acceleration. Much of the pickup reflects the strengthening of large advanced economies driven by substantial macroeconomic policy support and the nascent release of pent-up demand as pandemic control measures are relaxed. However, this pickup will do little to reverse significant debt and external vulnerabilities accumulated during the pandemic.

A. Central bank policy rate projections

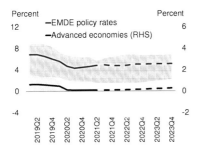

B. Quantitative easing in advanced economies and EMDEs since March 2020

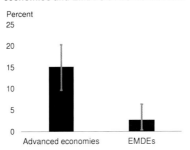

C. Fiscal support measures in response to COVID-19 since January 2020

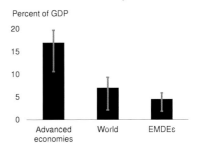

D. Personal savings

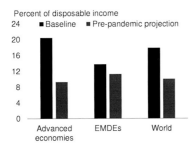

E. EMDE government and private debt

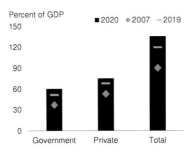

F. EMDE current account and fiscal balances

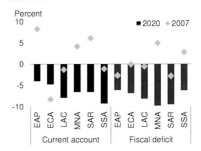

Sources: Bank of International Settlements; International Institute of Finance; International Monetary Fund; National accounts; Oxford Economics; World Bank.
Note: EMDEs = emerging market and developing economies; EAP = East Asia and Pacific, ECA = Europe and Central Asia, LAC = Latin America and the Caribbean, MNA = Middle East and North Africa, SAR = South Asia, SSA = Sub-Saharan Africa.
A. Blue and red lines show average policy rates for 27 advanced economies and 23 EMDEs. Dotted line shows projections as based on Oxford Economics May21_1 Oxford database. Shaded areas show interquartile range.
B. Announced or completed purchases (where no announcement exists) and of sovereign and private sector bonds in percent of nominal GDP as of May 2021. Sample for EMDEs consists of 17 countries. Sample for advanced economies consists of US, Euro area, Japan, and United Kingdom. Bars shows averages. Orange whiskers show regional range.
C. Bars show unweighted average of total fiscal support measures in response to COVID-19 pandemic. Sample includes 48 advanced economies and 143 EMDEs.
D. Figure shows average personal savings for 2021 H1 for baseline projection and pre-pandemic baseline approximated by Jan20_1 Oxford Economics database. Sample includes 27 advanced economies and 17 EMDEs.
E. Aggregates are calculated using real U.S. dollar GDP weights at average 2010-19 prices and market exchange rates, excluding China. Total debt is a sum of government and private debt. Government debt based on 149 EMDEs and private debt based on 126 EMDEs.
F. Averages across EMDE regions, consisting of 22 EAP (excluding China), 23 ECA, 31 LAC, 16 MNA, 8 SAR, and 46 SSA.

of them exposed to financial market disruptions (figure 1.1.1.E-F).

Beyond 2021, the baseline forecast anticipates a moderation of the global recovery with a continued divergence between advanced economies and EMDEs. Advanced economies are expected to continue to recover at a healthy pace, buoyed by reopening amid limited projected scarring of potential output (Das and Wingender 2021). Growth in the United States is forecast to remain strong, in part due to the likelihood that the Federal Reserve will keep policy rates near zero through early 2023, in line with market expectations. In doing so, the Federal Reserve is assumed to permit a modest overshoot of inflation above the 2 percent target over the next three years, consistent with its new Average Inflation Targeting

BOX 1.1 What is next? Growth scenarios beyond 2021 (*continued*)

regime (Brainard 2021).[b] In contrast, the pace of recovery in EMDEs is expected to be subdued and uneven, with growth in 2022 and 2023 averaging 4.5 percent—only modestly above a declining rate of potential output growth (averaging 4 percent over the same period). The factors weighing on EMDE recoveries include a slow pace of vaccination and reopening, the withdrawal of macro-economic support, the stabilization of commodity prices, and a sluggish rebound in global tourism.

Comparison with recoveries from previous global recessions

The baseline scenario envisages the fastest recovery from any of the five global recessions in the past 80 years, considerably faster than the initial rebound from the global financial crisis (figure B1.1.2.A-B). The recovery in advanced economies is projected to be particularly robust—their 2021 growth is expected to be nearly twice as fast as that after the 2009 recession (figure B1.1.2.C). In contrast, the recovery in EMDEs is expected to be more modest, with growth in 2021 about one fifth slower than after the 2009 recession.

Nevertheless, this global recovery is expected to be markedly less broad-based than previous ones. Only half of all countries are expected to have regained their pre-pandemic per capita income levels in 2022, two years after the global recession (figure B1.1.2.D). In contrast, by 2011, after the 2009 global recession induced by the global financial crisis, two thirds of countries had regained the pre-recession per capital output levels, a similar share of countries as after the average global recession in the 20th century. The weakness of the recovery is concentrated in EMDEs: Over 90 percent of advanced economies are expected to regain their pre-pandemic per capita income levels in 2022, while only about one third of EMDEs are expected to do so over that time (figure B1.1.2.E-F).

Downside scenario: A Faltering Recovery

The global recovery could falter once policy support is withdrawn and pent-up demand is exhausted, similar to

the experience following the global recession of 2009 (Kose and Ohnsorge 2021). A lingering pandemic, with new variants causing recurring local resurgences of infections, would leave households and businesses wary of future prospects (Kozlowski 2020; Ilut and Schneider 2012). This would keep savings elevated and limit the scope for further improvement in private consumption and investment.

At the same time, a rapid demand-driven increase in growth in the United States absent large supply-side improvement would generate sustained inflation pressures and potentially cause a de-anchoring of inflation expectations (Tauber and Van Zandweghe 2020). The Federal Reserve could have no choice but to respond by quickly tightening monetary policy, likely triggering a sharp repricing of risk by financial markets, and exacerbating already heightened macroeconomic vulnerabilities.[c] The macroeconomic effects of a sharp tightening of global financial conditions, as well as weaker consumer and business confidence, would compound the expected unwinding of global fiscal support.[d] Growth in advanced economies would slow sharply from 5.4 percent in 2021 to 2.6 percent in 2022 and 1.4 percent in 2023 (figure B1.1.3.A).

The slowdown would also be sharp in EMDEs as negative spillovers via confidence, trade, and commodity price channels would reduce private sector activity.[e] These countries would experience significant capital outflows in response to heightened investor risk aversion, leading to sharp currency depreciations, which in turn would worsen debt burdens and boost inflation. Domestic credit spreads would significantly widen, triggering a notable rise in defaults, especially in those countries with pre-existing balance sheet vulnerabilities (figure B1.1.3.B; Arteta et al.

---

b. Under average inflation targeting, the inflation rate is expected to exceed its target during expansions to compensate for below-target inflation during downturns. The modest overshoot in core PCE inflation envisioned by the Federal Reserve in its March 2021 Summary of Economic Projections would bring average core PCE inflation to 1.9 percent over 2020-23 and to 1.6 percent over 2015-23, still below the 2 percent target. Critically, the projection for U.S. inflation assumes that inflation expectations remain anchored and the Phillips Curve—the relationship between inflation and the level of excess demand—is nearly flat (Hazell et al. 2020).

c. The Federal Reserve is assumed to begin raising rates while rapidly tapering its quantitative easing program starting in 2022Q1.

d. In this scenario, financial market volatility would spike in 2022Q1 and 2022Q2, with the VIX experiencing a rise on par with the COVID-19 crisis due in large part to an unexpected acceleration in the unwinding of U.S. monetary policy stimulus in the face of rising inflation expectations. The sharp rise in global risk aversion is assumed to precipitate a persistent downward shift in global confidence starting in early 2022.

e. Major EMDEs are assumed to face significant adverse domestic confidence shocks in addition to negative spillovers from abroad. These shocks are calibrated to broadly match recent episodes of domestic economic weakness such as what occurred during the Taper Tantrum (2013Q2) and what happened during the global financial crisis for certain EMDEs.

BOX 1.1 What is next? Growth scenarios beyond 2021 (*continued*)

FIGURE B1.1.2 Global recovery in historical context

The baseline forecast envisages the strongest post-recession rebound in global output growth in 80 years. Much of the strength reflects a remarkably swift recovery in advanced economies, in contrast to the recovery that followed the global financial crisis. That said, the recovery is expected to be unusually narrow in per capita terms, with only 50 percent of countries expected to exceed their pre-recession peaks in 2022. The global recovery is also expected to be markedly uneven across advanced economies and EMDEs.

A. Global output recoveries over history

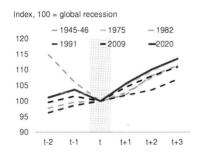

B. Global output per capita recoveries over history

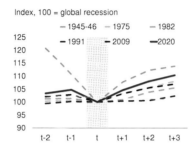

C. Advanced economy and EMDE output: 2020 vs 2009

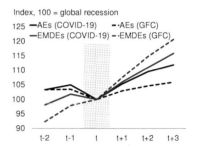

D. Share of countries exceeding pre-recession per capita peaks after 2 years

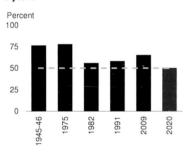

E. Share of advanced economies exceeding pre-recession per capita peaks after 2 years

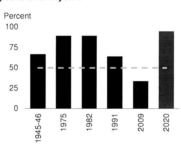

F. Share of EMDEs exceeding pre-recession per capita peaks after 2 years

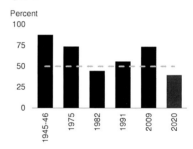

Sources: Bolt et al. (2018); Kose, Sugawara, and Terrones (2020); World Bank.
Note: A.-F. Data for 2021-23 used in the "2020" episode are forecasts. GFC = global financial crisis.
A.-B. Lines show global recession episodes. Multiple years are used when the global recession lasted for more than one year.
C. t = 2020 for COVID-19 and t = 2009 for GFC.
D.-F. Dashed yellow line is 50 percent.

2015). [f] Increased debt servicing costs amid heightened rollover risks would force governments in many EMDEs, particularly in countries with limited fiscal space, to cut consumption and delay investment projects. [g]

EMDEs would experience renewed downturns, with growth falling sharply from 6.0 percent to 2.9 percent in 2022, well below the 5.1 percent average of the previous decade (figure B1.1.3.C). Relative to the baseline scenario, EMDE growth in 2022 and 2023 would be 1.8 and 1.3 percentage point lower, respectively, and the additional slowdown would cut across all EMDE sub-regions.

Growth in China would remain resilient, averaging nearly 5 percent in 2022 and 2023 as policy makers would be

---

f. The domestic credit spread is calculated as a difference between the short-term lending rate and the 10-year government bond yield. Credit spreads in advanced economies are endogenously determined, whereas in EMDEs they are set to be consistent with (1) the levels prevailing during the GFC or (2) the period of rising concerns in anticipation of weaker-than-expected global growth and a no-deal Brexit in 2018.

g. The magnitude of the fiscal consolidation shock is calibrated to match recent historical episodes of rapid fiscal consolidation in major EMDEs. The degree of fiscal consolidation varies across major EMDEs

according to the size of their fiscal sustainability gap based on Kose et al. (2017). The fiscal sustainability gap widened considerably in most EMDEs in 2020.

BOX 1.1 What is next? Growth scenarios beyond 2021 (*continued*)

FIGURE B1.1.3 Alternative scenarios for global growth

Global growth is expected to pick up strongly in 2021, buttressed by increased but unequal vaccination, policy support, and the release of pent-up demand. For 2022, growth outcomes will depend on the extent to which the initial rebound can catalyze a durable recovery in private sector activity and potential output growth. In a "Faltering Recovery" scenario, the global recovery may prove short-lived, as recurring local resurgences of the pandemic combined with the de-anchoring of inflation expectations in the United States lead to a sharp repricing of risk and a tightening of global and especially EMDE financial conditions. In contrast, in a "Sustained Expansion" scenario, rising global confidence amid brighter pandemic prospects, an accelerated pace of technological change, and growth-enhancing reforms in EMDEs provide a strong growth boost through 2023.

A. Advanced economy GDP growth

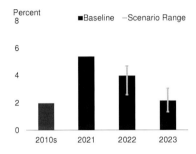

B. Major EMDE credit spreads

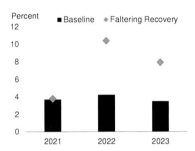

C. EMDE GDP Growth

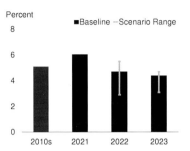

D. World GDP growth

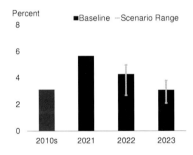

E. Episodes of rising advanced economy total factor productivity growth

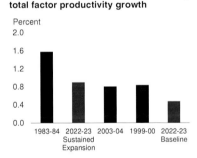

F. EMDE output growth and potential output growth with reforms

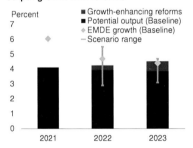

Sources: Dieppe (2020); Kilic Celik, Kose, and Ohnsorge (2020); Oxford Economics; UN Population Projections; World Bank.
Note: A.C.D. Red bars show average of 2010-2019 GDP growth. Blue bars show baseline data from *Global Economic Prospects* June 2021 database. Yellow whiskers indicate the scenario ranges from Oxford Global Economic Model simulations compared to the baseline scenario.
B. Major EMDE countries comprise Argentina, Brazil, China, India, Indonesia, Malaysia, Mexico, Russian Federation, South Africa, and Turkey.
E. TFP is total factor productivity. Advanced economies comprise France, Germany, Italy, Japan, United Kingdom, and United States. Episodes of rising advanced economy TFP growth are instances when TFP growth accelerated above its historical 1981-2018 average for two consecutive years. The sustained recovery scenario is based on the acceleration witnessed during the two most recent acceleration episodes of 2003-04 and 1999-00.
F. Potential output estimates and projections are based on a production function approach as described in Kilic Celik, Kose, and Ohnsorge (2020). Sample includes 82 economies (including 30 advanced economies and 52 EMDEs, of which 12 are low-income countries) for 1995-2029. These countries accounted for 95 percent of global GDP over the past five years. Yellow diamonds show the baseline data from *Global Economic Prospects* June 2021 database. Green whiskers denote scenario range.

expected to roll out additional policy support measures to cushion the effect of adverse spillovers. Excluding China, growth in EMDEs would fall more sharply, from 4.4 percent to 1.4 percent in 2022—2.8 percentage points below the baseline scenario—resulting in nearly zero growth in per capita terms in that year. The pace of activity in EMDEs would barely tick up in 2023 and at 2 percent would still be 1.7 percentage points below the baseline forecast.

In sum, this scenario would mean that global growth would slow sharply, by nearly 3 percentage points from 5.6 percent in 2021 to 2.7 percent in 2022, and further to 2.1 percent in 2023 (figure B1.1.3.D). This would leave the recovery from the COVID-19 pandemic roughly similar to the anemic recovery that followed the global financial crisis.

BOX 1.1 What is next? Growth scenarios beyond 2021 (*continued*)

Upside scenario: A Sustained Expansion

Alternatively, the global recovery could prove more robust and broad-based than expected. For instance, the policy-supported surge in global growth in 2021, coupled with faster and more equitable global vaccination, could catalyze a self-sustaining period of rapid growth in which the private sector becomes a powerful engine of growth starting in 2022. In effect, strong pro-cyclical policy support would trigger a process of "reverse hysteresis" in which a robust cyclical upturn lifts long-run growth prospects (Reifschneider, Wascher, and Wilcox 2013; Coibion, Gorodnichenko, and Ulate 2017).

In particular, this scenario envisages that technological adoption would accelerate, along with rising investment and labor force participation, causing potential output to strengthen. Starting in the first quarter of 2022, total factor productivity growth in advanced economies would accelerate to levels similar to those seen during previous episodes of productivity surges, as corporations deepen their use of digital technologies and work from home policies adopted during the pandemic (figure B1.1.3.E; Barrero, Bloom, and Davis 2021; McKinsey 2020). Knowledge spillovers and faster installation of new productive capital would also raise productivity in other countries.[h] At the same time, this scenario assumes that EMDE policy makers, faced with high levels of sovereign debt and slowing long-run growth prospects, implement growth-enhancing reforms, including reforms to strengthen economic governance, diversify economies reliant on commodities or tourism, and facilitate the reallocation of resources towards more productive activities (World Bank 2021a). This comprehensive package of reforms would raise EMDE potential output growth gradually starting in 2022 (figure B1.1.3.F).

Consumer confidence would surge, anchoring strong private consumption growth as consumers rapidly draw down their savings.[i] At the same time, rising potential output and well-anchored inflation expectations would help keep inflationary pressures in check, allowing advanced economy central banks to keep monetary policy accommodative for a prolonged period. In turn, continued monetary accommodation would support investment and consumption by alleviating debt service burdens and supporting asset prices.

Growth in advanced economies would remain near 5 percent in 2022 before slowing to a still strong 3.1 percent in 2023. The investment- and productivity-driven growth in advanced economy growth would have greater spillovers to EMDEs, boosting export demand while ensuring that global financial conditions remain benign (World Bank 2017). As a result, EMDEs would experience a robust expansion, with growth averaging over 5 percent in 2022 and 2023—0.6 percentage point higher on average than in the baseline scenario. Overall, global growth would be notably stronger, averaging 4.4 percent over 2022-23 compared to 3.7 percent in the baseline scenario (figure B1.1.4.A-C).

Policy implications

COVID-19 continues to spread across the world, making pandemic control the top priority for policy makers. Launching durable economic recoveries will not be possible until containment is achieved through widespread and equitable vaccination efforts. Still, there have been encouraging signs of a solid macroeconomic recovery from the deleterious effects of the pandemic in recent months. A supportive external environment has helped buoy activity: strengthened external demand has boosted exports of raw commodities and traded goods, while still-benign global financial conditions have helped ease the burden of heavy debt loads among many EMDE governments and corporates.

Looking beyond 2021, EMDE policy makers can help realize a Sustained Expansion scenario of the global economy by decisively implementing growth-enhancing reforms. The benefits of the ongoing global trade rebound can be leveraged by reforms that lower trade costs (chapter 3), including streamlining trade processes and customs clearance procedures, lowering tariffs, and implementing policies that support trade infrastructure and services. Ambitious reforms to facilitate the transition of labor and capital to high-growth sectors, strengthen social safety nets, and fund environmentally sustainable investments can help entrench a domestically driven green, resilient, and inclusive recovery.

---

h. TFP spillovers are calibrated using estimates from Coe, Helpman and Hoffmaister (2008) and differentiated across advanced economies and EMDEs based on the results of multi-country vector autoregression models. The installation of new productive capital is also assumed to raise total factor productivity (World Bank 2018a).

i. The global increase in confidence is modeled using globally correlated confidence shocks that simultaneously increase private consumption and business investment. The magnitude of the shock is calibrated to raise EMDE growth in 2022 by a similar magnitude to the acceleration in growth that occurred in 2006 (about 0.9 percentage point).

BOX 1.1 What is next? Growth scenarios beyond 2021 (*continued*)

FIGURE B1.1.4 Global recovery scenarios in historical context

From a historical perspective, global activity could follow alternative paths as it recovers from the 2020 recession. In the Faltering Recovery scenario, the global recovery could lose momentum, with global output evolving broadly in line with the recovery that followed the global financial crisis. Alternatively, in the Sustained Expansion scenario, the post-recession recovery could be notably stronger.

A. Global output around historical recessions

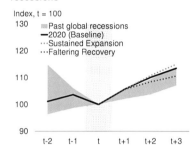

B. Advanced economy output around historical recessions

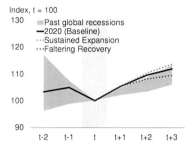

C. EMDE output around historical recessions

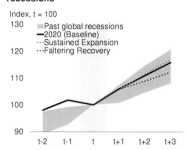

Sources: Bolt et al. (2018); Kose, Sugawara, and Terrones (2019, 2020); World Bank.
Note: EMDEs = emerging market and developing economies.
A.-C. Sample includes 183 economies, though the sample size varies significantly by year. Past global recessions shading includes 1945-46, 1975, 1982, 1991, and 2009 global recession episodes.

As highlighted by the Faltering Recovery scenario, however, the favorable external environment may not last, and many EMDEs are vulnerable to a sudden shift in external conditions. This underscores the need for policy makers to take full advantage of the currently favorable external environment to implement reforms that increase the resilience of financial systems and improve fiscal sustainability. On the macroprudential front, steps can include enhancing macroprudential supervision, closely monitoring systemic risks in the financial system, and incentivizing domestic banks to rebuild capital buffers. At

the same time, fiscal authorities can address investor concerns about long-run debt sustainability by strengthening fiscal frameworks, enhancing debt transparency, and improving debt management by issuing long-duration debt denominated in local currency. If fiscal revenues surprise temporarily on the upside, these can be used to replenish depleted fiscal buffers or to fund critical investment and development needs. When combined, these policies can go a long way in making economies more resilient to external shocks and less susceptible to episodes of financial stress.

Price pressures associated with supply bottlenecks are likely to abate over time as global growth moderates and shippers expand capacity.

High-frequency data point to a pickup in some components of services trade, such as telecommunications and financial services (figure 1.4.C). Tourism remains depressed, however, even in countries that have not experienced major outbreaks, such as small island economies. International travel is expected to be constrained for some time owing to lingering mobility

restrictions and reluctance to travel so long as the virus is not completely under control (figure 1.4.D; UNWTO 2021).

Trade growth is hampered by high trade costs, which remain particularly elevated in EMDEs (chapter 3). Trade costs primarily arise from transportation expenses and cumbersome customs procedures, and are likely to have increased further as a result of protectionist measures, such as tariffs on U.S.-China trade and export controls on food and medical products (WTO 2020). In all, global

FIGURE 1.4 **Global trade**

The global trade recovery has been boosted by a rotation in demand toward trade-intensive goods; as the low-trade-intensity domestic services sector picks up and accounts for a greater share of the economic recovery, trade momentum is likely to slow. Manufacturing trade is being constrained by supply bottlenecks amid localized shortages of shipping containers. Incoming data point to a pickup in some components of services trade, such as telecommunications and financial services, whereas tourism activity is expected to remain weak until the virus is brought under control.

A. Impact of a $1 increase in sectoral demand on imports

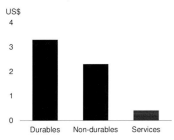

B. Global shipping times and costs

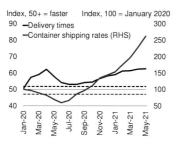

C. State of the recovery in global services trade, by component share of total

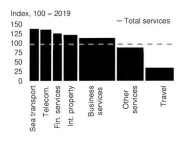

D. Global survey expectations for international tourism to return to pre-pandemic levels

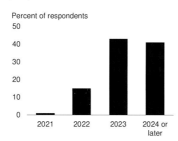

Sources: Auboin and Borino (2017); Bems, Johnson, and Yi (2010); Harper Petersen & Co. (database); Haver Analytics; United Nations World Tourism Organization; World Bank; World Trade Organization.

A. Figure shows the impact of a $1 increase in demand from a given sector on imports, as estimated by Bems, Johnson, and Yi (2010).

B. Figure shows the global manufacturing suppliers' delivery times Purchasing Managers' Index (PMI) and the Harper Petersen Charter Rates Index (HARPEX) for container shipping rates. PMI data are inverted by subtracting data from 100; therefore, increasing (decreasing) PMI data indicate faster (slower) delivery times. Container shipping rates are monthly averages of weekly data and reflect price developments on the charter market for container ships. Dashed lines indicate long term averages over the period January 1998 – December 2019 for delivery times and February 2018 – December 2019 for container shipping rates. Last observation is May 2021 for delivery times and May 25, 2021 for container shipping rates.

C. Trade is measured as the average of import and export volumes. Sample includes 12 advanced economies and 12 EMDEs in March 2021. The height of the bars shows latest data relative to the corresponding month of 2019 whereas the width of bars shows the pre-pandemic share of each component in total services trade. Telecom. = Telecommunications, computer, and information services; Fin. services = financial services; Int. property = charges for the use of intellectual property. Dashed orange line indicates the level of trade in total services as compared to the average of 2019.

D. Figure shows the expectations for international tourism to return to 2019 levels according to a global survey conducted by UNWTO in January 2021.

trade is forecast to grow 8.3 percent this year and 6.3 percent in 2022, reflecting firming global output and investment, but also the diminishing trade intensity of the global recovery.

Financial markets

Financial conditions have tightened but remain generally supportive. Global borrowing costs have increased as expectations of stronger future growth and higher inflation have pushed up long-term yields on government bonds. Thus far, these developments have been substantially less disruptive to global and EMDE financial conditions than the 2013 taper tantrum, when expectations of tighter U.S. monetary policy triggered volatility in global financial markets.

Global corporate borrowing costs have also risen, but spreads have been stable and stock market valuations in most regions are still close to multi-year highs. Business bankruptcies, which had been limited considering the depth of the global recession, have picked up in some industries and countries but remain below pre-pandemic levels amid easy access to credit and the extension of some COVID-19 relief measures. The extent of post-pandemic credit losses may be limited by the fact that crisis-hit sectors account for a small share of total non-financial-sector debt (Mojon, Rees, and Schimieder 2021).

EMDE sovereign debt yields have risen slightly more than U.S. borrowing costs, particularly for some more-indebted countries, resulting in modest increases in spreads (figure 1.5.A-B). Portfolio flows to EMDEs have lost momentum (figure 1.5.C). Some EMDEs have experienced currency depreciation, contributing to above-target inflation (figure 1.5.D). As has been the case in the past, currency depreciation has led some EMDE central banks to start removing monetary policy accommodation. Large output gaps in many countries may limit the extent of EMDE policy tightening in the near future.

Remittances to many countries have been resilient. Strong activity in the U.S. construction sector, for example, has supported flows to many countries in Latin America and the Caribbean (LAC). The extent of this resilience may be overstated, however, by mobility constraints that encourage a shift from informal methods of transporting money across borders toward wire transfers, which are more easily measured (Dinarte et al. 2021).

The recovery of foreign direct investment (FDI) flows to EMDEs is largely attributable to investors' optimism about prospects in China and a few large foreign acquisitions in India. FDI flows to other EMDEs remain subdued due to concerns about the course of the pandemic and uncertainty about growth prospects.

Commodity markets

Commodity prices have seen a sharp rise in 2021, with many now well above their pre-pandemic levels (figure 1.6.A; World Bank 2021b). Oil prices have rallied markedly, averaging $60/bbl in 2021 so far. Prices have been supported by a gradual firming in demand and continued production restraint among OPEC+, even if the group is gradually reducing the extent of its production cuts as the market recovers. However, the pickup in oil prices has been partly dampened by uncertainty regarding the evolution of the pandemic and its potential impact on future oil demand.

Oil prices are projected to average $62/bbl in 2021 and 2022. Oil demand is expected to continue to firm in the second half of 2021 but will not regain its pre-pandemic level until next year, with the shortfall mainly due to subdued jet fuel consumption (IEA 2021). A key risk to the forecast is the speed at which OPEC+ increases production—the group currently has spare production capacity of up to 9 million barrels per day, equivalent to 9 percent of global consumption in 2019 (figure 1.6.B). A further increase in drilling activity among U.S. shale oil producers is also a potential risk to the oil price forecast. In the longer term, the outlook for oil and other energy commodities will be dependent on the pace of transition toward renewable energy sources.

Base metal prices have increased sharply this year, supported by continued strong demand from China as well as recovery in the rest of the world (figure 1.6.C). The forecast for metals prices in 2021 has been revised sharply upwards, and prices are now expected to be 36 percent higher in 2021 on average relative to last year, before falling back in 2022 as some supply constraints ease.

FIGURE 1.5 Global finance

Global financial conditions have tightened, with larger increases in borrowing costs for some more-indebted emerging market and developing economies (EMDEs). The recent rise in global yields has been driven by increasing U.S. bond yields, but has been substantially less disruptive than the 2013 taper tantrum. Sovereign credit spreads in EMDEs have increased modestly, whereas capital flows have lost momentum. Some EMDEs have experienced currency depreciations in recent months.

A. Cumulative change in 10-year EMDE government bond yields

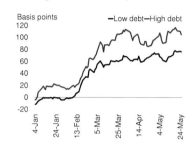

B. Response of EMDE credit spreads to rising U.S. yields

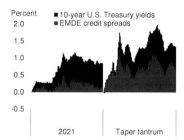

C. EMDE portfolio flows

D. EMDE exchange rates

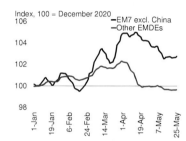

Sources: Bloomberg; Haver Analytics; Institute of International Finance; International Monetary Fund; J.P. Morgan; World Bank.

Note: EMDEs = emerging market and developing economies.

A. Aggregates are calculated using unweighted averages. "Low debt" indicates EMDEs with the 2020 general government debt below the median for the sample (60.5 percent of GDP). Sample includes 15 EMDEs. Last observation is May 25, 2021.

B. Cumulative change after the beginning of each episode, which is January 1, 2021 for 2021 and May 22, 2013 for taper tantrum. EMDE credit spreads refer to JP Morgan Emerging Markets Bond Index (EMBI) spread. Last observation is May 25, 2021.

C. Four-week cumulative net debt and equity portfolio flows to 18 EMDEs (excluding China). Last observation is May 28, 2021.

D. Figure shows the 5-day moving average nominal exchange rates versus the U.S. dollar; an increase indicates depreciation. Sample includes 32 EMDEs with floating or free-floating exchange rate; "EM7 excl. China" refers to India, Brazil, Mexico, the Russian Federation, Indonesia, and Turkey. Last observation is May 25, 2021.

Agricultural prices have also seen a substantial rise, particularly those of food commodities, and concerns about food insecurity persist in some countries, especially those afflicted by conflict or experiencing adverse weather events. While most global agricultural commodity markets remain well supplied, production growth for the main crops has been below trend for the past few years (figure 1.6.D). Agricultural prices are expected to rise by 16 percent in 2021 before plateauing in 2022.

FIGURE 1.6 Commodity markets

Commodity prices have increased markedly this year, with many now well above their pre-pandemic levels. While oil demand has picked up, significant spare capacity remains among the OPEC+ countries. Demand for metals remains robust. Despite recent price increases, agricultural markets remain generally well supplied.

A. Commodity price indexes

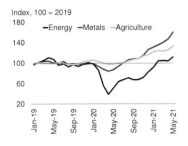

B. Estimates of OPEC+ spare capacity

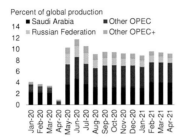

C. Global metals demand growth

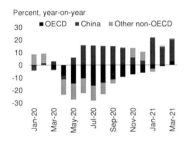

D. Food stock-to-use ratio

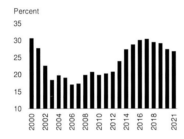

Sources: Bloomberg; International Energy Agency; U.S. Department of Agriculture; World Bank; World Bureau of Metal Statistics.
A. Last observation is May 2021.
B. Spare production capacity estimated as the difference between a country's current production and their maximum level of output since 2018, shown as a percent of global supply in 2019. "Other OPEC" includes all current OPEC countries except the Islamic Republic of Iran, Libya, Saudi Arabia, and República Bolivariana de Venezuela, which are exempt from production cuts. Other OPEC+ includes Azerbaijan, Bahrain, Brunei Darussalam, Kazakhstan, Malaysia, Oman, South Sudan, and Sudan.
C. Last observation is March 2021.
D. May 12, 2021 update. Years represent crop seasons (for example, 2019 refers to 2019-20 crop season).

Major economies: Recent developments and outlook

In advanced economies, progress in containing the pandemic, primarily through a ramping up of vaccinations, is expected to unlock significant pent-up demand, allowing a gradual narrowing of the gap between advanced-economy output and its pre-pandemic trend. The recovery is projected to strengthen first in the United States on the back of rapid vaccination and a new round of fiscal support, followed gradually by other advanced economies. The pronounced recovery in China is expected to moderate as macroeconomic policy support is with-drawn.

Activity among advanced economies has been propelled so far this year by a solid recovery in the United States, partly due to the effects of massive fiscal support. Vaccination campaigns are generally proceeding at a faster pace than envisioned in the January baseline forecast, albeit at varying degrees across countries (figure 1.7.A). Still, most advanced economies have maintained some pandemic control measures to dampen COVID-19 caseloads and guard against possible resurgences.

More generally, advanced economies continue to experience a two-track recovery, with sales and production of goods nearing or exceeding their pre-pandemic levels, while services sectors struggle to overcome headwinds from the pandemic and associated lockdown measures (figure 1.7.B). Although labor markets so far are healing at a faster pace than during the global financial crisis, employment in early 2021 remains well below its pre-pandemic level (figure 1.7.C).

Growth in advanced economies is forecast to reach 5.4 percent in 2021—2.1 percentage points higher than envisioned in January, powered by stronger-than-expected momentum leading into 2021, faster vaccination in several countries, additional U.S. fiscal support, and the release of sizable pent-up demand (figure 1.7.D). U.S. growth is expected to outperform that of other major advanced economies due to its more rapid vaccine rollout and larger fiscal support. After this year's rebound, growth is expected to moderate but remain robust in 2022 as the removal of pandemic control measures continues.

United States

The U.S. economy is recovering more quickly than its peers from the pandemic shock, supported by greater amounts of fiscal relief. Surging personal income has boosted consumption, which is expected to firm as households reduce their savings rate from historically high levels. The signing of the American Rescue Act in March offered $1.9 trillion in additional fiscal support, bringing the cumulative fiscal relief provided since the beginning of the pandemic to over one-quarter of GDP—a level of support that is unprecedented in peacetime. Vaccination is proceeding at a robust pace and is set to become widespread by mid-2021.

In all, U.S. growth is projected to reach 6.8 percent in 2021—its fastest pace since 1984—reflecting additional large-scale fiscal relief and the ongoing easing of pandemic restrictions. It is then expected to soften to a still-strong 4.2 percent in 2022 as the fiscal impulse begins to fade.

Euro area

A slow and inconsistent vaccine rollout and the need to maintain stringent mobility restrictions in the face of more transmissible variants have constrained the pace of recovery in the first half of the year. The euro area is set to experience a strong recovery in the second half of 2021, alongside the expected acceleration of vaccinations and a relaxation of pandemic restrictions.

Growth in 2021 is projected to reach 4.2 percent—0.6 percentage point above January forecasts—and pick up further to 4.4 percent in 2022 as member countries steadily unwind pandemic controls, enabling the continued release of pent-up demand. Disbursement of Next Generation EU grants and loans will also contribute to the recovery over the forecast horizon, helping to finance various growth-enhancing investments, including green and digital infrastructure.

Japan

Following a bounce back in the second half of 2020, Japan's economy again contracted at the start of 2021, weighed down by targeted lockdown measures amid a resurgence of COVID-19. Activity is expected to recover as sharply diminished COVID-19 caseloads allow for a continued relaxation of lockdown measures and fiscal support increasingly feeds through to domestic activity.

Japanese output is projected to expand 2.9 percent in 2021—0.4 percentage point higher than January forecasts, reflecting firming domestic economic activity alongside robust external

FIGURE 1.7 **Advanced economies**

Faster-than-expected vaccination in some advanced economies is strengthening the growth outlook. Retail sales, industrial production, and construction have exceeded or are approaching pre-pandemic levels, while consumption of services remains weak. Despite a nascent rebound, employment remains well below pre-pandemic trends, and below levels at a similar time during the recovery that followed the global financial crisis. The eventual containment of the pandemic is expected to unlock sizable pent-up demand as households spend their excess savings.

A. Effective daily vaccination rate in major advanced economies

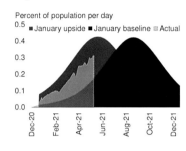

B. Activity indicators for advanced economies

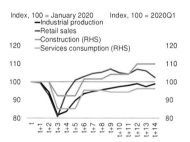

C. Employment in advanced economies

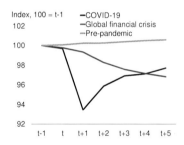

D. Household savings rate in advanced economies

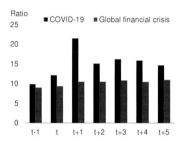

Sources: CPB Netherlands Bureau for Economic Policy Analysis; Guénette and Yamazaki (2021); Haver Analytics; Organisation for Economic Co-operation and Development; Our World in Data (database); Oxford Economics; World Bank.
A. Figure shows the average seven-day moving average of effective daily COVID-19 vaccinations administered per hundred people across the Group of Seven (G7) member countries which include Canada, France, Germany, Italy, Japan, the United Kingdom, and the United States. As in Guénette and Yamazaki (2021), effective vaccinations are computed by multiplying the total number of vaccinations by 0.5 to account for multi-dose vaccines and by 0.85 to account for imperfect vaccine effectiveness. Baseline and upside assumption as described in box 1.4 of the January 2021 edition of the *Global Economic Prospects* report (World Bank 2021a). Last observation is May 31, 2021.
B. For industrial production the weights represent country shares in global nominal, dollar-denominated value added in industry. Aggregates for construction, retail sales and services consumption are calculated using 2020 real U.S. dollar GDP weights at 2010-19 prices and market exchange rates. Sample includes 35 advanced economies for the industrial production, 20 advanced economies for the retail sales, 24 advanced economies for construction, and 14 advanced economies for services consumption. Last observation is March 2021 for retail sales and industrial production, and 2021Q1 for construction and services consumption.
C. Figure shows quarterly employment reindexed to equal 100 at t-1 quarters from the onset of respective shocks. "t-1" refers to 2019Q4 for COVID-19, 2008Q2 for the global financial crisis, and 2019Q4 from January 2020 vintage data for pre-pandemic. COVID-19 data for "t+5" are forecasts. Sample includes 20 advanced economies.
D. Figure shows quarterly ratio of personal savings over personal disposable income. "t-1" refers to 2019Q4 for COVID-19, and 2008Q2 for Global financial crisis. Sample includes 27 advanced economies.

demand. The 2021 Tokyo Olympic Games are to be held without foreign spectators, limiting its economic benefits. Growth is envisioned to

FIGURE 1.8 China

China's economic recovery has broadened from public investment to consumption. Policy efforts have shifted from supporting activity to reducing financial stability risks.

A. Growth and contributions to real GDP

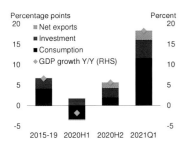

B. Liquidity injections and growth of money supply

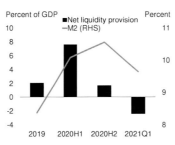

Sources: Haver Analytics; National Bureau of Statistics of China; World Bank.
A. Figure shows year-on-year GDP growth and contributions to real GDP. Investment stands for gross capital formation. Last observation is 2021Q1.
B. Figure shows year-on-year growth of money supply and net liquidity provision as share of GDP. Money supply is the M2 from China's Banking Survey. Net liquidity injection provided by the People's Bank of China (PBOC) through standing lending facility (SLF), the medium-term lending facility (MLF), the targeted medium-term lending facility (TMLF), the pledged supplementary lending (PSL), the special-purpose refinancing (SPRF), and the special relending or rediscounting facilities. Last observation is March 2021 for M2 and 2021Q1 for net liquidity provision.

moderate in 2022, to 2.6 percent, held back by lingering weakness in consumption amid subdued wage growth.

China

After expanding 2.3 percent in 2020, output in China has continued to recover, gradually broadening from public investment and exports to domestic consumption (figure 1.8.A). Policy has been shifting away from buttressing activity and toward reducing financial stability risks (figure 1.8.B). Credit support and infrastructure spending, which initially fueled much of the acceleration in investment, have moderated. Debt defaults, including for state-owned enterprises, have continued to rise (World Bank 2021c).

China's growth is forecast to rebound to 8.5 percent this year, reflecting the release of pent-up demand. This represents an upward revision of 0.6 percentage point, largely owing to expectations of stronger foreign demand. Amid diminishing fiscal and monetary support and tighter property and macroprudential regulations, growth is expected to moderate in 2022, to 5.4 percent.

Emerging market and developing economies

Although improving external demand and higher commodity prices are lifting aggregate activity in emerging market and developing economies (EMDEs), the recovery in many of them is being constrained by a severe resurgence of new COVID-19 cases and lagging vaccination, as well as a partial withdrawal of macroeconomic policy support. The pandemic continues to have a particularly dampening effect on tourism-reliant economies and is further exacerbating domestic challenges in low-income countries. In all, the pace of recovery in two-thirds of EMDEs will be insufficient to recoup the per capita income losses caused by the pandemic by 2022, and poverty rates are expected to rise further. The long-term outlook has also deteriorated, owing to the pandemic's lasting impact on potential output.

Recent developments

Aggregate EMDE output in 2020 fell 1.7 percent, less severe than the expected contraction of 2.3 percent. This reflected better-than-expected activity in some large economies, such as China, as well as among industrial commodity exporters, which benefited from rising energy and metals prices toward the end of last year. The upgrade in 2020 was not broad-based, however. Growth estimates were upgraded in just over half of EMDEs, and outturns for most tourism-reliant economies were weaker than expected (figure 1.9.A-B). Excluding China, the contraction in EMDE output was far more severe, at 4.3 percent, as many countries faced continued headwinds from the pandemic.

Uneven progress at vaccination has allowed for sharp resurgences of COVID-19 cases, often featuring new variants, which have dampened the recovery in many EMDEs (figure 1.10.A). Services activity remains feeble amid ongoing social-distancing and lockdown measures, while depressed international tourism and travel weigh on services trade (figure 1.10.B). Retail sales are stabilizing below pre-pandemic levels, reflecting renewed softness in countries grappling with high

COVID-19 caseloads (figure 1.10.C). Private investment has been constrained by an earlier collapse in FDI and, in some cases, escalations in political tensions or heightened policy uncertainty (figure 1.10.D; UNCTAD 2021). Nevertheless, the drag from the pandemic has been offset by a continued recovery in industrial production and goods trade, with both surpassing pre-crisis levels faster than in the aftermath of the global financial crisis (figure 1.10.E). Moreover, robust remittance inflows have partly cushioned household incomes amid widespread unemployment (figure 1.10.F; ILO 2021b).

The pace of recovery has diverged across EMDE regions (box 1.2; chapter 2). A strong rebound in goods exports has underpinned activity in East Asia and Pacific (EAP), helping to offset soft domestic demand. Elsewhere, the recovery in goods trade volumes and industrial production has been more tepid. In Europe and Central Asia (ECA) and Latin America and the Caribbean (LAC), high COVID-19 caseloads continue to constrain growth. In the Middle East and North Africa (MENA), OPEC+ oil production restraint is weighing on extractive activity. In Sub-Saharan Africa (SSA), the continuation of COVID-19 restrictions has curbed business activity, with weakness in some industrial sectors compounded by power outages and subdued oil production. In South Asia (SAR), a robust rebound in services has been interrupted by a sharp worsening of COVID-19 cases and a deterioration in mobility indicators.

Following a sharp slowdown in 2020, activity in LICs has recovered somewhat this year, as some countries benefit from improving industrial commodity exports. Nonetheless, growth continues to be dampened by the effects of the pandemic and the very slow pace of vaccinations, which have delayed the relaxation of control measures and inhibited activity that relies on face-to-face interaction (Afghanistan, Guinea, Madagascar; box 1.3). Some fragile and conflict-affected LICs have also had to contend with floods, droughts, locust infestations, and rising insecurity (Central African Republic, Eritrea, Mali, Sudan).

FIGURE 1.9 Recent developments in emerging market and developing economies

The collapse in activity in 2020 was shallower than anticipated for a number of emerging market and developing economies (EMDEs), especially industrial commodity exporters. In contrast, growth forecasts for most tourism-reliant economies were downgraded.

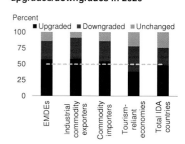

A. Revisions to 2020 GDP estimates

B. Share of EMDEs with GDP upgrades/downgrades in 2020

Sources: United Nations World Tourism Organization; World Bank.
Note: EMDEs = emerging market and developing economies. Tourism-reliant EMDEs are defined as EMDEs with average 2015-19 inbound tourism expenditures as a share of GDP above the fourth quartile. Aggregates are calculated using real U.S. dollar GDP weights at average 2010-19 prices and market exchange rates.
A. Figure shows revisions of country groups 2020 growth estimates relative to the January 2021 edition of the *Global Economic Prospects* report (World Bank 2021a). EMDE average calculated using 2019 nominal U.S. dollar GDP. Sample includes 140 EMDEs, among which 48 are industrial commodity exporters and 37 are tourism reliant. Yellow whiskers show interquartile range.
B. Figure shows the share of EMDEs whose 2020 growth estimates have been upgraded or downgraded relative to the January 2021 edition of the *Global Economic Prospects* report (World Bank 2021a). Dashed yellow line indicates 50 percent threshold. Total IDA countries are those eligible to receive IDA resources, including IDA blend countries. Sample includes 144 EMDEs, among which 47 are industrial commodity exporters, 58 are commodity importers, 36 are tourism-reliant economies, and 71 are Total IDA countries.

Outlook

EMDE near-term outlook

The recovery in aggregate EMDE activity is anticipated to gather further pace in the second half of 2021 as vaccine deployment, while still uneven, gradually proceeds, particularly in large countries. Aggregate EMDE growth is forecast to reach 6 percent in 2021, supported by improving external demand and elevated commodity prices. The 2021 forecast is 0.8 percentage point higher than earlier projections; however, this mostly reflects sizable upgrades to some large economies, as well as strong momentum from late 2020 (figure 1.11.A-B). In particular, the projection for China's growth for 2021 has been revised up due to expectations of more robust external demand.

The recovery in EMDEs excluding China is projected to be more modest, at 4.4 percent in 2021, with about 40 percent of countries facing downward revisions to growth this year, reflecting

FIGURE 1.10 Recent developments in emerging market and developing economies, excluding China

Sharp resurgences of new COVID-19 cases have continued to weigh on the recovery in many emerging market and developing economies. Services trade remains anemic, as international tourism continues to be dampened by ongoing travel restrictions, while retail sales have stabilized below pre-pandemic trends. Subdued FDI is constraining investment. Nevertheless, activity has benefited from improving goods trade and robust remittance inflows, which are recovering more quickly than in the aftermath of the global financial crisis.

A. Quarterly GDP

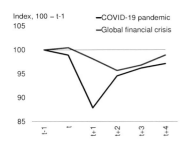

B. Services trade and tourist arrivals

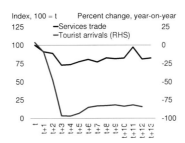

C. Retail sales

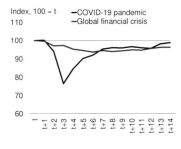

D. FDI flows to EMDEs

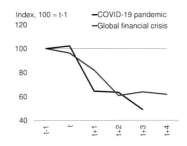

E. Goods trade and industrial production

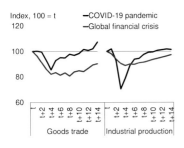

F. Remittances flows to EMDEs

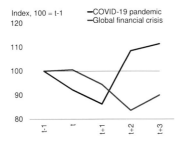

Sources: CPB Netherlands Bureau for Economic Policy Analysis; Haver Analytics; International Monetary Fund; United Nations World Tourism Organization; World Bank; World Trade Organization.
Note: EMDEs = emerging market and developing economies; FDI = foreign direct investment. Unless otherwise noted, t = 100 for the global financial crisis in September 2008; t = 100 for the COVID-19 pandemic in January 2020.
A. D.F. t-1 = 100 for the global financial crisis in 2008Q2; t-1 = 100 for the COVID-19 pandemic in 2019Q4.
B. Services trade measured as the average of import and export values. Last observation is January 2021 for tourist arrivals and February 2021 for services trade.
C. Last observation is March 2021.
D. Balanced sample includes 52 EMDEs.
E. Goods trade is measured as the average of import and export volumes. Last observation is March 2021.
F. Last observation is 2020Q4. Unbalanced sample includes up to 94 EMDEs for global financial crisis and up to 122 EMDEs for COVID-19 pandemic.

continued disruptions from the pandemic and the partial removal of monetary and, especially, fiscal support (figure 1.11.C). Although vaccine procurement and distribution are expected to gradually accelerate over the forecast horizon, it will remain uneven in the near term, with bottlenecks in the equitable distribution of vaccines anticipated to weigh on the recovery in many EMDEs (figure 1.11.D-E).

Aggregate EMDE growth is projected to edge down to 4.7 percent in 2022, as macroeconomic support continues to be withdrawn and commodity prices stabilize. Tourism-dependent economies, such as small island countries, are expected to continue to experience the consequences of subdued international travel next year, which will delay the recovery (UNWTO 2021). More generally, the recovery in EMDEs will not be sufficient to recoup earlier losses, with output in 2022 expected to remain 4.1 percent below pre-pandemic projections (figure 1.11.F).

EMDE long-term outlook

In the longer term, the EMDE outlook will likely be dampened by the pandemic's lasting legacies. EMDE potential output—the activity EMDEs can sustain at full capacity and employment—is expected to remain below pre-pandemic projections over the next decade. Major drivers of growth had been projected to lose momentum even before the COVID-19 crisis, and this trend is likely to be exacerbated by the scarring effects of the pandemic (figure 1.12.A; Kilic Celik, Kose, and Ohnsorge 2020; World Bank 2021a). The pandemic is expected to worsen the slowdown in labor productivity growth, as it has damaged the process of both physical and human capital accumulation (Dieppe 2020). It is possible that the pandemic spurs productivity by accelerating technology adoption, innovation, and a shift in activity toward more productive sectors, but this has not yet been observed on a global scale, whereas the damage to investment and human capital is readily apparent (di Mauro and Syverson 2020).

Investment—both public and private—is expected to remain well below pre-pandemic projections for a prolonged period, which will result in a smaller capital stock and lower productivity (figure 1.12.B; World Bank 2018a). Impaired corporate productivity and heightened risk aversion will likely impede private investment, whereas the need to unwind fiscal support in some EMDEs will constrain public investment (Caballero and Simsek 2020; Stiglitz 2020; World Bank 2021a). Sizable investment needs of many EMDEs, and particularly LICs, are likely to go unmet, putting development goals further out of reach (World Bank 2021d).

The pandemic has also eroded earlier gains in human capital through its impact on health outcomes, school closures, and prolonged spells of unemployment. Beyond its direct effects on morbidity and mortality, the pandemic has also delayed essential primary health services and increased food insecurity, which could lead to higher maternal and early childhood deaths (Roberton et al. 2020). These effects are also likely to weigh on longer-term productivity, as malnutrition early in life can permanently impair learning abilities. Education has also been disrupted as partial and full school closures continue to interrupt learning continuity, which could worsen learning outcomes (figure 1.12.C). This, combined with the deskilling associated with prolonged unemployment, could lead to sizable future earnings losses.[1] In EMDEs, COVID-19 triggered a fall in working hours equivalent to the loss of roughly 200 million full-time jobs in 2020, with employment not expected to recover to pre-pandemic levels by 2022, particularly in LICs (figure 1.12.D; ILO 2021b; Khamis et al. 2021). The longer unemployment remains high, the more pronounced will be the loss of human capital.

LIC outlook

In LICs, growth is expected to pick up in 2021, reaching 2.9 percent, aided by firming external demand from LICs' trading partners and elevated

---

FIGURE 1.11 Prospects for growth in emerging market and developing economies

The forecast for aggregate growth in emerging market and developing economies (EMDEs) for 2021 has been revised up, to 6 percent; however, this mainly reflects substantial upgrades to some large economies as well as strong carryover from growth in late 2020. Firming external demand and higher commodity prices will help offset macroeconomic policy tightening. The recovery will critically depend on the pace of vaccination. For tourism-reliant economies, activity will continue to be constrained by subdued international travel. In all, the pickup in EMDE growth will be insufficient to restore GDP to pre-pandemic projections.

A. Forecast revisions to EMDE growth

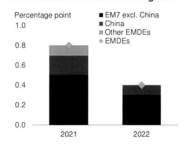

B. Contributions to 2021 GDP growth

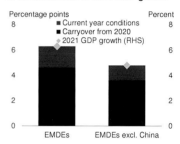

C. Fiscal and monetary policy stance in 2021

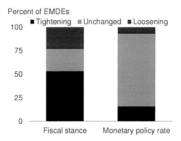

D. Vaccine procurement in 2021

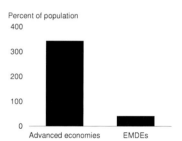

E. Forecast revisions to EMDE growth in 2021, by vaccination progress

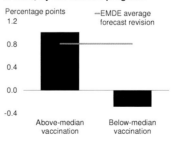

F. EMDE growth forecasts and gaps with pre-pandemic projections

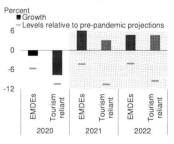

Sources: Duke Global Health Innovation Center (2021); Haver Analytics; International Monetary Fund; Our World in Data (database); World Bank.
Note: EMDEs = emerging market and developing economies; EM7 = Brazil, China, India, Indonesia, Mexico, the Russian Federation, and Turkey. Aggregate growth rates calculated using GDP weights at average 2010-19 prices and market exchange rates. Shaded area indicates forecasts.
A.E. Figure shows contributions to revision of EMDE growth forecasts relative to World Bank (2021a).
A. Sample includes 147 EMDEs.
B. Figure shows contribution to annual growth using quarterly data. Sample includes 48 EMDEs.
C. Fiscal loosening/tightening threshold is a fiscal impulse of +/- 0.5 percentage point of potential GDP. Fiscal impulse is the negative change in the cyclically-adjusted primary balance from the previous year. Monetary policy stance is measured using year-to-date net policy rate hikes/cuts. Sample includes 30 EMDEs for fiscal balance and 70 EMDEs for monetary policy rate.
D. Figure shows the share of confirmed vaccine doses purchased as a share of total population. Sample includes 16 advanced economies and 67 EMDEs. Data are as of May 27, 2021.
E. GDP-weighted forecast revisions above and below the EMDE median share of population that has received at least one COVID-19 vaccine dose as of June 1, 2021. Sample includes 132 EMDEs.
F. GDP levels are relative to World Bank (2020d) forecasts. Sample includes 144 EMDEs, of which 37 are tourism reliant (defined as having average 2015-19 inbound tourism expenditures as a share of GDP above the fourth quartile).

---

[1] See Azevedo et al. (2021); Bundervoet, Davalos, and Garcia (2021); UNESCO (2021); and UNICEF (2021) for a discussion of the impact of COVID-19 on education. See Azevedo et al. (2020) and Fasih, Patrinos, and Shafiq (2020) for a discussion of the impact of COVID-19 on future labor earnings through its disruptions to education and employment.

FIGURE 1.12 Long-term outlook in emerging market and developing economies

The pandemic is likely to lead to a lasting reduction in the level of potential output in emerging market and developing economies (EMDEs) and may cause potential growth to lose further momentum over the next decade. Investment will remain well below pre-pandemic projections for a prolonged period, hindering long-term growth. COVID-related school closures are expected to worsen learning outcomes in EMDEs, while prolonged spells of unemployment may lead to a deterioration in skills.

A. EMDE potential growth prospects

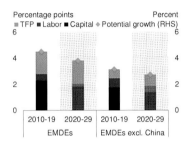

B. Investment gaps with pre-pandemic projections

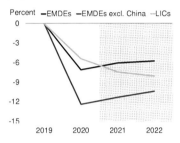

C. Learning-poverty rates

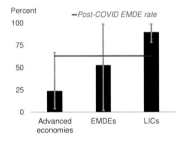

D. Working-hour losses, deviation from pre-pandemic levels

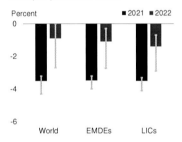

Sources: Azevedo et al. (2021); International Labour Organization (2021b); Kilic Celik, Kose, and Ohnsorge (2020); World Bank.
Note: EMDEs = emerging market and developing economies; LICs = low-income countries; TFP = total factor productivity.
A. Potential growth estimates based on a production function approach as described in Kilic Celik, Kose, and Ohnsorge (2020). 2010-19 aggregates are calculated using 2009 constant GDP-weighted average for 68 EMDEs. 2020-29 aggregates are calculated using post-COVID prospects and 2019 constant GDP-weighted average for 68 EMDEs. Post-COVID prospects assume that investment grows as expected by forecasts from *Consensus Economics* and secondary attainment rates decline by 2.5 percentage points. Shaded areas indicate forecasts.
B. Figure shows investment levels relative to January 2020 projections in World Bank (2021a).
C. The learning-poverty rate is the proportion of 10-year-olds unable to read a short, age-appropriate text, as described in Azevedo et al. (2021). Blue bars show the pre-COVID estimations and red horizontal line denotes the expected impact of COVID-19 on learning poverty due to education disruptions. Orange whiskers show the minimum-maximum ranges for each country group.
D. International Labour Organization (ILO) model-based data are expressed as a percentage difference between the projected number of total hours worked assuming that there had been no pandemic and total hours worked as projected under the three scenarios. Bars represent working-hour losses, yellow whiskers show ILO pessimistic and optimistic scenarios.

commodity prices. Despite this year's recovery, the pace of expansion will be the slowest of the past two decades excluding 2020 amid a very slow pace of vaccination. Growth is subsequently projected to firm to 4.7 in 2022, as vaccine distribution bolsters activity. In tourism-reliant countries, a wider administration of the vaccine is also envisioned to support the recovery (Madagascar,

Uganda; UNWTO 2021; World Bank 2021a). Nevertheless, the level of aggregate LIC output in 2022 will still be 4.9 percent below pre-pandemic projections.

Furthermore, LIC forecasts for this year and next have been downgraded—especially in fragile and conflict-affected countries, where the outlook is particularly dire (figure 1.13.A). For this subset of LICs, growth is expected to average 2.5 percent in 2021-22—0.7 percentage point below previous forecasts, as an improved external context is more than offset by increased debt burdens, policy uncertainty, social unrest, and rising insecurity.

Per capita income growth and poverty

With economic activity rebounding this year, EMDE per capita income growth is projected to reach 4.9 percent in 2021 and edge down to 3.6 percent next year (figure 1.13.B). Among LICs, however, per capita income growth is expected to be essentially zero this year and a meager 2 percent in 2022. At this rate, per capita income growth in many EMDEs—especially in fragile and conflict-affected LICs—will fall short of the pace of recovery in advanced economies over the next two years. In many economies, this will slow or even reverse the pace of per capita income catch-up (figure 1.13.C). In all, per capita income losses incurred in 2020 will not be fully unwound by 2022 in about two-thirds of EMDEs—including 75 percent of fragile and conflict-affected LICs—as the lingering effects of job losses and heightened uncertainty continue to dampen domestic demand (figure 1.13.D; Furceri et al. 2021; ILO 2021a).

The per capita income losses incurred due to COVID-19 are anticipated to worsen deprivation along multiple dimensions in health, education, and living standards, with large increases in poverty headcounts, particularly in Sub-Saharan Africa and South Asia (figure 1.13.E; Alkire et al. 2020). In all, it is projected that about 100 million people will have fallen back into extreme poverty by the end of this year due to the pandemic, making the Sustainable Development Goals (SDGs) more elusive (World Bank 2020b).

In addition to reversing gains in global poverty reduction for the first time in a generation last

BOX 1.2 Regional perspectives: Recent developments and outlook

The recovery in most EMDE regions is expected to be insufficient to reverse the damage from the pandemic. By 2022, output in all regions is expected to remain below pre-pandemic projections, weighed down by the ongoing pandemic and its legacies, which include higher debt loads and damage to many of the drivers of potential output. The recovery in small, tourism-dependent economies is expected to be particularly weak as some travel restrictions will remain in place until the pandemic is brought under control. The pace of vaccine rollout varies across countries, with low-income countries lagging considerably. The recovery is expected to be strongest in East Asia and the Pacific, primarily due to strength in China. In South Asia, India's recovery is being hampered by the largest outbreak of any country since the beginning of the pandemic. In the Middle East and North Africa and Latin America and the Caribbean, the pace of growth in 2021 is expected to be less than the magnitude of the contraction in 2020, while the tepid recovery in Sub-Saharan Africa will make little progress in reversing the increase in extreme poverty caused by the pandemic. In most regions, risks to the outlook are tilted to the downside. All regions remain vulnerable to renewed outbreaks of COVID-19, which could feature variant strains of the virus; financial stress amplified by elevated debt levels; deeper -than-expected scarring from the pandemic; and rising social unrest, potentially triggered by rising food prices.

East Asia and Pacific. Growth in the region is projected to accelerate to 7.7 percent in 2021, largely reflecting a strong rebound in China. Nevertheless, output in two-thirds of the countries in the region will remain below pre-pandemic levels until 2022. The pandemic is expected to dampen potential growth in many economies, especially those that suffered most from extended outbreaks of COVID-19 and the collapse of global tourism and trade. Downside risks to the forecast include the possibility of repeated and large COVID-19 outbreaks amid delayed vaccinations; heightened financial stress amplified by elevated debt levels; and the possibility of more severe and longer-lasting effects from the pandemic, including subdued investment and eroded human capital. Disruptions from natural disasters are a constant source of severe downside risk for many countries, especially island economies. On the upside, risks include accelerated vaccination rollouts and greater-than-expected spillovers from recoveries in the United States and other major economies.

Europe and Central Asia. The regional economy is projected to grow 3.9 percent in 2021, with firming external demand and higher industrial commodity prices offsetting the negative impact of recent resurgences in new COVID-19 cases. Regional growth is forecast to remain at 3.9 percent in 2022 as the recovery in domestic demand gains traction. The outlook remains uncertain, however, with uneven vaccine rollouts and the withdrawal of macroeconomic support measures weighing on the regional recovery. Growth could be weaker than projected if the pandemic takes longer than expected to abate, external financing conditions tighten, or geopolitical

tensions rise further. Legacies of the pandemic, including slowdowns in physical and human capital accumulation, loom over the medium-term outlook if left unaddressed.

Latin America and the Caribbean. Activity is projected to grow 5.2 percent in 2021—a rebound insufficient to return GDP to 2019 levels this year after a historically deep recession in 2020. The rebound will be supported by moderate progress in vaccine rollouts, relaxation of mobility restrictions, and improved external economic conditions. Per capita income losses will still be deep in 2022, particularly for small island economies in the Caribbean. Although spillovers from robust growth and additional fiscal support in the United States through trade and confidence channels are an upside risk to the baseline forecast, the balance of risks is tilted to the downside. Key downside risks include a slower-than-expected COVID-19 vaccine rollout; further surges in new COVID-19 cases, including from variant strains of the virus; adverse market reactions from social unrest or strained fiscal conditions; and disruptions related to social unrest or to climate change and natural disasters.

Middle East and North Africa. Regional output is projected to grow by a subdued 2.4 percent in 2021, only half the pace of the recovery following the 2009 global recession. Higher oil prices have bolstered growth prospects in oil exporters, but the improvement has been limited by new virus outbreaks and mixed progress at vaccine rollout. COVID-19 resurgences have also worsened the outlook for oil importers. By 2022, regional activity is expected to remain 6 percent below pre-pandemic projections. Risks to the regional outlook remain predominantly to the downside. Limited vaccine progress suggests that the pandemic may intensify again, new variants may emerge, and mobility restrictions may be reimposed. The region is also exposed to risks from conflict and social unrest, high debt in some economies,

---

Note: This box was prepared by Patrick Kirby with contributions from Cedric Okou, Franz Ulrich Ruch, Ekaterine Vashakmadze, Dana Vorisek, and Collette Wheeler.

BOX 1.2 Regional perspectives: Recent developments and outlook (*continued*)

FIGURE B1.2.1 Regional growth

The recovery in most EMDE regions this year is expected to be insufficient to reverse the damage from the pandemic. In the Middle East and North Africa and Latin America and the Caribbean, the rebound of growth in 2021 is expected to be smaller than the contraction in 2020, while the tepid recovery in Sub-Saharan Africa (SSA) will make little progress in reversing the increase in extreme poverty caused by the pandemic. The global pandemic has left behind a legacy of higher debt and scarring to potential output that is expected to impede the recovery of activity back to its pre-pandemic trend. In all regions, per capita income catch-up with advanced economies is projected to either slow or go into reverse.

A. Regional growth

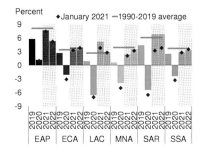

B. Gaps with pre-pandemic projections by 2022

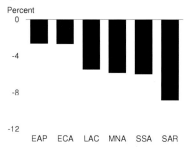

C. Per capita income convergence

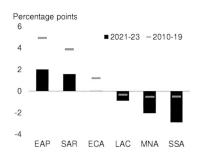

Source: World Bank.
Note: EAP = East Asia and Pacific, ECA = Europe and Central Asia, LAC = Latin America and the Caribbean, SAR = South Asia, SSA = Sub-Saharan Africa.
A. Bars denote latest forecast; diamonds correspond to January 2021 forecasts in the *Global Economic Prospects* report. Aggregate growth rates calculated using constant GDP weights at average 2010-19 prices and market exchange rates. Since largest economies account for more than 50 percent of GDP in some regions, weighted averages predominantly reflect the developments in the largest economies in each region.
B. Figure shows the gaps between the current projections and the forecasts in the January 2020 edition of the *Global Economic Prospects* report.
C. Relative per capita income growth is computed as a difference in per capita GDP growth between each respective region and advanced economies, expressed in percentage points.

and unfavorable commodity price developments. These risks could interact and further undermine living standards, increase deprivation for vulnerable communities, and heighten food insecurity.

South Asia. Output in the region is expected to expand 6.8 percent in 2021, a pace on par with average growth over the previous decade. Stronger-than-expected momentum at the beginning of the year has been disrupted by a large surge of COVID-19 cases. Despite continued recovery, output in 2022 is forecast to be 9 percent below pre-pandemic projections. Poverty rates have risen, and by the end of this year more than half the new global poor are expected to live in the region. The outlook could be weaker if vaccination does not proceed as quickly as assumed. Financial sector balance sheets are at risk of deteriorating, as policy measures put in place at the peak of the pandemic are scaled back, which could constrain the provision of credit and investment needed to support the recovery.

Sub-Saharan Africa. Regional activity is expected to expand a modest 2.8 percent in 2021 and 3.3 percent next year. Positive spillovers from strengthening global activity, better international control of COVID-19, and strong domestic activity in agricultural commodity exporters are expected to gradually help lift growth. Nonetheless, the recovery is envisioned to remain fragile, given the legacies of the pandemic and the slow pace of vaccinations in the region. In a region where tens of millions more people are estimated to have slipped into extreme poverty because of COVID-19, per capita income growth is set to remain feeble, averaging 0.4 percent a year in 2021-22, reversing only a small part of last year's loss. Risks to the outlook are tilted to the downside, and include lingering procurement and logistical impediments to vaccinations, further increases in food prices that could worsen food insecurity, rising internal tensions and conflicts, and deeper-than-expected long-term damage from the pandemic.

year, COVID-19 is set to cause lasting damage to the living conditions of the most vulnerable populations. In LICs, this compounds the challenges faced by the 112 million people who are already facing food insecurity and the 223 million who are exposed to significant flood risk (figure 1.13.F; Furceri et al. 2020; WFP and FAO 2021; World Bank 2021e). The pandemic is also bound to worsen income and gender inequality given its outsized negative effect on women, children, and unskilled and informal workers, as well as its adverse effects on education, health, and living standards (Bundervoet, Davalos, and Garcia 2021; Lakner et al. 2020; Ohnsorge and Yu 2021).

Global outlook and risks

Global growth is recovering unevenly. The pickup in many emerging market and developing economies (EMDEs) remains constrained by high COVID-19 caseloads and the partial withdrawal of macroeconomic support, while activity in major economies—particularly the United States—is rebounding markedly. Aggregate global activity is not expected to be strong enough to fully recoup last year's output losses in the near term. New variants of COVID-19 could extend the duration of the pandemic, and a sudden rise in interest rates or an increase in corporate defaults could trigger financial stress, resulting in weaker-than-expected activity. Conversely, global and EMDE growth could be more robust if the virus is controlled more quickly or if spillovers from rapid growth in major economies catalyze a sustained, broad-based global rebound.

Global outlook

The global economy is recovering, and is expected to expand by 5.6 percent in 2021 and 4.3 percent in 2022 (figure 1.14.A). The strength of the near-term recovery is, to a large extent, attributable to a few major economies, such as the United States and China (figure 1.14.B-C). In many other economies, the pickup is projected to be less robust than previously envisioned, partly due to the continued spread of the virus and slow vaccine distribution (figure 1.14.D). On aggregate, the global forecast has been upgraded as a result of the diminishing economic impact of subsequent waves

FIGURE 1.13 Poverty and per capita income in emerging market and developing economies

GDP growth forecasts in low-income countries (LICs) have been downgraded for 2021-22; in per capita terms, LIC growth will be essentially zero this year. Per capita income catch-up with advanced economies could slow or even reverse in many emerging market and developing economies (EMDEs). The pandemic has erased at least three years of per capita income gains in about two-thirds of EMDEs, including 75 percent of fragile and conflict-affected LICs. Poverty headcounts are set to rise sharply, especially in Sub-Saharan Africa and South Asia, leaving millions of the world's poorest even more vulnerable to future shocks, including adverse weather.

A. Forecast revisions to LIC growth

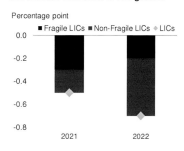

B. Per capita GDP growth

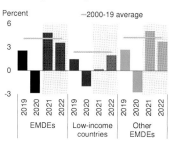

C. Per capita income growth relative to advanced economies

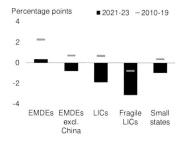

D. Share of countries with lower per capita GDP level in 2022 than 2019

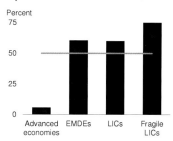

E. Increase in poverty headcounts due to the pandemic by end-2021

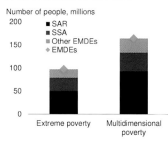

F. Number of poor exposed to flood risk

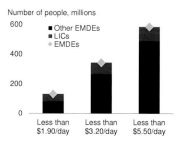

Sources: Mahler et al. (2021); Rentschler and Salhab (2020); World Bank; World Bank (2020b).
Note: EMDEs = emerging market and developing economies; LICs = low-income countries; Fragile LICs = fragile and conflict-affected LICs; Other EMDEs = EMDEs that are not low-income countries; SAR = South Asia; SSA = Sub-Saharan Africa. Shaded areas indicate forecasts.
A.B.D. Aggregates calculated using GDP weights at average 2010-19 prices and market exchange rates.
C. Relative per capita income growth is computed as a difference in per capita GDP growth between respective EMDE groups and advanced economies. For more information on "Small states," see: https://www.worldbank.org/en/country/smallstates/overview.
D. Sample includes 36 advanced economies and 147 EMDEs, including 25 LICs and 16 fragile and conflict-affected LICs. Orange line is 50 percent line.
E. Figure shows the estimated number of people pushed into poverty as a result of the pandemic. This is calculated by comparing poverty using pre- and post-pandemic growth forecasts (Lakner et al. 2020). Extreme poverty reflects the international poverty line of $1.90/day. Multidimensional poverty also includes deprivations in health, education, and living standards (UNDP and OPHI 2020; World Bank 2020b). Percent increase in multidimensional poverty as a result of the pandemic is estimated to be the same as for extreme poverty.
F. Number of poor exposed to significant flood risk, by poverty line (Renschler and Salhab 2020).

FIGURE 1.14 Global outlook and risks

The global economy is recovering. The faster-than-expected rebound is to a large extent attributable to a few major economies, such as the United States and China. In many emerging market and developing economies, growth forecasts have been downgraded and output is projected to remain well below pre-pandemic trends, weighed down by the effects of the pandemic. Although risks to the outlook have become more balanced, downside risks are significant.

A. Global growth

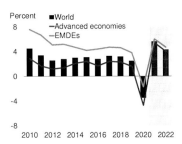

B. Share of global growth

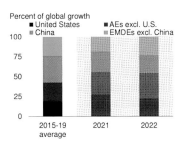

C. Contributions to global growth

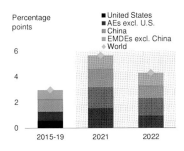

D. Share of countries with forecast revisions

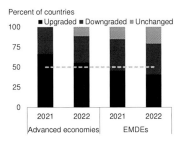

E. GDP gaps relative to pre-pandemic projections

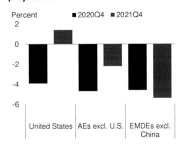

F. Probability distribution around global growth forecasts

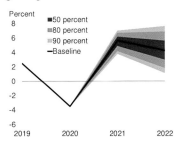

Sources: Bloomberg; Consensus Economics; Oxford Economics; World Bank.
Note: AEs = advanced economies; EMDEs = emerging market and developing economies. Aggregate growth rates are calculated using GDP weights at average 2010-19 prices and market exchange rates.
A.-C. Shaded area indicates forecasts.
A. Data for 2020 are estimates.
B. Figure shows the contribution of various countries and aggregates to growth of global GDP in 2021 and 2022 in the baseline forecast and average of 2015-19 period.
C. Figure shows contributions to global growth forecast for 2021 and 2022 compared to average contributions to growth in the 2015-19 period.
D. Figure shows the share of EMDEs and advanced economies with forecast upgrades, downgrades, and no forecast changes since January 2021 edition of the *Global Economic Prospects* report (World Bank 2021a). Dashed yellow line indicates 50 percent threshold.
E. Deviation calculated as the percent difference between the level of current projections and January 2020 projections. Sample includes 28 advanced economies and 18 EMDEs.
F. Probabilities for the forecast distribution of global growth are generated using time-varying estimates of the standard deviation and skewness extracted from the forecast distribution of oil price futures, S&P 500 equity price futures, and term spread forecasts, as described in Ohnsorge, Stocker, and Some (2016). Values for 2022 are based on 18-month-ahead forecast distributions. Last observation for S&P 500 and oil price futures is May 26, 2021, whereas term spread forecasts are from May 2021.

of COVID-19, faster-than-expected pace of vaccination in many advanced economies, and additional fiscal relief in the United States.

U.S. output is rebounding particularly sharply, fueled by substantial fiscal support, and it is now expected to exceed its pre-pandemic projection by the end of this year (figure 1.14.E). Growth in other major advanced economies is also firming, albeit to a lesser extent due in part to the resurgence of COVID-19 caseloads. In China, whose economy led the initial stages of the recovery last year, activity remains robust, but the pace of growth has moderated amid diminished policy support.

Across most EMDEs, however, the recoveries taking place will not be sufficient to erase the damage from the pandemic, whose legacies are expected to weigh on global activity for a protracted period. Many countries will take a prolonged period to regain their pre-COVID-19 levels of activity, and a return to pre-pandemic output trends may become unattainable in the absence of major reform efforts (World Bank 2020a; World Bank 2021a). The erosion of skills from lost education and employment are likely to reduce productivity, as will the smaller stock of physical capital resulting from last year's sharp decline in investment. Debt burdens and financial vulnerabilities have risen in many parts of the global economy, which will make the recovery susceptible to financial market stress. This is expected to be accompanied by a gradual withdrawal of macroeconomic policy support over the forecast horizon.

The evolution of the pandemic and the pace of vaccination will be the most crucial factor driving the outlook. The baseline assumes that progress at vaccination will help to effectively contain COVID-19 in advanced economies by the end of the year, with most major EMDEs also making substantial progress at reducing transmission. This would allow most control measures in these economies to be lifted, with a few—such as restrictions on some international travel—being maintained to minimize possible flare-ups linked to new variants of COVID-19. In many other EMDEs, vaccination campaigns will be ongoing throughout the forecast horizon. The virus will continue to disrupt activity to varying degrees, but growth will still benefit from vaccine deployment as well as spillovers from the rapid recovery in major economies.

Risks to the outlook

Forecasts of the pace of the global recovery are subject to considerable uncertainty, especially given the volatile nature of the pandemic (figure 1.14.F). Positive surprises to growth since the January forecast suggest that risks to the outlook have become more balanced; however, downside risks to the near-term outlook continue to predominate.

On the downside, the pandemic could prove more persistent than expected, a wave of corporate bankruptcies or financial market stress could derail the recovery, and an unequal pickup in growth could exacerbate social unrest in various parts of the world. On the upside, more rapid vaccine production—along with more equitable distribution—could lead to faster-than-expected control of the pandemic; moreover, the current upturn in growth, currently concentrated in some major economies, could lead to sizable spillovers and trigger a broader and stronger global economic recovery.

Downside risks

Continued COVID-19 flare-ups and new variants

COVID-19 caseloads are likely to remain high in many parts of the world, including in EMDEs where vaccination progress has been slow, or LICs where vaccinations have barely begun. Bottlenecks in production, vaccine hoarding by some countries, and logistical impediments could continue to slow the pace of vaccine rollouts, particularly in EMDEs. Within many countries, a substantial share of the population is hesitant about inoculation (figure 1.15.A). The continued circulation of the virus in these places means that countries risk repeatedly cycling between making progress in reducing COVID-19 caseloads and relaxing restrictions, followed by the re-emergence of the virus, triggering new lockdowns and renewed declines in activity. The effectiveness of

FIGURE 1.15 Downside risk: Continued COVID-19 flare-ups and new variants

The virus may continue to circulate in areas where populations are hesitant about vaccination, and may mutate and re-emerge from these reservoirs. The effectiveness of persistent pandemic control measures may be eroded by "lockdown fatigue."

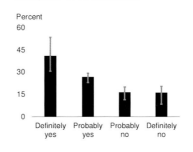

A. Response to survey question about willingness to be vaccinated

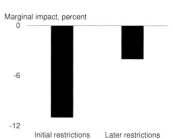

B. Impact of lockdowns on mobility over time

Sources: Delphi Group (database); Fan et al. (2021); Goldstein, Yeyati, and Sartorio (2021); World Bank.
A. Bars indicate the share of responses to the question "If a vaccine to prevent COVID-19 were offered to you today, would you choose to get vaccinated?". Orange whiskers indicate interquartile range across countries. Survey includes 3.9 million respondents in 114 countries. Data as of May 2021, last observation is May 15, 2021.
B. The graph represents the impact of a one standard deviation in the OxCGRT Stringency Index on mobility after 40 days, with an interaction variable representing whether lockdowns had been in effect in the preceding 120 days, as estimated in Goldstein, Yeyati, and Sartorio (2021).

pandemic control measures is also likely being progressively eroded by a rising degree of "lockdown fatigue" (figure 1.15.B).

In addition, COVID-19 has a demonstrated ability to mutate. The appearance and spread of new variants that are more transmissible or more severe could significantly set back the fight against the virus, as well as the economic recovery. The emergence of new strains that are able to circulate even within vaccinated or previously infected populations could prove especially damaging. The prevalence of virus variants in foreign countries would encourage policy makers to maintain stringent travel restrictions, and further delay the recovery in economies dependent on international tourism.

Financial market stress

Governments and corporations amassed considerable debt as they weathered last year's global recession (figure 1.16.A-B). This followed a decade of rapidly accumulating debt after the global financial crisis (Kose et al. 2021). Elevated

BOX 1.3 Recent developments and outlook for low-income countries

Following a sharp slowdown last year, growth among low-income countries (LICs) is expected to pick up to an average of 3.8 percent a year in 2021-22, still lower than its 2010-19 average pace and below January projections. Fragile and conflict-affected LICs are expected to face a particularly dire outlook, with growth of 2.5 percent in 2021-22. In about 60 percent of LICs and 75 percent of fragile and conflict-affected LICs, last year's per capita income losses will not be fully unwound by 2022. Risks to the growth outlook are tilted to the downside and include further impediments to widescale vaccinations, debt distress, worsening food insecurity, and a rise in violence. With tens of millions of people expected to have slipped into extreme poverty last year, the legacies of the pandemic are set to weigh on human and physical capital accumulation, income growth, and poverty reduction for years to come.

Recent developments

In 2020, the COVID-19 pandemic pushed growth in low-income countries (LICs) down to 0.7 percent—the slowest pace in 27 years—with per capita income contracting by 2 percent. Activity has since picked up somewhat, aided by stronger activity in major trading partners and higher commodity prices (figure B1.3.1.A-B). Nonetheless, growth continues to be held back by the ongoing pandemic and its legacies. Continued infections have delayed the resumption of activity in some sectors, particularly in those dependent on face-to-face interactions. The pace of vaccination has been extremely slow in LICs, in part due to procurement hurdles and limited financing. As of late May, only about 0.3 percent of the population in LICs has received at least one dose of vaccine—a mere one-tenth of the share of the population vaccinated in EMDEs and just one-hundredth of the share in advanced economies.

Fragile and conflict-affected LICs have been hit the hardest by the pandemic, with GDP falling by an estimated 1.2 percent in 2020 (Afghanistan, Eritrea, Haiti, Liberia, Sudan). In per capita terms, output in these countries contracted by an estimated 3.8 percent last year, setting back per capita income gains by at least a decade (World Bank 2021a). In some countries, the negative effects of the pandemic were exacerbated by severe floods, droughts, locust infestations, and rising insecurity (Afghanistan, Eritrea, Mali, Sudan).

Activity in other LICs also decelerated sharply last year, with GDP growth falling to a two-decade low of 2.7 percent, equivalent to zero per capita income growth. The adverse effects of COVID-19 and related control measures have disrupted exports, impeded consumption and investments, and eroded tourism revenues (Ethiopia, Guinea, Rwanda).

The evolution of sovereign borrowing costs has been uneven among LICs. With still-benign global financing conditions, sovereign bond yields have fallen back to pre-pandemic levels in some countries (figure B1.3.1.C). In other LICs, however, sovereign borrowing costs have remained elevated, reflecting investors' concerns about public debt sustainability, subdued growth, and political risk (Chad, Ethiopia, Mozambique). Fairly resilient remittance inflows have partially cushioned household income losses (ILO 2021a).

Outlook

Activity in LICs is forecast to grow by 2.9 percent in 2021—the second slowest growth rate of the past 20 years after that of 2020—and by 4.7 percent in 2022 (figure B1.3.2.A; table B1.3.1). The projected rebound hinges on stronger demand from LICs' trading partners—notably China and the United States—higher commodity prices, and some progress at vaccination in LICs. Nonetheless, growth forecasts in 2021-22 have been downgraded by an average 0.6 percentage point, reflecting further delays in vaccination campaigns; natural disasters such as floods, droughts, and insect infestations; and rising geopolitical risks and conflicts. The group's output level in 2022 is projected to be 4.9 percent lower than pre-pandemic projections, as the lingering adverse effects of the pandemic weigh on the recovery. The weakness of the rebound implies that most LICs will make little progress toward recovering to pre-pandemic output levels.

Firming metals and oil prices and strengthening global activity are projected to support growth in industrial commodity-exporting LICs (Central African Republic, Guinea, Tajikistan) to 3.1 percent a year on average in 2021-22. Nevertheless, this pace will be 1.4 percentage point lower than the 2010-19 average and 1.1 percentage points below previous projections, as policy uncertainty, social tensions, and insecurity are expected to delay some investments in new production capacity in the extractive sector (Chad, Mozambique, Niger). In commodity importers (Eritrea, Haiti), activity is expected to stall, with

Note: This section was prepared by Cedric Okou.

BOX 1.3 Recent developments and outlook for low-income countries *(continued)*

FIGURE B1.3.1 Recent developments

Despite improved external conditions and relatively low infection rates, the pandemic and the very slow pace of vaccination have inhibited the resumption of activity in low-income countries (LICs). Sovereign borrowing costs have increased in some LICs.

A. GDP growth in major LIC trading partners

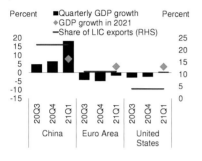

B. COVID-19 infections in LICs

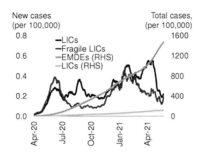

C. Sovereign borrowing costs in selected LICs

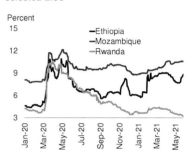

Sources: Bloomberg; Haver Analytics; International Monetary Fund; Johns Hopkins University (database); World Bank
Note: EMDEs = emerging market and developing economies; Fragile LICs = fragile and conflict-affected LICs; LICs = low-income countries.
A. "Share of LIC exports" reflects goods exports.
B. Shows the seven-day moving average of daily new infections in Fragile LICs and LICs. Seven-day moving average of total number of infections in EMDEs and LICs are on the right-hand side axis. Sample includes 147 EMDEs, 28 LICs, and 19 Fragile LICs. Last observation is May 25, 2021.
C. Data for Ethiopia, Mozambique, and Rwanda reflect the yields on 2024, 2031, and 2023 Eurobonds, respectively. Last observation is May 26, 2021.

essentially zero growth this year followed by 2.4 percent growth in 2022.

In fragile and conflict-affected LICs (Afghanistan, Eritrea, Sudan), the recovery is also expected to be subdued, with GDP growth reaching 1.7 percent in 2021 and firming to 3.4 percent in 2022. For this subset of LICs, the growth forecasts for 2021-22 will be 1.1 percentage point below the 2010-19 average and 0.7 percentage point lower than January forecasts. Persistently weak growth reflects the ongoing effects of COVID-19 compounded by the limited administrative capacity of some governments, the high prevalence of extreme poverty, and exposure to frequent natural disasters and violence (Corral et al. 2020).

In other LICs, the recovery is projected to be less subdued, with growth averaging 5 percent a year in 2021-22—still 0.4 percentage point below previous projections. Activity in Ethiopia, the largest LIC, is forecast to expand by 4.2 percent a year in the near term amid geopolitical tensions. In some countries, more stable political and business environments are expected to support growth, including by boosting private sector investment and reinvigorating entrepreneurship (Rwanda, Togo).

Per capita GDP growth in LICs is expected to tick up modestly, averaging 1 percent a year in 2021-22, after falling by 2 percent last year (figure B1.3.2.B). As a result of limited gains in per capita incomes, many of the tens of millions of people projected to fall into extreme poverty due to the pandemic will struggle to escape, as per capita incomes in 2022 will be marginally lower, by 0.1 percent, than in 2019 (figure B1.3.2.C; World Bank 2020b). Among LICs affected by fragility, conflict, and violence—which already have a higher incidence of extreme poverty—per capita income growth is forecast to contract by 0.2 percent a year, on average, in 2021-22. In about three-fifths of LICs and three-quarters of fragile and conflict-affected LICs, last year's per capita income losses will not be fully recouped by 2022. The weak recovery is also unlikely to reverse the increase in inequality caused by the outsized negative effects of the pandemic on women, children, and unskilled and informal workers (IMF 2021a).

After a steep increase last year, government debt in LICs is projected to stabilize at 65 percent of GDP by 2022. As the pandemic recedes and economic activity picks up, a gradual unwinding of fiscal support could help slow

BOX 1.3 Recent developments and outlook for low-income countries *(continued)*

FIGURE B1.3.2 **Outlook**

Growth in low-income countries (LICs) is projected to edge up after the sharpest growth slowdown in a generation last year. The outlook is particularly challenging in fragile and conflict-affected LICs, as the adverse effects of the pandemic are compounded by limited administrative capacity, widespread extreme poverty, natural disasters, and violence. Although per capita incomes are expected to recover somewhat in 2021-22, this will only partially reverse the COVID-related per capita income losses, leaving millions of people in extreme poverty.

A. GDP growth

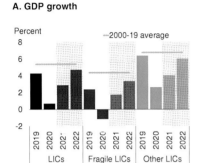

B. GDP growth per capita

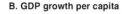
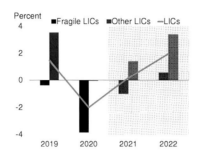

C. Poverty headcount and rate

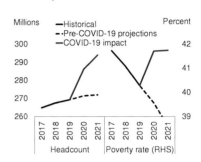

Sources: Mahler et al. (2021); World Bank; World Bank (2020b).
Note: Shaded area indicates forecasts. Fragile LICs = fragile and conflict-affected LICs; LICs = low-income countries.
A.B. Aggregate GDP growth rates calculated using constant GDP weights at average 2010-19 prices and market exchange rates. Aggregate per capita GDP growth rates calculated using the total GDP for each subgroup divided by its total population. Sample comprises 25 LICs, which include 16 Fragile LICs.
C. Red line reflects the baseline projection for the impact of the pandemic on poverty headcounts and rates in LICs.

somewhat the build-up of government debt in some LICs (The Gambia, Togo).

Risks

Downside risks to the outlook predominate. More contagious variants of COVID-19 could spread to populous LICs and weaken the recovery if not quickly contained (Democratic Republic of Congo, Ethiopia, Uganda). Chronic impediments to vaccine delivery and administration, alongside vaccine hesitancy could put widescale vaccination out of reach for some time. The COVAX facility could fail to receive adequate multilateral and bilateral financial and logistical support, causing further delays in LIC vaccination campaigns, with particularly outsized negative effects in tourism-reliant countries (Ethiopia, Madagascar, Uganda).[a]

The pandemic has caused a deterioration in public finances and sharply increased debt service costs in some

LICs, especially those that were already in financial stress (figure B1.3.3.A). Heightened sovereign debt sustainability concerns may further raise borrowing costs, increase debt burdens, exacerbate debt distress, and dampen the recovery in some countries (World Bank 2020c).

Oil-exporting LICs are set to benefit from stronger oil prices (Chad, South Sudan). However, higher oil prices could prompt a rise in global oil supply—in particular from U.S. shale fields. The current OPEC+ production cut agreement could fail, possibly leading to a sharp increase in supply and weaker oil prices. If this happens, oil-exporting LICs could experience revenue shortfalls and, as a result, be forced to decide between growth-damaging fiscal consolidation and risking financial stress. Lower-than-assumed oil prices would, however, benefit net oil importers.

Food insecurity continues to weigh on the livelihoods of more than 112 million people in LICs (figure B1.3.3.B; FSIN 2021). Currency depreciations, localized supply disruptions, and natural disasters have pushed food price inflation well above pre-pandemic rates in some LICs, and many households are set to suffer real income losses and lower food consumption (Afghanistan, Ethiopia,

---

a. The COVAX facility is a multilateral initiative that aims at assisting the poorest countries to secure equitable access to about 2 billion vaccine doses by the end of 2021. It provides demand guarantees to vaccine manufacturers to encourage them to expand and accelerate the production of vaccine doses.

BOX 1.3 Recent developments and outlook for low-income countries *(continued)*

TABLE B1.3.1 Low-income country forecasts [a]
(Real GDP growth at market prices in percent, unless indicated otherwise)

Percentage point differences from January 2021 projections

	2018	2019	2020e	2021f	2022f	2023f	2021f	2022f
Low-Income Country, GDP [b]	**4.7**	**4.3**	**0.7**	**2.9**	**4.7**	**5.6**	**-0.5**	**-0.7**
Afghanistan	1.2	3.9	-1.9	1.0	2.6	3.0	-1.5	-0.7
Burkina Faso	6.7	5.7	0.6	3.1	5.0	5.7	0.7	0.3
Burundi	1.6	1.8	0.3	2.0	2.5	3.0	0.0	0.0
Central African Republic	3.7	3.1	0.0	0.7	2.8	4.4	-2.5	-1.3
Chad	2.4	3.2	-0.9	1.0	2.5	2.9	-1.4	-0.8
Congo, Dem. Rep.	5.8	4.4	0.8	2.5	3.0	4.1	0.4	0.0
Eritrea	13.0	3.7	-0.6	2.0	4.9	3.8	-1.5	-0.6
Ethiopia [c]	6.8	8.4	6.1	2.3	6.0	7.5	2.3	-2.7
Gambia, The	7.2	6.1	0.0	3.5	5.5	7.0	0.4	0.2
Guinea	6.2	5.6	4.7	5.5	5.2	5.2	0.0	0.0
Guinea-Bissau	3.8	4.6	-2.4	3.0	4.0	5.0	0.0	0.0
Haiti [c]	1.7	-1.7	-3.3	-0.5	1.5	2.0	-1.9	0.0
Liberia	1.2	-2.3	-2.9	3.3	4.2	4.7	0.1	0.3
Madagascar	4.6	4.9	-4.2	2.0	5.8	5.4	0.0	0.0
Malawi	4.4	5.4	0.8	2.8	3.0	4.5	-0.5	-1.9
Mali	4.7	4.8	-2.0	2.5	5.2	5.0	0.0	0.0
Mozambique	3.4	2.3	-1.3	1.7	4.1	6.3	-1.1	-0.3
Niger	7.2	5.9	0.8	4.7	8.9	12.1	-0.4	-2.9
Rwanda	8.6	9.4	-3.3	4.9	6.4	7.5	-0.8	-0.4
Sierra Leone	3.4	5.5	-2.2	3.0	3.7	4.0	-1.1	-0.9
South Sudan [c]	-3.5	-0.3	9.5	-3.4	1.5	3.0	0.0	1.5
Sudan	-2.3	-2.5	-3.6	0.4	1.1	2.6	-2.1	-2.0
Tajikistan	7.6	7.4	4.5	5.3	5.6	6.0	1.8	0.1
Togo [d]	4.9	5.3	0.7	3.4	4.6	5.0	0.4	0.1
Uganda [c]	6.3	6.4	3.0	3.3	4.7	6.4	0.5	-1.2

Source: World Bank.
Note: e = estimate; f = forecast. World Bank forecasts are frequently updated based on new information and changing (global) circumstances. Consequently, projections presented here may differ from those contained in other Bank documents, even if basic assessments of countries' prospects do not significantly differ at any given moment in time.
a. The Democratic People's Republic of Korea, Somalia, the Syrian Arab Republic, and the Republic of Yemen are not forecast due to data limitations.
b. Aggregate growth rates are calculated using GDP weights at average 2010-19 prices and market exchange rates.
c. GDP growth based on fiscal year data. For South Sudan, the year 2019 refers to FY2018/19.
d. For Togo, growth figures in 2018 and 2019 are based on pre-2020 rebasing GDP estimates.

Mozambique, Rwanda, Tajikistan, chapter 4). Absent additional aid, acute hunger and poverty could soar in countries where the prevalence of extreme poverty is already highest, particularly in those grappling with fragility or conflict situations (UNFAO 2021; World Bank 2021e).

Rising violence against civilians threatens growth prospects in some LICs (figure B1.3.3.C). Insurgencies in the Sahel and political tensions in some countries are taking a heavy humanitarian and economic toll on the most vulnerable populations and exacerbating the negative effects of COVID-19.

BOX 1.3 Recent developments and outlook for low-income countries *(continued)*

FIGURE B1.3.3 Risks

In addition to further impediments to vaccination, elevated sovereign debt costs and food insecurity continue to cloud the outlook in low-income countries (LICs). Rising violence against civilians could also jeopardize the recovery.

A. Debt service costs in LICs, by risk of debt distress

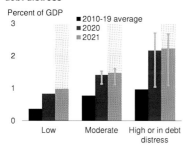

B. Food insecurity in LICs

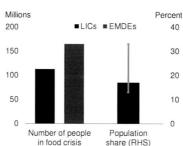

C. Violence against civilians

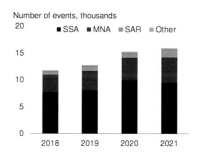

Sources: Armed Conflict Location & Event Data Project (ACLED), https://www.acleddata.com; FSIN and Global Network Against Food Crises; International Monetary Fund; World Bank.
Note: Shaded area indicates forecasts. EMDEs = emerging market and developing economies; LICs = low-income countries.
A. Aggregates represent external debt service payments of the general government sector as a share of current GDP.
B. "Number of people in food crisis" reflects those classified as Integrated Food Security Phase Classification (IPC/CH) Phase 3, i.e., in acute food insecurity crisis or worse, in 2019-20. "Population share" reflects the sample median. Whiskers reflect the interquartile range. Sample includes 55 EMDEs and 25 LICs.
C. Number of acts of violence against civilians. Last observation is May 21, 2021. Values in 2021 are estimated.

debt levels and the resultant vulnerability to higher financing costs have contributed to credit downgrades for nearly 40 percent of EMDEs since the beginning of 2020 (Barnes, Casey, and Jordan -Doak 2021; Reinhart et al. 2021).

In an environment of elevated debt, financial stress can be triggered by any of a number of shocks that increase borrowing costs (Rogoff 2021). Significant fiscal support could lead to rapidly rising inflation and monetary tightening in some major advanced economies, with important international spillover effects (Kose et al. 2017; box 1.1). For example, in the past, U.S. monetary tightening has often contributed to currency depreciation in EMDEs, followed by domestic monetary tightening and, in some countries, financial turmoil (figure 1.16.C; Arteta et al. 2015).

Alternatively, in some countries there is a risk that the recent acceleration in inflation due to commodity price increases and currency depreciation could de-anchor inflation expectations

(figure 1.16.D). Especially for those countries that have borrowed heavily in foreign currency, that have substantial upcoming redemptions that need to be rolled over, or that have limited foreign exchange reserves, a sustained pickup in inflation would drive further depreciation, exacerbating currency mismatches, and could result in significant outflows of the volatile portfolio flows that are often used to finance current account deficits (chapter 4). As has been shown in the past, several vulnerabilities in a country can interact to become severe conglomerate crises, and financing difficulties in one country can cause contagion and trigger broad-based financial crises as investors move capital to safe havens (Devereux and Changhua 2020; Reinhart 2021).

Corporate defaults and deleveraging

In many countries, government support programs were successful in limiting the number of companies that failed during the pandemic. A combination of loan guarantees, payment moratoria, monetary easing, and regulatory forbearance helped maintain liquidity during a period of plunging sales revenues. It also helped lower the number of bankruptcies below those seen during the global financial crisis (figure 1.17.A; Banerjee, Noss, and Vidal Pastor 2021). As these programs are gradually withdrawn, major corporate solvency crises may emerge, especially in those countries where corporate indebtedness is high and weak recoveries reduce profits, or in those with a high proportion of "zombie" firms dependent on low interest rates (Helmersson et al. 2021).

The global banking system entered the pandemic with substantial capital buffers and has proved resilient during the downturn (IMF 2021b). Many indicators of banking health appear robust—for example, the average share of non-performing loans (NPLs) in many countries' financial systems has declined during the pandemic (figure 1.17.B). Nonetheless, the apparent strength of many banks may be overstated by pandemic-related relaxations of the regulations surrounding loan classification and provisioning (Alonso Gispert et al. 2020). If bankruptcies rise as support policies are phased out, bank balance sheets could quickly become impaired.

A wave of corporate defaults could trigger banking crises, particularly in countries where recapitalization by the government may not be possible because of already-strained fiscal positions. The interlinkages between public and private balance sheets have tightened in many countries as a result of pandemic relief programs, suggesting that banking crises could also be triggered by sovereign weakness. Even if a full-fledged banking crisis is averted, a persistently weak banking system would reduce credit availability, hindering the ability of firms to finance investment once demand picks up. This would be particularly damaging for small- and medium-sized enterprises, which have been disproportionately damaged by the pandemic and rely heavily on the banking system for credit (Diez et al. 2021; Gourinchas et al. 2021). At the aggregate level, attempts at deleveraging can fail to gain traction as efforts to reduce debt are hampered by weak nominal output growth.

FIGURE 1.16 Downside risk: Financial market stress

Governments and corporations amassed considerable debt as they weathered last year's global recession. In the past, large currency depreciation in emerging market and developing economies (EMDEs) has often led central banks to tighten monetary policy, regardless of the strength of the domestic economy. Currency depreciation and the recent rise in energy and input prices could also de-anchor inflation expectations and trigger destabilizing capital outflows in some countries.

A. Cumulative change in government debt in EMDEs

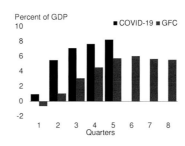

B. Cumulative change in nonfinancial corporations' debt in EMDEs

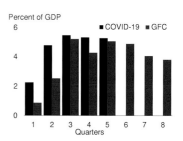

C. EMDE policy rates after large depreciations

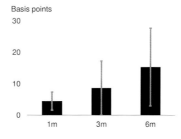

D. Input, output, and oil prices

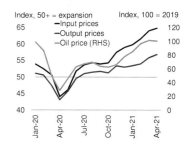

Sources: Haver Analytics; Institute of International Finance; World Bank.
Note: EMDEs = emerging market and developing economies; GFC = global financial crisis.
A.B. Figures show the cumulative change in debt since the start of the episode, which is 2008Q3 for GFC and 2020Q1 for COVID-19. Sample includes 25 EMDEs, excluding China.
C. Bars show estimated impact of a 10-percent monthly currency depreciation at t = 0 on EMDE policy rates at t+1, t+3, and t+6 months horizons using a local projections model. Orange whiskers indicate 90 percent confidence intervals. Sample includes 33 EMDEs with floating or free-floating exchange rates.
D. Figure shows the composite Purchasing Managers' Index (PMI) for input and output prices. PMI readings above 50 indicate expansion in economic activity; readings below 50 indicate contraction. Last observation is April 2021.

Region-specific downside risks

The global recession impacted some regions and groups harder than others, and the global recovery is leaving many behind. Weak and unequal growth or policy missteps could worsen the social discontent already seen in some countries in regions such as EAP, ECA, and LAC. Some governments may address fiscal deficits through austerity measures that reduce support to vulnerable groups. Climate-related events can cause large economic losses (Fernando, Liu, and

FIGURE 1.17 Downside risk: Corporate defaults and deleveraging

Government support programs were successful at averting a rise in bankruptcies such as that which occurred during the global financial crisis, but many of these programs are being withdrawn. Although the global financial system appears to be healthy, as suggested by declining shares of nonperforming loans in many countries, risks may be obscured by regulatory forbearance in many countries.

A. Evolution of bankruptcies in advanced economies during GFC and pandemic

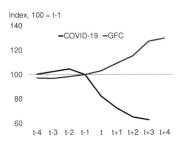

B. Nonperforming loans as a share of total, cumulative change relative to 2019Q1

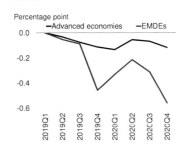

Sources: Bloomberg; European Banking Authority; European Central Bank; Federal Deposit Insurance Corporation; International Monetary Fund; Organisation for Economic Co-operation and Development; World Bank.
Note: EMDEs = emerging market and developing economies; GFC = global financial crisis.
A. Figure shows the median index of bankruptcies for 10 advanced economies. "t" is 2008Q1 for the GFC and 2020Q1 for COVID-19.
B. Figure shows unweighted averages for 22 advanced economies and 33 EMDEs with available data.

McKibbin 2021). These are likely to become increasingly frequent if climate change abatement targets are not met, also often have a disproportionate impact on the poor and risk further magnifying social inequality. For example, the storms that affect small island states in EAP and LAC generally do more damage to the less well-built and uninsured houses of the poor, and droughts in ECA and SAR weigh heavily on subsistence farmers.

Geopolitical tensions remain elevated in regions such as ECA, MENA, and SSA, which face simmering conflicts that could escalate. Conflict and disasters displace millions of people every year, which could result in waves of refugees that exacerbate political tensions or have destabilizing economic effects in neighboring countries (IDMC 2021). In addition, all economies are vulnerable to cyber-attacks, which could affect key infrastructure such as power grids, financial systems, or telecommunications networks.

Many countries are experiencing a sharp rise in food prices, which account for about one-third of the consumption basket in EMDEs, on average, and close to half in some countries. A sustained rise in food prices would exacerbate food insecurity, erode real incomes, and potentially contribute to more widespread malnutrition. Oil supplies may increase suddenly if OPEC+ changes course, or if U.S. shale operators ramp up production. This could lead to a sharp fall in oil prices that could cause difficulties in many oil-exporting countries, including those concentrated in MENA and SSA.

Upside risks

Rapid end of the pandemic at the global level

Vaccine rollouts at the global level, while unequal, have proceeded somewhat more quickly than anticipated at the beginning of the year (figure 1.18.A). At least 10 separate manufacturers have set production targets of more than 1 billion vaccines each by the end of the year (Wouters et al. 2021). If vaccine-makers' projections prove accurate, the world will have almost 13 billion doses available by December, more than enough to fully inoculate about 80 percent of the world's population (figure 1.18.B; Duke Global Health Innovation Center 2021). Temporary waivers on intellectual property protections for COVID-19 vaccines could allow for additional manufacturers to enter the market, further accelerating production.

As domestic supplies exceed demand in countries where vaccination is proceeding rapidly, some excess vaccines will be channeled abroad, accelerating progress in lagging countries. Unless distribution and demand challenges hinder progress, increased vaccine production could result in more rapid and globally equitable vaccination distribution and remove the need for stringent control measures. Accelerated COVID-19 vaccination is likely to have economic benefits that heavily outweigh its costs (Gagnon, Kamin, and Kearns 2021). A rapid, effective, and global containment of COVID-19 would strengthen the medium-term global recovery and make it subject to fewer setbacks.

Sustained, broad-based global upturn

The global recovery is now being driven by the United States and a few other major economies. It is possible that spillovers from activity in these economies help to undam a large reserve of pent-up demand, bolster confidence, and catalyze a synchronized and self-sustaining boom that pushes global activity above baseline forecasts, even if outbreaks persist in some EMDEs (figure 1.19.A-B; box 1.1).

A stronger, more durable, and more broad-based global upturn would reduce the scarring caused by the pandemic. A more robust labor market would attract a greater share of discouraged workers back to the labor force. Faster growth would propel the recovery in investment above the baseline forecast. The need to meet surging demand could also encourage faster adoption of new technologies, particularly in the services sector as companies invest in the digital remote service practices pioneered during the pandemic (McKinsey Global Institute 2021). Stronger potential output growth would help keep inflation pressures in check and help reduce debt ratios. A more broad-based recovery would also likely be more inclusive, with a greater reach to those vulnerable groups that have been most affected by the crisis, and thus help move a larger number of people out of poverty.

Policy challenges

Globally-coordinated efforts are essential to secure equitable vaccine distribution and far-reaching debt relief, particularly for low-income countries. As the health crisis abates, policy actions will be needed to address the adverse legacies of the pandemic, including high debt and weak productivity growth. This will require a difficult balancing act as policy makers seek to nurture the recovery while safeguarding macroeconomic stability. Policies to facilitate employment in high-growth sectors, protect vulnerable groups, and reduce trade costs—combined with increased investments in education, connectivity, and green infrastructure—will be needed to bolster growth prospects and steer the recovery onto a green, resilient, and inclusive development path.

FIGURE 1.18 Upside risk: Rapid end of the pandemic at the global level

The pace of vaccine rollout at the global level, while highly unequal, has exceeded expectations. Vaccine makers have committed to producing almost 13 billion doses by the end of the year, enough to fully inoculate most of the world if distribution issues can be resolved and vaccine access becomes more equitable.

A. Pace of vaccination compared to January assumptions

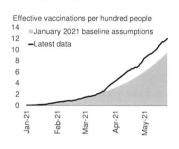

B. Vaccine production targets for 2021

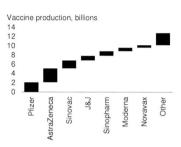

Sources: Duke Global Health Innovation Center (2021); Guénette and Yamazaki (2021); Our World in Data (database); World Bank.
A. Figure shows the average seven-day moving average of effective daily COVID-19 vaccinations administered per hundred people across the Group of Seven (G7) member countries which include Canada, France, Germany, Italy, Japan, the United Kingdom, and the United States and the Emerging Seven (EM7) member countries including China, India, Brazil, Mexico, the Russian Federation, Indonesia, and Turkey. As in Guénette and Yamazaki (2021), effective vaccinations are computed by multiplying the total number of vaccinations by 0.5 to account for multi-dose vaccines and by 0.85 to account for imperfect vaccine effectiveness. Baseline assumption is for advanced economies and major EMDEs as described in box 1.4 of the January 2021 edition of the *Global Economic Prospects* report (World Bank 2021a). Last observation is May 25, 2021.
B. Global planned vaccine production in 2021. "Other" includes CanSino Biologics, COVAXX United Biomedical, Gamaleya, CureVac, Bharat Biotech, Valneva, Inovio, Zydus Cadila, Medicago, and Vector Institute. Data are as of May 25, 2021.

FIGURE 1.19 Upside risk: Sustained, broad-based global upturn

A stronger, more durable, and more broad-based global upturn would help reduce the scarring caused by the pandemic. Spillovers from faster growth in major economies would increase growth elsewhere.

A. Response of growth in EMDEs excl. China to 1-percentage-point higher growth in major economies

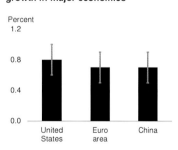

B. GDP growth in 2022 in baseline and upside scenario

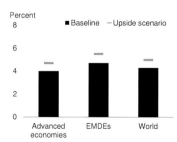

Sources: Oxford Economics; World Bank.
Note: EMDEs = emerging market and developing economies.
A. Figure shows impulse response of growth in EMDEs excluding China after one year to a 1-percentage-point growth acceleration in the United States, the euro area, or China. Estimates are based on the methodology in World Bank (2020a).
B. Bars show baseline data from *Global Economic Prospects* June 2021 database. Orange markers reflect growth in the "sustained boom" scenario from Oxford Global Economic Model simulations.

Key global challenges

Ending the COVID-19 pandemic will require a global deployment of vaccines. Accelerating the pace of vaccinations will require policy makers to bolster public trust in vaccine safety and work with the private sector to improve the production and distribution of vaccines. International support is also critical to hastening global control of the virus by providing vaccines to EMDEs and LICs where availability is limited. Global initiatives, including COVAX, can redistribute excess vaccine doses and ensure more equitable access to vaccine supplies (Gavi 2021). Until widespread vaccination is achieved, growth-friendly control measures—including universal masking, social distancing, and test and trace strategies—are needed to help contain domestic flare-ups, including those resulting from the spread of new virus strains (Prettner et al. 2021).

In addition, health systems must be strengthened to confront the lingering health consequences of the pandemic, including chronic COVID-19 symptoms and delayed treatment of other conditions. Increasing global pandemic preparedness can also help reduce the risk of future global health crises. Moreover, it is essential to avoid the lure of protectionism in favor of a rules-based international trade regime that safeguards global supply chains for vaccines and other essential traded goods.

Sustaining the global recovery and tackling the many legacies from the pandemic will necessitate close cooperation across governments, multilateral organizations, and the private sector. For instance, the collective benefits of exceptional fiscal and monetary policy support measures are more likely to be sustained if their eventual withdrawal is carefully coordinated (Yoshino et al. 2020). International cooperation can play an important role in helping poorer countries address liquidity and solvency issues through interventions that mobilize development finance, as well as spur the design of government credit guarantees, helping to alleviate financing constraints in EMDEs with fragile banking systems. For LICs facing very large debt burdens, far-reaching and globally-coordinated debt relief efforts involving all creditors will be needed to address long-term debt

sustainability challenges (Malpass 2021). At the same time, global cooperation can be instrumental in facilitating the transformational investments in agriculture, transportation, and energy systems needed to entrench a green recovery, reduce global emissions, and ultimately tackle the long-term challenge of climate change.

Challenges in advanced economies

Continued support from monetary and fiscal policy will be needed to ensure a durable recovery in the short term. As the pandemic abates, a gradual normalization of macroeconomic policy will be required to achieve price stability and public debt sustainability. Reforms will be also needed to foster green, resilient, and inclusive growth. These include facilitating the reallocation of labor across sectors and harnessing the accelerated pace of technological adoption brought on by the pandemic. They also include expanded green infrastructure and proper carbon tax policy, which would accelerate a low-carbon transition.

Monetary and financial policies

Inflation pressures are appearing earlier than was the case following the global financial crisis, due to an increase in commodity prices and global supply bottlenecks (figure 1.20.A; chapter 4). Still, most advanced economies are in the early stages of recovery and face the prospect of sizable excess supply (figure 1.20.B). A continued high degree of monetary accommodation will therefore be essential to cementing a strong recovery. In the United States, however, the Federal Reserve's intention to keep policy rates near zero for a prolonged period may be tested by a rapidly narrowing negative output gap and the possibility that additional fiscal support, coupled with continued reopening, leads to unexpectedly strong domestic demand. Effective communication with market participants will continue to be crucial to ensure that the eventual withdrawal of monetary policy support does not trigger undue volatility in financial markets.

In most advanced economies, authorities will need to carefully manage the unwinding of debt and payment moratoria, especially given elevated nonfinancial corporate debt levels (figure 1.20.C).

Although the level of nonperforming bank loans is much lower than it was during the global financial crisis, it will likely rise once forbearance policies are allowed to expire. The risk of insolvency has also increased for small- and medium-sized enterprises with limited means to raise new capital (Gourinchas et al. 2021). Therefore, it would be important to proactively improve a menu of policies to safeguard the health of the banking system, including debt restructuring, asset separation, and recapitalization that could be used to facilitate an early resolution of corporate and household insolvencies (Beck, Carletti, and Bruno 2021; Boot et al. 2021; Diez et al. 2021).

Fiscal policy

The historically sharp and ongoing rise of sovereign debt levels highlights the need to use fiscal support wisely and efficiently (figure 1.20.D). Providing continued support to the nascent recovery remains the near-term priority of advanced-economy fiscal authorities, although at this stage in the crisis fiscal support can be more narrowly targeted. For example, focusing support on hard-hit vulnerable populations, such as the unemployed and lower-income families with children, would have a greater macroeconomic impact given their higher marginal propensities to consume (Klein and Smith 2021; Wilson 2020).

In economies already experiencing a rapid recovery, such as the United States, additional fiscal support, over and above historically large increases in spending, would need to be employed efficiently and weighed carefully against its potential consequences for inflation and long-term debt sustainability (figure 1.20.E-F; Furman and Summers 2020). Although the near-term growth impacts of infrastructure investments may be limited, they can be particularly useful in generating long-run economic benefits (Ramey 2020). In the euro area, enhanced coordination of national fiscal relief measures across member countries can help strengthen the recovery and reduce trade imbalances (Aussilloux et al. 2021).

Although record-high public debt and fiscal deficit ratios among advanced economies do not pose an imminent threat given currently low interest rates, there will soon be a need to rebuild fiscal space

FIGURE 1.20 Monetary, financial, and fiscal policies in advanced economies

Inflation pressures are appearing earlier than at a similar time during the recovery that followed the global financial crisis. Nonetheless, they may not persist outside of the United States, as most advanced economies face substantial excess supply. Nonfinancial corporate debt levels have risen above their global financial crisis average. Moreover, the historically large increase in sovereign debt levels highlights the need to use fiscal support efficiently.

A. Inflation pressures in advanced economies

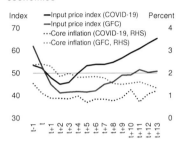

B. Output gaps and deviations of output from pre-pandemic projections

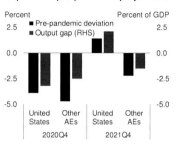

C. Nonfinancial corporate leverage

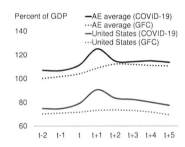

D. Gross government debt to GDP

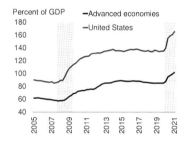

E. Fiscal support in the United States and euro area

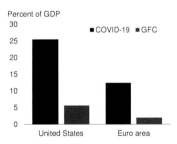

F. General government balance in the United States and euro area

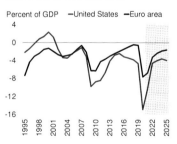

Sources: Congressional Budget Office; Haver Analytics; International Monetary Fund; Oxford Economics; World Bank.
Note: AE = advanced economies; GFC = global financial crisis.
A. Solid lines show 3-month moving average of the Purchasing Managers' Index (PMI) composite input price index for Developed Markets. PMI readings above (below) 50 indicate expansion (contraction) in economic activity. Dotted lines show median year-over-year core inflation rate for 29 advanced economies. "t" refers to November 2008 for GFC and March 2020 for COVID-19. Last observation is April 2021.
B. Deviation is percent change in real GDP levels between current projections and January 2020 vintage as pre-pandemic estimate. Other AEs calculated using GDP weights at average 2010-19 prices and market exchange rates. Sample includes 25 advanced economies.
C. "t" refers to 2020Q1 for COVID-19 and 2008Q3 for global financial crisis.
D. Average of 25 advanced economies. Recent data are estimates by Oxford Economics. Shaded areas are global financial crisis and COVID-19 pandemic. Last observation is 2021Q1.
E. COVID-19 fiscal support is "above the line" measures as compiled by the International Monetary Fund. COVID-19 fiscal support in euro area includes measures announced by euro area member countries and the European Commission.
F. Figure shows percent of nominal GDP. Shaded area over 2021-2025 indicates projections from the Congressional Budget Office (for the United States) and the International Monetary Fund (for euro area).

FIGURE 1.21 Structural policies in advanced economies

In contrast to the global financial crisis, the COVID-19 recession caused a collapse of activity and employment in the services sector. Policies to facilitate employment of displaced workers are needed as many jobs in sectors adversely affected by the pandemic can be automated.

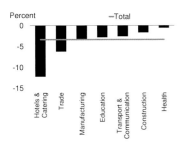

A. Change in employment in 2020, by sector

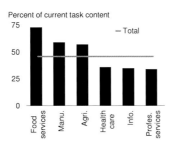

B. Potential for automation across industries in the United States

Sources: Muro et al. (2019); Oxford Economics; World Bank.
A. Aggregates calculated using GDP weights at average 2010-19 prices and market exchange rates. Unbalanced sample includes 33 advanced economies.
B. Figure shows the automation potential for specific industry groups in the United States as presented in Muro et al. (2019). Food services = accommodation and food services, Manu. = manufacturing, Agri. = agriculture, forestry, fishing and hunting, Health care = health care and social assistance, Info. = Information, and Profes. services = professional, scientific, and technical services.

and ensure medium-term debt sustainability (Bartsch et al. 2020). Achieving these goals will be more likely if early action is taken to establish credible medium-term fiscal plans and develop carefully calibrated consolidation strategies. These efforts can be complemented with comprehensive reform of tax and social security systems (Orszag, Rubin and Stiglitz 2021).

Structural policies

In advanced economies, the pandemic has caused far greater disruption to output and employment in services sectors than the global financial crisis (figure 1.21.A). A comprehensive set of labor market policies can strengthen the recovery and accelerate an appropriate reallocation of labor across sectors. In particular, policies to facilitate employment of displaced workers—notably women and young workers—are crucial given that many of the occupations in the hardest-hit sectors are highly susceptible to automation (figure 1.21.B; Albanesi and Kim 2021; Hallward-Driemeier and Nayyar 2018). Policy makers can consider expanding worker retraining opportunities and increasing social protection funded by a broader and more progressive tax structure

(Sedik and Yoo 2021). Education systems can also be improved to counter pandemic-related learning losses, particularly in vulnerable populations (Rose et al. 2021).

In contrast to the global financial crisis, productivity and output growth are likely to rebound in the near term, at least temporarily, as pandemic restrictions on activity and mobility are lifted (Bloom et al. 2021). Policy efforts will be needed to sustain this recovery, especially through cementing rapid gains in digitalization. For instance, providing a secure and fast digital communications environment, coupled with regulatory reforms, can harness the flexibility and productivity inherent in allowing workers to work remotely (Barrero, Bloom, and Davis 2021; Morikawa 2021). Behavioral change in favor of digital services and telecommuting stemming from the pandemic may exacerbate inequalities across firms and households. Policies that enhance the accessibility of financial and public services, support small- and medium-sized enterprises, and promote research and development are essential (OECD 2021a).

Fostering green, resilient, and inclusive growth is also a key policy priority. Government authorities can engage the private sector to increase the economy's resilience to climate change, working together to accelerate a low-carbon transition, strengthen biodiversity, and enhance environmental health (Disparte 2021; OECD 2021b). Implementing carbon taxes can help reduce harmful emissions and better align incentives with economic objectives, while raising the revenues required to fund green investments, strengthen social safety nets, and improve long-run debt sustainability (IMF 2019; OECD 2020).

Challenges in emerging market and developing economies

As the health emergency abates, EMDE policy makers need to cement a durable, resilient, and inclusive recovery while tackling the pandemic's longer-lasting and harmful legacies. Millions of lives and livelihoods have been lost, progress at poverty reduction has been reversed, and the policy space available to support growth has been eroded. Emerging inflation pressures mean that some central banks will have to balance the need to support the economic recovery against risks to price stability (chapter 4). The deterioration of fiscal positions and record-high levels of debt in many countries have heightened financial vulnerabilities and may force a premature removal of fiscal support.

These challenges highlight the need to pursue policies that help rebuild fiscal space without unduly weighing on growth. Such policies include efforts to improve spending efficiency and to better target social protection measures. As the recovery gains traction, these policies can be complemented with those that bolster domestic revenue mobilization. Over the longer term, entrenching a green, resilient, and inclusive recovery amid reduced fiscal space will require policies that prioritize raising long-run growth prospects. These include helping workers transition to high-growth sectors while protecting vulnerable groups, raising human capital, increasing access to digital connectivity, reducing trade costs, and spurring green investments.

Policy challenges in China

Although China's recovery from COVID-19 is becoming more broad-based, the public investment-led support measures to confront the pandemic-induced downturn have disrupted progress at rebalancing aggregate demand toward domestic consumption. Corporate and household debt levels, which were already high before the pandemic, have risen further, eroding previous deleveraging gains and increasing financial stability risks.

As authorities resume de-risking and deleveraging, they may need to avoid premature policy tightening until private domestic demand strengthens further. Improving insolvency and bank resolution frameworks would facilitate an orderly exit of weak or failing corporates and banks and free up resources for more productive activities.

After this year's cyclical rebound, China's economy is projected to slow over the medium term, reflecting the legacies of excessive borrowing as well as structural trends, including declining labor supply and softening productivity growth.

To bolster potential growth, China needs to pursue structural reforms that boost market-based resource allocation toward more productive activities (World Bank 2020d; World Bank 2021f).

EMDE monetary and financial policies

Average core inflation in EMDEs has ticked up to slightly above pre-pandemic levels, with a more pronounced increase in countries that experienced depreciations (figure 1.22.A-B). Headline inflation has also increased due to rising energy prices and, particularly in LICs, food prices. Model-based forecasts and inflation expectations point to an increase in inflation in 2021 that will exceed target ranges in about one-half of inflation-targeting EMDEs (chapter 4; figure 1.22.C).

EMDEs have generally maintained their expansionary monetary stance, supported by continued benign global financial conditions. Amid some tightening in financial conditions, average EMDE 10-year bond yields have increased by slightly more than those in the United States (BIS 2021). However, further increases in advanced-economy yields may result in larger transmissions into EMDE yields and financial conditions, which could weigh on the recovery.

Some EMDE central banks are already facing difficult policy trade-offs in ensuring that inflation pressures remain contained, particularly after large currency depreciations, in the presence of substantial output gaps. EMDEs with larger current account deficits and higher external debt-to-GDP ratios experienced larger depreciations, on average, over the past year. Countries with weakly-anchored inflation expectations face a higher and more persistent pass-through from currency depreciations to inflation; accordingly, larger increases in interest rates may be required in these economies to prevent a persistent rise in inflation (Ha, Stocker, and Yilmazkuday 2019).

On average, capital adequacy ratios remain high and NPLs low in EMDEs, reflecting forbearance measures, government guarantees, and a delay in loan defaults that has also been typical in previous recessions (World Bank 2021g). Some EMDE banking sectors are likely to face significant challenges as government support measures for

FIGURE 1.22 Monetary and financial policies in EMDEs

Core inflation in emerging market and developing economies (EMDEs) has risen slightly above pre-pandemic levels, with a more pronounced increase in EMDEs that experienced depreciations. In about half of inflation-targeting EMDEs, inflation is expected to exceed targets for 2021, albeit only slightly. Price pressures and depreciations have required policy tightening in some countries, even as output gaps remain large. EMDE banks remain well capitalized, but asset quality could deteriorate as government support measures end. Improvements in insolvency frameworks could bolster recovery rates from defaulted loans and facilitate a redeployment of productive capital.

A. Core and headline inflation in EMDEs

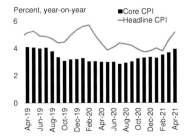

B. Core inflation in EMDEs and exchange rate adjustments

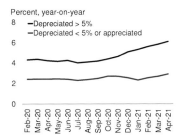

C. Model-based conditional forecast for EMDE inflation

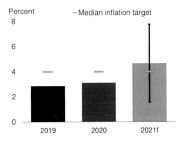

D. Time to resolve insolvency

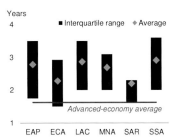

Sources: Consensus Economics; Haver Analytics; World Bank.

Note: CPI = consumer price index; EMDEs = emerging market and developing economies; EAP = East Asia and Pacific, ECA = Europe and Central Asia, LAC = Latin America and the Caribbean, MNA = Middle East and North Africa, SAR = South Asia, SSA = Sub-Saharan Africa.

A. Aggregates calculated using 2020 real U.S. dollar GDP weights at average 2010-19 prices and market exchange rates. Sample for "Headline CPI" and "Core CPI" includes up to 89 and 50 EMDEs respectively. Last observation is April 2021.

B. Sample includes 14 EMDEs where the currency depreciated by more than 5 percent and 28 EMDEs where the currency depreciated by less than 5 percent, or appreciated, between February 2020 and April 2021.

C. Based on median inflation in 125 EMDEs and inflation target in 30 inflation-targeting EMDEs. 2021 EMDE inflation forecast described in chapter 4. Vertical line indicates 16-84 confidence bands.

D. Time to resolve insolvency is the number of years from the filing for insolvency in court until the resolution of distressed assets. Bars show interquartile range whereas orange diamonds show average number of years.

credit provision are withdrawn and regulatory guidance is tightened on loan classifications. Measures to assess credit quality need to be strengthened to identify the scale of potential loan losses and insolvency frameworks improved to maximize recovery rates as government guarantees and forbearance measures are reviewed (figure 1.22.D; World Bank 2021h).

EMDE fiscal policy

EMDE fiscal support packages announced last year were sizable, with discretionary measures averaging 4 percent of GDP. They were also broad based, with nearly all countries easing their fiscal stance. Relative to advanced economies, EMDE fiscal support was largely front-loaded, with announced COVID-19 revenue and spending measures mostly deployed in 2020 (figure 1.23.A; Gaspar et al. 2021). In addition to this discretionary fiscal support, sharp declines in revenues contributed to rapidly widening fiscal deficits in EMDEs, whereas in advanced economies, widening deficits reflected a surge in spending.

This year, many EMDEs, including some large economies, are expected to pivot toward fiscal tightening to improve the sustainability of public finances, despite large spending needs and sizable output losses relative to pre-pandemic projections (figure 1.23.B-C). For about one-third of those EMDEs with fiscal rules, this will be aided by a gradual transition back to rules-based frameworks after invoking escape clauses in response to the pandemic. These efforts notwithstanding, government debt is anticipated to continue to rise over the forecast horizon, which will further limit fiscal space. Moreover, fiscal sustainability gaps are expected to remain negative, even under current benign financing conditions; in this context, a sudden tightening of financing conditions or worse-than-expected growth could result in higher adjustment needs to stabilize government debt.

Policy makers continue to face the challenge of balancing the need to support the incipient recovery with that of ensuring fiscal sustainability and containing vulnerabilities to financial market stress. Although many EMDEs are still able to tap international capital markets, a sudden shift in investor sentiment could result in a jump in borrowing costs, worsen fiscal positions, and increase debt rollover and currency mismatch risks (Blanchard, Felman, and Subramanian 2021; Kalemli-Özcan, Shim, and Liu 2021). To address these challenges, authorities can prioritize and streamline spending, including by targeting social expenditures more effectively.

For smaller EMDEs and LICs, many of which currently face liquidity or solvency issues, international debt relief and financing support have been critical in providing fiscal space. These include the Debt Service Suspension Initiative and the G20 Common Framework, with the latter also helping to facilitate coordination among creditors. Other initiatives, such as the World Bank Group's Sustainable Development Financing Policy, can help some countries address debt vulnerabilities and achieve more sustainable debt, including through the provision of technical assistance. However, additional resources are likely to be needed, including grants and highly concessional funding, as well as increased private sector participation. Measures to further strengthen the debt restructuring framework could also help increase the efficiency and effectiveness of restructuring in circumstances where it proves necessary (Group of Thirty 2021).

As the pandemic is contained and the recovery firms, governments will need to shore up medium-term fiscal sustainability by realigning expenditures with revenues. This can include measures to improve domestic revenue mobilization, such as broadening revenue bases with new tax instruments to help close sizable gaps with advanced economies (figure 1.23.D; De Mooij et al. 2020; Kose et al. 2021). On the spending side, strengthening the efficiency of public expenditures could help ensure that additional spending yields dividends to growth (figure 1.23.E; Mathai et al. 2020; Schwartz et al. 2020). Such measures would also help restore the fiscal space that is needed to address sizable investment gaps and broaden social safety net coverage, which could build resilience against future shocks. These efforts can be supported by confidence-enhancing measures to strengthen fiscal credibility, such as fortifying medium-term fiscal frameworks, providing clear policy direction, and increasing debt transparency (Reinhart et al. 2021).

The pandemic has also created additional fiscal challenges for EMDEs with less diversified economies, including energy exporters. For these economies, earlier oil price declines and the subsequent need for fiscal adjustment highlight

FIGURE 1.23 Fiscal policy in emerging market and developing economies

Nearly all emerging market and developing economies (EMDEs) implemented fiscal support packages to confront the pandemic. Fiscal support was mostly front-loaded in 2020, however, and many EMDEs are expected to unwind these measures and adopt a tighter fiscal stance starting this year. Strengthening domestic revenue mobilization to close tax revenue gaps, and reducing public spending inefficiencies to yield higher growth dividends, will be critical to ensure debt sustainability and rebuild fiscal space, particularly in low-income countries and energy exporters.

A. Fiscal support and stance

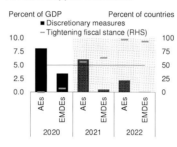

B. Fiscal impulses and output gaps

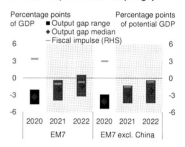

C. Cumulative change in cyclically-adjusted primary balances

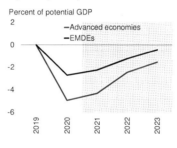

D. EMDE tax revenue gaps with advanced economies

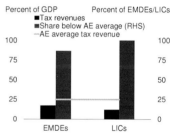

E. Inefficiencies in public spending

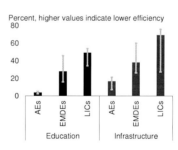

F. Revenue impact of low-carbon scenario in EMDE energy exporters

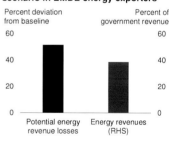

Sources: Baum, Mogues, and Verdier (2020); Carbon Tracker; IMF; World Bank.
Note: AEs = advanced economies; EMDEs = emerging market and developing economies; EM7 = China, India, Brazil, Mexico, the Russian Federation, Indonesia, and Turkey; LICs = low-income-countries. Fiscal impulse is defined as the negative change in the cyclically-adjusted primary balance (CAPB) from the previous year. Declines (increases) in the fiscal impulse indicate fiscal tightening (expansion). Shaded areas indicate forecasts.
A. Discretionary fiscal support measured as additional spending and foregone revenues, as in IMF (2021a). Sample includes 34 advanced economies and 30 EMDEs.
B. Output gaps estimated using a modified multivariate filter model of World Bank (2018). Blue bars reflect range around one standard deviation.
C. Figure shows the median cumulative change in the CAPB, as measured in IMF (2021a). Sample includes 34 advanced economies and 30 EMDEs.
D. Data reflect the last observation available between 2016 and 2018. Sample includes 36 advanced economies, 127 EMDEs, and 21 LICs.
E. Figure shows median efficiency gap: The difference between the country's spending efficiency and that of best performers, as measured in Baum, Mogues, and Verdier (2020). Yellow whiskers show interquartile ranges. Sample includes 34 advanced economies, 139 EMDEs, and 24 LICs.
F. Figure shows the share of oil and gas revenue in total government revenue and potential government energy revenue loss under a low-carbon scenario, as measured by Carbon Tracker. Potential energy revenue losses reflect shortfalls over 2021-40 relative to 2015-19 average, whereas energy revenues are the 2015-18 average. Aggregates are calculated using 2019 real U.S. dollar GDP weights at average 2010-19 prices and market exchange rates. Sample includes 25 EMDE energy exporters.

the urgency of diversifying sources of fiscal revenue (Stocker et al. 2018). Although global oil prices in the near term have been revised up, broadening the fiscal revenue base could help reduce the vulnerability of EMDE energy exporters to adverse external shocks, particularly as other countries shift toward greener energy (figure 1.23.F). These efforts can be further complemented by other reforms that promote diversification, including those that bolster competition and improve the business environment, as well as fiscal measures that reduce costly energy subsidies and strengthen macroeconomic policy frameworks (Wheeler et al. 2020).

EMDE structural policies

The pandemic is expected to exacerbate the slowdown in EMDE potential growth that had already been projected over the next decade. The accumulated scars on human capital will be slow to heal, while the pace of accumulation of physical capital is likely to remain subdued for a prolonged period (World Bank 2021a). Productivity may have also been impaired by disruptions to organizational effectiveness, increased transaction costs, and reduced dynamism, even if some firms have taken the opportunity to increase technological adoption (di Mauro and Syverson 2020; Apedo-Amah et al. 2020).

The policy response to the crisis provides an opportunity to bolster a green, resilient, and inclusive recovery that addresses both the scars brought about by COVID-19 and the longer-term challenges of climate change (World Bank 2021d). To this end, authorities can carefully sequence a package of growth-enhancing reforms, prioritizing policies aimed at alleviating the damage caused to human capital, investment, and productivity by the pandemic, while better aligning private sector incentives with broader economic policy objectives. These include policies that would facilitate the transition of labor across sectors while protecting vulnerable groups, deepen human capital, expand access to digital connectivity, reduce trade costs, and boost green investments.

Reinvigorating human capital

The COVID-19 recession caused a severe yet uneven collapse in employment across sectors, and some of those jobs are at risk of automation. EMDEs suffered particularly large declines in working hours (figure 1.24.A; ILO 2021a). Policy action needs to underpin a resilient and inclusive recovery in employment and limit the damage to human capital originating from long spells of unemployment. Active labor market policies—such as providing employment services, entrepreneurship support, and worker retraining programs—can be pursued to encourage employment in sectors experiencing higher growth (Card, Kluve, and Weber 2018; Schmillen 2020; Trebilcock 2014). Coupled with income support programs geared toward vulnerable populations, such as targeted cash transfers, active labor market policies can facilitate the movement of labor across sectors and enhance employment prospects in low-income countries (Escudero and Liepermann 2020).

Investing in education is also needed to mitigate the disruptions to human capital brought about by the pandemic, including learning losses and youth disengagement. About 60 percent of low- and lower-middle-income countries have cut their public education budgets since the onset of the crisis, reversing a decade-long trend of increased funding (figure 1.24.B; UNESCO 2021). Education budgets can be bolstered with additional financing deployed to incentivize attendance and educational attainment, improve school facilities, and reform incentive structures for teachers, which can also increase the efficiency of existing education spending (Hui, La-Bhus, and Baoping 2019; World Bank 2018b; World Bank 2021i). Investment in learning infrastructure leads to improved educational outcomes and higher incomes in the long term (Akresh, Halim, and Kleemans 2021). Moreover, governments can facilitate access to existing free and open-source education technologies in a way that favors the inclusion of disadvantaged groups (Burns et al. 2019; UNESCO 2020).

Expanding access to digital connectivity

Policies aimed at expanding access to digital connectivity can also be pursued to accelerate digital transformation and support higher productivity and potential output. In many EMDEs, this requires liberalizing telecommunications sectors while expanding investment in communications infrastructure. Properly liberalized telecommunications, coupled with regulatory independence and efficient taxation of digital services, can catalyze private sector investment that lowers the cost of access and increases internet adoption and access to digital services, with significant spillovers to the rest of the economy (Arezki et al. 2021; Rodriguez-Castelan et al. 2021; World Bank 2019).

Policy makers can also play a key role in accelerating the pace of adoption of digital technologies by firms (World Bank 2016). Efforts to foster equitable internet access for distance learning can help avoid the widening of a digital divide across income levels. In addition, policies that enhance data transparency and security can strengthen institutions, including by holding governments more accountable, which in the long run is associated with higher levels of per capita income (Islam and Lederman 2020). Fostering data transparency is important to guarantee an efficient allocation of resources, and it can also help reduce borrowing costs by instilling market discipline and reducing uncertainty (Kubota and Zeufack 2020).

Reducing trade costs

Trade integration can yield significant productivity gains, especially when it involves participation in global value chains (Constantinescu, Matoo, and Ruta 2017; World Bank 2020e). Trade openness can raise incomes across sectors, lower poverty, and reduce gender bias in wages (World Bank and WTO 2020). Conversely, high trade costs hinder competitiveness, limit participation in global value chains, and erode consumer welfare by reducing the availability of goods and services for consumption (Diakantoni et al. 2017).

Trade costs have declined steadily in EMDEs since the mid-1990s. Still, in many countries, they remain well in excess of 100 percent of the value of traded goods and substantially higher than in advanced economies (figure 1.24.C-D). Trade costs are particularly elevated in small island states. Poor communication and transportation infrastructure, a lack of logistics services, lengthy

FIGURE 1.24 Structural policies in emerging market and developing economies

The pandemic severely reduced working hours in emerging market and developing economies (EMDEs). Disruptions to education have been particularly large in lower-income countries, a majority of which have cut education budgets since the pandemic began. In order to sustain the nascent recovery, authorities can prioritize policies to boost productivity, including measures that reduce trade costs. There remains significant scope to improve environmental performance in EMDEs, including by reducing greenhouse gas emissions and accelerating investments in green infrastructure.

A. Changes in working hours in 2020

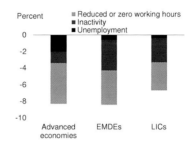

B. Share of countries with recent declines in education budgets

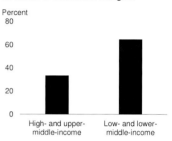

C. Trade costs and tariff rates

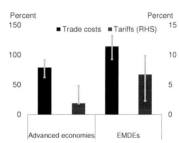

D. EMDE trade costs and tariff rates

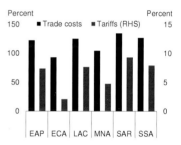

E. Environmental performance

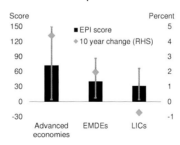

F. Global greenhouse gas emissions

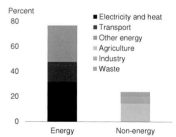

Sources: Al-Samarrai et al. (2021); Comtrade (database); Environmental Performance Index, Yale University (database); ESCAP-World Bank Trade Cost Database; International Labour Organization (2021a); World Bank; World Resources Institute.

Note: EMDEs = emerging market and developing economies; EPI = Environmental Performance Index; LICs = low-income countries; EAP = East Asia and Pacific, ECA = Europe and Central Asia, LAC = Latin America and the Caribbean, MNA = Middle East and North Africa, SAR = South Asia, SSA = Sub-Saharan Africa.

A. Unemployment and inactivity converted into working-hour equivalents. EMDE aggregate calculated as the unweighted average of lower middle-income countries and upper middle-income countries. Advanced economies refers to ILO's classification of high-income countries.

B. Figure shows share of countries with declines in education budgets between March 2020 and February 2021. Budget changes extracted from country documents for 29 EMDEs.

C.D. Data are for 2018. Blue bars show average trade costs expressed as ad valorem (tariff) equivalent of the value of traded goods. Red bars show average tariffs. Bilateral trade costs aggregated using 2018 bilateral country export shares. Yellow whiskers show interquartile ranges.

E. EPI is a proxy measure of environmental health calculated by Yale University for 180 countries based on 32 performance indicators. Countries ranked according to their relative performance across all categories. Orange whiskers show interquartile range.

F. Data are for 2018. "Other energy" includes energy used by industry, construction, and other emissions from energy production.

border processes, and elevated tariff barriers all contribute to high trade costs (chapter 3).

Authorities can facilitate trade integration by implementing policies that reduce the cost of trading, including streamlining border procedures and reducing border fees through simplification of border clearance procedures, automation, and digitalization of border processes. Adoption of digital technologies can also enhance information flows between exporters and shippers, supporting global value chains. In addition, enhancing transparency in the provision of customs information can reduce corruption and uncertainty. In lower-income countries, investments can improve connectivity by modernizing communications and road, railway, and port infrastructure, while trade liberalization can reduce tariff barriers. Swift implementation of reforms included in the WTO Trade Facilitation Agreement—such as provisions for expediting the movement, release, and clearance of goods in transit—can also be encouraged, including through close cooperation between customs authorities. Trade and global value chain integration could also be promoted through policies aimed at attracting FDI and fostering interactions of domestic firms with multinational corporations (Qiang, Zhenwei, and Steenbergen 2021).

Deploying and financing green infrastructure

The post-pandemic recovery represents an opportunity to pursue long-term strategies to put countries on a greener development path. Investments in green infrastructure, climate-smart agricultural technologies, and climate resilience, combined with sustainable energy policies, can play a pivotal role to this end. There is tremendous scope to improve environmental performance through green investments in EMDEs, including retrofitting buildings for energy efficiency and increasing the use of

renewable energy sources to lower greenhouse gas emissions (figure 1.24.E-F). Enhancing environmental clean-up activities and monitoring and deterring the illicit extraction of natural resources can also bolster growth prospects (Strand and Toman 2010).

Attracting private investment is essential to realizing ambitious green investment goals. This requires a supportive domestic environment, with reduced risks, strong competition, and measures to promote capital flows. Providing an effective regulatory environment, while enforcing environmental standards, is paramount to this endeavor (Ambec et al. 2011). Authorities can also buttress the capacity of domestic financial sectors to attract capital to fund green investments in collaboration with international financial institutions, including by strengthening regulation and supervision of local financial institutions. Moreover, concessional finance can play a key role in supporting climate-smart investments. Authorities can also introduce regulations that "green" the financial sector, such as reporting requirements that highlight environmental, social, and governance risks to financial institutions.

As governments adopt policy measures to reinvigorate growth, they can further prioritize objectives related to climate change adaptation and resilience, including enhancing climate risk information systems (Tall et al. 2021). Infrastructures in EMDEs remain particularly vulnerable to climate risks (Miller and Swann 2016). In this regard, ensuring adequate infrastructure maintenance can promote resilience against climate disasters, which is particularly important for small island states (Rozenberg and Fay 2019). Moreover, promoting the issuance of green bonds can also increase investments in climate change mitigation and adaptation, especially if combined with carbon pricing policies (Heine et al. 2019).

TABLE 1.2 **Emerging market and developing economies[1]**

Commodity exporters[2]		Commodity importers[3]	
Afghanistan	Lao PDR	Albania	Romania
Algeria*	Liberia	Antigua and Barbuda	Samoa
Angola*	Libya*	Bahamas, The	Serbia
Argentina	Madagascar	Bangladesh	Sri Lanka
Armenia	Malawi	Barbados	St. Kitts and Nevis
Azerbaijan*	Mali	Belarus	St. Lucia
Bahrain*	Mauritania	Bhutan	St. Vincent and the Grenadines
Belize	Mongolia	Bosnia and Herzegovina	Thailand
Benin	Morocco	Bulgaria	Tonga
Bolivia*	Mozambique	Cambodia	Tunisia
Botswana	Myanmar*	China	Turkey
Brazil	Namibia	Croatia	Tuvalu
Burkina Faso	Nicaragua	Djibouti	Vanuatu
Burundi	Niger	Dominica	Vietnam
Cabo Verde	Nigeria*	Dominican Republic	
Cameroon*	Oman*	Egypt, Arab Rep.	
Central African Republic	Papua New Guinea	El Salvador	
Chad*	Paraguay	Eritrea	
Chile	Peru	Eswatini	
Colombia*	Qatar*	Georgia	
Comoros	Russian Federation*	Grenada	
Congo, Dem. Rep.	Rwanda	Haiti	
Congo, Rep.*	São Tomé and Príncipe	Hungary	
Costa Rica	Saudi Arabia*	India	
Côte d'Ivoire	Senegal	Jamaica	
Ecuador*	Seychelles	Jordan	
Equatorial Guinea*	Sierra Leone	Kiribati	
Ethiopia	Solomon Islands	Lebanon	
Fiji	South Africa	Lesotho	
Gabon*	South Sudan*	Malaysia	
Gambia, The	Sudan	Maldives	
Ghana*	Suriname	Marshall Islands	
Guatemala	Tajikistan	Mauritius	
Guinea	Tanzania	Mexico	
Guinea-Bissau	Timor-Leste*	Micronesia, Fed. Sts.	
Guyana	Togo	Moldova	
Honduras	Uganda	Montenegro	
Indonesia*	Ukraine	Nauru	
Iran, Islamic Rep.*	United Arab Emirates*	Nepal	
Iraq*	Uruguay	North Macedonia	
Kazakhstan*	Uzbekistan	Pakistan	
Kenya	West Bank and Gaza	Palau	
Kosovo	Zambia	Panama	
Kuwait*	Zimbabwe	Philippines	
Kyrgyz Republic		Poland	

* Energy exporters.

1. Emerging market and developing economies (EMDEs) include all those that are not classified as advanced economies and for which a forecast is published for this report. Dependent territories are excluded. Advanced economies include Australia; Austria; Belgium; Canada; Cyprus; the Czech Republic; Denmark; Estonia; Finland; France; Germany; Greece; Hong Kong SAR, China; Iceland; Ireland; Israel; Italy; Japan; the Republic of Korea; Latvia; Lithuania; Luxembourg; Malta; the Netherlands; New Zealand; Norway; Portugal; Singapore; the Slovak Republic; Slovenia; Spain; Sweden; Switzerland; the United Kingdom; and the United States.
2. An economy is defined as commodity exporter when, on average in 2017-19, either (i) total commodities exports accounted for 30 percent or more of total exports or (ii) exports of any single commodity accounted for 20 percent or more of total exports. Economies for which these thresholds were met as a result of re-exports were excluded. When data were not available, judgment was used. This taxonomy results in the classification of some well-diversified economies as importers, even if they are exporters of certain commodities (for example, Mexico).
3. Commodity importers are all EMDEs that are not classified as commodity exporters.

References

Akresh, R., D. Halim, and M. Kleemans. 2021. "Long-Term and Intergenerational Effects of Education: Evidence from School Construction in Indonesia." Policy Research Working Paper 9559, World Bank, Washington, DC.

Albanesi, S., and J. Kim. 2021. "The Gendered Impact of the COVID-19 Recession on the US Labor Market." NBER Working Paper 28505, National Bureau of Economic Research, Cambridge, MA.

Alkire, S., R. Nogales, N. N. Quinn, and N. Suppa. 2020. "On Track or Not? Projecting the Global Multidimensional Poverty Index." OPHI Research Paper 58a, University of Oxford.

Alonso Gispert, T., E. Feyen, T. Kliatskova, D. S. Mare, and M. Poser. 2020. "COVID-19 Pandemic: A Database of Policy Responses Related to the Financial Sector" (database). World Bank, Washington, DC.

Al-Samarrai, S., P. Cerdan-Infantes, A. Bigarinova, J. Bodmer, M. J. Vital, M. Antoninis, B. F. Barakat, and Y. Murakami. 2021. "Education Finance Watch 2021." World Bank, Washington, DC.

Ambec, S., M. A. Cohen, S. Elgie, and P. Lanoie. 2011. "The Porter Hypothesis at 20: Can Environmental Regulation Enhance Innovation and Competitiveness?" Resources for the Future Discussion Paper 11-01, *SSRN Electronic Journal.* https://papers.ssrn.com/sol3/papers.cfm?abstract_id=1754674.

Apedo-Amah, M. C., B. Avdiu, X. Cirera, M. Cruz, E. Davies, A. Grover, L. Iacovone, et al. 2020. "Unmasking the Impact of COVID-19 on Businesses: Firm Level Evidence from Across the World." Policy Research Working Paper 9434, World Bank, Washington, DC.

Arezki, R., V. Dequiedt, R. Y. Fan, and C. M. Rossotto. 2021. "Liberalization, Technology Adoption, and Stock Returns: Evidence from Telecom." Policy Research Working Paper 9561, World Bank, Washington, DC.

Arteta, C., M. A. Kose, F. Ohnsorge, and M. Stocker. 2015. "The Coming U.S. Interest Rate Tightening Cycle: Smooth Sailing or Stormy Waters?" Policy Research Note 15/02, World Bank, Washington, DC.

Auboin, M., and F. Borino. 2017. "The Falling Elasticity of Global Trade to Economic Activity: Testing the Demand Channel." WTO Staff Working Paper ERSD-2017-09, World Trade Organization, Geneva.

Aussilloux, V., A. Baïz, M. Garrigue, P. Martin, and D. Mavridis. 2021. "Fiscal Plans in Europe: No Divergence but no Coordination." VoxEU.org, CEPR Policy Portal, February 19, https://voxeu.org/article/fiscal-plans-europe-no-divergence-no-coordination.

Azevedo, J. P., D. Goldemberg, S. Montoya, R. Nayar, H. Rogers, J. Saavedra, and B. W. Stacy. 2021. "Will Every Child Be Able to Read by 2030? Defining Learning Poverty and Mapping the Dimensions of the Challenge." Policy Research Working Paper 9588, World Bank, Washington, DC.

Azevedo, J. P., A. Hasan, D. Goldemberg, S. A. Iqbal, and K. Geven. 2020. "Simulating the Potential Impacts of Covid-19 School Closures on Schooling and Learning Outcomes: A Set of Global Estimates." Policy Research Working Paper 9284, World Bank, Washington, DC.

Banerjee, R. N., J. Noss, and J. M. Vidal Pastor. 2021. "Liquidity to Solvency: Transition Cancelled or Postponed?" BIS Bulletin, No. 40, Bank for International Settlements, Basel.

Barnes, S., E. Casey, and E. Jordan-Doak. 2021. "Managing Government Debt at High Altitude: Velocity, Instability and Headwinds." IFAC Working Paper 15, Irish Fiscal Advisory Council, Dublin.

Barrero, J. M., N. Bloom, and S. J. Davis. 2021. "Why Working from Home Will Stick." Becker Friedman Institute Working Paper 2020-174, University of Chicago.

Bartsch, E., A. Bénassy-Quéré, G. Corsetti, and X. Debrun. 2020. "Stronger Together? The Policy Mix Strikes Back." VoxEU.org, CEPR Policy Portal, December 15, https://voxeu.org/article/stronger-together-policy-mix-strikes-back.

Baum, A., T. Mogues, and G. Verdier. 2020. "Getting the Most from Public Investment." In *Well Spent: How Strong Infrastructure Governance Can End Waste in Public Investment*, edited by G. Schwartz, M. Fouad, T. Hansen, and G. Verdier, 30–49. Washington, DC: International Monetary Fund.

Beck, T., E. Carletti, and B. Bruno. 2021. "Unwinding COVID Support Measures for Banks." VoxEU.org, CEPR Policy Portal, March 17, https://voxeu.org/article/unwinding-covid-support-measures-banks.

Bems, R., R. C. Johnson, and K. Yi. 2010. "Demand Spillovers and the Collapse of Trade in Global Recession." IMF Working Paper 10/142, International Monetary Fund, Washington, DC.

Bhattacharyya, R., R. Bhaduri, R. Kundu, S. Salvatore, B. Mukherjee. 2020. "Reconciling Epidemiological Models with Misclassified Case-counts for SARS-CoV-2 with Seroprevalence urveys: A Case Study in Delhi, India." COVID-19 SARS-CoV-2 preprints from medRxiv and bioRxiv.

BIS (Bank for International Settlements). 2021. *BIS Quarterly Review.* March. Basel: Bank for International Settlements.

Blanchard, O. J., J. Felman, and A. Subramanian. 2021. "Does the New Fiscal Consensus in Advanced Economies Travel to Emerging Markets?" PIIE Policy Brief 21-7, Peterson Institute for International Economics, Washington, DC.

Bloom, N., P. Bunn, P. Mizen, P. Smietanka, and G. Thwaites. 2021. "The Impact of Covid-19 on Productivity." VoxEU.org, CEPR Policy Portal, January 18, https://voxeu.org/article/impact-covid-19-productivity.

Bolt, J., R. Inklaar, H. de Jong, and J. L. van Zanden. 2018. "Rebasing 'Maddison': New Income Comparisons and the Shape of Long-Run Economic Development." GGDC Research Memorandum 174, University of Groningen, Groningen.

Boot, A., E. Carletti, H-H. Kotz, J. P. Krahnen, L. Pelizzon, and M. Subrahmanyam. 2021. "Coronavirus and Banking: Evaluating Policy Options for Avoiding a Financial Crisis." VoxEU.org, CEPR Policy Portal, January 25, https://voxeu.org/article/coronavirus-and-banking-evaluating-policy-options-avoiding-financial-crisis.

Brainard, L. 2021. "Remaining Patient as the Outlook Brightens." Board of Governors of the Federal Reserve System Speech at the National Association for Business Economics Virtual 37th Annual Economic Policy Conference, Washington, DC, March 23. https://www.federalreserve.gov/newsevents/speech/brainard20210323b.htm.

Bundervoet, T., M. E. Davalos, and N. Garcia. 2021. "The Short-Term Impacts of COVID-19 on Households in Developing Countries: An Overview Based on a Harmonized Data Set of High-Frequency Surveys." Policy Research Working Paper 9582, World Bank, Washington, DC.

Burns, M., M. Santally, Y. Rajabalee, R. Halkhoree, and R. Sungkur. 2019. "Information and Communications Technologies in Secondary Education in Sub-Saharan Africa: Policies, Practices, Trends and Recommendations." Mastercard Foundation, Toronto.

Caballero, R. J., and A. Simsek. 2020. "Asset Prices and Aggregate Demand in a 'Covid-19' Shock: A Model of Endogenous Risk Intolerance and LSAPs." NBER Working Paper 27044, National Bureau of Economic Research, Cambridge.

Çakmaklı, C., S. Demiralp, S. Kalemli-Özcan, S. Yeşiltaş, and M. A. Yıldırım. 2021. "The Economic Case for Global Vaccinations: An Epidemiological Model with International Production Networks?" NBER Working Paper 28395, National Bureau of Economic Research, Cambridge, MA.

Carbon Tracker. 2021. "Beyond Petrostates: The Burning Need to Cut Oil Dependence in the Energy Transition." *Carbon Tracker Initiative.* February 11. https://carbontracker.org/reports/petrostates-energy-transition-report/.

Card, D., J. Kluve, and A. Weber. 2018. "What Works? A Meta Analysis of Recent Active Labor Market Program Evaluations." *Journal of the European Economic Association* 16 (3): 894–93.

Coe, D. T., E. Helpman, and A. W. Hoffmaister. 2008. "International R&D Spillovers and Institutions." IMF Working Paper 08/104, International Monetary Fund, Washington, DC.

Coibion, O., Y. Gorodnichenko, and M. Ulate. 2017. "The Cyclical Sensitivity in Estimates of Potential Output." NBER Working Paper 23580, National Bureau of Economic Research, Cambridge, MA.

Comtrade (database). United Nations. Accessed May 25, 2021. https://comtrade.un.org.

Corral, P., A. Irwin, N. Krishnan, D. Gerszon Mahler, and T. Vishwanath. 2020. *Fragility and Conflict: On the Front Lines of the Fight against Poverty.* Washington, DC: World Bank.

Constantinescu, C., A. Matoo, and M. Ruta. 2017. "Does Vertical Specialization Increase Productivity?" Policy Research Working Paper 7978, World Bank, Washington, DC.

Das, S., and P. Wingender. 2021. "Slow-Healing Scars: The Pandemic's Legacy." *IMF Blog.* March 31, 2021. https://blogs.imf.org/2021/03/31/slow-healing-scars-the-pandemics-legacy/.

Davies, N. G., S. Abbott, R. C. Barnard, C. I. Jarvis, A. J. Kucharski, J. D. Munday, C. A. Pearson, et al. 2021. "Estimated Transmissibility and Impact of SARS-CoV-2 Lineage B.1.1.7 in England." COVID-19 SARS-CoV-2 preprints from medRxiv and bioRxiv.

De Mooij, R., R. Fenochietto, S. Hebous, S. Leduc, and C. Osorio-Buitron. 2020. "Tax Policy for Inclusive Growth after the Pandemic." Special Series on COVID-19. December. International Monetary Fund, Washington, DC.

Delphi Group at Carnegie Mellon University (database). "COVIDcast." Accessed May 24, 2021. https://delphi.cmu.edu/covidcast/.

Devereux, M., and Y. Changhua. 2020. "International Financial Integration and Crisis Contagion." *The Review of Economic Studies* 87 (3): 1174-1212.

di Mauro, F., and C. Syverson. 2020. "The COVID Crisis and Productivity Growth." VoxEU.org, CEPR Policy Portal, April 16, https://voxeu.org/article/covid-crisis-and-productivity-growth.

Diakantoni, A., E. Escaith, M. Roberts, and T. Verbeet. 2017. "Accumulating Trade Costs and Competitiveness in Global Value Chains." WTO Staff Working Paper ERSD-2017-02, World Trade Organization, Geneva.

Dieppe, A. ed. 2020. *Global Productivity: Trends, Drivers, and Policies.* Washington, DC: World Bank.

Diez, F. J., R. A. Duval, J. Fan, J. Garrido, S. Kalemli-Ozcan, C. Maggi, M. S. Martinez Peria, and N. Pierri. 2021. "Insolvency Prospects Among Small and Medium Enterprises in Advanced Economies: Assessment and Policy Options." IMF Staff Discussion Note 21/02, International Monetary Fund, Washington, DC.

Dinarte, L., E. Medina-Cortina, D. Jaume, and H. Winkler. 2021. "Neither by Land nor by Sea: The Rise of Electronic Remittances during COVID-19." World Bank, Washington, DC.

Disparte, D. 2021. *Preparing for the Next Pandemic: Early Lessons from COVID-19.* Washington, DC: Brookings Institution.

Doing Business (database). World Bank. Accessed May 25, 2021. https://www.doingbusiness.org.

Duke Global Health Innovation Center. 2021. "Launch and Scale Speedometer." Duke University, Durham, NC. https://launchandscalefaster.org/covid-19.

ECB (European Central Bank). 2021. "The Impact of Containment Measures across Sectors and Countries during the COVID-19 Pandemic." ECB Economic Bulletin 2/2021, European Central Bank, Frankfurt.

Escudero, V., and H. Liepmann. 2020. "The Joint Provision of Active Labour Market Policies and Income Support Can Be a Powerful Solution for Improving Workers' Perspectives." VoxEU.org, CEPR Policy Portal, September 19, https://voxeu.org/article/combined-active-labour-market-policies-and-income-support-can-improve-workers-perspectives.

Fan, J., Y. Li, K. Stewart, A. R. Kommareddy, A. Garcia, J. Ma, A. Bradford, et al. 2021. "COVID-19 World Symptom Survey Data API." University of Maryland, College Park. https://covidmap.umd.edu/api.html.

Fasih, T., H. A. Patrinos, and M. J. Shafiq. 2020. "The Impact of COVID-19 on Labor Market Outcomes: Lessons from Past Economic Crises." *Education for Global Development* (blog), World Bank. https://blogs.worldbank.org/education/impact-covid-19-labor-market-outcomes-lessons-past-economic-crises.

Fernando, R., W. Liu, and W. J. McKibbin. 2021. "Global Economic Impacts of Climate Shocks, Climate Policy and Changes in Climate Risk Assessment." CEPAR Working Paper 2021/12, ARC Centre of Excellence in Population Ageing Research.

Ferrantino, M. J., J. F. Arvis, I. C. Constantinescu, K. S. Dairabayeva, I. J. Gillson, K. Souza Muramatsu, and D. Ulybina. 2021. "COVID-19 Trade Watch #11: Sunny Skies Behind, Trouble Ahead." March. Washington, DC, World Bank.

FSIN (Food Security Information Network) and Global Network Against Food Crises. 2021. *Global Report on Food Crises 2021.* Rome: Food Security Information Network.

Furceri, D., M. Ganslmeier, J. D. Ostry, and N. Yang. 2021. "Initial Output Losses from the COVID Pandemic: Robust Determinants." CEPR Discussion Paper 13601, Centre for Economic Policy Research, London.

Furceri, D., P. Loungani, J. D. Ostry, and P. Pizzuto. 2020. "Will Covid-19 Affect Inequality? Evidence from Past Pandemics." *Covid Economics: Vetted and Real-Time Papers* 12 (May): 138-157.

Furman, J., and L. Summers. 2020. "A Reconsideration of Fiscal Policy in the Era of Low Interest Rates." Discussion draft, Brookings Institution, Washington, DC.

Gagnon, J. E., S. Kamin, and J. Kearns. 2021. 21-11 Economic Costs and Benefits of Accelerated COVID-19 Vaccinations. Washington, DC: Peterson Institute for International Economics.

Gaspar, V., W. R. Lam, P. Mauro, and M. Raissi. 2021. "Tailoring Government Support." *IMF Blog,*

April 7, 2021. https://blogs.imf.org/2021/04/07/tailor ing-government-support/.

Gavi, The Vaccine Alliance. 2021. *COVAX Global Supply Forecast.* Geneva: Gavi.

Goldstein, P., E. L. Yeyati, and L. Sartorio. 2021. "Lockdown Fatigue: The Diminishing Effects of Quarantines on the Spread of COVID-19." *Covid Economics: Vetted and Real-Time Papers* 67 (February): 1-23.

Gourinchas, P.-O., Ş. Kalemli-Özcan, V. Penciakova, and N. Sander. 2021. "COVID-19 and SMEs: A 2021 'Time Bomb'?" NBER Working Paper 28418, National Bureau of Economic Research, Cambridge, MA.

Guénette, J.-D., and T. Yamazaki. 2021. "Projecting the Economic Consequences of the COVID-19 Pandemic." Policy Research Working Paper 9589, World Bank, Washington, DC.

Group of Thirty. 2021. *Sovereign Debt and Financing for Recovery After the COVID-19 Shock: Next Steps to Build a Better Architecture.* Washington, DC: Group of Thirty.

Ha, J., M. Stocker, and H. Yilmazkuday. 2019. "Inflation and Exchange Rate Pass-Through." Policy Research Working Paper 8780, World Bank, Washington, DC.

Hallward-Driemeier, M., and G. Nayyar. 2018. *Trouble in the Making? The Future of Manufacturing-Led Development.* Washington, DC: World Bank.

Harper Petersen & Co. (database). "Harper Petersen Charter Rates Index (HARPEX)." Accessed May 24, 2021. https://www.harperpetersen.com.

Hazell, J., J. Herreno, E. Nakamura, and J. Steinsson. 2020. "The Slope of the Phillips Curve: Evidence from U.S. States." NBER Working Paper 28005, National Bureau of Economic Research, Cambridge, MA.

Heine, D., W. Semmler, M. Mazzucato, J. P. Braga, M. Flaherty, A. Gevorkyan, E. Hayde, and S. Radpour. 2019. "Financing Low-Carbon Transitions through Carbon Pricing and Green Bonds." Policy Research Working Paper 8991, World Bank, Washington, DC.

Helmersson, T., L. Mingarelli, B. Mosk, A. Pietsch, B. Ravanetti, T. Shakir, and J. Wendelborn. 2021. "Corporate Zombification: Post-Pandemic Risks in the Euro Area." Financial Stability Review, May 2021, European Central Bank, Frankfurt.

Hui, J., F. J. La-Bhus, and S. Baoping. 2019. "Improving the Efficiency and Equity of Public Education Spending: The Case of Moldova." IMF Working Paper 19/42, International Monetary Fund, Washington, DC.

IEA (International Energy Agency). 2021. *Oil 2021.* Paris: International Energy Agency.

IDMC (Internal Displacement Monitoring Centre). 2021. "Internal displacement in a changing climate." Norwegian Refugee Council. May 24, 2021. https://www.internal-displacement.org/sites/default/files/publications/documents/grid2021_idmc.pdf

ILO (International Labour Organization). 2021a. *ILO Monitor: COVID-19 and the world of work.* Seventh edition. Geneva: International Labour Organization.

ILO (International Labour Organization). 2021b. *World Employment and Social Outlook.* Geneva: International Labour Organization.

Ilut, C., and M. Schneider. 2012. "Ambiguous Business Cycles." NBER Working Paper 17900, National Bureau of Economic Research, Cambridge, MA.

IMF (International Monetary Fund). 2019. *Fiscal Monitor: How to Mitigate Climate Change.* October. Washington, DC: International Monetary Fund.

IMF (International Monetary Fund). 2021a. *Fiscal Monitor: A Fair Shot.* April. Washington, DC: International Monetary Fund.

IMF (International Monetary Fund). 2021b. *Global Financial Stability Report: Preempting a Legacy of Vulnerabilities.* April. Washington, DC: International Monetary Fund.

Islam, A. M., and D. Lederman. 2020. "Data Transparency and Long-Run Growth." Policy Research Working Paper 9493, World Bank, Washington, DC.

Johns Hopkins University (database). "Coronavirus Resource Center." Accessed May 26, 2021. https://coronavirus.jhu.edu/.

Kalemli-Özcan, S., I. Shim, and X. Liu. 2021. "Exchange Rate Fluctuations and Firm Leverage." NBER Working Paper 28608, National Bureau of Economic Research, Cambridge, MA.

Khamis, M., D. Prinz, D. Newhouse, A. Palacios-Lopez, U. Pape, and M. Weber. 2021. "The Early Labor Market Impacts of COVID-19 in Developing

Countries: Evidence from High-Frequency Phone Surveys." Jobs Working Paper 58, World Bank, Washington, DC.

Kilic Celik, S., M. A. Kose, and F. Ohnsorge. 2020"Subdued Potential Growth: Sources and Remedies." In *Growth in a Time of Change: Global and Country Perspectives on a New Agenda*, edited by H.-W. Kim and Z. Qureshi. Washington, DC: Brookings Institution.

Klein, A., and E. Smith. 2021. "Explaining the Economic Impact of COVID-19: Core Industries and the Hispanic Workforce." Brookings Institution, Washington, DC. https://www.brookings.edu/research/explaining-the-economic-impact-of-covid-19-core-industries-and-the-hispanic-workforce/.

Kose, M. A., S. Kurlat, F. Ohnsorge, and N. Sugawara. 2017. "A Cross-Country Database of Fiscal Space." Policy Research Working Paper 8157, World Bank, Washington, DC.

Kose, M. A., C. Lakatos, F. L. Ohnsorge, and M. Stocker. 2017. "The Global Role of the U.S. Economy: Linkages, Policies and Spillovers." Policy Research Working Paper 7962, World Bank, Washington, DC.

Kose, M. A., P. Nagle, F. Ohnsorge, and N. Sugawara. 2021. *Global Waves of Debt: Causes and Consequences.* Washington, DC: World Bank.

Kose, M. A., and F. Ohnsorge. 2021. "The 2020s: Roaring or Disappointing?" *Voices* (blog), March 29, 2021. https://blogs.worldbank.org/voices/2020s-roaring-or-disappointing.

Kose, M. A., N. Sugawara, and M. E. Terrones. 2020. "Global Recessions." CEPR Discussion Paper 14397, Center for Economic Policy Research, London.

Kozlowski, J. 2020. "COVID-19: Scarring Body and Mind." Economics Synopses 43, Federal Reserve Bank of St. Louis.

Kubota, M., and A. Zeufack. 2020. "Assessing the Returns on Investment in Data Openness and Transparency." Policy Research Working Paper 9139, World Bank, Washington, DC: World Bank.

Lakner, C., D. G. Mahler, M. Negre Rossignoli, and E. B. Prydz. 2020. "How Much Does Reducing Inequality Matter for Global Poverty?" Global Poverty Monitoring Technical Note 13, World Bank, Washington, DC.

Mahler, D. G., N. Yonzan, C. Lakner, R. A. Castaneda Aguilar, and H. Wu. "Updated Estimates of the Impact of COVID-19 on Global Poverty." *Data Blog*, June 2021. https://blogs.worldbank.org/opendata.

Malpass, D. 2021. "Building a Green, Resilient, and Inclusive Recovery: Speech by World Bank Group President David Malpass." *World Bank News.* March 29, 2021. https://www.worldbank.org/en/news/speech/2021/03/29/building-a-green-resilient-and-inclusive-recovery-speech-by-world-bank-group-president-david-malpass.

Mathai, K., C. Duenwald, A. Guscina, A. R. Al-Farah, H. Bukhari, A. Chaudry, M. El-Said, F. Fareed, et al. 2020. "Social Spending for Inclusive Growth in the Middle East and Central Asia." IMF Departmental Paper 20/12, International Monetary Fund, Washington, DC.

McKinsey & Company. 2020. "How COVID-19 has Pushed Companies over the Technology Tipping Point—and Transformed Business Forever." October 5, 2020. https://www.mckinsey.com/business-functions/strategy-and-corporate-finance/our-insights/how-covid-19-has-pushed-companies-over-the-technology-tipping-point-and-transformed-business-forever.

McKinsey Global Institute. 2021. "Will Productivity and Growth Return after the COVID-19 Crisis?" *McKinsey Global Institute.* March 30, 2021. https://www.mckinsey.com/industries/public-and-social-sector/our-insights/will-productivity-and-growth-return-after-the-covid-19-crisis.

Miller, A., and S. Swann. 2016. "How to Make Infrastructure Climate Resilient." *EMCompass 14.* International Finance Corporation, Washington, DC.

Mojon, B., D. Rees, and C. Schimieder. 2021. "How Much Stress Could Covid Put on Corporate Credit? Evidence Using Sectoral Data." *BIS Quarterly Review (*March): 55-70.

Morikawa, M. 2021. "The Productivity of Working from Home: Evidence from Japan." VoxEU.org, CEPR Policy Portal, March 12, https://voxeu.org/article/productivity-working-home-evidence-japan.

Muro, M., R. Maxim, J. Whiton, and I. Hathaway. 2019. *Automation and Artificial Intelligence: How Machines are Affecting People and Places.* Washington, DC: Brookings Institution.

OECD (Organisation for Economic Co-operation and Development). 2020. "Making the Green Recovery Work for Jobs, Income and Growth." OECD Policy Responses to Coronavirus (COVID-19). October 6.

http://www.oecd.org/coronavirus/policy-responses/making-the-green-recovery-work-for-jobs-income-and-growth-a505f3e7/.

OECD (Organisation for Economic Co-Operation and Development). 2021a. *OECD Science, Technology and Innovation Outlook 2021: Times of Crisis and Opportunity.* Paris: OECD Publishing.

OECD (Organisation for Economic Co-operation and Development). 2021b. "Focus on Green Recovery." OECD Policy Responses to Coronavirus (COVID-19). http://www.oecd.org/coronavirus/en/themes/green-recovery.

Ohnsorge, F., and S. Yu. 2021. *The Long Shadow of Informality: Challenges and Policies.* Washington, DC: World Bank.

Orszag, P. R., R. E. Rubin, and J. E. Stiglitz. 2021. "Fiscal Resiliency in a Deeply Uncertain World: The Role of Semiautonomous Discretion." PIIE Policy Brief 21-2, Peterson Institute for International Economics, Washington, DC.

Our World in Data (database). "Coronavirus Pandemic (COVID-19)." Accessed May 25, 2021. https://ourworldindata.org/coronavirus.

Oxford Economics. 2019. "Global Economic Model." July. Oxford Economics, Oxford, U.K.

Prettner, K., S. Chen, M. Kuhn, and D. Bloom. 2021. "Effective Pandemic Management that Minimises Economic Harm." VoxEU.org, CEPR Policy Portal, January 4, https://voxeu.org/article/effective-pandemic-management-minimises-economic-harm.

Qiang, C., L. Y. Zhenwei, and V. Steenbergen. 2021. *An Investment Perspective on Global Value Chains.* Washington, DC: World Bank.

Ramey, V. A. 2020. "The Macroeconomic Consequences of Infrastructure Investment." NBER Working Paper 27625, National Bureau of Economic Research, Cambridge, MA.

Reifschneider, D., W. Wascher, and D. Wilcox. 2013. "Aggregate Supply in the United States: Recent Developments and Implications for the Conduct of Monetary Policy." Finance and Economics Discussion Series Working Paper 2013-77, Federal Reserve Board of Governors, Washington, DC.

Reinhart, C. M. 2021. "From Health Crisis to Financial Distress." Policy Research Working Paper 9616, World Bank, Washington, DC.

Reinhart, C., J. Meyer, C. Trebesch, and C. G. von Luckner. 2021. "External sovereign debt restructurings: Delay and replay." VoxEU.org, CEPR Policy Portal, March 30, https://voxeu.org/article/external-sovereign-debt-restructurings-delay-and-replay.

Reinhart, C., and V. Reinhart. 2020. "The Pandemic Depression: The Global Economy Will Never Be the Same." *Foreign Affairs,* September/October. https://www.foreignaffairs.com/articles/united-states/2020-08-06/coronavirus-depression-global-economy.

Rentschler, J., and M. Salhab. 2020. "People in Harm's Way: Flood Exposure and Poverty in 189 Countries." Policy Research Working Paper 9447, World Bank, Washington, DC.

Roberton, T., E. D. Carter, V. B. Chou, A. R. Stegmuller, B. D. Jackson, Y. Tam, T. Sawadogo-Lewis, and N. Walker. 2020. "Early Estimates of the Indirect Effects of the COVID-19 Pandemic on Maternal and Child Mortality in Low-income and Middle-income Countries: A Modelling Study." *The Lancet Global Health* 8 (7): e901-e908.

Rodriguez-Castelan, C., R. Granguillhome Ochoa, S. Lach, and T. Masaki. 2021. "Mobile Internet Adoption in West Africa." Policy Research Working Paper 9560, World Bank, Washington, DC.

Rogoff, K. 2021. "Fiscal Sustainability in the Aftermath of the Great Pause." *Journal of Policy Modeling* (in press).

Rose, S., L. Twist, P. Lord, S. Rutt, K. Badr, C. Hope, and B. Styles. 2021. "Impact of School Closures and Subsequent Support Strategies on Attainment and Socio-emotional Wellbeing." *National Foundation for Education Research.* January 28. https://www.nfer.ac.uk/impact-of-school-closures-and-subsequent-support-strategies-on-attainment-and-socio-emotional-wellbeing/.

Rozenberg, J., and M. Fay. 2019. "Beyond the Gap: How Countries Can Afford the Infrastructure They Need while Protecting the Planet." Sustainable Infrastructure Series. Washington, DC: World Bank.

Saurav, A., P. Kusek, R. Kuo, and B. Viney. 2020. *The Impact of COVID-19 on Foreign Investors: Evidence from the Second Round of a Global Pulse Survey.* Washington, DC: World Bank.

Schmillen, A. D. 2020. "Causes and Impacts of Job Displacements and Public Policy Responses." Research and Policy Brief 33, Malaysia Hub, World Bank.

Schwartz, G., M. Fouad, T. Hansen, and G. Verdier. 2020. *Well Spent: How Strong Infrastructure Governance*

Can End Waste in Public Investment. Washington, DC: International Monetary Fund.

Sedik, T. S., and J. Yoo. 2021. "Pandemics and Automation: Will the Lost Jobs Come Back?" IMF Working Paper 2021/11, International Monetary Fund, Washington, DC.

Stiglitz, J. E. 2020. "The Pandemic Economic Crisis, Precautionary Behavior, and Mobility Constraints: An Application of the Dynamic Disequilibrium Model with Randomness." NBER Working Paper 27992, National Bureau of Economic Research, Cambridge, MA.

Stocker, M., J. Baffes, Y. Some, D. Vorisek, and C. M. Wheeler. 2018. "The 2014-16 Oil Price Collapse in Retrospect: Sources and Implications." Policy Research Working Paper 8419, World Bank, Washington, DC.

Strand, J., and M. Toman. 2010. "'Green Stimulus,' Economic Recovery, and Long-Term Sustainable Development." Policy Research Working Paper 5163, World Bank, Washington, DC.

Tall, A., S. Lynagh, C. Blanco Vecchi, P. Bardouille, F. Montoya Pino, E. Shabahat, V. Stenek, et al. 2021. *Enabling Private Investment in Climate Adaptation and Resilience: Current Status, Barriers to Investment and Blueprint for Action.* Washington, DC: World Bank.

Trebilcock, M. J. 2014. *Dealing with Losers: The Political Economy of Policy Transition.* New York: Oxford University Press.

UNCTAD (United Nations Conference on Trade and Development). 2021. *Investment Trends Monitor. Issue 38.* Geneva: UNCTAD.

UNDP (United Nations Development Programme) and OPHI (Oxford Poverty and Human Development Initiative). 2020. *Global Multidimensional Poverty Index 2020—Charting Pathways out of Multidimensional Poverty: Achieving the SDGs.* New York: UNDP; Oxford, UK: OPHI.

UNESCO (United Nations Educational, Scientific, and Cultural Organization). 2020. *Education in a Post-COVID World: Nine Ideas for Public Action.* International Commission on the Futures of Education. Paris: UNESCO.

UNESCO (United Nations Educational, Scientific, and Cultural Organization). 2021. *COVID-19 Educational Disruption and Response.* https://en.unesco.org/covid19/educationresponse.

UNICEF (United Nations Children's Fund). 2021. "How the COVID-19 Pandemic has Scarred the World's Children." *UNICEF Stories.* March 10. https://www.unicef.org/coronavirus/COVID-19-pandemic-scarred-world-children.

United Nations Economic and Social Commission for Asia and the Pacific (database). "ESCAP-World Bank Trade Cost Database." Accessed May 25, 2021. https://www.unescap.org/resources/escap-world-bank-trade-cost-database.

UNWTO (United Nations World Tourism Organization). 2021. "2020: Worst Year in Tourism History With 1 Billion Fewer International Arrivals." UNWTO News, January 28, 2021.

Wang, P., M. S. Nair, L. Liu, S. Iketani, Y. Luo, Y. Guo, M. Wang, et al. 2021. "Antibody Resistance of SARS-CoV-2 Variants B.1.351 and B.1.1.7." COVID-19 SARS-CoV-2 preprints from medRxiv and bioRxiv.

WFP (World Food Program) and FAO (Food and Agriculture Organization of the United Nations). 2021. "Hunger Hotspots. FAO-WFP Early Warnings on Acute Food Insecurity." March to July 2021 outlook. Rome: WFP and FAO.

Wheeler, C. M., J. Baffes, A. Kabundi, G. Kindberg-Hanlon, P. S. Nagle, and F. Ohnsorge. 2020. "Adding Fuel to the Fire: Cheap Oil during the COVID-19 Pandemic." Policy Research Working Paper 9320, World Bank, Washington, DC.

Wilson, D. J. 2020. "The COVID-19 Fiscal Multiplier: Lessons from the Great Recession." *Federal Reserve Bank San Francisco Economic Letter.* May 26. https://www.frbsf.org/economic-research/publications/economic-letter/2020/may/covid-19-fiscal-multiplier-lessons-from-great-recession/.

World Bank. 2016. *World Development Report 2016: Digital Dividends.* Washington, DC: World Bank.

World Bank. 2017. *Global Economic Prospects: Weak Investment in Uncertain Times.* June. Washington, DC: World Bank.

World Bank. 2018a. *Global Economic Prospects: Broad-Based Upturn, but for How Long?* January. Washington, DC: World Bank.

World Bank. 2018b. *World Development Report 2018: Learning to Realize Education's Promise.* Washington, DC: World Bank.

World Bank. 2019. *Africa's Pulse: An Analysis of Issues Shaping Africa's Economic Future.* Volume 19. Washington, DC: World Bank.

World Bank. 2020a. *Global Economic Prospects.* June. Washington, DC: World Bank.

World Bank. 2020b. *Poverty and Shared Prosperity Report 2020: Reversing Reversals of Fortune.* Washington, DC: World Bank.

World Bank. 2020c. "COVID-19: Debt Service Suspension Initiative." Brief. Updated on September 15, 2020. World Bank, Washington, DC.

World Bank. 2020d. *Global Economic Prospects: Slow Growth, Policy Challenges.* January. Washington, DC: World Bank.

World Bank. 2020e. *World Development Report. Trading for Development in the Age of Global Value Chains.* Washington, DC: World Bank.

World Bank. 2021a. *Global Economic Prospects.* January. Washington, DC: World Bank.

World Bank. 2021b. *Commodity Markets Outlook: Causes and Consequences of Metal Price Shocks.* April. Washington, DC: World Bank.

World Bank. 2021c. *China Economic Update.* Washington, DC: World Bank.

World Bank. 2021d. "From COVID-19 Crisis Response to Resilient Recovery—Saving Lives and Livelihoods while Supporting Green, Resilient and Inclusive Development (GRID)." World Bank, Washington.

World Bank. 2021e. "Food Security and COVID-19." World Bank Brief. May 7. https://www.worldbank.org/en/topic/agriculture/brief/food-security-and-covid-19.

World Bank. 2021f. *East Asia and Pacific Economic Update: Uneven Recovery.* March. Washington, DC: World Bank.

World Bank. 2021g. "The Calm Before the Storm: Early Evidence on Business Insolvency Filings After the Onset of COVID-19." COVID-19 Notes: Finance Series. Washington DC: World Bank.

World Bank. 2021h. "How Insolvency and Creditor/Debtor Regimes Can Help Address Nonperforming Loans." EFI Note-Finance. Washington, DC: World Bank.

World Bank. 2021i. "Investing in Human Capital for a Resilient Recovery: The Role of Public Finance." *Human Capital Project.* Ministerial Conclave Conference Draft. April. World Bank, Washington, DC.

World Bank and WTO (World Trade Organization). 2020. *Women and Trade: The Role of Trade in Promoting Women's Equality.* Washington, DC: World Bank.

World Resources Institute. 2019. *Climate Watch.* Washington, DC: World Resources Institute. www.climatewatchdata.org.

Wouters, O. J., K. C. Shadlen, M. Salcher-Konrad, A. J. Pollard, H. J. Larson, Y. Teerawattananon, and M. Jit. 2021. "Challenges in Ensuring Global Access to COVID-19 Vaccines: Production, Affordability, Allocation, and Deployment." *The Lancet* 397 (10278): 1023-1034.

WTO (World Trade Organization). 2020. "Exports Restrictions and Prohibitions." Information Note. World Trade Organization, Geneva. https://www.wto.org/english/tratop_e/covid19_e/export_prohibitions_report_e.pdf.

Yale University (database). "Environmental Performance Index." Accessed May 25, 2021. https://epi.yale.edu/epi-results/2020/component/epi.

Yoshino, N., J. Dong, N. S. Hendriyetty, and P. J. Morgan. 2020. "Coordinated and Comprehensive Fiscal and Monetary Stimulus for Tackling the Covid-19 Crisis." Policy Brief, G20 Insights. https://www.g20-insights.org/wp-content/uploads/2020/11/T20_TF11_PB9.pdf.

CHAPTER 2

REGIONAL OUTLOOK

EAST ASIA and PACIFIC

Growth in East Asia and Pacific (EAP) is projected to accelerate to 7.7 percent in 2021, largely reflecting a strong rebound in China. Nevertheless, output in two-thirds of the countries in the region will remain below pre-pandemic levels until 2022. The pandemic is expected to dampen potential growth in many economies, especially those that suffered most from extended outbreaks of COVID-19 and the collapse of global tourism and trade. Downside risks to the forecast include, the possibility of repeated and large COVID-19 outbreaks amid delayed vaccinations; heightened financial stress amplified by elevated debt levels; and the possibility of more severe and longer-lasting effects from the pandemic, including subdued investment and eroded human capital. Disruptions from natural disasters are a constant source of severe downside risk for many countries, especially island economies. On the upside, risks include accelerated vaccination rollouts and greater-than-expected spillovers from recoveries in the United States and other major economies.

Recent developments

After sharply slowing to 1.2 percent in 2020, regional growth has bounced back, but with the speed of recovery differing considerably among countries (tables 2.1.1 and 2.1.2). With a few exceptions, recovery to pre-COVID-19 output levels is far from complete. Among the region's three largest economies (China, Indonesia, Thailand), only China has seen its output already surpassing pre-pandemic levels (figure 2.1.1.A).

In China, COVID-19 infections remain low and the recovery has broadened from public investment to consumption (figure 2.1.1.B). Goods export growth has been strong, and goods import growth has accelerated, helped by recovering domestic demand (figure 2.1.1.C). The authorities have recently started to shift policy efforts away from supporting activity and toward addressing financial stability risks by reducing net liquidity provision (figure 2.1.1.D). The Indonesian economy initially suffered a shallower output contraction than many other emerging market and developing economies (EMDEs), but

this has been followed by a more gradual recovery. Indonesia's initial resilience reflected in part the greater insulation from the collapse of global tourism and trade combined with decentralized and gradual lock-downs despite a severe and persistent COVID-19 outbreak. By contrast, in Thailand, which depends heavily on trade and tourism, the initial contraction was much sharper despite the low incidence of infection, because of the sizable drop in external demand combined with domestic policy uncertainty.

Among the other large ASEAN countries (Malaysia, the Philippines, and Vietnam), only Vietnam, has seen output surpassing its pre-pandemic levels (figure 2.1.2.A). Vietnam has been successful in containing COVID-19 and has benefitted from fiscal measures supporting public investment and robust foreign direct investment (FDI) inflows. By contrast, output remains 8 percent below its pre-pandemic level in the more tourism-dependent Philippines, which has implemented extended periods of strict lockdowns in response to a severe COVID-19 outbreak and has also suffered from a series of natural disasters including super-typhoon Goni and a volcanic eruption. Several small island economies (Fiji, Samoa, Palau, Vanuatu), which have been largely spared from direct health effects of the pandemic

Note: This section was prepared by Ekaterine Vashakmadze.

FIGURE 2.1.1 China: Recent developments

Among the region's three largest economies, only China has seen output surpassing pre-pandemic levels. The recovery has gradually broadened from public investment to consumption. Goods export growth has been strong, and goods import growth has accelerated. Authorities have started to shift policy efforts away from supporting activity toward reducing financial stability risks.

A. GDP

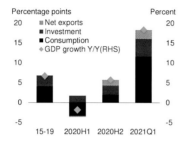

B. Contributions to GDP growth

C. Goods exports and imports

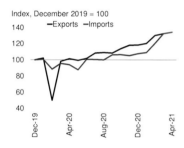

D. Net liquidity provision

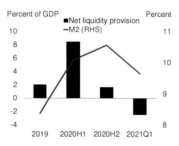

Sources: Haver Analytics; National Bureau of Statistics of China.
A. Last observation is 2021Q1 for China, Indonesia, and Thailand. Last observation is 2020Q4 for other EMDEs.
B. Figure shows year-on-year real GDP growth and expenditure contributions. Data is based on official estimates published by the Chinese National Statistics agency. Last observation is 2021Q1.
C. Value of goods imports and exports. Last observation is April 2021.
D. "Net liquidity provision" refers to liquidity injections by the People's Bank of China through its lending facility (SLF), medium-term lending facility (MLF), targeted medium-term lending facility (TMLF), pledged supplementary lending facility (PSL), special-purpose refinancing facility (SPRF) and the special relending or rediscounting facilities. Red line denotes year-on-year money supply (M2) growth. Last observation is 2021Q1.

have been devastated by the collapse of global tourism and travel, as well as the effects of cyclones Harold and Yasa.

COVID-19 infection rates remain elevated in Indonesia, Malaysia, and the Philippines and have recently increased in Cambodia and Thailand. Social distancing measures to stem the pandemic have been reimposed across the region in response to sporadic outbreaks. Mobility around workplaces and retail areas remains subdued in many economies, reflecting lingering infection and slow progress at vaccination (figure 2.1.2.B). These factors, along with significant income and job losses and persistent policy uncertainty,

continue to weigh on consumer confidence and limit private spending (figure 2.1.2.C). A strong rebound of regional goods exports, helped by robust global manufacturing trade, is providing some support to regional growth (figure 2.1.2.D). Fear of the virus and ongoing travel restrictions, however, continue to limit economic activity in tourism-dependent economies of the region (Cambodia, Fiji, Palau, Thailand, Vanuatu).

Outlook

Regional growth is projected to strengthen to 7.7 percent in 2021, primarily reflecting strong activity in China (figure 2.1.3.A). In China, growth is projected to accelerate to 8.5 percent this year, faster than projected in January, supported by buoyant exports and the release of pent-up demand amid effective control of the outbreak. Output in the rest of the region is projected to grow by 4.0 percent in 2021, more slowly than in the January forecasts, because of continued pandemic-related headwinds and a delayed recovery of global tourism and travel.

The regional forecast is slightly above the January projections, as an upgrade for China more than offsets downgrades elsewhere. The regional recovery is expected to moderate in 2022 as China's growth edges down toward its potential rate. Growth in China is projected to moderate to 5.4 percent in 2022, reflecting diminishing fiscal and monetary support and tighter property and macroprudential regulations. By contrast, growth in the rest of the region is projected to accelerate to 5.0 percent in 2022 as the economic recovery takes hold.

The projected growth would not be sufficient to fully undo the pandemic-related output losses in many regional economies, with output in two-thirds of them expected to remain below pre-pandemic levels until 2022 (figure 2.1.3.B). Output gaps are expected to remain negative and large for an extended period (figure 2.1.3.C). In one-third of the economies in the region, output is expected to recover to its pre-pandemic levels over the course of 2021 or early 2022 but to remain below pre-pandemic projections, with gaps ranging from about one percent in China to more than 10 percent in Cambodia and the Philippines (figure 2.1.3.D).

There is considerable uncertainty about the outlook. COVID-19 caseloads are expected to remain elevated in several regional economies this year, owing to the limited vaccination progress and the spread of new variants, requiring many governments to keep various pandemic-control measures in place. Rising vaccination rates are expected to reduce caseloads throughout 2022 and 2023 in most regional economies. The strength of the region's recovery will depend particularly on the ability of the major regional economies to meet their vaccination commitments, the magnitude of spillovers from other economies, and country-specific conditions.

In Indonesia, growth is expected to rebound to 4.4 percent in 2021 and strengthen further to 5 percent in 2022. But many jobs in low value-added services—such as trade, transport, and hospitality—were lost during the crisis and will be slow to come back. Thailand's economy is expected to recover gradually over the next two years, with growth picking up to 2.2 percent in 2021 before accelerating to 5.1 percent in 2022, helped by the recovery of global tourism and travel.

In the Philippines, GDP growth is projected at 4.7 percent in 2021 and 5.9 percent in 2022, with output expected to reach its pre-pandemic levels in the course of 2022. In Malaysia, growth is expected to rebound to 6 percent in 2021, provided the COVID-19 outbreak remains in check and vaccine distribution accelerates. Output in Vietnam is projected to expand by 6.6 percent on average in 2021 and 2022, resulting in only a small gap between the current forecast of GDP and pre-pandemic projections.

In February 2021, the military assumed power in Myanmar, resulting in significant supply and demand-side impacts on an economy that had already been weakened by COVID-19. The economic outlook is now highly uncertain. Any recovery from the deep GDP contraction that is likely in 2021 will require a normalization of domestic conditions, of which there is little evidence to date. The outlook for international

FIGURE 2.1.2 **EAP: Recent developments**

Among the smaller ASEAN countries, only Vietnam has seen output surpassing its pre-pandemic levels. Mobility around retail areas remains subdued, reflecting continued spread of the virus amid slow progress of vaccination. Consumer spending has therefore been lagging, but industrial output has mostly recovered, helped by a quick rebound of regional goods exports.

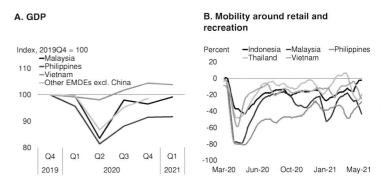

A. GDP

B. Mobility around retail and recreation

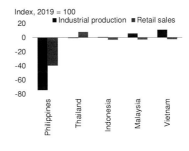

C. Industrial production and retail sales: Deviation from pre-pandemic levels

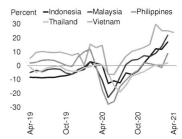

D. Export growth

Sources: Google Maps; Haver Analytics; World Bank.
A. Last observation is 2021Q1 for Malaysia, the Philippines, and Vietnam. Last observation is 2020Q4 for "Other EMDEs excl. China."
B. 21-day moving average. Mobility refers to changes in visits to (or time spent in) retail and recreation facilities compared to the baseline. The baseline day represents a normal value of visits for that day of the week. Retail and recreation facilities include restaurants, cafes, shopping centers, theme parks, museums, libraries, and movie theaters. Last observation is May 29, 2021.
C. For industrial production, last observation is March 2021 for Malaysia, the Philippines, and Thailand, and April 2021 for Vietnam; Indonesia is an estimate. For retail sales, last observation is March 2021 for Malaysia and Thailand and April 2021 for Indonesia and Vietnam; the Philippines is an estimate.
D. Value of goods exports. 3-month moving average of year-on-year change. Last observation is March 2021 for Indonesia, Malaysia, Thailand, and the Philippines. Last observation is April 2021 for Vietnam.

trade and foreign investment has worsened due to severe finance and logistics constraints and a sharp deterioration of the busines environment, as well as the reactions of foreign governments and firms.

Among the smaller countries, the recovery is expected to be particularly feeble in the tourism-dependent island economies. These countries have suffered severely from the collapse of global tourism, which is expected to remain below pre-pandemic levels until at least 2023.

FIGURE 2.1.3 **EAP: Outlook**

Regional growth is projected to rebound in 2021, partly reflecting a rapid recovery in China. The rest of the region is expected to grow more moderately, and output in two-thirds of the countries in the region is projected to remain below pre-pandemic levels until 2022. Output gaps are expected to remain negative and large for an extended period. Output in the region excluding China is projected to remain about 10 percent below pre-pandemic projections in 2022.

A. GDP growth

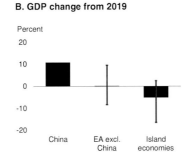

B. GDP change from 2019

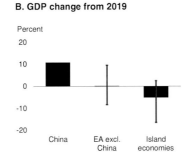

C. Output gap

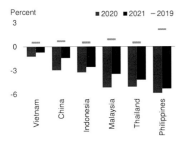

D. Deviation of GDP from January 2020 forecasts

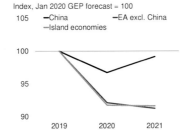

Sources: Bank for International Settlements; Haver Analytics; Institute of International Finance; Penn World Tables; World Bank.

A. Year-on-year change of real GDP in 2010-19 average prices. EAP excl. China = Cambodia, Indonesia, Lao PDR, Malaysia, Mongolia, Myanmar, the Philippines, Thailand, and Vietnam. Island economies = Fiji, Kiribati, Marshall Islands, Micronesia, Palau, Papua New Guinea, Samoa, Solomon Islands, Timor-Leste, Tonga, Tuvalu, and Vanuatu. Aggregate growth rates are calculated using average 2010-19 GDP weights and market exchange rates. Data in shaded areas are forecasts.

B. Cumulative GDP in 2020 and projected for 2021. The aggregate is a simple average. EA excl. China = Cambodia, Indonesia, Lao PDR, Malaysia, Mongolia, Myanmar, the Philippines, Thailand, and Vietnam. Island economies = Fiji, Kiribati, Marshall Islands, Micronesia, Nauru, Palau, Papua New Guinea, Samoa, Solomon Islands, Timor-Leste, Tonga, Tuvalu, and Vanuatu. Error bars denote the largest and smallest change in the aggregates.

C. Based on estimates from a modified multivariate filter model (World Bank 2018).

D. Deviation from the levels under the baseline scenario implied by January 2020 GEP forecasts.

The pandemic is expected to dampen potential growth in many regional economies, especially those that have suffered most from extended and severe outbreaks of COVID-19 (World Bank 2020a). Rising indebtedness along with increased uncertainty and risk aversion are likely to inhibit investment. School closures and job losses have severely eroded human capital (World Bank 2020b). Obstacles to the reallocation of resources away from firms and sectors with limited potential in a post-COVID-19 world is hurting productivity growth (De Nikola et al. 2021).

Risks

Risks to the regional outlook are more balanced than in January but the downside risks predominate. On the downside, vaccination delays in the context of new virus variants could lead to a more persistent pandemic and the possibility of repeated and large outbreaks. Slow global suppression of the disease would increase the risk of the emergence of new variants that could be more infectious, lethal, and resistant to existing vaccines. Vaccine administration has been proceeding unevenly across countries. In China, the share of population which had received at least one dose of vaccine is estimated to have surpassed 30 percent reflecting the accelerated pace of vaccination (figure 2.1.4.A). None of the other major regional economies have surpassed 10 percent vaccine coverage. The current pace of vaccination could make it difficult to achieve widescale vaccination in many countries for some time, which increases the probability of the protracted and weaker-than-projected regional economic recovery. The protracted recovery may worsen balance sheets further and could lead to financial stress in some countries. All tourism-dependent countries are expected to suffer from a delay in the recovery of international tourism and travel and longer-than-expected recovery of output.

There is also a risk that favorable global financial conditions of recent years may not persist. Significant fiscal support could lead to concerns about rising inflation or monetary tightening in the United States, with important international spillover effects (Chapter 1). In the past, U.S. monetary tightening has often contributed to currency depreciation in EMDEs, followed by domestic monetary tightening and, in some countries, capital outflows, and financial turmoil in the region's most vulnerable economies. The impact is likely to be concentrated in countries with deeper financial markets, elevated external debt levels, large current account deficits, and high external financing needs (Cambodia, Lao People's Democratic Republic, Mongolia; figures 2.1.4.B-C). Alternatively, in some countries there is a risk that the recent acceleration in inflation due to commodity price increases and currency depreciation could de-anchor inflation expectations.

Disruptions and damages related to frequent natural disasters and weather-related events are a persistent source of severe downside risk for many economies in the region. Small island countries are particularly vulnerable, losing about 0.8 percent of aggregate GDP per year during 1980-2019, on average, to damages related to natural disasters, compared to 0.3 percent in all EMDEs (figure 2.1.4.D).

Finally, the region is also facing a risk of more severe and longer-lasting effects from the pandemic than expected, including more subdued investment than assumed and eroded human capital. Annual growth in the next decade could be more than one percentage point lower than pre-COVID-19 projections in the region excluding China, even considering the positive impact of technological advancements (World Bank 2018, 2021a).

Upside risks include faster vaccination and more rapid control of the pandemic than currently assumed. The policy support and recoveries in the United States and other major economies could have greater than assumed spillovers that boost regional growth, especially through stronger trade and remittances. The most export-oriented or competitive regional economies—including China, Cambodia, Malaysia, Thailand, and Vietnam—would be expected to benefit most from higher growth in the United States and other advanced economies (World Bank 2021a).

FIGURE 2.1.4 **EAP: Risks**

The regional forecast is subject to a number of downside risks. Repeated and large COVID-19 outbreaks and delays in vaccine rollout could lead to a more persistent pandemic and the possibility of repeated outbreaks. Countries with large current account deficits and large external financing needs are highly exposed to the risk related to heightened financial stress amplified by possible tightening of financing conditions. Disruptions from natural disasters and weather-related events are a persistent source of severe downside risk for many countries, especially island economies.

A. Share of population with at least one vaccine dose

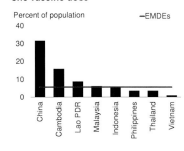

B. Domestic and external debt, 2020

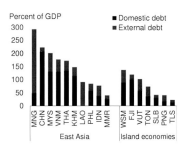

C. External financing needs

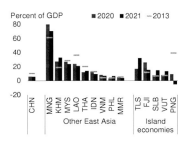

D. Cost and frequency of natural disasters, 1980-2019

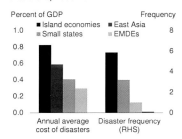

Sources: Bank for International Settlements; EM-DAT, CRED/UCLouvain, https://www.emdat.be; Haver Analytics; International Monetary Fund; Institute of International Finance; Our World in Data; World Bank.
A. Percent of population that has received at least one vaccine dose. Data for China is an estimate. Last observation is June 1, 2021.
B. Chart shows an estimated stock of domestic and external debt. Island economies = Fiji, Papua New Guinea, Samoa, the Solomon Islands (SLB), Timor-Leste (TLS), Tonga, Vanuatu. Domestic debt stock data for China, Indonesia, Malaysia, the Philippines, Thailand, and Vietnam are based on Institute of International Finance (IIF) database. Last observation is 2020 for China, Indonesia, the Philippines, and Thailand. Last observation is 2019 for Malaysia and Vietnam. Domestic debt stock data for Cambodia, Fiji, Mongolia, Myanmar, Papua New Guinea, Samoa, the Solomon Islands, Timor-Leste, Tonga, and Vanuatu are based on World Development Indicators (WDI) data. Last observation is 2019. External debt stock data for Cambodia, China, Fiji, Indonesia, Lao PDR, Malaysia, Mongolia, Papua New Guinea, the Philippines, the Solomon Islands, and Thailand are calculated based on Quarterly External Debt Statistics (QEDS). Last observation is 2020Q4. External debt stock data for Kiribati, Myanmar, Timor-Leste, Tonga, Vanuatu, and Vietnam are based on World Development Indicators (WDI) data. Last observation is 2019.
C. Estimated as a difference between current account and debt obligations coming due. Debt obligations coming due include the sum of principal repayment and interest in currency, goods, or services on long-term debt, on short-term debt, and repayments (repurchases and charges) to the IMF in corresponding year and short-term external debt stocks in corresponding year. External debts in 2020 and 2021 are estimated. GDP and current account in 2021 are projected.
D. East Asia = Cambodia, China, Indonesia, Lao PDR, Malaysia, Mongolia, Myanmar, the Philippines, Thailand, and Vietnam. Island economies = Fiji, Kiribati, Marshall Islands, Micronesia, Nauru, Palau, Papua New Guinea, Samoa, Solomon Islands, Timor-Leste, Tonga, Tuvalu, and Vanuatu. Annual average cost of disasters in percent of GDP. Disaster frequency is the annual average of natural disaster incidents from 1980-2019 per 10,000 square kilometers of land.

TABLE 2.1.1 East Asia and Pacific forecast summary

(Real GDP growth at market prices in percent, unless indicated otherwise)

Percentage point differences from January 2021 projections

	2018	2019	2020e	2021f	2022f	2023f	2021f	2022f
EMDE EAP, GDP [1]	**6.5**	**5.8**	**1.2**	**7.7**	**5.3**	**5.2**	**0.3**	**0.1**
GDP per capita (U.S. dollars)	5.8	5.1	0.6	7.1	4.8	4.8	0.3	0.1
(Average including countries that report expenditure components in national accounts) [2]								
EMDE EAP, GDP [2]	6.5	5.8	1.2	7.8	5.4	5.3	0.3	0.2
PPP GDP	6.4	5.7	0.8	7.6	5.4	5.3	0.4	0.2
Private consumption	8.6	6.4	-1.5	9.9	5.8	5.7	0.2	0.0
Public consumption	9.7	7.8	8.9	6.8	7.6	7.5	0.0	0.1
Fixed investment	5.7	4.4	0.3	5.7	4.3	4.2	-0.8	0.5
Exports, GNFS [3]	4.9	1.9	-1.5	6.9	5.5	4.6	3.2	1.9
Imports, GNFS [3]	8.4	0.4	-4.0	7.4	6.5	5.6	2.3	2.7
Net exports, contribution to growth	-0.8	0.4	0.6	0.0	-0.1	-0.2	0.3	-0.1
Memo items: GDP								
East Asia excluding China	5.3	4.8	-3.8	4.0	5.0	5.0	-0.9	-0.2
China	6.8	6.0	2.3	8.5	5.4	5.3	0.6	0.2
Indonesia	5.2	5.0	-2.1	4.4	5.0	5.1	0.0	0.2
Thailand	4.2	2.3	-6.1	2.2	5.1	4.3	-1.8	0.4
Island economies [4]	0.6	4.2	-6.3	2.7	4.7	3.2	-0.2	0.0

Source: World Bank.
Note: e = estimate; f = forecast; PPP = purchasing power parity; EMDE = emerging market and developing economy. World Bank forecasts are frequently updated based on new information and changing (global) circumstances. Consequently, projections presented here may differ from those contained in other Bank documents, even if basic assessments of countries' prospects do not differ at any given moment in time.
1. GDP and expenditure components are measured in average 2010-19 prices and market exchange rates. Excludes the Democratic People's Republic of Korea and dependent territories.
2. Subregion aggregate excludes the Democratic People's Republic of Korea, dependent territories, Fiji, Kiribati, the Marshall Islands, the Federated States of Micronesia, Myanmar, Palau, Papua New Guinea, Samoa, Timor-Leste, Tonga, and Tuvalu, for which data limitations prevent the forecasting of GDP components.
3. Exports and imports of goods and nonfactor services (GNFS).
4. Includes Fiji, Kiribati, the Marshall Islands, the Federated States of Micronesia, Nauru, Palau, Papua New Guinea, Samoa, the Solomon Islands, Timor-Leste, Tonga, and Tuvalu.

TABLE 2.1.2 East Asia and Pacific country forecasts [1]

(Real GDP growth at market prices in percent, unless indicated otherwise)

Percentage point differences from January 2021 projections

	2018	2019	2020e	2021f	2022f	2023f	2021f	2022f
Cambodia	7.5	7.1	-3.1	4.0	5.2	6.0	0.0	0.0
China	6.8	6.0	2.3	8.5	5.4	5.3	0.6	0.2
Fiji	3.5	-0.4	-19.0	2.6	8.2	6.9	0.0	0.0
Indonesia	5.2	5.0	-2.1	4.4	5.0	5.1	0.0	0.2
Lao PDR	3.8	3.9	-1.9	3.0	2.6	2.5	0.0	0.0
Kiribati	6.3	5.5	0.4	4.0	4.6	4.7	-0.9	-0.2
Malaysia	4.8	4.3	-5.6	6.0	4.2	4.4	-0.7	-0.6
Marshall Islands	3.3	6.6	-4.5	-1.0	3.0	2.0	0.5	-1.0
Micronesia, Fed. Sts.	0.2	1.2	-1.5	-3.5	2.5	1.0	-2.0	-2.0
Mongolia	7.0	5.0	-5.4	5.9	6.1	7.0	1.6	0.7
Myanmar [2]	6.4	6.8	1.7	-10.0	..	..	-12.0	..
Nauru	5.7	1.0	0.7	1.3	0.9	1.0	1.3	-1.1
Palau	4.1	-4.2	-10.0	-4.0	12.0	6.0	2.0	-3.0
Papua New Guinea	-0.3	5.9	-3.9	3.5	4.2	2.4	0.0	0.0
Philippines	6.3	6.0	-9.6	4.7	5.9	6.0	-1.2	-0.1
Samoa	-2.2	3.5	-3.5	-7.7	5.6	4.9	0.0	0.0
Solomon Islands	3.9	1.2	-5.0	2.0	4.5	4.3	-1.2	1.0
Thailand	4.2	2.3	-6.1	2.2	5.1	4.3	-1.8	0.4
Timor-Leste	-1.1	1.8	-7.3	1.8	3.7	4.3	-1.3	-0.5
Tonga	0.3	0.7	-1.5	-3.0	2.3	2.8	2.3	0.0
Tuvalu	4.3	4.1	-0.5	3.0	4.0	3.0	-0.5	0.0
Vanuatu	2.8	3.0	-10.0	4.0	3.9	3.3	-2.0	-0.1
Vietnam	7.1	7.0	2.9	6.6	6.5	6.5	-0.1	0.0

Source: World Bank.
Note: e = estimate; f = forecast. World Bank forecasts are frequently updated based on new information and changing (global) circumstances. Consequently, projections presented here may differ from those contained in other Bank documents, even if basic assessments of countries' prospects do not significantly differ at any given moment in time.
1. Data are based on GDP measured in average 2010-19 prices and market exchange rates. Values for Timor-Leste represent non-oil GDP. For the following countries, values correspond to the fiscal year: the Marshall Islands, Myanmar, the Federated States of Micronesia, and Palau (October 1– September 30); Nauru, Samoa, and Tonga (July 1–June 30).
2. Forecasts beyond 2021 are excluded due to a high degree of uncertainty.

EUROPE and CENTRAL ASIA

Growth in Europe and Central Asia (ECA) is projected to reach 3.9 percent in 2021, with firming external demand and elevated industrial commodity prices offsetting the negative impact of recent resurgences in new COVID-19 cases. Regional growth is forecast to remain at 3.9 percent in 2022 as the recovery in domestic demand gains traction. The outlook remains uncertain, however, with uneven vaccine rollouts and the withdrawal of domestic macroeconomic support measures weighing on the regional recovery. Growth could be weaker than projected if the pandemic takes longer than expected to abate, external financing conditions tighten, or policy uncertainty and geopolitical tensions rise further. Legacies of the pandemic, including slowdowns in physical and human capital accumulation, loom over the medium-term outlook if left unaddressed.

Recent developments

Europe and Central Asia (ECA) continues to grapple with containing COVID-19 and remains among the emerging market and developing economy (EMDE) regions with the highest cases and deaths per capita. The true death toll is likely even higher, with excess death statistics indicating double-digit percentage increases in deaths relative to pre-pandemic years in half of the region's economies. After declining in early 2021, daily new COVID-19 cases accelerated rapidly along-side the emergence of new variants and increased population mobility—restrictions on mobility, including lockdowns, have helped bend the epidemiological curve and are gradually being lifted (figure 2.2.1.A). Although the start of vaccinations in most regional economies is a positive development, progress remains uneven across the region, partly reflecting procurement challenges (figure 2.2.1.B).

The 2.1 percent fall in regional output in 2020 was shallower than expected, as firming external demand from the euro area buoyed industrial production and goods trade volumes. Household incomes were supported by robust remittance

inflows amid increases in official transfers and the drawdown of savings of migrant workers (figure 2.2.1.C; Dinarte et al. 2021; Quayyum and Kpodar 2020; ILO 2021). The resilience of activity also reflected adaptation to containment measures, as schools and storefronts pivoted toward virtual settings, where feasible, while job retention schemes reduced job losses (Demirgüç-Kunt, Lokshin, and Torre 2020; ILO 2021; World Bank 2021a).

The resurgence of COVID-19 cases in early 2021 has interrupted the incipient economic recovery. Manufacturing and composite PMIs have faltered across the region in recent months. Services activity remains subdued, weighed down by continuing social distancing measures and sustained weakness in international tourism. Elevated pandemic cases and spikes in geopolitical tensions and policy uncertainty in some countries have also triggered portfolio outflows, which were already larger than in other EMDEs, exacerbating currency depreciations. EMBI spreads have widened in countries facing elevated geopolitical tensions, policy uncertainty, or external financing pressures (Belarus, Turkey, Ukraine).

Recent currency depreciations have put further upward pressure on prices. Of the 17 ECA central banks with inflation targets, nearly half reported headline inflation above the upper bound of the

Note: This section was prepared by Collette Mari Wheeler.

FIGURE 2.2.1 **ECA: Recent developments**

A resurgence of new COVID-19 cases has weighed on the recovery in Europe and Central Asia (ECA). Vaccinations across the region are progressing, but unevenly, with many countries below the world average of vaccinations per person owing to bottlenecks in procurement and administration. Despite continued disruptions from the pandemic, ECA economies are expected to start to unwind policy support measures in 2021.

A. New daily COVID-19 cases and mobility

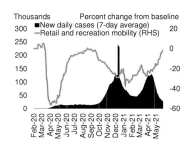

B. COVID-19 vaccine doses administered and procured

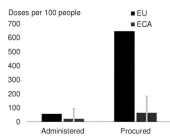

C. Economic activity and inward remittances

D. Fiscal and monetary policy in 2021

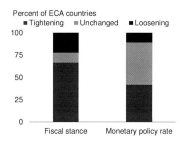

Sources: Duke Global Health Innovation Center (2021); Haver Analytics; International Monetary Fund; Johns Hopkins University; World Bank.
Note: ECA = Europe and Central Asia; EU = European Union.
A. Figure shows 7-day moving average of new daily COVID-19 cases and of retail and recreation mobility. Retail and recreation mobility refers to mobility trends for places like restaurants, cafes, shopping centers, theme parks, museums, libraries, and movie theaters. The baseline for mobility is the median value, for the corresponding day of the week, during the 5-week period January 3–February 6, 2020. Last observation is May 28, 2021 for both COVID-19 cases and retail and recreation mobility.
B. Figure shows last observation of total vaccination administration, which is May 28, 2021, and confirmed procurement of vaccine dose purchases, which is May 14, 2021. Yellow whiskers show the minimum-maximum range of ECA countries.
C. Last observation is March 2021.
D. Figure shows the share of countries with a positive (loosening fiscal stance), negative (tightening fiscal stance), and unchanged fiscal impulse in 2021 using +/- 0.5 percentage point of potential GDP threshold, and the share of countries that experienced a policy rate hike (tightening monetary policy rate) and cut (loosening monetary policy rate). Fiscal impulse is defined as the change in the cyclically adjusted primary balance (CAPB) from the previous year. Sample includes 10 ECA countries for fiscal stance and 19 ECA countries for monetary policy rate.

target band in early 2021. As a result of inflationary pressures, policy interest rates have been raised in one-third of the region's economies thus far in 2021 (Armenia, Belarus, Georgia, Kyrgyz Republic, the Russian Federation, Tajikistan, Turkey, Ukraine). Although the banking sector has adequate liquidity and buffers

in many ECA economies, increases in non-performing and distressed loans are expected as countries continue to phase out regulatory relief and moratoriums on credit obligations.

The large fiscal support packages delivered in 2020—equivalent, on average, to 7.5 percent of GDP—are expected to be partially unwound this year (figure 2.2.1.D). The fiscal response to the pandemic, together with last year's contraction in output, is expected to leave median public debt at 54 percent of GDP by end-2022—nearly 15 percentage points higher than in 2019. Nevertheless, targeted fiscal support, such as wage subsidies and cash transfers, is estimated to have helped avert a larger spike in poverty and job losses (Kazakhstan, Turkey, Western Balkans; World Bank 2021a). As countries gradually withdraw support measures, however, job losses could increase again.

Outlook

ECA's economy is forecast to expand 3.9 percent in 2021, stronger than previously projected partly owing to a more robust than anticipated recovery in neighboring euro area (figure 2.2.2.A-B; chapter 1). Nonetheless, the outlook remains challenging especially given continued disruptions from the pandemic, combined with tighter monetary policy as well as elevated policy uncertainty and geopolitical tensions. The outlook is predicated on a faster pace of vaccination in the second half of the year in ECA's largest economies. Widespread vaccination in other regional economies is expected to lag the region's largest economies by about one to two quarters. Several countries Central Asia, Eastern Europe, and the Western Balkans face bottlenecks related to the production, procurement, or delivery of vaccines secured through the COVAX facility or other agreements.

Growth is expected to remain at 3.9 percent in 2022, as the recovery in domestic demand offsets a continued drag from the withdrawal of macroeconomic policy support. Despite the improvement, per capita GDP in 2022 is forecast to be 5.3 percent below the level expected prior to the pandemic. Meanwhile, the continued disrupttion of education for millions of school-children and a sharp decline in investment, particularly foreign direct investment (FDI), are expected to contribute to a further slowdown in productivity growth over a prolonged period (figure 2.2.2.C-D; UNCTAD 2021, World Bank 2021a, World Bank 2021b).

The strength and speed of countries' recoveries will depend on the effectiveness of pandemic management, the duration of lockdowns, and the pace of vaccine deployment. Tourism-dependent economies will continue to face particular challenges amid depressed international travel (UNWTO 2021). The recovery is also expected to be slower in countries suffering from heightened geopolitical tensions, as weak investor confidence weighs on private investment.

The Russian economy is projected to grow 3.2 percent in 2021, supported by firming domestic demand and elevated energy prices. Although new COVID-19 cases have somewhat stabilized, vaccine reluctance is impeding inoculation. The escalation of geopolitical tensions in 2021, including additional U.S. sanctions, and increases in the policy rate from record lows are also weighing on the outlook. Nonetheless, the recovery is expected to remain steady in 2022, at 3.2 percent, as the pandemic's effects wane and industrial commodity prices stabilize. Despite this improvement, per capita income in 2022 will be 1.8 percent below the level expected before the pandemic.

In Turkey, following three years of subdued growth amid recurring financial market pressures and the COVID-19 crisis, growth is projected to rise to 5 percent in 2021, as exports benefit from firming external demand, particularly in the euro area. The expansion is then set to moderate to 4.5 percent in 2022, with activity supported by a gradual pick up in domestic demand. The projected pace of recovery will buoy income relative to the regional average. The forecast masks growing vulnerabilities (World Bank 2021a). The economy's vulnerabilities include reoccurring COVID-19 outbreaks and a slowdown in vaccination progress, weak international tourism, sharp tightening of external financing conditions,

FIGURE 2.2.2 **ECA: Outlook**

Forecasts for growth in Europe and Central Asia (ECA) have been revised upward, as supportive external conditions help offset an intensifying pandemic. Nevertheless, the recovery in 2021-22 will not be sufficient to recoup losses from 2020, with output in 2022 projected to be below pre-pandemic projections in most of the region's economies.

A. Contributions to forecast revisions for ECA GDP growth

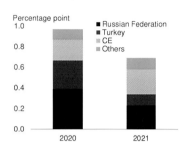

B. GDP forecast revisions for 2021, by vaccination progress

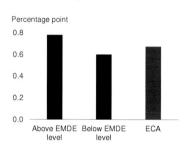

C. GDP growth in ECA, by subregion

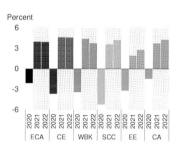

D. GDP per capita changes from pre-pandemic projections for 2022, by region and country

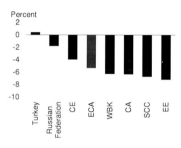

Sources: Our World in Data; World Bank.
Note: EMDE = emerging market and developing economies; CA = Central Asia; CE = Central Europe; ECA = Europe and Central Asia; EE = Eastern Europe; EU = European Union; SCC = South Caucasus; WBK = Western Balkans. Aggregates calculated using constant GDP weights at average 2010-19 prices and market exchange rates. Shaded areas indicate forecasts.
A. Figure shows the contribution to forecast revisions between the current and January 2021 editions of the *Global Economic Prospects* report.
B. Figure shows unweighted average of percentage-point difference between the current and January 2021 editions of the *Global Economic Prospects* report. Vaccine progress above (below) EMDE level refers to ECA countries with a total number of doses administered per hundred people of the national population higher (lower) than the ratio for EMDEs.
D. Figure shows the gaps between the current projections and January 2020 editions of the *Global Economic Prospects* report.

and a recent rise in policy uncertainty, especially about monetary policy

Growth in Central Europe is projected to rebound to 4.6 percent in 2021 and remain at that pace in 2022, supported by a recovery in trade as activity improves in the euro area. Exceptional policy accommodation is expected to continue through 2021, including near-zero policy interest rates in Hungary and Poland. The sizable European Union (EU) fund packages for members states—including for all Central European economies—

FIGURE 2.2.3 **ECA: Risks**

Although countries in ECA were among the first to begin vaccination campaigns, widespread progress has been constrained by logistical challenges and general vaccine reluctance. Meanwhile, continued weakness in investment could exacerbate the slowdown in long-run growth, especially absent progress on reforms to strengthen governance. Aside from the pandemic, ECA faces the risk of financial stress. Inflationary pressures are rising across the region and may limit monetary authorities' ability to respond to adverse shocks.

A. Willingness to receive a COVID-19 vaccine

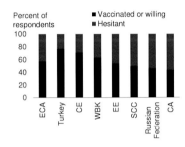

B. Long-term investment growth forecasts

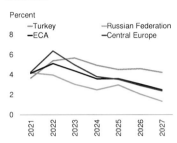

C. Sources of reform advances and setbacks in ECA countries, 1998-2018

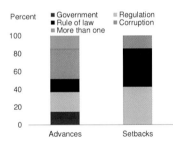

D. Consumer price inflation versus target

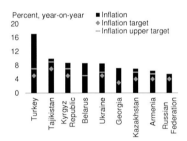

Sources: Consensus Economics; Fan et al. (2021); Haver Analytics; Our World in Data; Worldwide Governance Indicators, World Bank.

Note: BiH = Bosnia and Herzegovina; CA = Central Asia; CE = Central Europe; ECA = Europe and Central Asia; EE = Eastern Europe; RUS = Russian Federation; SCC = South Caucasus; WBK = Western Balkans. Shaded areas indicate forecasts. Aggregates calculated using constant GDP weights at average 2010-19 prices and market exchange rates.

A. Survey results are based on 236,000 interviews conducted in 18 countries between April 1-30, 2021. Bars indicate data on share of population receiving at least one vaccine dose and responses to a vaccine acceptance question. Responses to the vaccine acceptance question are weighted to reflect the share of population who have not yet received a vaccine. Survey respondents are asked, "If a vaccine to prevent COVID-19 were offered to you today, would you choose to get vaccinated?" Aggregates are calculated using population weights.

B. Long-term prospects refer to 10-year-ahead forecasts. The horizontal axis shows the year when long-term forecasts are surveyed. Sample includes 8 ECA countries.

C. Based on 27 episodes of reform advances and 7 episodes of reform setbacks identified in 23 ECA countries using the World Bank's *Worldwide Governance Indicators*.

D. Last observation is March 2021 for Tajikistan and Ukraine, and April 2021 for others.

should help mitigate the weakness in investment. The boost, however, could be tempered by low absorption of the funds due to challenges relating to administrative capacity and governance.

Growth in the Western Balkans is expected to rebound to 4.4 percent in 2021 and to moderate to 3.7 percent in 2022, assuming that consumer

and business confidence is restored as vaccination rollout accelerates, and that political instability eases. Activity in tourism-dependent economies, particularly Albania and Montenegro, will continue to be hampered by international travel restrictions. Meanwhile, medium-term growth in Albania and North Macedonia should be boosted by accelerating structural reforms in preparation for EU membership, provided negotiations surrounding the accession process are not further delayed (Rovo 2020). The subregion is also expected to benefit from the EU's recently adopted Economic and Investment Plan, which will mobilize funding to support competitiveness and inclusive growth, as well as the green and digital transition.

After suffering the sharpest collapse in output among the ECA subregions in 2020 amid armed conflict, the South Caucasus is projected to return to positive growth, expanding 3.6 percent in 2021; growth is then expected to strengthen to 4.2 percent in 2022. The recovery in early 2021 remains muted, reflecting subdued domestic demand due to the pandemic, as well as an escalation in domestic political tensions (Armenia) and continued weakness in transport and tourism (Georgia). Monetary policy has also tightened, with Armenia and Georgia having hiked policy rates. The current forecast is predicated on the dissipation of the shocks related both to the pandemic and to conflict, and on a recovery in tourism alongside improving consumer and business confidence. Growth in Azerbaijan is expected to be supported by stabilization of oil prices as well as investment and reconstruction spending. The November 2020 ceasefire agreement between Armenia and Azerbaijan have alleviated geopolitical tensions in the region, although risks to stability remain elevated.

Growth in Eastern Europe in the near term is projected to be the weakest among the ECA subregions, rising only to 1.9 percent in 2021 and 2.8 percent in 2022. The banking sector remains fragile amid high dollarization in some economies, with sharp currency depreciations and weak activity having eroded bank asset quality. A surge in inflation, especially in Ukraine—the subregion's largest economy—triggered more restrictive monetary policy in early 2021. The recovery is constrained by continued challenges related to subdued domestic demand and structural weakness, as well as policy uncertainty over upcoming elections in Moldova and ongoing geopolitical tensions in Ukraine and Belarus, with the latter facing newly imposed international sanctions. Growing external imbalances, slower reform momentum, and political tensions will continue to weigh on private investment.

In Central Asia, growth is forecast to recover to 3.7 percent in 2021 and 4.3 percent in 2022—well below historical averages. The economy is expected to be supported by a modest rise in commodity prices, relaxation of OPEC+ production cuts (Kazakhstan), and firming FDI as the subregion deepens its global and regional integration. In Uzbekistan, growth should continue to benefit from the implementation of an ambitious reform agenda, which progressed last year despite formidable headwinds from the pandemic. However, the rebound in Central Asia has been dampened by rising policy uncertainty, particularly in the Kyrgyz Republic, following political tensions and social unrest. Geopolitical tensions have also increased in Central Asia amid conflict over a border dispute between the Kyrgyz Republic and Tajikistan. Rising inflationary pressures prompted increases in key policy interest rates in the Kyrgyz Republic and Tajikistan.

Risks

The forecast is subject to predominantly downside risks, including those related to the pandemic (World Bank 2021a; World Bank 2021c). Although the region has administered more vaccine doses per person relative to the world average, vaccine distribution and progress remain highly uneven; only about one-third of ECA's economies are above the world average, while the rest continue to trail the world average due to logistical challenges and vaccine hesitancy. Absent clear and consistent communication to strengthen public trust, the suspension of vaccines due to safety concerns could contribute to higher-than-expected vaccine reluctance (figure 2.2.3.A; World Bank 2021a). The combination of supply bottlenecks and subdued vaccine demand in some ECA countries, juxtaposed with widespread

vaccination in others, could contribute to an uneven regional recovery.

The pandemic could also exacerbate the slowdown in investment in physical and human capital, which was already steep in ECA due to longstanding structural challenges (Dieppe 2020; World Bank 2020a). Following a collapse in fixed investment, forecasts for long-term investment growth point to a decline 1.7 percentage points over the next decade (figure 2.2.3.B; Consensus Economics 2021, UNCTAD 2021). The pandemic has also dented the accumulation of human capital through school closures and sustained spells of unemployment. On the upside, however, the pandemic offers opportunities to lift long-term growth. Digitalization could be harnessed to strengthen governance by enhancing public efficiency and transparency (figure 2.2.3.C; World Bank 2021a).

The risk of financial stress also looms over the region's outlook. Renewed policy uncertainty has exacerbated the decline in portfolio inflows and reignited currency depreciation and reserve losses. As a result, external financing pressures are building, particularly in countries with a large share of foreign-currency-denominated debt. An acceleration in inflation has further constrained the capacity of some central banks to buffer the impact of additional negative external shocks, with about one-third of the region's economies forced to raise policy rates in 2021 (figure 2.2.3.D). A sharper erosion of investor sentiment could abruptly tighten financing conditions, and lead to cascading defaults and rising non-performing loans. Corporate balance sheet pressures have continued to rise as authorities unwind liquidity support and regulatory forbearance, putting strain on the banking sector.

The possibility of intensifying geopolitical tensions is also a downside risk in ECA, and could be accompanied by additional sanctions and financial market pressures. The region could be destabilized by an escalation of conflict in Ukraine or between the Kyrgyz Republic and Tajikistan, as well as by elevated stability risks linked to post-conflict settlements between Armenia and Azerbaijan. Additional political pressures in Belarus or the

Kyrgyz Republic could weaken the outlook in Eastern Europe and Central Asia. Disagreements between the EU and other major economies could also lead to additional sanctions that could have spillover effects into some ECA countries. A further rise in policy uncertainty, particularly in some of the region's large economies, could also undermine the recovery if it triggers financial stress.

TABLE 2.2.1 Europe and Central Asia forecast summary

(Real GDP growth at market prices in percent, unless indicated otherwise)

Percentage point differences from January 2021 projections

	2018	2019	2020e	2021f	2022f	2023f	2021f	2022f
EMDE ECA, GDP [1]	3.5	2.7	-2.1	3.9	3.9	3.5	0.6	0.1
GDP per capita (U.S. dollars)	3.1	2.3	-2.4	3.7	3.7	3.4	0.7	0.1
EMDE ECA, GDP excl. Turkey	3.7	3.1	-3.2	3.7	3.7	3.2	0.8	0.2
(Average including countries that report expenditure components in national accounts) [2]								
EMDE ECA, GDP [2]	3.4	2.5	-2.1	4.0	3.9	3.4	0.7	0.1
PPP GDP	3.4	2.4	-2.1	3.9	3.8	3.3	0.6	0.0
Private consumption	3.9	3.6	-3.8	3.7	3.9	3.6	0.0	0.8
Public consumption	2.9	3.3	2.9	0.8	0.7	1.6	1.5	-0.1
Fixed investment	2.2	-0.2	-2.3	4.9	6.6	5.0	0.3	0.1
Exports, GNFS [3]	5.9	3.6	-7.2	5.6	5.5	5.4	-0.3	-0.4
Imports, GNFS [3]	3.3	2.9	-5.2	5.1	7.0	5.6	-1.7	-0.3
Net exports, contribution to growth	1.1	0.4	-1.0	0.3	-0.3	0.1	0.5	0.0
Memo items: GDP								
Commodity exporters [4]	3.0	2.5	-2.9	3.3	3.4	2.8	0.6	0.2
Commodity importers [5]	4.0	2.8	-1.3	4.6	4.4	4.2	0.8	-0.1
Central Europe [6]	4.9	4.4	-3.7	4.6	4.6	4.0	1.0	0.4
Western Balkans [7]	4.0	3.6	-3.4	4.4	3.7	3.8	0.9	0.0
Eastern Europe [8]	3.4	2.7	-3.2	1.9	2.8	2.6	0.7	0.3
South Caucasus [9]	2.8	3.6	-5.2	3.6	4.2	4.0	1.1	-0.6
Central Asia [10]	4.5	4.9	-1.5	3.7	4.3	5.1	0.7	0.4
Russian Federation	2.8	2.0	-3.0	3.2	3.2	2.3	0.6	0.2
Turkey	3.0	0.9	1.8	5.0	4.5	4.5	0.5	-0.5
Poland	5.4	4.7	-2.7	3.8	4.5	3.9	0.3	0.2

Source: World Bank.

Note: e = estimate; f = forecast; PPP = purchasing power parity; EMDE = emerging market and developing economy. World Bank forecasts are frequently updated based on new information and changing (global) circumstances. Consequently, projections presented here may differ from those contained in other Bank documents, even if basic assessments of countries' prospects do not differ at any given moment in time. Due to lack of reliable data of adequate quality, the World Bank is currently not publishing economic output, income, or growth data for Turkmenistan, and Turkmenistan is excluded from cross-country macroeconomic aggregates.

1. GDP and expenditure components are measured in average 2010-19 prices and market exchange rates.
2. Aggregates presented here exclude Azerbaijan, Bosnia and Herzegovina, Kazakhstan, Kosovo, the Kyrgyz Republic, Montenegro, Serbia, Tajikistan, Turkmenistan, and Uzbekistan, for which data limitations prevent the forecasting of GDP components.
3. Exports and imports of goods and nonfactor services (GNFS).
4. Includes Armenia, Azerbaijan, Kazakhstan, the Kyrgyz Republic, Kosovo, the Russian Federation, Tajikistan, Ukraine, and Uzbekistan.
5. Includes Albania, Belarus, Bosnia and Herzegovina, Bulgaria, Croatia, Georgia, Hungary, Moldova, Montenegro, North Macedonia, Poland, Romania, Serbia, and Turkey.
6. Includes Bulgaria, Croatia, Hungary, Poland, and Romania.
7. Includes Albania, Bosnia and Herzegovina, Kosovo, Montenegro, North Macedonia, and Serbia.
8. Includes Belarus, Moldova, and Ukraine.
9. Includes Armenia, Azerbaijan, and Georgia.
10. Includes Kazakhstan, the Kyrgyz Republic, Tajikistan, and Uzbekistan.

TABLE 2.2.2 Europe and Central Asia country forecasts [1]

(Real GDP growth at market prices in percent, unless indicated otherwise)

Percentage point differences from January 2021 projections

	2018	2019	2020e	2021f	2022f	2023f	2021f	2022f
Albania	4.1	2.2	-3.3	4.4	3.7	3.7	-0.7	-0.7
Armenia	5.2	7.6	-7.6	3.4	4.3	5.3	0.3	-0.2
Azerbaijan	1.5	2.2	-4.3	2.8	3.9	3.4	0.9	-0.6
Belarus	3.1	1.4	-0.9	-2.2	1.9	1.2	0.5	1.0
Bosnia and Herzegovina [2]	3.7	2.8	-4.3	2.8	3.5	3.7	0.0	0.0
Bulgaria	3.1	3.7	-4.2	2.6	3.3	3.4	-0.7	-0.4
Croatia	2.8	2.9	-8.0	5.5	6.2	5.7	0.1	2.0
Georgia	4.9	5.0	-6.1	6.0	5.0	5.0	2.0	-1.0
Hungary	5.4	4.6	-5.0	6.0	4.7	4.3	2.2	0.4
Kazakhstan	4.1	4.5	-2.6	3.2	3.7	4.8	0.7	0.2
Kosovo	3.8	4.9	-6.9	4.0	4.5	4.1	0.3	-0.4
Kyrgyz Republic	3.8	4.6	-8.6	3.8	4.3	4.5	0.0	-0.2
Moldova	4.3	3.6	-7.0	3.8	3.7	3.8	0.0	0.0
Montenegro	5.1	4.1	-15.2	7.1	4.5	3.5	1.0	0.6
North Macedonia	2.9	3.2	-4.5	3.6	3.5	3.4	0.0	0.0
Poland	5.4	4.7	-2.7	3.8	4.5	3.9	0.3	0.2
Romania	4.5	4.1	-3.9	6.0	4.5	3.9	2.5	0.4
Russian Federation	2.8	2.0	-3.0	3.2	3.2	2.3	0.6	0.2
Serbia	4.4	4.2	-1.0	5.0	3.7	3.9	1.9	0.3
Tajikistan	7.6	7.4	4.5	5.3	5.6	6.0	1.8	0.1
Turkey	3.0	0.9	1.8	5.0	4.5	4.5	0.5	-0.5
Ukraine	3.4	3.2	-4.0	3.8	3.1	3.1	0.8	0.0
Uzbekistan	5.4	5.8	1.6	4.8	5.5	5.8	0.5	1.0

Source: World Bank.
Note: e = estimate; f = forecast. World Bank forecasts are frequently updated based on new information and changing (global) circumstances. Consequently, projections presented here may differ from those contained in other Bank documents, even if basic assessments of countries' prospects do not significantly differ at any given moment in time. Due to lack of reliable data of adequate quality, the World Bank is currently not publishing economic output, income, or growth data for Turkmenistan, and Turkmenistan is excluded from cross-country macroeconomic aggregates.
1. Data are based on GDP measured in average 2010-19 prices and market exchange rates, unless indicated otherwise.
2. GDP growth rate at constant prices is based on production approach.

LATIN AMERICA and THE CARIBBEAN

Growth in Latin America and the Caribbean (LAC) is projected to be 5.2 percent in 2021—a rebound insufficient to return GDP to 2019 levels this year after a historically deep recession in 2020. The rebound will be supported by moderate progress in vaccine rollouts, relaxation of mobility restrictions, and improved external economic conditions. Per capita income losses will still be deep in 2022, particularly for small island economies in the Caribbean. Although spillovers from robust growth and additional fiscal support in the United States through trade and confidence channels are an upside risk to the baseline forecast, the balance of risks is tilted to the downside. Key downside risks include a slower-than-expected COVID-19 vaccine rollout; further surges in new COVID-19 cases, including from variant strains of the virus; adverse market reactions from social unrest or strained fiscal conditions; and disruptions related to social unrest or to climate change and natural disasters.

Recent developments

Latin America and the Caribbean (LAC) continues to be severely affected by COVID-19. After slowing in the first two months of this year, new cases have spiked again, surpassing 2020 peaks in many countries. The region accounts about 30 percent of confirmed deaths worldwide, nearly four times its share of the global population. Some countries are grappling with the widescale spread of COVID-19 variants.

Mobility restrictions were tightened in numerous countries (including Argentina, Barbados, Brazil, Colombia, Ecuador, Paraguay, Peru, and Uruguay) in the first half of this year, hindering economic activity especially in the services sector, which was already lagging the rebound in the industrial sector (figure 2.3.1.A). Vaccine administration is proceeding unevenly across countries. About half of the population of Chile and Uruguay had received at least one dose of vaccine as of late May, as had approximately one-quarter in the Dominican Republic, Dominica, Barbados, and Guyana. But many other countries have scarcely begun.

Note: This section was prepared by Dana Vorisek.

In several respects, external economic conditions have improved since the start of the year. Prices of key commodities have risen, bolstering government revenues (figure 2.3.1.B). Remittance inflows remain robust, supporting consumer spending in a swath of highly remittance-reliant economies (El Salvador, Guatemala, Honduras, Jamaica, Nicaragua), in part reflecting substantial income support and social transfers in the United States. Although international tourist arrivals remain a small fraction of pre-pandemic levels in most of the Caribbean, arrivals have approached half of pre-pandemic levels in recent months in the Dominican Republic and Mexico (figure 2.3.1.C).

Sovereign borrowing costs have risen in recent months, after an earlier narrowing of spreads over 10-year U.S. Treasury bonds in much of the region between April 2020 and January 2021. Spreads are especially elevated in countries including Argentina, Belize, and Ecuador, although they have fallen in Ecuador since early March. Portfolio inflows to the region have slowed, and currencies have depreciated against the U.S. dollar. Headline inflation has risen in many countries, but from a low level, in part due to increasing energy and food prices in many countries. Inflation has recently breached the upper bound of inflation target bands in three of

FIGURE 2.3.1 LAC: Recent developments

Economic conditions in Latin America and the Caribbean (LAC) are improving after a deep recession in 2020. External conditions have become increasingly supportive in important respects: key commodity prices have risen, remittance inflows remain robust, and new fiscal support in the United States will likely benefit the region. But tourism remains subdued. The damage from the pandemic—including job and income losses and poverty increases—is severe.

A. Services and industry sector growth

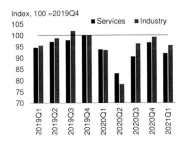

B. Commodity prices

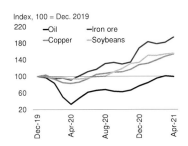

C. International tourist arrivals

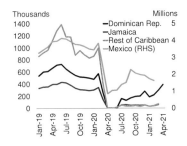

D. Change in employment, end-2019 to present

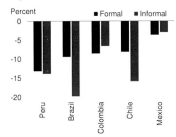

Sources: Haver Analytics; national sources; World Bank.
Note: LAC = Latin America and the Caribbean.
A. Bars show the GDP-weighted average of Argentina, Brazil, Chile, Colombia, Mexico, and Peru. Growth rates for Argentina for 2021Q1 are estimated based on available information.
B. Last observation is April 2021.
C. "Rest of Caribbean" includes Antigua and Barbuda, The Bahamas, Belize, Grenada, and St. Lucia. Data are seasonally adjusted. Last observation is April 2021 for the Dominican Republic, March 2021 for Jamaica and for rest of the Caribbean, and February 2021 for Mexico.
D. Bars show the decline in the number of people employed between December 2019 and the latest available month. Bars show three-month moving averages. For Peru, formal employment covers only metropolitan Lima. Last observation for both formal and informal employment is March 2021 for Brazil, Chile, and Mexico; February 2021 for Colombia; and December 2020 for Peru.

the eight countries using them—Brazil, the Dominican Republic, and Mexico.

With fiscal strains already severe and the worst economic effects of the pandemic assumed to have passed, additional spending and tax relief related to the pandemic is winding down in most countries. Uncertainty about the direction of economic policy has become more prominent, however, with countries accounting for 45 percent of the region's GDP holding elections in 2021 (general elections in Chile, Ecuador, Honduras,

Nicaragua, Peru, and St. Lucia; legislative elections in Argentina, El Salvador, and Mexico).

The scars of the pandemic are severe. Although employment has risen from mid-2020 lows, it has not returned to pre-pandemic levels (figure 2.3.1.D). Female, young, informal, and low-wage workers have disproportionately suffered job losses (ECLAC 2021; World Bank 2021e). Labor force participation has declined substantially, increasing concerns that professional skills are being eroded. Income losses have raised poverty and food insecurity in many countries, despite the substantial expansion in social safety nets (Bracco et al. forthcoming; Busso et al. 2020; Mahler et al. 2021).

Outlook

Regional growth is projected to be 5.2 percent in 2021. This is a modest recovery after a 6.5 percent contraction in 2020, deeper than recessions during World War I and the Great Depression (figure 2.3.2.A). Although the forecast for 2021 has been revised upward since January, the rebound in the region is still weak relative to other EMDE regions. LAC is one of the two emerging market and developing economy (EMDE) regions, along with the Middle East and North Africa, where real GDP is expected to be lower in 2021 than in 2019.

The baseline near-term outlook for the region assumes moderate progress in vaccine rollouts in most countries, less stringent mobility restrictions than in 2020, positive spillovers from strong growth in advanced economies and fiscal support in the United States, and a broad-based rise in commodity prices. Growth in 2022 is projected to soften, to 2.9 percent, as the boost from these factors wanes (tables 2.3.1, 2.3.2). Tourism-reliant economies are projected to take longer than commodity-exporting economies to reach 2019 levels of output (figure 2.3.2.B).

Still benign global financing conditions and a faster-than-expected resumption of economic activity is supporting more robust investment growth this year than projected in January. This upturn follows a seven-year declining trend.

However, even by 2022, the level of investment is projected to only have returned to about where it stalled prior to the pandemic, and will still be well below the high reached in 2013, prior to a sharp drop in global commodity prices (figure 2.3.2.C). This will continue to weigh on potential growth prospects (World Bank 2021c).

By 2022, per capita real GDP in LAC is projected to be 1.5 percent below its 2019 level. Numerous economies, particularly tourism-reliant economies (The Bahamas, Barbados, Belize, Dominica, Grenada, Jamaica, Panama, St. Lucia), face substantially deeper losses (figure 2.3.2.D).

Brazil's economy is projected to expand by 4.5 percent in 2021. Private consumption will be boosted by a fresh round of emergency payments to households, although social transfers will be substantially smaller than in 2020. Investment growth will be supported by benign domestic and international credit conditions. Growth in services output is expected to continue lagging industrial output growth in the short term, owing to the effects of COVID-19. Growth is projected to moderate to 2.5 percent in 2022 as domestic policy support is withdrawn and external conditions become less supportive.

In Mexico, growth of 5 percent is projected for 2021, after an 8.3 percent contraction in 2020. The manufacturing industry, but also the services sector, is expected to benefit from increased export demand associated with robust growth in the United States, which receives four-fifths of Mexico's exports. Growth is envisaged to soften to 3 percent in 2022 as the fiscal impulse in the United States fades, but domestic demand will be supported by growing COVID-19 vaccination coverage.

In Argentina, growth is expected to rebound to 6.4 percent in 2021, reflecting ample spare capacity following a three-year contraction that pushed real GDP back to approximately its 2009 level. Thereafter, the temporary growth boost will moderate, with growth projected to be 1.7 percent in 2022.

In Colombia, growth is projected to reach 5.9 percent in 2021, underpinned by improved

FIGURE 2.3.2 LAC: Outlook

Growth in LAC is expected to reach 5.2 percent in 2021, a modest rebound after a historically deep recession in 2020. A pickup in investment is expected to follow several years of weakness; however, investment in 2022 is still expected to return only to about the level where it stalled from 2016 to 2019. Tourism-reliant economies are projected to take longer than commodity-exporting economies to reach 2019 levels of output. Many countries in LAC, especially those in the Caribbean, will still have per capita GDP below 2019 levels in 2022 and beyond.

A. LAC growth

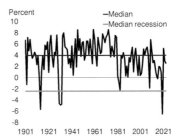

B. LAC GDP, by subgroup

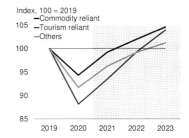

C. LAC GDP components

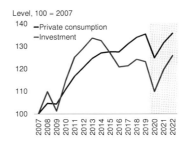

D. Change in per capita GDP, 2019 to 2022

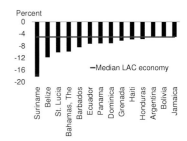

Sources: University of Groningen (Maddison Project Database, Penn World Table); Haver Analytics; national sources; World Bank.
Note: LAC = Latin America and the Caribbean.
B.C. Grey area indicates forecasts.
D. Figure shows economies with the largest gaps. Antigua and Barbuda and St. Kitts and Nevis are not shown but have gaps larger than the regional median.

external conditions and a rebound in domestic demand. After a slow start, any further delays in the COVID-19 vaccination would be a drag on the recovery.

Chile's economy is forecast to expand by 6.1 percent in 2021 as COVID-19 vaccines continue to be administered at a robust pace and private consumption is boosted by pension fund withdrawals allowed during the pandemic. Export growth will improve in line with rising demand in advanced economies and China.

Growth in Peru is projected to rebound to 10.3 percent in 2021—after a deep recession in 2020, supported by private consumption growth and an

FIGURE 2.3.3 **LAC: Risks**

The balance of risks to the regional growth forecast is to the downside. Key downside risks are slower-than-expected COVID-19 vaccine rollouts, continued surges in new cases, adverse market reactions to strained fiscal conditions, and disruptions related to social unrest and natural disasters. Spillovers through trade and confidence channels as the U.S. economy gains momentum are an upside risk to the growth forecast for the region, particularly for Mexico and several Central American economies.

A. COVID-19 vaccination

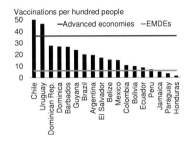

B. Debt

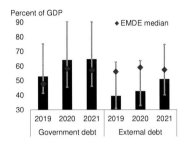

C. Duration of full school closures

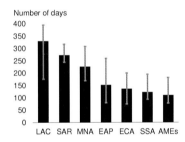

D. Exports to the United States, 2015-19

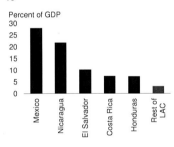

Sources: Hale et al. (2021); International Monetary Fund; Our World in Data (database); World Integrated Trade Solution (WITS); World Bank.

Note: AMEs = advanced economies; EAP = East Asia and Pacific; ECA = Europe and Central Asia; EMDEs = emerging market and developing economies; LAC = Latin America and the Caribbean; MNA = Middle East and North Africa; SAR = South Asia; SSA = Sub-Saharan Africa.

A. Bars show cumulative share of the population of each country or group of countries that has received at least one vaccination. Sample includes 152 EMDEs and 37 advanced economies. Last observation is May 26, 2021.

B. Orange whiskers represent interquartile range for LAC sample. Sample includes 24 LAC economies and 151 EMDEs for government debt and 16 LAC economies and 47 EMDEs for external debt.

C. Blue bars are medians of the countries in each group. Days are counted from January 25, 2020 to May 26, 2021. Orange whiskers represent interquartile ranges. Sample contains 32 LAC, 7 SAR, 19 MNA, 23 ECA, 20 EAP, and 43 SSA economies and 33 advanced economies.

D. Bars show averages for 2015-19 except for the Dominican Republic (2015-18) and Panama (2015-17). "Rest of LAC" includes Argentina, Belize, Bolivia, Brazil, Chile, Colombia, the Dominican Republic, Ecuador, Guatemala, Jamaica, Panama, Peru, Paraguay, and Uruguay.

acceleration in investment, particularly public investment. The economy is benefiting from easy credit conditions and supportive external condition, including a 10-year high in copper prices.

Growth in Central America is projected to reach 4.8 percent this year as robust growth and additional fiscal support in the United States supports remittance inflows and exports,

international tourist arrivals partially recover from steep declines in 2020, and key commodity prices rise. In Panama, which suffered the highest per capita number of COVID-19 cases and one of the most severe GDP contractions in LAC in 2020, the economy is expected to benefit from a rapid decline in new COVID-19 cases in the first half of 2021. Public transportation projects will support a rebound in investment. Reconstruction after two major hurricanes in late 2020 will support the 2021 growth rebound in Guatemala and Honduras, although agricultural production capacity may take longer to recover.

Growth in the Caribbean is projected to reach 4.7 percent this year, supported in part by low COVID-19 caseloads in most countries. With the recovery in tourism still sluggish, however, the 2021 growth outlook for most of the tourism-reliant economies in the Caribbean has been revised downward since January.

Risks

Risks to the regional growth outlook continue to be predominantly to the downside, including slower-than-expected COVID-19 vaccination, continued surges in new cases, adverse market reactions to strained fiscal conditions, and disruptions related to social unrest and natural disasters.

Across the region, the durability of the economic recovery is highly contingent on control of the pandemic. Although the share of the regional population that has received at least one vaccination is higher than the EMDE average, the pace suggests that widescale vaccination will not be reached until well into 2022 or beyond in most of the region (figure 2.3.3.A). In this context, renewed surges of infections, or widespread circulation of new variants, could set back the region's economic recovery and put additional strain on already overburdened health systems. Further, frustration about the stringency and duration of mobility restrictions related to COVID-19, combined with entrenched inequality of opportunity and a worsening perception of government effectiveness over time, could fuel social unrest.

Concerns about fiscal sustainability, a constant vulnerability for the region, have intensified. Last year's extra spending to cushion households, firms, and banks from the economic shocks of the pandemic, together with a sharp drop in tax revenues, has caused government deficits and debt levels to increase sharply. Gross government debt in the median LAC economy rose from 53 percent of GDP in 2019, to 64 percent in 2020, and is estimated to remain at about that level through the forecast period (figure 2.3.3.B). External debt has also risen substantially.

Larger financing needs and debt burdens make sovereigns more susceptible to spikes in borrowing costs, currency depreciation, and capital outflows in the face of shifts in investor sentiment. Risks related to contingent liabilities have also risen. Deteriorating investor sentiment in reaction to poor fiscal conditions could be compounded by, or catalyzed by, market reactions in response to heightened uncertainty about the direction of policy.

Disruptions related to natural disasters are a persistent, and significant, source of downside risk to the region's economic activity. A recent drought in portions of South America, hurricanes in Central America, and volcanic eruptions in St. Vincent and the Grenadines underscore the need for concrete action to improve resilience to natural disasters and climate-induced shocks (World Bank 2021f).

Failure to pursue policies to offset the damage from the pandemic, such as the promotion of investment in new technologies and infrastructure that boost productivity, would weaken long-term growth prospects. Schools in LAC have been fully closed for longer than in other EMDE regions (figure 2.3.3.C). The learning losses incurred by students during extended school closures in the region will likely have long-lasting repercussions on lifetime earnings and impede already sluggish growth of labor productivity and potential output (Kilic Celik, Kose, and Ohnsorge 2020; World Bank 2021g, 2021h).

An upside risk to the forecast in the near term is stronger-than-expected spillovers from a strong growth rebound in the United States through trade and confidence channels. Mexico, Nicaragua, El Salvador, Costa Rica, and Honduras, in particular, stand to benefit from stronger export demand from the United States (figure 2.3.3.D).

TABLE 2.3.1 Latin America and the Caribbean forecast summary

(Real GDP growth at market prices in percent, unless indicated otherwise)

Percentage point differences from January 2021 projections

	2018	2019	2020e	2021f	2022f	2023f	2021f	2022f
EMDE LAC, GDP[1]	**1.8**	**0.9**	**-6.5**	**5.2**	**2.9**	**2.5**	**1.4**	**0.1**
GDP per capita (U.S. dollars)	0.7	-0.2	-7.4	4.2	2.1	1.7	1.3	0.1
(Average including countries that report expenditure components in national accounts)[2]								
EMDE LAC, GDP[2]	1.8	0.9	-6.5	5.2	2.9	2.5	1.4	0.1
PPP GDP	1.8	0.9	-6.8	5.2	2.9	2.5	1.3	0.0
Private consumption	2.2	1.1	-7.7	5.3	3.2	2.7	1.2	0.2
Public consumption	1.7	0.1	-1.9	0.7	0.5	0.5	0.1	0.1
Fixed investment	2.4	-0.9	-10.7	8.8	5.3	4.3	3.4	0.4
Exports, GNFS[3]	4.3	0.8	-8.3	7.3	4.9	3.9	1.1	0.5
Imports, GNFS[3]	5.3	-0.8	-13.8	9.7	5.4	4.9	2.9	0.4
Net exports, contribution to growth	-0.3	0.4	1.3	-0.5	-0.1	-0.2	-0.4	0.0
Memo items: GDP								
South America[4]	1.5	1.0	-5.8	5.2	2.7	2.5	1.4	-0.1
Central America[5]	2.7	2.6	-7.5	4.8	4.5	3.6	1.2	1.0
Caribbean[6]	4.9	3.2	-6.8	4.7	6.1	5.7	0.3	2.2
Brazil	1.8	1.4	-4.1	4.5	2.5	2.3	1.5	0.0
Mexico	2.2	-0.2	-8.3	5.0	3.0	2.0	1.3	0.4
Argentina	-2.6	-2.1	-9.9	6.4	1.7	1.9	1.5	-0.2

Source: World Bank.
Note: e = estimate; f = forecast; PPP = purchasing power parity; EMDE = emerging market and developing economy. World Bank forecasts are frequently updated based on new information and changing (global) circumstances. Consequently, projections presented here may differ from those contained in other Bank documents, even if basic assessments of countries' prospects do not differ at any given moment in time. Due to lack of reliable data of adequate quality, the World Bank is currently not publishing economic output, income, or growth data for República Bolivariana de Venezuela, and República Bolivariana de Venezuela is excluded from cross-country macroeconomic aggregates.
1. GDP and expenditure components are measured in average 2010-19 prices and market exchange rates.
2. Aggregate includes all countries in notes 4, 5, and 6, plus Mexico, except Antigua and Barbuda, Barbados, Dominica, Grenada, Guyana, Haiti, St. Kitts and Nevis, St. Lucia, St. Vincent and the Grenadines, and Suriname.
3. Exports and imports of goods and nonfactor services (GNFS).
4. Includes Argentina, Bolivia, Brazil, Chile, Colombia, Ecuador, Paraguay, Peru, and Uruguay.
5. Includes Costa Rica, El Salvador, Guatemala, Honduras, Nicaragua, and Panama.
6. Includes Antigua and Barbuda, The Bahamas, Barbados, Belize, Dominica, the Dominican Republic, Grenada, Guyana, Haiti, Jamaica, St. Kitts and Nevis, St. Lucia, St. Vincent and the Grenadines, and Suriname.

TABLE 2.3.2 **Latin America and the Caribbean country forecasts** [1]

(Real GDP growth at market prices in percent, unless indicated otherwise)

Percentage point differences from January 2021 projections

	2018	2019	2020e	2021f	2022f	2023f	2021f	2022f
Argentina	-2.6	-2.1	-9.9	6.4	1.7	1.9	1.5	-0.2
Bahamas, The	3.0	1.2	-16.2	2.0	8.5	4.0	-2.6	3.0
Barbados	-0.6	-0.1	-18.0	3.3	8.5	4.8	-4.1	4.6
Belize	2.9	1.8	-14.1	1.9	6.4	4.2	-5.0	4.2
Bolivia	4.2	2.2	-8.8	4.7	3.5	3.0	0.8	0.0
Brazil	1.8	1.4	-4.1	4.5	2.5	2.3	1.5	0.0
Chile	3.7	0.9	-5.8	6.1	3.0	2.5	1.9	-0.1
Colombia	2.6	3.3	-6.8	5.9	4.1	4.0	1.0	-0.2
Costa Rica	2.1	2.2	-4.1	2.7	3.4	3.1	0.1	-0.3
Dominica	2.3	3.6	-10.0	1.0	3.0	2.5	0.0	0.0
Dominican Republic	7.0	5.1	-6.7	5.5	4.8	4.8	0.7	0.3
Ecuador	1.3	0.1	-7.8	3.4	1.4	1.8	-0.1	0.1
El Salvador	2.4	2.6	-7.9	4.1	3.1	2.4	-0.5	0.0
Grenada	4.1	1.9	-12.6	3.5	5.0	4.9	0.5	0.0
Guatemala	3.3	3.9	-1.5	3.6	4.0	3.8	0.0	0.2
Guyana	4.4	5.4	43.5	20.9	26.0	23.0	13.1	22.4
Haiti[2]	1.7	-1.7	-3.3	-0.5	1.5	2.0	-1.9	0.0
Honduras	3.8	2.7	-9.0	4.5	3.9	3.8	0.7	0.0
Jamaica	1.9	0.9	-10.0	3.0	3.8	3.2	-1.0	1.8
Mexico	2.2	-0.2	-8.3	5.0	3.0	2.0	1.3	0.4
Nicaragua	-3.4	-3.7	-2.0	0.9	1.2	1.4	1.8	0.0
Panama	3.6	3.0	-17.9	9.9	7.8	4.9	4.8	4.3
Paraguay	3.2	-0.4	-0.6	3.5	4.0	3.8	0.2	0.0
Peru	4.0	2.2	-11.1	10.3	3.9	3.5	2.7	-0.6
St. Lucia	2.6	1.7	-20.4	2.6	11.5	8.1	-5.5	6.3
St. Vincent and the Grenadines	2.2	0.5	-3.8	-6.1	8.3	6.1	-6.1	3.3
Suriname	2.6	0.3	-14.5	-1.9	0.1	1.3	0.0	1.6
Uruguay	0.5	0.4	-5.9	3.4	3.1	2.5	0.0	-0.1

Source: World Bank.
Note: e = estimate; f = forecast. World Bank forecasts are frequently updated based on new information and changing (global) circumstances. Consequently, projections presented here may differ from those contained in other Bank documents, even if basic assessments of countries' prospects do not significantly differ at any given moment in time.
1. Data are based on GDP measured in average 2010-19 prices and market exchange rates.
2. GDP is based on fiscal year, which runs from October to September of next year.

MIDDLE EAST and NORTH AFRICA

Output in the Middle East and North Africa region is projected to grow by a subdued 2.4 percent in 2021, only half the pace of the recovery that followed the 2009 global recession. Higher oil prices have bolstered growth prospects in oil exporters, but the improvement has been limited by new virus outbreaks and mixed vaccination progress. COVID-19 resurgences have also worsened the outlook for oil importers. By 2022, regional activity is expected to remain 6 percent below pre-pandemic projections. Risks to the regional outlook remain predominantly to the downside. Limited vaccine progress suggests that the pandemic may intensify again, new variants may emerge, and mobility restrictions may be reimposed. The region is also exposed to risks from conflict and social unrest, high debt in some economies, and unfavorable commodity price developments. These risks could interact and further undermine living standards, increase deprivation for vulnerable communities, and heighten food insecurity.

Recent developments

Most economies in the Middle East and North Africa (MENA) experienced their sharpest contraction in decades in 2020. In 2021, new confirmed cases per day again reached all-time highs in two-thirds of economies (figure 2.4.1.A). The resurgent virus has forced renewed mobility restrictions in many economies. The economic implications of rising infections, however, has so far been limited. Mobility around work and retail spaces has again contracted relative to pre-pandemic levels since April, but considerably less than last year. Administered COVID-19 vaccine doses are still a small fraction of the population and even confirmed purchases (not necessarily delivered) amount to only about half of the regional population (figure 2.4.1.B).

The economic damage done by the pandemic remains particularly evident in the transport and tourism sectors (figure 2.4.1.C). Transport activity in late 2020 was still 7 percent below pre-pandemic levels. International tourist arrivals have hardly started to recover and are only partly

compensated by domestic tourism. This is a sharp deceleration from before the pandemic, when revenue from inbound tourists accounted for 5 percent of GDP on average and exceeded 10 percent of GDP in Jordan and Lebanon. The recovery has yet to generate employment increases, with the employment sub-index of the purchasing managers' indexes in the region still showing contraction (figure 2.4.1.D).

Despite continued pandemic-related disruptions, rising oil prices and faster-than-expected recoveries in most regional economies, are supporting activity in oil exporters. The Islamic Republic of Iran avoided an expected contraction in fiscal year 2020/21, which ended in March, with both the oil and non-oil sectors rebounding in the second half of the year, benefiting from higher oil prices and currency depreciation, respectively. In Saudi Arabia, oil production cuts deepened the contraction in the oil sector but was offset by a continued recovery in the non-oil sector. High frequency data suggest the recovery has gained momentum. In Qatar and the United Arab Emirates, significant progress of vaccination campaigns helped boost activity in early 2021. Rising oil prices, and a recovery in demand, are expected to return current account balances to surplus and increase inflation in many oil exporters.

Note: This section was prepared by Franz Ulrich Ruch.

FIGURE 2.4.1 MENA: Recent developments

New COVID-19 cases have reached all-time highs in the Middle East and North Africa (MENA), although vaccine rollouts have begun in earnest in some. Economic recovery is underway, but hard-hit sectors, such as transport and hospitality, are still lagging. Although activity has been expanding in the region, employment has continued to fall, and unemployment remains elevated.

A. COVID-19 cases

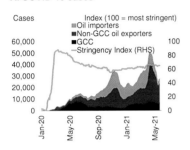

B. COVID-19 vaccinations

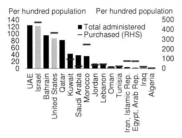

C. Growth in sectoral activity

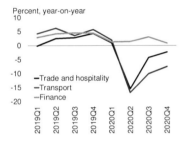

D. Purchasing managers' indexes

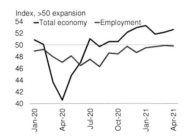

Sources: Duke Global Health Innovation Center, Duke University; Haver Analytics; Johns Hopkins University Coronavirus Resource Center; Our World in Data; University of Oxford Coronavirus Government Policy Tracker; World Bank.
Note: GCC = Gulf Cooperation Council; MENA = Middle East and North Africa; UAE = United Arab Emirates.
A. Seven-day average new confirmed COVID-19 cases. Last observation is May 25, 2021.
"Stringency Index" is a GDP-weighted average where the last available country observation is extended to most recent date.
B. Yellow bars reflect advanced economies. "Purchased" refers to total vaccines purchased as of May 2021. It excludes vaccines from the COVAX initiative and potential future purchases. Last observation for administered doses is May 25, 2021.
C. 2019 GDP-weighted average for the Arab Republic of Egypt, the Islamic Republic of Iran, Iraq, Morocco, Qatar, and Saudi Arabia. Last observation is 2020Q4.
D. 2019 GDP-weighted average of Arab Republic of Egypt, Lebanon, Qatar, Saudi Arabia, and the United Arab Emirates. Last observation is April 2021.

Several oil importers experienced a resurgence of COVID-19 cases in early 2021, clouding economic activity in the Arab Republic of Egypt, Jordan, Lebanon, and Tunisia. In Egypt, high-frequency indicators suggest that the economy remains sluggish in the first half of 2021 despite an easing of lockdown restrictions. In Morocco, the combination of drought, the collapse of tourism, and tight lockdown restrictions continues to hinder economic activity. High new cases of COVID-19 in Lebanon and West Bank and Gaza, and recent conflict in the latter are compounding already challenging economic and humanitarian situations.

Bond market conditions have improved in 2021, with sovereign spreads narrowing in most countries, although Lebanon is an exception. There has been renewed pressure on portfolio inflows recently, however. Regional equity prices are mixed remaining below pre-pandemic levels in Bahrain, Egypt, and Morocco.

Governments have taken further policy steps in 2021 to address the effects of the pandemic. In Saudi Arabia, an instant payment system has been launched, guarantees and forbearance measures have been extended, and working rules for expatriates loosened. In Egypt, the minimum wage for public sector workers was increased by 20 percent (starting July), charges on most financial transactions were cancelled for an additional six months from the start of 2021, and further measures were undertaken to encourage lending. In the United Arab Emirates, steps have been taken to encourage foreign ownership in the economy, including through the removal of limits on the banking sector, board composition, and majority ownership.

Outlook

GDP in the region is expected to grow by 2.4 percent in 2021, 0.3 percentage points more than projected in January but still below the average during the past decade (figure 2.4.2.A). The region should benefit from the recent rebound in oil prices, stronger external demand, and less economically disruptive new outbreaks. Growth is expected to strengthen further in 2022, to 3.5 percent, but ease to 3.2 percent in 2023. Firming activity in 2022 will be underpinned by increasingly robust private consumption and investment growth, as mobility restrictions ease and vaccinations progress (figure 2.4.2.B). Yet the outlook is still highly uncertain and tied to the course of the pandemic and vaccine rollouts.

In oil exporters, a stronger-than-expected rebound in GDP in the second half of 2020 has created the foundation for growth to accelerate to a projected 2.3 percent in 2021. This reflects an upgrade of 0.5 percentage point relative to previous forecasts. Higher oil prices, as oil production cuts are tapered, will support growth and government revenue recoveries (figure 2.4.2.C). Oil prices are expected to average $62 a barrel in 2021 and 2022, significantly higher than assumed in January. Nevertheless, GDP in 2022 in oil exporters is projected to be 5 percent below its pre-pandemic trend.

GDP in Saudi Arabia is expected to grow by 2.4 percent this year and 3.3 percent in 2022, reflecting positive pandemic developments, higher oil prices, and the start of a new government investment program, financed through the sovereign wealth fund, equivalent to about 5 percent of GDP per year over the next five years. In the Islamic Republic of Iran, growth is forecast to recover to 2.1 percent in 2021 and 2.2 percent in 2022 with a rebound in industrial production outweighing continued suppressed demand for services due to a high number of COVID-19 cases.

Higher oil prices were not enough to improve prospects in all oil exporters, however. The recovery in Algeria has been downgraded as better hydrocarbon output is more than offset by private sector weakness and the recovery in public investment is increasingly constrained by fiscal policy.

Prospects for economies that have recently faced fragility, conflict, and violence are mixed. In Libya, the creation of an interim unity government in March, following years of division, and the lifting of the oil blockade are expected to restore economic activity this year close to 2019 levels after a collapse last year. In Iraq, output is projected to expand by 1.9 percent in 2021 and strengthen to 8.4 percent in 2022, after a double-digit percentage point contraction last year, as oil production rebounds. Growth over the forecast horizon, however, will only gradually reverse a substantial rise in poverty rates that occurred in 2020 (World Bank 2021i). In Lebanon, the 20.3 percent contraction of GDP in 2020 is expected to be followed by another large decline in 2021.

Oil importers are expected to grow by 2.8 percent in 2021, 0.2 percentage point slower than projected in January, as the pandemic undermines recoveries in several economies. As caseloads are brought under control and restrictions are

FIGURE 2.4.2 MENA: Outlook

The regional economy is expected to grow by 2.4 percent in 2021, driven by stronger consumption and investment. Higher oil prices should support a tapering of oil production cuts and boost government revenue in oil exporters. Per capita income will not regain its 2019 level over the forecast horizon.

A. GDP growth

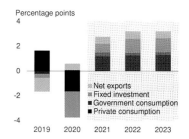

B. Contributions to GDP growth

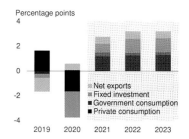

C. Oil output and prices

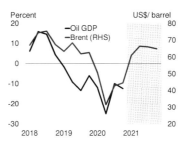

D. GDP per capita

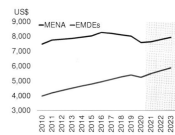

Sources: Bloomberg; BP Statistical Review; Haver Analytics; World Bank.
Note: EMDEs = emerging market and developing economies; MENA = Middle East and North Africa.
B. Includes countries that report expenditure components of GDP in their national accounts and excludes change in inventories and residuals.
C. "Oil GDP" shows a 2019 GDP-weighted average of 9 MENA oil exporters. Quarterly data. Brent crude oil price forecasts based on oil futures. Last observation is May 21, 2021.
D. Based on real GDP in USD using 2010-19 prices and market exchange rates.

removed, growth should pick up further, to 3.8 percent and 4.2 percent in 2022 and 2023, respectively. In Egypt, growth, having been solid in fiscal year 2019/20, is expected to slow to 2.3 percent in 2020/21, starting July, before strengthening again in 2021/22. The slower growth expected this year reflects damage to tourism, manufacturing, and oil and gas extractives from the pandemic and the lingering impact of a decline in domestic demand, notably from a collapse in fixed investment. In Morocco, output is expected to rebound to 4.6 percent in 2021 as drought conditions ease, policy remains accommodative, and favorable virus and vaccine trends provide scope for easing domestic mobility restrictions.

Fiscal policy is envisioned to be less accommodative this year following unprecedented

FIGURE 2.4.3 **MENA: Risks**

Limited access to vaccines is hindering progress in bringing down COVID-19 caseloads. Oil activity remains a large part of oil exporters' economies, and regional growth prospects may be more sensitive than expected to an ongoing decline in global reliance on oil. Conflict and social unrest may present downside risks for the region.

A. COVID-19 vaccine purchases

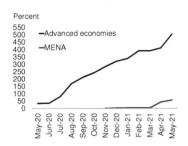

B. Oil share in activity

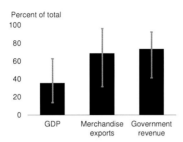

C. Energy intensity of global output

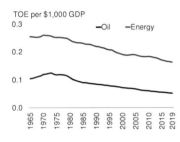

D. Recurring conflicts in MENA

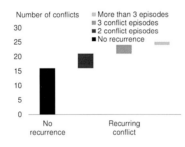

Sources: BP Statistical Review; Duke Global Health Innovation Center, Duke University; Haver Analytics; Jarland et al. (2020); UNCTAD; World Bank.

Note: MENA = Middle East and North Africa.

A. "Vaccine purchases" reflect total purchases as a ratio to total population in each region. This data excludes the COVAX initiative and potential future purchases. Last observation is May 2021.

B. Unweighted averages. "GDP" is based on real GDP data for 8 MENA oil exporters, "Revenue" is based on 7 oil exporters, "Merchandise exports" are based on SITC commodity code 3 which includes petroleum, petroleum products and related materials, gas, natural and manufactured for 9 oil exporters. Orange lines reflect minimum and maximum values. Based on 2019 data.

C. Energy includes coal, natural gas and oil; "TOE" stands for tonnes of oil equivalent; GDP is in constant 2010-19 U.S. dollars.

D. Based on Jarland et al. (2020) and includes all conflicts in MENA between 1989 and 2018. Conflicts are considered as recurring when there is at least one calendar year between the last event in the previous episode, and the first event in the following episode.

support in 2020. The average primary fiscal deficit is expected to be about 4 percent of GDP in 2021, about two-thirds its level in 2020. The scope for further fiscal support is limited by vulnerabilities related to rising debt from already high levels in a number of economies (Bahrain, Egypt, Lebanon, Morocco, Oman, Tunisia) and buffers used up following the oil price collapse of 2015. Monetary policy should remain accommodative with policy interest rates likely to remain flat through 2021 and at historically low levels in many economies.

Despite the economic recovery in 2021, per capita incomes will grow by less than 1 percent in the region this year, still 5 percent below their level in 2019, and will remain below this level over the forecast horizon (figure 2.4.2.D). The damage to incomes means that an estimated 192 million people in the region, 14.2 million more than expected before the pandemic, are estimated to live on less than $5.50 per day in 2021 (World Bank 2021j). This represents about half of the region's population. The incidence of poverty is higher among refugees (Joint Data Center of Forced Displacement, World Bank, and UNHCR 2021). Economies facing fragility and conflict are likely to see rising cases of food insecurity, compounded by a large increase in global agricultural prices. Lebanon (facing rapid food inflation and damage to food security infra-structure), the Republic of Yemen, the Syrian Arab Republic, and West Bank and Gaza are particularly vulnerable. An estimated 28.5 million people are suffering high or acute food insecurity in Syria and Yemen (FAO and WFP 2021).[1]

Risks

Risks to the regional outlook are predominantly to the downside and relate to the possibilities of resurgent COVID-19 cases, vaccination delays, weaker oil prices in the context of limited economic diversification, higher agricultural prices and food insecurity, and conflict and social unrest. The materialization of several of these risks could have compound effects that severely worsen economic, institutional, and political outcomes.

Limited vaccine availability and ineffective vaccine rollouts could cause the pandemic to worsen in the region, with additional virus variants possibly emerging. Vaccines access remains an important limiting factor in durably bringing down caseloads in the region (figure 2.4.3.A). On the upside, concerted efforts to accelerate vaccination rollout globally could ease regional mobility restrictions, improve confidence, and release pent-up demand.

Limited economic diversification in oil-exporting economies continues to present risks to the region

---

[1] Food insecurity is based on the Integrated Food Security Phase Classification and refers to food deprivation that threatens lives or livelihoods.

as oil demand is expected to remain below pre-pandemic levels through 2023 (IEA 2021). Oil revenue accounted for about one-third of output, two-thirds of merchandise exports, and three-quarters of government revenue in these economies in 2019 (figure 2.4.3.B). In the short run, oil prices may remain volatile, with the main risk posed by lower global demand if pandemic containment falters. The unravelling of oil production cut agreements may also lead to lower oil prices. In the long run, post-pandemic initiatives for a greener development path make diversification even more urgent. The oil intensity of global output declined by about one-third in the two decades to 2019, and this trend will likely continue (figure 2.4.3.C).

The possibility of social unrest and conflict is a downside risk to the outlook and could extend existing economic disruptions and food security challenges already present in some economies. Close to half of conflicts globally, and one-third in MENA, have recurred in the past, often over the same or similar issues (figure 2.4.3.D; Jarland et al. 2020). Recent conflict in the West Bank and Gaza present significant downside risk to its growth outlook. Countries affected by conflict have some of the worst gender gaps in education, labor force participation and political participation, making gender-specific provision of opportunities vital in supporting medium and long-term development in these economies (Bakken and Buhaug 2020; World Bank and German Development Cooperation 2020). Separately, sporadic attempted attacks on Saudi Arabian oil facilities underline security threats in the region and risks of a surge in tensions.

Additional increases in food price inflation, which have accelerated rapidly in Lebanon and Yemen, may further erode real incomes and reduce consumption. Agricultural prices have already increased by 30 percent over the past year and may further increase food insecurity (World Bank 2021k).

TABLE 2.4.1 Middle East and North Africa forecast summary

(Real GDP growth at market prices in percent, unless indicated otherwise)

Percentage point differences from January 2021 projections

	2018	2019	2020e	2021f	2022f	2023f	2021f	2022f
EMDE MENA, GDP[1]	0.6	0.6	-3.9	2.4	3.5	3.2	0.3	0.3
GDP per capita (U.S. dollars)	-1.1	-1.1	-5.4	0.8	2.0	1.8	0.3	0.3
(Average including countries that report expenditure components in national accounts)[2]								
EMDE MENA, GDP[2]	0.8	0.3	-3.3	2.3	3.1	3.0	0.3	0.3
PPP GDP	1.0	0.4	-2.6	2.5	3.3	3.3	0.2	0.2
Private consumption	0.7	3.5	-3.4	2.4	2.6	2.7	0.9	0.1
Public consumption	2.9	-1.6	0.6	1.9	1.3	1.4	0.9	-0.4
Fixed investment	-0.9	-1.3	-9.6	3.5	5.4	5.3	-2.1	1.9
Exports, GNFS[3]	1.4	-4.4	-10.3	4.6	5.3	5.2	1.4	0.9
Imports, GNFS[3]	-4.5	-2.5	-13.8	4.2	5.0	5.1	1.6	1.1
Net exports, contribution to growth	2.5	-1.1	0.5	0.5	0.6	0.6	0.0	0.1
Memo items: GDP								
Oil exporters[4]	-0.1	0.1	-4.2	2.3	3.5	3.0	0.5	0.6
GCC countries[5]	1.9	1.5	-4.8	2.2	3.4	3.2	0.5	0.7
Saudi Arabia	2.4	0.3	-4.1	2.4	3.3	3.2	0.4	1.1
Iran, Islamic Rep.	-6.0	-6.8	1.7	2.1	2.2	2.3	0.6	0.5
Oil importers[6]	3.8	2.7	-2.4	2.8	3.8	4.2	-0.2	-0.5
Egypt, Arab Rep.[7]	5.3	5.6	3.6	2.3	4.5	5.5	-0.4	-1.3

Source: World Bank.
Note: e = estimate; f = forecast; PPP = purchasing power parity; EMDE = emerging market and developing economy. World Bank forecasts are frequently updated based on new information and changing (global) circumstances. Consequently, projections presented here may differ from those contained in other Bank documents, even if basic assessments of countries' prospects do not differ at any given moment in time.
1. GDP and expenditure components are measured in average 2010-19 prices and market exchange rates. Excludes the Syrian Arab Republic and the Republic of Yemen due to data limitations, and Libya due to the high degree of uncertainty.
2. Aggregate includes all economies in notes 4 and 6 except Djibouti, Iraq, Qatar, and West Bank and Gaza, for which data limitations prevent the forecasting of GDP components.
3. Exports and imports of goods and nonfactor services (GNFS).
4. Oil exporters include Algeria, Bahrain, the Islamic Republic of Iran, Iraq, Kuwait, Oman, Qatar, Saudi Arabia, and the United Arab Emirates.
5. The Gulf Cooperation Council (GCC) includes Bahrain, Kuwait, Oman, Qatar, Saudi Arabia, and the United Arab Emirates.
6. Fiscal-year based numbers. The fiscal year runs from July 1 to June 30 in the Arab Republic of Egypt, with 2020 reflecting FY2019/20. For the Islamic Republic of Iran, it runs from March 21 through March 20, with 2020 reflecting FY2020/21.
7. Oil importers include Djibouti, the Arab Republic of Egypt, Jordan, Lebanon, Morocco, Tunisia, and West Bank and Gaza.

TABLE 2.4.2 Middle East and North Africa economy forecasts[1]

(Real GDP growth at market prices in percent, unless indicated otherwise)

Percentage point differences from January 2021 projections

	2018	2019	2020e	2021f	2022f	2023f	2021f	2022f
Algeria	1.2	0.8	-5.5	3.6	2.3	1.6	-0.2	0.2
Bahrain	2.0	1.9	-5.4	3.3	3.2	3.2	1.1	0.7
Djibouti	8.4	7.8	0.5	5.5	6.0	6.2	-1.6	-1.2
Egypt, Arab Rep.[2]	5.3	5.6	3.6	2.3	4.5	5.5	-0.4	-1.3
Iran, Islamic Rep.[2]	-6.0	-6.8	1.7	2.1	2.2	2.3	0.6	0.5
Iraq	-1.2	4.4	-10.4	1.9	8.4	4.2	-0.1	1.1
Jordan	1.9	2.0	-1.6	1.4	2.2	2.3	-0.4	0.2
Kuwait	1.2	0.4	-5.4	2.4	3.6	2.8	1.9	0.5
Lebanon[3]	-1.9	-6.7	-20.3	-9.5	..	..	3.7	..
Libya[3]	15.1	2.5	-31.3	66.7	..	..	62.7	..
Morocco	3.1	2.5	-7.1	4.6	3.4	3.7	0.6	-0.3
Oman	0.9	-0.8	-6.3	2.5	6.5	4.2	2.0	-1.4
Qatar	1.2	0.8	-3.7	3.0	4.1	4.5	0.0	1.1
Saudi Arabia	2.4	0.3	-4.1	2.4	3.3	3.2	0.4	1.1
Tunisia	2.9	0.9	-8.8	4.0	2.6	2.2	-1.8	0.6
United Arab Emirates	1.7	4.8	-6.1	1.2	2.5	2.5	0.2	0.1
West Bank and Gaza	1.2	1.4	-11.5	3.5	3.6	3.7	1.2	1.2

Source: World Bank.
Note: e = estimate; f = forecast. World Bank forecasts are frequently updated based on new information and changing (global) circumstances. Consequently, projections presented here may differ from those contained in other Bank documents, even if basic assessments of economies' prospects do not significantly differ at any given moment in time.
1. Data are based on GDP measured in average 2010-19 prices and market exchange rates. Excludes the Syrian Arab Republic and the Republic of Yemen due to data limitations.
2. Fiscal-year based numbers. The fiscal year runs from July 1 to June 30 in the Arab Republic of Egypt, with 2020 reflecting FY2019/20. For the Islamic Republic of Iran, it runs from March 21 through March 20, with 2020 reflecting FY2020/21.
3. Forecasts for Lebanon and Libya beyond 2021 are excluded due to a high degree of uncertainty.

SOUTH ASIA

Output in South Asia is expected to expand 6.8 percent in 2021, a pace on par with average growth for the previous decade (2010-19). Stronger-than-expected momentum at the beginning of the year has been disrupted by a large surge of COVID-19 cases. Despite continued recovery, output in 2022 is forecast to be 9 percent below pre-pandemic projections. Poverty rates have risen, and by the end of this year more than half the new global poor are expected to live in the region. The outlook could be weaker if vaccination does not proceed as quickly as assumed. Moreover, financial sector balance sheets are at risk of deteriorating, as policy measures put in place at the peak of the pandemic are scaled back, which could constrain the provision of credit and investment needed to support the recovery.

Recent developments

COVID-19 cases have surged in South Asia (SAR) with peaks in daily new confirmed cases this year higher than anything seen before in three-quarters of economies (figure 2.5.1.A). The situation is particularly serious in India, where the number of daily deaths and cases is now higher than in any other country during the pandemic. For the region as a whole, peaks in daily new confirmed cases and deaths in 2021 are multiple times higher than last year. Although nearly all countries in the region have begun vaccinations, progress has been slow, and the region's largest economies—Bangladesh, India, and Pakistan—have vaccinated only a small fraction of their populations (figure 2.5.1.B). Bhutan and Maldives, however, have managed to vaccinate more than half of their populations.

The recovery in SAR has been faster than expected. Activity in most sectors has overtaken pre-pandemic levels, despite rising COVID-19 cases—including in construction, one of the initially hardest hit sectors (figure 2.5.1.C). Output in retail and wholesale trade, and hotels and restaurants, however, was still lower than the pre-pandemic level. Tourist arrivals to SAR have

risen from their trough but remain 70 percent below pre-pandemic levels. Bhutan and Maldives, two economies highly exposed to tourism, experienced larger-than-expected output declines in 2020. External balances improved in 2020, with the region's current account shifting to surplus for the first time in over a decade as imports plunged more than exports (figure 2.5.1.D). The current account balance, however, has already shifted back to deficit as stronger domestic demand boosted imports.

In India, an enormous second COVID-19 wave is undermining the sharper-than-expected rebound in activity seen during the second half of FY2020/21, especially in services. With surging COVID-19 cases, foot traffic around work and retail spaces has again slowed to more than one-third below pre-pandemic levels since March, in part due to greater restrictions on mobility. Recoveries in Bangladesh and Pakistan face new headwinds from a recent rise in COVID-19 cases accompanied by rising restrictions to stamp out the new surge. Mobility around places of work and retail has again dropped below pre-pandemic levels.

Benign global financial conditions have helped boost asset prices and narrow sovereign spreads; however, sentiment remains fragile. Equity prices in May were about 20 percent above pre-pandemic

Note: This section was prepared by Franz Ulrich Ruch.

FIGURE 2.5.1 **SAR: Recent developments**

New COVID-19 cases have risen sharply, most notably in India, and restrictions on mobility have been tightened in some countries. Vaccinations have begun in earnest with limited progress in the region's large economies. Economic recovery is underway, but activity in some sectors is still below pre-pandemic levels. External balances have shifted back to deficit after import compression brought about the first surplus in a decade.

A. COVID-19 cases

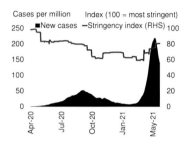

B. Total administered vaccinations

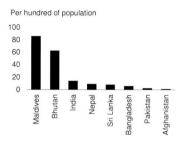

C. Sectoral activity

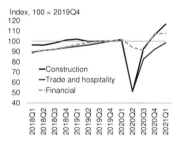

D. Current account balance

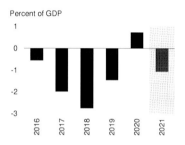

Sources: Haver Analytics; John Hopkins University Coronavirus Resource Center; Our World in Data; University of Oxford Coronavirus Government Policy Tracker; World Bank.
Note: EMDEs = emerging market and developing economies; SAR = South Asia.
A.B. Last observation is May 25, 2021. "Stringency index" shows a real 2019 GDP-weighted average for 7 economies and last available country observation extended to the latest date.
C. Lines show real 2019 GDP-weighted averages for India, Maldives, and Sri Lanka. "Trade and hospitality" includes wholesale and retail trade, and hotels and restaurants.
D. Based on data for 8 economies weighted using 2019 GDP at 2010-19 prices and market exchange rates.

levels in most of the region's large economies, and sovereign spreads were effectively back to pre-pandemic levels except in Sri Lanka. Despite low global interest rates and domestic forbearance measures, credit growth has slowed significantly, partly reflecting impaired bank, corporate, and household balance sheets. Sri Lanka, facing resurging COVID-19 cases and mounting government debt, experienced significant exchange rate depreciation since the onset of the pandemic—despite the halving of foreign exchange reserves and curbs on non-essential imports—and sovereign spreads remain about 14 percent above the risk-free rate.

Following an aggressive policy response in 2020 that included cuts in interest rates, increases in government expenditure, the extension of loans and guarantees, and steps to ensure financial stability, fiscal and monetary policies remain accommodative. A number of new measures have been implemented this year as economies have calibrated policy responses to support the still-uneven recovery. In India, the FY2021/22 budget marked a significant policy shift. The government announced health-related spending would more than double and set out a revised medium-term fiscal path intended to address the economic legacy of the pandemic. Following deteriorating pandemic-related developments, the Reserve Bank of India announced further measures to support liquidity provision to micro, small, and medium firms and loosened regulatory requirements on the provisioning for nonperforming loans. Debt relief under the Debt Service Suspension Initiative has been extended to December 2021 and will provide additional fiscal space for Afghanistan, Maldives, Nepal, and Pakistan (G20 2021).

Outlook

Growth in South Asia is expected to rebound to 6.8 percent in 2021, 3.6 percentage points higher than previously projected, partly reflecting stronger-than-expected momentum from the end of last year (figure 2.5.2.A). India accounts for nine-tenths of the upgrade to growth in 2021, as strong services activity more than offsets the economic effects of the worsening pandemic. The region's outlook for 2021 is underpinned by a rebound in private consumption, which is expected to account for about half of overall growth (figure 2.5.2.B). Near-term growth prospects have not improved in some countries, however. Projections for Afghanistan (suffering from drought, elevated political uncertainty, and security challenges) and Bhutan (with growth held back by weak tourism and the postponement of infrastructure spending) for 2021 have been downgraded by more than 1.0 percentage point. The recovery has also done little to narrow gaps with pre-pandemic trends. In 2022, regional GDP is expected to be 9 percent lower than projected prior to the pandemic. The shortfalls are expected to be largest in tourism-dependent Bhutan and

Maldives, at over 12 percent, and smallest in Pakistan at 5 percent (figure 2.5.2.C).

For India, GDP in fiscal year 2021/22, starting April 2021, is expected to expand 8.3 percent. Activity will benefit from policy support, including higher spending on infrastructure, rural development, and health, and a stronger-than-expected recovery in services and manufacturing. Although the forecast has been revised up by 2.9 percentage points, this masks significant expected economic damage from an enormous second COVID-19 wave and localized mobility restrictions since March 2021. Activity is expected to follow the same, yet less pronounced, collapse and recovery seen during the first wave. The pandemic will undermine consumption and investment as confidence remains depressed and balance sheets damaged. Growth in FY2022/23 is expected to slow to 7.5 percent reflecting lingering impacts of COVID-19 on household, corporate and bank balance sheets; possibly low levels of consumer confidence; and heightened uncertainty on job and income prospects.

In the region excluding India, the recovery is expected to be weaker than its historical growth average, with GDP growth at 3.1 percent in FY2021/22 and 4.0 percent in FY2022/23. In the decade prior to the pandemic, growth in the subregion exceeded 5 percent; however, COVID-19 outbreaks and mobility restrictions, weak confidence, and potential output losses make this growth performance seem unattainable in the near term. In Bangladesh, the recovery is expected to be gradual, with growth of 3.6 percent in fiscal year 2020/21, starting July, and 5.1 percent in FY2021/22 as private consumption, the main engine of growth, is supported by normalizing activity, moderate inflation, and rising ready-made garment exports. In Sri Lanka, the resurgence of COVID-19 cases, severe fiscal pressures, and depressed tourism are holding back the recovery. In Maldives, reviving tourism activity, with international arrivals now 30 percent below pre-pandemic levels (compared with virtually no arrivals at the trough), and a strong vaccination drive, are expected to contribute to a boost in GDP growth to 17.1 percent in 2021. The forecast for Pakistan has been revised up on

FIGURE 2.5.2 **SAR: Outlook**

Growth in SAR is expected to rebound to 6.8 percent in 2021 and 2022, compared to average growth of 6.7 percent in the previous decade. Growth would have been even stronger if not for the economic impact of surging cases. The rebound will be supported by firming consumption and investment, with net exports again turning negative as imports compression unwinds. Despite the rebound, output in 2022 will still be well below pre-pandemic projections. Fiscal and monetary policy is expected to remain accommodative in 2021. Government consumption is projected to contribute over 2 percentage points to 2021 regional growth, reflecting in part additional policy support in India.

A. GDP growth

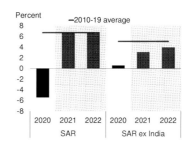

B. Contributions to GDP growth

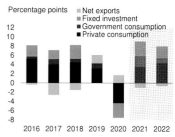

C. Output losses compared to pre-pandemic trend, 2022

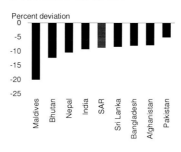

D. Primary fiscal balance

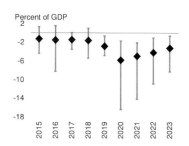

Source: World Bank.
Note: EMDEs = emerging market and developing economies; SAR = South Asia.
B. Includes countries that report expenditure components of GDP in their national accounts and excludes change in inventories and residuals.
C. Percent deviation in 2022 output between the January 2020 (pre-pandemic forecast) and June 2021 *Global Economic Prospects* forecasts.
D. Unweighted average for 9 SAR economies. Orange lines reflect the minimum and maximum values.

improving remittance inflows and a rebound in confidence, but the economy is expected to grow by only 1.3 percent in fiscal year 2020/21, reflecting contracting investment, fiscal consolidation, and depressed activity amid recurring COVID-19 flare-ups.

Fiscal and monetary policies are expected to remain accommodative in the forecast period. Real policy interest rates—an indicator of the policy support provided by central banks—are expected to remain negative in 2021. South Asian countries are expected to run an average primary fiscal

FIGURE 2.5.3 **SAR: Risks**

Amid a worsening pandemic, uncertainty about near-term growth remains elevated. Financing conditions remain benign but can reverse quickly on changes in risk perceptions amid elevated government debt levels. Deteriorating domestic bank balance sheets, already weakened by high nonperforming loans, risk undermining output growth. Rising food inflation remains a significant risk to regional incomes.

A. Uncertainty

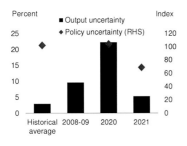

B. Global financing conditions

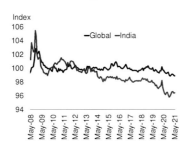

C. Gross government debt

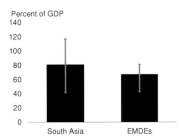

D. Financial sector developments

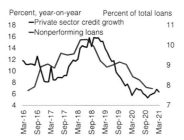

E. Nonperforming loans

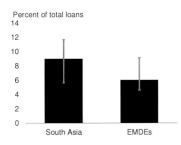

F. Food inflation

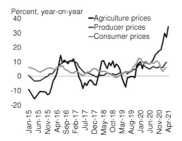

Sources: Baker, Bloom and Davis (2016); Bloomberg; Choudhary, Pasha, and Waheed (2020); Goldman Sachs; Haver Analytics; International Monetary Fund; World Bank.

Note: EMDEs = emerging market and developing economies; SAR = South Asia.

A. "Output volatility" from a Bayesian VAR model with stochastic volatility for India based on Ha et al. (2019). "Policy uncertainty" is a GDP-weighted average of Pakistan and India with the index normalized such that the mean prior to 2011 is equal to 100. "Historical average" is 2002Q2-2019Q4 for output volatility and August 2010 to December 2019 for policy uncertainty.

B. Based on Goldman Sachs Financial Conditions Indexes for the United States, United Kingdom, Japan, Euro Area, India, Indonesia, Brazil, Mexico, the Russian Federation, and Turkey. Lines show 2019 GDP-weighted averages. Last observation is May 2021. Higher values reflect tighter financial conditions.

C. Unweighted average. Based on 2021 forecasts for 8 South Asia economies and 134 EMDEs. Orange lines reflect interquartile range.

D. Lines show real 2019 GDP-weighted averages. Sample includes Bangladesh, India, Pakistan, and Sri Lanka.

E. Unweighted average. Based on the latest available quarterly data for 2020 for 6 economies in South Asia and 67 EMDEs. Orange lines reflect minimum and maximum values.

F. Consumer and producer food prices are real 2019 GDP-weighted averages for 6 South Asian economies, depending on data availability. Agricultural food prices are adjusted using exchange rates weighted by 2019 real GDP. Last observation is Apr 2021.

deficit of about 4 percent of GDP in 2021 (figure 2.5.2.D). Two-thirds of the region's economies are expected to have a larger primary deficit in 2021 than last year. High levels of public debt in the region—above 80 percent of GDP, on average—limit the ability of some economies to increase spending without the risk of negative market reactions. In India, fiscal policy shifted in the FY2021/22 budget toward higher expenditure targeted at health care and infrastructure to boost the post-pandemic recovery. The renewed outbreak, however, may require further targeted policy support to address the health and economic costs.

One of the most challenging legacies of the pandemic in South Asia will be its impact on poverty. The region is expected to see tens of millions more extreme poor—living below $1.90 per day—by the end of this year and to have more than half of the new global poor created by COVID-19 (Mahler et al. 2021; World Bank 2021l). Further deprivation could be caused by higher food prices, with global agricultural commodity prices already increasing by 30 percent over the past year (Sahibzada et al. 2021, World Bank 2021k, World Bank 2021l). Prospects for longer-term poverty reduction have also been adversely affected by the pandemic's impact on potential growth. With fixed investment in 2022 expected to be 10 percent below pre-pandemic trends, physical capital growth will likely be slower in the decade ahead than in the past decade. With schools closed in SAR for about one-third of the time so far during the pandemic—affecting about 390 million students—and an estimated 12 percent of labor hours lost, human capital will also be eroded (ILO 2021; World Bank 2021l).

Risks

With the recovery in its infancy and the pandemic still spreading rapidly, the outlook remains highly uncertain. Output uncertainty in the region in 2021 is not as high as last year, but it is still almost double its historical average (figure 2.5.3.A). Downside risks still dominate the outlook.

Downside risks emanate from high government debt, upward pressure on food prices, financial sector challenges, and—in particular—the uncertain path of COVID-19 cases and vaccinations. Export bans on vaccines, limited raw materials required in their production, inadequate financial resources, vaccine hoarding, and ineffective vaccination campaigns create space for the pandemic to worsen in the region and for variants to emerge and undermine the recovery. Renewed COVID-19 outbreaks may also disrupt cross-border supply chains and undermine the moderation in policy uncertainty. Most SAR economies are also lagging on vaccine procurement.

Global and domestic financial conditions remain accommodative, with abundant liquidity and low interest rates (figure 2.5.3.B). In India, domestic financial conditions are easier than they have been in decades. These conditions may change, however, if rapid recoveries in advanced economies lead to tightening monetary policy in these economies before recoveries are entrenched in EMDEs, including those in SAR. An unexpected rise in global inflation from unprecedented advanced economy policy support may also reverse easy financing conditions (chapter 4). Domestically, high debt levels may create the conditions for borrowing costs to surge if expectations change abruptly (figure 2.5.3.C).

Domestic financial sector stress remains a significant downside risk in the region. Nonperforming loans (NPLs) as a share of total loans were already elevated prior to the pandemic (Bangladesh, Bhutan, India), contributing to a precipitous slowdown in credit growth (figure 2.5.3.D-E). Although previous efforts to clean up bank balance sheets yielded some gains in bringing down NPLs, temporary forbearance measures extended in 2020 may have concealed a more severe deterioration in balance sheets experienced during the pandemic. Going forward, asset quality and bank profitability may worsen as temporary forbearance measures are removed or renewed outbreaks damage balance sheets, undermining credit and investment growth in these economies.

The intersection of higher food prices and resurgent COVID-19 outbreaks poses significant risks to vulnerable communities and could further undermine food security and economic growth. Although the region has seen food price inflation for consumers decline from over 10 percent in September 2020 to about 6 percent in March 2021, inflation for producers remains elevated and global agriculture prices rose rapidly (figure 2.5.3.F). Rising agricultural prices, which are expected to increase by double-digit rates in 2021, may lead to faster than assumed food price inflation for consumers, eroding real incomes and reducing consumption. SAR is particularly vulnerable to the impact of higher food prices, with food accounting for 44 percent of expenditure in the consumer basket, compared to 32 percent in EMDEs on average.

TABLE 2.5.1 South Asia forecast summary

(Real GDP growth at market prices in percent, unless indicated otherwise)

Percentage point differences from January 2021 projections

	2018	2019	2020e	2021f	2022f	2023f	2021f	2022f
EMDE South Asia, GDP [1,2]	**6.4**	**4.4**	**-5.4**	**6.8**	**6.8**	**5.2**	**3.6**	**3.0**
GDP per capita (U.S. dollars)	5.2	3.2	-6.5	5.6	5.7	4.1	3.5	3.0
(Average including countries that report expenditure components in national accounts)[3]								
EMDE South Asia, GDP [3]	6.5	4.4	-5.4	6.8	6.8	5.2	3.6	3.0
PPP GDP	6.5	4.4	-5.5	6.9	6.9	5.2	3.7	3.1
Private consumption	7.1	5.0	-7.0	5.7	7.1	5.3	3.1	2.8
Public consumption	8.3	10.2	-0.2	19.5	8.5	7.6	13.3	5.3
Fixed investment	10.1	0.5	-10.9	11.7	8.9	5.5	6.9	3.4
Exports, GNFS [4]	10.4	1.5	-7.9	12.1	6.8	9.1	8.0	-0.5
Imports, GNFS [4]	13.1	-4.9	-12.6	13.8	7.5	10.2	8.6	-1.7
Net exports, contribution to growth	-1.5	1.7	1.7	-1.0	-0.6	-0.8	-0.5	0.2
Memo items: GDP [2]	**2017/18**	**2018/19**	**2019/20e**	**2020/21f**	**2021/22f**	**2022/23f**	**2020/21f**	**2021/22f**
South Asia excluding India	6.1	5.3	2.6	0.6	3.1	4.0	1.2	1.0
India	6.8	6.5	4.0	-7.3	8.3	7.5	2.3	2.9
Pakistan (factor cost)	5.5	2.1	-0.5	1.3	2.0	3.4	0.8	0.0
Bangladesh	7.9	8.2	2.4	3.6	5.1	6.2	2.0	1.7

Source: World Bank.
Note: e = estimate; f = forecast; PPP = purchasing power parity; EMDE = emerging market and developing economy. World Bank forecasts are frequently updated based on new information and changing (global) circumstances. Consequently, projections presented here may differ from those contained in other Bank documents, even if basic assessments of countries' prospects do not differ at any given moment in time.
1. GDP and expenditure components are measured in average 2010-19 prices and market exchange rates.
2. National income and product account data refer to fiscal years (FY) while aggregates are presented in calendar year (CY) terms. (For example, aggregate under 2020/21 refers to CY 2020). The fiscal year runs from July 1 through June 30 in Bangladesh, Bhutan, and Pakistan; from July 16 through July 15 in Nepal; and April 1 through March 31 in India.
3. Subregion aggregate excludes Afghanistan, Bhutan, and Maldives, for which data limitations prevent the forecasting of GDP components.
4. Exports and imports of goods and nonfactor services (GNFS).

TABLE 2.5.2 South Asia country forecasts

(Real GDP growth at market prices in percent, unless indicated otherwise)

Percentage point differences from January 2021 projections

	2018	2019	2020e	2021f	2022f	2023f	2021f	2022f
Calendar year basis [1]								
Afghanistan	1.2	3.9	-1.9	1.0	2.6	3.0	-1.5	-0.7
Maldives	8.1	7.0	-28.0	17.1	11.5	8.3	7.6	0.0
Sri Lanka	3.3	2.3	-3.6	3.4	2.0	2.1	0.1	0.0
Fiscal year basis [1]	**2017/18**	**2018/19**	**2019/20e**	**2020/21f**	**2021/22f**	**2022/23f**	**2020/21f**	**2021/22f**
Bangladesh	7.9	8.2	2.4	3.6	5.1	6.2	2.0	1.7
Bhutan	3.8	4.3	-0.8	-1.8	5.0	5.6	-1.1	2.7
India	6.8	6.5	4.0	-7.3	8.3	7.5	2.3	2.9
Nepal	7.6	6.7	-2.1	2.7	3.9	5.1	2.1	1.4
Pakistan (factor cost)	5.5	2.1	-0.5	1.3	2.0	3.4	0.8	0.0

Source: World Bank.
Note: e = estimate; f = forecast. World Bank forecasts are frequently updated based on new information and changing (global) circumstances. Consequently, projections presented here may differ from those contained in other Bank documents, even if basic assessments of countries' prospects do not significantly differ at any given moment in time.
1. Historical data is reported on a market price basis. National income and product account data refer to fiscal years (FY) with the exception of Afghanistan, Maldives, and Sri Lanka, which report in calendar year. The fiscal year runs from July 1 through June 30 in Bangladesh, Bhutan, and Pakistan; from July 16 through July 15 in Nepal; and April 1 through March 31 in India.

SUB-SAHARAN AFRICA

Output in Sub-Saharan Africa (SSA) is expected to expand a modest 2.8 percent in 2021, and 3.3 percent next year. Positive spillovers from strengthening global activity, better international control of COVID-19, and strong domestic activity in agricultural commodity exporters are expected to gradually help lift growth. Nonetheless, the recovery is envisioned to remain fragile, given the legacies of the pandemic and the slow pace of vaccinations in the region. In a region where tens of millions more people are estimated to have slipped into extreme poverty because of COVID-19, per capita income growth is set to remain feeble, averaging 0.4 percent a year in 2021-22, reversing only a small part of last year's loss. Risks to the outlook are tilted to the downside, and include lingering procurement and logistical impediments to vaccinations, further increases in food prices that could worsen food insecurity, rising internal tensions and conflicts, and deeper-than-expected long-term damage from the pandemic.

Recent developments

Output in Sub-Saharan Africa (SSA) collapsed by an estimated 2.4 percent in 2020 as a result of the COVID-19 pandemic. This was the region's first economic contraction in a generation and the deepest recession since the 1960s. The recession was, however, milder than previously projected, as the virus spread more slowly than anticipated and agricultural activity was unexpectedly strong in some countries (Benin, Ethiopia, Kenya, Nigeria; World Bank 2021m). Growth in the region has gradually resumed this year, reflecting positive spillovers from strengthening global economic activity, including higher oil and metal prices, and some progress at containing COVID-19 outbreaks, especially in Western and Central Africa (figure 2.6.1.A). PMI readings for manufacturing and services suggest that activity in these sectors continued to expand in 2021, albeit at still modest rates (figure 2.6.1.B). The pandemic has contributed to a widening of budget deficits and a sharp increase in government debt. The debt-to-GDP ratio in the region jumped on average 8 percentage points to 70 percent of GDP last year, raising the risk of debt distress in some

---

Note: This section was prepared by Cedric Okou.

countries (IMF 2020). The adverse effects of the pandemic, fiscal pressures, and the very slow pace of vaccinations have dampened the resumption of growth, in particular in the hospitality and tourism sectors.

Activity in the three largest economies in the region—Angola, Nigeria, and South Africa—has partially recovered after falling by 4.2 percent in 2020. Many industrial and agricultural commodity exporters suffered deep contractions last year from depressed external demand and localized COVID-related disruptions (Angola, Cabo Verde, Mali, Republic of Congo; FAO 2020; World Bank 2021n). In tourism-reliant countries, international arrivals have been at a near-halt, and are likely to remain anemic until widescale vaccinations allow for a safe reopening of borders to international travel (Kenya, Mauritius, Seychelles; figure 2.6.1.C). Although conditions have improved in the region, COVID-19 and related control measures have continued to disrupt schooling, damage health, inhibit investment, and weigh on growth.

In countries with policy space, accommodative monetary and fiscal policies, combined with currency depreciations and rising energy and food prices, have fueled inflationary pressures in some

FIGURE 2.6.1. SSA: Recent developments

New COVID-19 infections in Sub-Saharan Africa (SSA) have declined after rising sharply in late 2020 and early 2021. Although PMI readings have remained in expansionary territory this year, the resumption in activity has been tepid. International tourist arrivals have remained close to zero over the past year. As vaccinations proceed, some countries will gradually lift travel restrictions. Inflation has picked up in some countries, reflecting currency depreciations and rising food prices.

A. Daily new COVID-19 infections in SSA

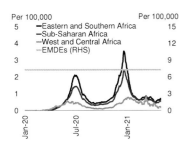

B. Median purchasing managers indexes for SSA countries

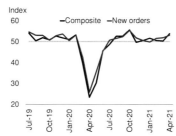

C. International tourist arrivals for selected SSA countries

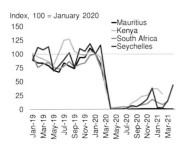

D. Inflation

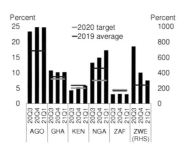

Sources: Haver Analytics; John Hopkins University; Seychelles National Statistics Agency; World Bank; Zimbabwe National Statistics.
Note: EMDEs = emerging market and developing economies; SSA = Sub-Saharan Africa.
A. Figure shows 7-day moving average of new COVID-19 cases. EMDEs line indicates the 7-day moving average ending on May 25, 2021.
B. Composite PMI covers manufacturing and services. Sample includes Ghana, Kenya, Mozambique, Nigeria, South Africa, Uganda, and Zambia. Last observation is April 2021.
C. Figure shows changes in tourist arrivals indexed to January 2020 = 100.
D. AGO = Angola; GHA = Ghana; KEN = Kenya; NGA = Nigeria; ZAF = South Africa; ZWE = Zimbabwe. Latest observation is 2021Q1. Orange lines show 2020 inflation targets for Ghana, Kenya, Nigeria, and South Africa.

countries (Angola, Nigeria; figure 2.6.1.D). In other countries in the region, however, subdued demand has kept inflation contained (Kenya, South Africa). Capital inflows to the region have lost momentum, owing to heightened uncertainty about the course of the pandemic and weak growth prospects in some recipient countries. Nonetheless, foreign direct investments in 2020 have been more resilient in SSA than the average EMDE excluding China, recouping about nine-tenths of their pre-pandemic levels. Workers'

remittances to the region—a lifeline for household consumption—have held up better than expected, partly reflecting a shift from informal or traditional non-digital cash payments to cheaper digital transfers and improving job opportunities in Sub-Saharan African migrant workers' destination countries.

Outlook

Growth is expected to resume in SSA this year, reaching 2.8 percent, and firm to 3.3 percent in 2022 (figure 2.6.2.A). This pickup is underpinned by stronger external demand from the region's trading partners—mainly China and the United States—higher commodity prices, and better containment of COVID-19. Despite the projected rebound, SSA will have the second-slowest growth this year among emerging market and developing economy (EMDE) regions. Although some countries have secured vaccine doses through the COVAX facility, procurement and logistical challenges are envisioned to further delay the already slow pace of vaccination in the region (figure 2.6.2.B). Policy uncertainty and the lingering negative effects of COVID-19 are also expected to delay some major investments in infrastructure and the extractives sector, and to weigh on the recovery (Central African Republic, Equatorial Guinea, Kenya, Niger). The regional forecast has been downgraded by an average 0.1 percentage point in 2021-22 below the January projections, mainly reflecting worse-than-expected weakness in investment, recurring bouts of conflict, and limited policy space to further support demand. Activity over the forecast horizon is now set to expand by 0.7 percentage point less than the average pace of 2010-19.

In per capita terms, income growth is forecast to remain subdued, averaging 0.4 percent a year in 2021-22, after a 5 percent decline last year. As a result, per capita income levels in 2022 will still be 4 percent, on average, lower than in 2019. Conditions in the region's fragile and conflict-affected countries are expected to be particularly challenging, with the average per capita GDP level in 2022 projected to be 5.3 percent below its 2019 level. In about half of this subset of SSA countries, a decade or more of per capita income will be lost by the end of the forecast horizon. The pandemic is also expected to worsen inequality through its outsized negative effects on women, children, and unskilled workers (IMF 2021). Feeble per capita GDP growth will be insufficient to improve conditions significantly in a region where 40 percent of the population struggles with extreme poverty (figure 2.6.2.C).

In Nigeria, growth is projected to resume at a modest rate of 1.8 percent in 2021 and edge up to 2.1 percent next year, assuming higher oil prices, a gradual implementation of structural reforms in the oil sector, and a market-based flexible exchange rate management (figure 2.6.2.D). The expected pickup is also predicated on continued vaccinations in the second half of this year and a gradual relaxation of COVID-related restrictions that will allow activity to improve. Nonetheless, output in Nigeria is not expected to return to its 2019 level until end-2022.

Following a sharp recession in 2020, growth in South Africa is forecast at 3.5 percent this year and 2.1 percent in 2022, with the recovery benefiting from a gradual relaxation of COVID-19 restrictions and stronger metal prices. Although expansionary monetary and fiscal policies have buoyed activity, GDP will remain well below its 2019 level through 2022. Heightened fiscal pressures and feeble public investment growth continue to dim South Africa's near-term growth prospects. Major structural impediments to potential growth remain, including labor market rigidities, reflected in continuing large-scale unemployment.

Angola's economy is projected to expand by 0.5 percent in 2021 and 3.3 percent in 2022, on the back of stronger oil prices and government consumption. Output is, however, not envisioned to regain its 2019 level until toward the end of the forecast horizon. Oil production, which plummeted last year, is forecast to remain below pre-pandemic levels in the near term if OPEC+ cuts are maintained. Fiscal pressures and increased policy uncertainty due to COVID-19 are expected to hamper the recovery by delaying critical

FIGURE 2.6.2 SSA: Outlook

Growth is forecast to resume at a modest pace, reflecting improved external demand and resilient commodity prices, but will remain below its pre-pandemic average. Lingering procurement and administration hurdles are expected to slow the pace of vaccinations in the region. The projected weak per capita income growth in 2021-22 will be insufficient to reverse setbacks in raising living standards caused by the pandemic last year in many SSA countries.

A. GDP growth

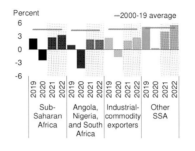

B. COVID-19 vaccinations

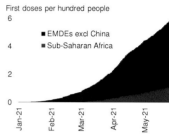

C. Evolution of per capita GDP

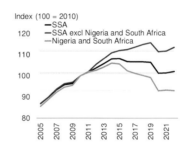

D. Changes in commodity prices between November 2020 and May 2021

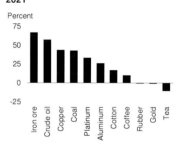

Sources: Our World in Data (database); World Bank
Note: EMDEs = emerging market and developing economies; SSA = Sub-Saharan Africa.
A. "Industrial-commodity exporters" represents oil and metal exporting countries. Aggregate growth rates calculated using constant GDP weights at average 2010-19 prices and market exchange rates. "Industrial commodity exporters" excludes Angola, Nigeria, and South Africa.
B. Total number of people who received at least one vaccine dose. Last observation is May 25, 2021.
C. Chart reflects the evolution of real per capita GDP in constant U.S. dollars at average 2010-19 prices and market exchange rates, rebased to 2010 = 100. "SSA" sample comprises 47 countries.
D. Bars represent the percentage change in the May 2021 monthly price relative to November 2020.

investments to revamp aging oil fields and increase production capacity in the oil sector.

Elsewhere in the region, growth is forecast to edge up to 3.8 percent a year on average in 2021-22, substantially below the 2010-19 average pace of 5.1 percent. Growth in industrial commodity exporters—excluding Angola, Nigeria, and South Africa—is expected to pick up to 2.4 percent in 2021-22; however, it will remain 1.5 percentage points below its 2010-19 average (Cameroon, Central African Republic, Democratic Republic of

FIGURE 2.6.3 SSA: Risks

Recent currency depreciations in some Sub-Saharan African countries may contribute to inflationary pressures. Food insecurity, rising conflicts, and violence against civilians, fueled by political unrest and economic disputes, could dampen the economic recovery. Fiscal deficits are projected to gradually narrow, as the pandemic is brought under control; however, a sharp increase in long-term sovereign bond yields could raise fiscal pressures in some SSA countries.

A. Changes in U.S. dollar exchange rates versus SSA currencies

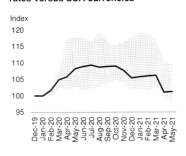

B. Food insecurity in SSA

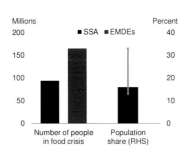

C. Forcibly displaced populations

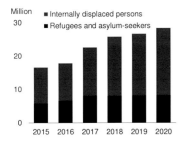

D. Fiscal balance

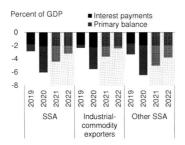

Sources: FSIN and Global Network Against Food Crises; Haver Analytics; IMF; UNHCR; World Bank.

Note: EMDEs = emerging market and developing economies; SSA = Sub-Saharan Africa.

A. Change in U.S. dollar exchange rates versus SSA currencies since December 2019. Monthly averages. Last observation is April 2021. Index (100 = December 2019). Values above 100 indicate depreciation. Shaded area indicates the 25-75 percentile range.

B. "Number of people in food crisis" reflects those classified as Integrated Food Security Phase Classification (IPC/CH) Phase 3, i.e., in acute food insecurity crisis or worse, in 2020. "Population share" reflects the sample median. Whiskers reflect the interquartile range. Sample includes 55 EMDEs and 35 SSA countries.

C. Asylum-seekers and refugees are people that flee their countries to seek asylum abroad or person that need international protection. Internally displaced persons are people that have been forced to leave or abandon their homes, and who have not crossed an internationally recognized border.

D. Simple averages of sub-groups.

Congo). In Botswana, growth is projected to rebound to 5.6 percent, on average, in 2021-22, as stronger metals and minerals prices, particularly for diamonds and nickel, rekindle activity after a precipitous collapse in the mining sector last year. For many industrial commodity-exporting economies, higher oil and metal prices will boost export revenues, but will not be sufficient to close fiscal deficits opened by last year's shortfalls.

In agricultural commodity exporters, growth is forecast to resume at a faster pace of 4.5 percent a year on average in 2021-22 (Benin, Côte d'Ivoire, Ethiopia). Projections for a number of countries assume sustained investment in infrastructure, greater export diversification, and continued implementation of reforms to improve business environments (Rwanda, Senegal, Togo). However, output growth in agricultural com-modity exporters over the next couple of years is projected to remain lower than the 2010-19 average growth rate of 5.7 percent.

Risks

Risks to the forecasts are tilted to the downside. Some countries in SSA have invested in upgrades to national vaccine distribution systems (Ghana, Nigeria, South Africa). Nevertheless, persistent procurement and logistical hurdles in many other countries could delay widescale vaccinations more severely than assumed. In South Africa, new outbreaks of a more transmittable strain of COVID-19 have contributed to the spread of the virus and slowed the distribution of vaccinations. Despite the strong scientific consensus that they are safe and effective, there is some skepticism about the vaccines among the public, with positive opinions of COVID-19 vaccines' safety and efficacy at just 21 percent in Senegal and 34 percent in Liberia (Afrobarometer 2021).[1] In addition to COVID-19, new Ebola outbreaks, if not contained, could spread and increase the viral threat in the region (Democratic Republic of Congo, Guinea).

Oil prices could fall, owing to continued weakness in global oil demand or a rapid increase in OPEC+ oil production (World Bank 2021k). In this scenario, some oil exporters could lose revenues, especially those that have structural capacity constraints and limited scope to quickly ramp up their production.

Food insecurity remains a key risk. Food price inflation has been exacerbated in some countries

---

[1] Afrobarometer surveys show that 79 and 66 percent of people were reluctant to get vaccinated in Senegal and Liberia, repectively (Afrobarometer 2021). Another survey across 15 African countries showed that 59 percent (Democratic Republic of Congo) to 94 percent (Ethiopia) of respondents were willing to take COVID-19 vaccines (Africa CDC 2021; Lazarus et al. 2020).

by currency depreciations: about half of the currencies in the region have depreciated since the start of 2021 (Ethiopia, Mozambique, Zambia; figure 2.6.3.A). Currency depreciation and supply constraints raised food prices by more than 20 percent in some countries early this year (Angola, Ethiopia, Nigeria). Flood and drought could also destroy crops, exacerbate food price inflation, and further weigh on household consumption, with outsized negative effects on the most vulnerable populations. Heavy rains, floods, cyclones, and wetter-than-normal weather conditions could lead to more locust breeding and infestation, and put large swaths of the population, especially in Eastern and Southern Africa, at a higher risk of hunger (World Bank 2021n). Conflicts could damage agricultural production, disrupt food supply, cause forced population displacements and make food insecurity more acute, with significantly greater negative effects on women and children (Brück and d'Errico 2019). With about 100 million people in food crisis and 4 out of 10 extremely poor people, the region could see many millions more slip into severe food insecurity in the next couple of years (figure 2.6.3.B; FSIN 2021).

Rising conflicts and insecurity could also weaken recoveries. There are concerns that the humanitarian and economic toll of conflicts could dampen the projected growth pickup. Insurgencies and abductions in the Sahel, as well as political and electoral violence, could weigh more heavily on growth and erode the living standards of the most vulnerable people (figure 2.6.3.C).

A sudden rise in sovereign borrowing costs could exacerbate fiscal pressures in some countries. Despite still-benign global financial conditions, sovereign borrowing costs have remained higher than before the pandemic in some countries (Angola, Ghana, Nigeria, South Africa). As COVID-19 recedes, budget deficits, which have widened substantially, are expected to gradually narrow (Chad, Ethiopia, Zambia; IMF 2020; figure 2.6.3.D). However, high debt burden and fiscal pressures could become more acute and precipitate financial distress in some countries, especially if borrowing costs increase sharply in line with further possible increases in long-term yields on government bonds in advanced economies and major EMDEs. Heightened fiscal pressures could also delay government payments to suppliers and contractors, cause revenue shortfalls and bankruptcies among these firms, and increase the likelihood of financial stress (Bosio et al. 2021).

There are also upside risks to the projections. The pace of vaccinations could surpass expectations, for example, if the COVAX facility and bilateral partners assist SSA countries in scaling up their vaccination programs. This could restore consumer and business confidence, stimulate consumption and investment, lower unemployment, and strengthen the recovery. Also, a stronger-than-expected rally in metals and oil prices could boost exports, increase government revenues, and ease fiscal pressures in industrial commodity exporters.

TABLE 2.6.1 Sub-Saharan Africa forecast summary

(Real GDP growth at market prices in percent, unless indicated otherwise)

Percentage point differences from January 2021 projections

	2018	2019	2020e	2021f	2022f	2023f	2021f	2022f
EMDE SSA, GDP [1]	**2.7**	**2.5**	**-2.4**	**2.8**	**3.3**	**3.8**	**0.0**	**-0.2**
GDP per capita (U.S. dollars)	0.0	-0.2	-4.9	0.2	0.7	1.2	0.0	-0.2
(Average including countries that report expenditure components in national accounts) [2]								
EMDE SSA, GDP [2,3]	2.7	2.5	-2.5	2.8	3.3	3.7	0.0	-0.1
PPP GDP	2.8	2.6	-2.2	2.8	3.3	3.9	-0.1	-0.3
Private consumption	4.5	2.7	-3.6	1.9	2.6	2.6	0.0	-0.1
Public consumption	5.9	3.7	3.8	1.1	2.1	2.2	-0.1	0.0
Fixed investment	6.9	5.2	-7.7	1.7	3.3	5.7	-1.1	-2.1
Exports, GNFS [4]	2.4	4.6	-8.5	6.8	5.4	5.5	0.1	-0.2
Imports, GNFS [4]	8.4	5.8	-9.2	3.1	3.4	3.5	0.3	0.0
Net exports, contribution to growth	-1.6	-0.4	0.4	0.9	0.5	0.5	0.0	0.0
Memo items: GDP								
Eastern and Southern Africa	2.6	1.9	-3.4	3.2	3.6	3.9	-0.3	-0.3
Western and Central Africa	2.9	3.2	-1.2	2.3	2.9	3.6	0.4	0.0
SSA excluding Nigeria, South Africa, and Angola	4.7	4.1	-0.5	3.3	4.4	5.3	-0.4	-0.6
Oil exporters [5]	1.4	2.1	-2.2	1.5	2.2	2.7	0.4	0.0
CFA countries [6]	3.9	4.1	-0.8	3.3	4.2	5.5	0.1	-0.7
CEMAC	0.3	1.5	-2.9	1.6	1.5	2.9	0.1	-1.2
WAEMU	6.4	5.8	0.7	4.3	5.8	7.1	0.0	-0.3
SSA3	1.0	1.1	-4.2	2.3	2.2	2.2	0.4	0.2
Nigeria	1.9	2.2	-1.8	1.8	2.1	2.4	0.7	0.3
South Africa	0.8	0.2	-7.0	3.5	2.1	1.5	0.2	0.4
Angola	-2.0	-0.6	-5.2	0.5	3.3	3.5	-0.4	-0.2

Source: World Bank.

Note: e = estimate; f = forecast; PPP = purchasing power parity; EMDE = emerging market and developing economy. World Bank forecasts are frequently updated based on new information and changing (global) circumstances. Consequently, projections presented here may differ from those contained in other Bank documents, even if basic assessments of countries' prospects do not differ at any given moment in time.

1. GDP and expenditure components are measured in average 2010-19 prices and market exchange rates.

2. Subregion aggregate excludes the Central African Republic, Eritrea, Guinea, São Tomé and Príncipe, Somalia, and South Sudan, for which data limitations prevent the forecasting of GDP components.

3. Subregion growth rates may differ from the most recent edition of Africa's Pulse (https://www.worldbank.org/en/region/afr/publication/africas-pulse) due to data revisions and the inclusion of the Central African Republic and São Tomé and Príncipe in the subregion aggregate of that publication.

4. Exports and imports of goods and nonfactor services (GNFS).

5. Includes Angola, Cameroon, Chad, the Republic of Congo, Equatorial Guinea, Gabon, Ghana, Nigeria, and South Sudan.

6. The Financial Community of Africa (CFA) franc zone consists of 14 countries in Sub-Saharan Africa, each affiliated with one of two monetary unions. The Central African Economic and Monetary Union (CEMAC) comprises Cameroon, the Central African Republic, Chad, the Republic of Congo, Equatorial Guinea, and Gabon; the West African Economic and Monetary Union (WAEMU) comprises Benin, Burkina Faso, Côte d'Ivoire, Guinea-Bissau, Mali, Niger, Senegal, and Togo.

TABLE 2.6.2 Sub-Saharan Africa country forecasts[1]

(Real GDP growth at market prices in percent, unless indicated otherwise)

Percentage point differences from January 2021 projections

	2018	2019	2020e	2021f	2022f	2023f	2021f	2022f
Angola	-2.0	-0.6	-5.2	0.5	3.3	3.5	-0.4	-0.2
Benin	6.7	6.9	2.0	5.0	6.0	6.5	0.0	-0.5
Botswana	4.5	3.0	-7.9	6.9	4.3	4.1	1.2	0.3
Burkina Faso	6.7	5.7	0.6	3.1	5.0	5.7	0.7	0.3
Burundi	1.6	1.8	0.3	2.0	2.5	3.0	0.0	0.0
Central African Republic	3.7	3.1	0.0	0.7	2.8	4.4	-2.5	-1.3
Cabo Verde	4.5	5.7	-14.0	3.9	5.2	6.1	-1.6	-0.8
Cameroon	4.1	3.7	-2.1	2.1	2.7	3.8	-0.9	-0.7
Chad	2.4	3.2	-0.9	1.0	2.5	2.9	-1.4	-0.8
Comoros	3.4	2.0	-0.5	0.2	2.2	4.2	-2.2	-1.4
Congo, Dem. Rep.	5.8	4.4	0.8	2.5	3.0	4.1	0.4	0.0
Congo, Rep.	-6.2	-3.5	-7.9	-0.1	2.3	3.1	1.9	1.0
Côte d'Ivoire	6.9	6.2	1.8	5.7	6.0	6.5	0.2	0.2
Equatorial Guinea	-6.4	-5.6	-4.9	2.4	-5.6	-2.3	5.2	-4.4
Eritrea	13.0	3.7	-0.6	2.0	4.9	3.8	-1.5	-0.6
Eswatini	2.4	2.2	-3.1	1.3	1.1	1.5	-0.2	0.2
Ethiopia[2]	6.8	8.4	6.1	2.3	6.0	7.5	2.3	-2.7
Gabon	0.8	3.9	-1.9	1.5	2.5	3.6	-0.4	-1.3
Gambia, The	7.2	6.1	0.0	3.5	5.5	7.0	0.4	0.2
Ghana	6.3	6.5	1.1	1.4	2.4	3.6	0.0	0.0
Guinea	6.2	5.6	4.7	5.5	5.2	5.2	0.0	0.0
Guinea-Bissau	3.8	4.6	-2.4	3.0	4.0	5.0	0.0	0.0
Kenya	6.3	5.4	-0.3	4.5	4.7	5.8	-2.4	-1.0
Lesotho	1.5	1.4	-5.8	2.9	3.1	3.2	-0.2	-0.7
Liberia	1.2	-2.3	-2.9	3.3	4.2	4.7	0.1	0.3
Madagascar	4.6	4.9	-4.2	2.0	5.8	5.4	0.0	0.0
Malawi	4.4	5.4	0.8	2.8	3.0	4.5	-0.5	-1.9
Mali	4.7	4.8	-2.0	2.5	5.2	5.0	0.0	0.0
Mauritania	2.1	5.9	-1.5	2.7	3.7	6.0	-1.0	-1.1
Mauritius	3.8	3.0	-15.6	3.6	5.9	4.3	-1.7	-0.9
Mozambique	3.4	2.3	-1.3	1.7	4.1	6.3	-1.1	-0.3
Namibia	1.1	-1.6	-7.3	1.8	1.8	1.5	-0.4	-0.2
Niger	7.2	5.9	0.8	4.7	8.9	12.1	-0.4	-2.9
Nigeria	1.9	2.2	-1.8	1.8	2.1	2.4	0.7	0.3
Rwanda	8.6	9.4	-3.3	4.9	6.4	7.5	-0.8	-0.4
São Tomé and Príncipe	2.9	1.3	3.1	2.7	3.5	4.0	-0.3	-2.0
Senegal	6.4	5.3	-0.7	3.1	4.9	8.9	-0.4	-0.7
Seychelles	3.8	5.3	-13.3	1.8	4.3	4.2	-1.3	0.5
Sierra Leone	3.4	5.5	-2.2	3.0	3.7	4.0	-1.1	-0.9
South Africa	0.8	0.2	-7.0	3.5	2.1	1.5	0.2	0.4
Sudan	-2.3	-2.5	-3.6	0.4	1.1	2.6	-2.1	-2.0
South Sudan[2]	-3.5	-0.3	9.5	-3.4	1.5	3.0	0.0	1.5
Tanzania	5.4	5.8	2.0	4.5	5.5	6.0	-1.0	-0.5
Togo[3]	4.9	5.3	0.7	3.4	4.6	5.0	0.4	0.1
Uganda[2]	6.3	6.4	3.0	3.3	4.7	6.4	0.5	-1.2
Zambia	3.5	1.4	-3.0	1.8	2.9	3.8	-0.1	-0.5
Zimbabwe	4.8	-8.1	-8.0	3.9	5.1	5.0	1.0	2.0

Source: World Bank.

Note: e = estimate; f = forecast. World Bank forecasts are frequently updated based on new information and changing (global) circumstances. Consequently, projections presented here may differ from those contained in other Bank documents, even if basic assessments of countries' prospects do not significantly differ at any given moment in time.

1. Data are based on GDP measured in average 2010-19 prices and market exchange rates.
2. Fiscal-year based numbers.
3. For Togo, growth figures in 2018 and 2019 are based on pre-2020 rebased GDP estimates.

References

Africabarometer. 2021. "Who Wants COVID-19 Vaccination? In 5 West African Countries, Hesitancy is High, Trust Low." Afrobarometer Dispatch 432. https://afrobarometer.org/sites/default/files/publications/Dispatches/ad432-covid-19_vaccine_hesitancy_high_trust_low_in_west_africa-afrobarometer-8march21.pdf.

Africa CDC (Africa Centres for Disease Control and Prevention). 2021. "Majority of African Would Take a Safe and Effective COVID-19." *Africa CDC* (blog), March 13, 2021. https://africacdc.org/news-item/majority-of-africans-would-take-a-safe-and-effective-covid-19-vaccine/.

Azevedo, J. P., A. Hasan, D. Goldemberg, S. A. Iqbal, and K. Geven. 2020. "Simulating the Potential Impacts of Covid-19 School Closures on Schooling and Learning Outcomes: A Set of Global Estimates." Policy Research Working Paper 9284, World Bank, Washington, DC.

Baker, S. R., N. Bloom, and S. J. Davis. 2016. "Measuring Economic Policy Uncertainty." *The Quarterly Journal of Economics* 131 (4): 1593-1636.

Bakken, I. V., and H. Buhaug. 2020. "Civil War and Female Empowerment." *Journal of Conflict Resolution* 65 (5): 982-1009.

Bosio, E., R. Ramalho, C. Reinhart. 2021. "The Invisible Burden: How Arrears Could Unleash a Banking Crisis." VoxEU.org, CEPR Policy Portal, March 22, https://voxeu.org/article/how-arrears-could-unleash-banking-crisis.

Bracco, J., L. Galeano, P. Juarros, D. Riera-Crichton, and G. Vuletin. Forthcoming. "Social Transfer Multipliers in Developed and Emerging Countries: The Role of Hand-to-Mouth Consumers." Policy Research Working Paper, World Bank, Washington, DC.

Brück, T., and M. d'Errico. 2019. "Food Security and Violent Conflict: Introduction to the Special Issue." *World Development* 117 (May): 167-171.

Busso, M., J. Camacho, J. Messina, and G. Montenegro. 2020. "Social Protection and Informality in Latin America during the COVID-19 Pandemic." Working Paper 10849, Inter-American Development Bank, Washington, DC.

Choudhary, M. A., F. Pasha, and M. Waheed. 2020. "Measuring Economic Policy Uncertainty in Pakistan.

"MPRA Paper 100013, University Library of Munich, Germany.

De Nicola, F., A. Mattoo, J. D. Timmis, and T. T. Tran. 2021. "Productivity in the Time of COVID-19: Evidence from East Asia and Pacific." Research & Policy Brief 46, World Bank, Washington, DC.

Demirgüç-Kunt, A., M. Lokshin, and I. Torre. 2020. "Opening-up Trajectories and Economic Recovery: Lessons after the First Wave of the COVID-19 Pandemic." Policy Research Working Paper 9480, World Bank, Washington, DC.

Demirgüç-Kunt, A., A. Pedraza, and C. Ruiz-Ortega. 2020. "Banking Sector Performance during the COVID-19 Crisis." Policy Research Working Paper 9363, World Bank, Washington, DC.

Dieppe, A., ed. 2020. *Global Productivity: Trends, Drivers, and Policies.* Washington, DC: World Bank.

Dinarte, L., E. Medina-Cortina, D. Jaume, and H. Winkler. 2021. "Not by Land nor by Sea: The Rise of Formal Remittances during COVID-19." World Bank, Washington, DC. https://devpolicy.org/Events/2021/Not-by-land-nor-by-sea-the-rise-of-formalremittances-during-COVID-19-Dinarte-13Apr/Full-paper.pdf.

Duke Global Health Innovation Center. 2021. *Launch and Scale Speedometer.* Duke University. https://launchandscalefaster.org/covid-19.

ECLAC (United Nations Economic Commission for Latin America and the Caribbean). 2021. "The Economic Autonomy of Women in a Sustainable Recovery with Equality." COVID-19 Special Report 9, ECLAC, Santiago.

Fan, J., Y. Li, K. Stewart, A. R. Kommareddy, A. Garcia, J. Ma, A. Bradford, et al. 2021. "COVID-19 World Symptom Survey Data API." University of Maryland, College Park. https://covidmap.umd.edu/api.html.

FAO (Food and Agricultural Organization). 2020. *Monthly Report on Food Price Trends.* October. Rome: Food and Agricultural Organization.

FAO (Food and Agriculture Organization) and WFP (World Food Programme). 2021. *Hunger Hotspots: FAO-WFP Early Warnings on Acute Food Insecurity.* March to July 2021 Outlook. Rome: FAO and WFP.

Fasih, T., H. A. Patrinos, and M. J. Shafiq. 2020. "The Impact of COVID-19 on Labor Market

Outcomes: Lessons from Past Economic Crises." *Education for Global Development* (blog), World Bank, May 20, 2021. https://blogs.worldbank.org/education/impact-covid-19-labor-market-outcomes-lessons-past-economic-crises.

G20 (Group of Twenty). 2021. "Italian G20 Presidency: Second G20 Finance Ministers and Central Bank Governors Meeting Communique." April 7, 2021.

Ha, J., M. Kose, F. Ohnsorge, and H. Yilmazkuday. 2019. "Sources of Inflation: Global and Domestic Drivers." In *Inflation in Emerging and Developing Economies*, edited by J. Ha, M. A. Kose, and F. Ohnsorge. Washington, DC: World Bank.

Hale, T., N. Angrist, R. Goldszmidt, B. Kira, A. Petherick, T. Phillips, S. Webster, E. Cameron-Blake, L. Hallas, S. Majumdar, and H. Tatlow. 2021. "A Global Panel Database of Pandemic Policies (Oxford COVID-19 Government Response Tracker." *Nature Human Behavior* 5: 529-538.

IEA (International Energy Agency). 2021. *Oil 2021: Analysis and Forecast to 2026.* Paris: International Energy Agency.

ILO (International Labour Organization). 2021. "ILO Monitor: COVID-19 and the World of Work." Seventh edition updated estimates and analysis. January. International Labour Organization, Geneva.

IMF (International Monetary Fund). 2020. *Fiscal Monitor: Policies for the Recovery*. October. Washington, DC: International Monetary Fund.

IMF (International Monetary Fund). 2021. *Fiscal Monitor: A Fair Shot*. April. Washington, DC: International Monetary Fund.

Jarland, J., H. M. Nygård, S. Gates, E. Hermansen, and V. B. Larsen. 2020. "How Should We Understand Patterns of Recurring Conflict?" Conflict Trends 3, Peace Research Institute Oslo, Norway.

Joint Data Center of Forced Displacement, World Bank, and UNHCR (United Nations High Commissioner for Refugees). 2021. *Compounding Misfortunes: Changes in Poverty Since the Onset of COVID-19 on Syrian Refugees and Host Communities in Jordan, the Kurdistan Region of Iraq and Lebanon (Vol. 2)*. Washington, DC: World Bank.

Kilic Celik, S., M. A. Kose, and F. Ohnsorge. 2020. "Subdued Potential Growth: Sources and Remedies." Policy Research Working Paper 9177, World Bank, Washington, DC.

Lazarus, J.V., S.C. Ratzan, A. Palayew, L.O Gostin, H.J. Larson, K. Rabin, S. Kimball, and A. El-Mohandes. 2020. "A Global Survey of Potential Acceptance of a COVID-19 Vaccine." *Nature Medicine* 27: 225-228.

Mahler, D. G., N. Yonzan, C. Lakner, R. A. Castaneda Aguilar, and H. Wu. "Updated Estimates of the Impact of COVID-19 on Global Poverty." *Data Blog*, June 2021. https://blogs.worldbank.org/opendata.

Marcec, R., M. Matja, and R. Likic. 2020. "Will Vaccination Refusal Prolong the War on SARS-CoV-2?" *Postgraduate Medical Journal 2021* (97): 143-149.

Quayyum, S. N., and R. K. Kpodar. 2020. "Supporting Migrants and Remittances as COVID-19 Rages On." IMFBlog, September 11, 2020. https://blogs.imf.org/2020/09/11/supporting-migrants-and-remittances-as-covid-19-rages-on/.

Rovo, N. 2020. "Structural Reforms to Set the Growth Ambition." Policy Research Working Paper 9175, World Bank, Washington, DC.

Sahibzada, H., S. M. Muzaffari, T. A. Haque, and M. Waheed. 2021. *Afghanistan Development Update: Setting Course to Recovery*. Washington, DC: World Bank.

Shmis, T., A. Sava, J. E. N. Teixeira, and H. A. Patrinos. 2020. "Response Note to COVID-19 in Europe and Central Asia: Policy and Practice Recommendations." World Bank, Washington, DC.

UNCTAD (United Nations Conference on Trade and Development). 2021. *Investment Trends Monitor*. Issue 38. Geneva: UNCTAD.

UNWTO (United Nations World Tourism Organization). 2021. "2020: Worst Year In Tourism History With 1 Billion Fewer International Arrivals." UNWTO News, Madrid.

WFP (World Food Programme) and FAO (Food and Agriculture Organization). 2021. "Hunger Hotspots. FAO-WFP Early Warnings on Acute Food Insecurity." March to July 2021 outlook. Rome: WFP and FAO.

World Bank. 2018. "Building Solid Foundations: How to Promote Potential Growth." In *Global Economic Prospects: Broad-based Upturn, But for How Long?* 157-217. Washington, DC: World Bank.

World Bank. 2020a. "Lasting Scars of the COVID-19 Pandemic." In *Global Economic Prospects* (January), 143-88. Washington, DC: World Bank.

World Bank. 2020b. *East Asia and Pacific Economic Update: From Containment to Recovery.* October. Washington, DC: World Bank.

World Bank. 2020c. *Europe and Central Asia Economic Update: COVID-19 and Human Capital.* October. Washington, DC: World Bank.

World Bank. 2021a. *East Asia and Pacific Economic Update: Uneven Recovery.* March. Washington, DC: World Bank.

World Bank. 2021b. *Europe and Central Asia Economic Update: Data, Digitalization, and Governance.* March. Washington, DC: World Bank.

World Bank. 2021c. *Global Economic Prospects.* January. Washington, DC: World Bank.

World Bank. 2021d. *Western Balkans Economic Update.* April. Washington, DC: World Bank.

World Bank. 2021e. "The Gendered Impact of COVID-19 on Labor Markets in Latin America and the Caribbean." Policy Brief, Innovation Lab for Latin America and the Caribbean, World Bank, Washington, DC.

World Bank. 2021f. "Promoting Climate Change Action in Latin America and the Caribbean." Results Brief, April 14, 2021. https://www.worldbank.org/en/results/2021/04/14/promoting-climate-change-action-in-latin-america-and-the-caribbean.

World Bank. 2021g. *Renewing with Growth—Semiannual Report of the Latin America and the Caribbean Region.* Washington, DC: World Bank.

World Bank. 2021h. "Acting Now to Protect the Human Capital of Our Children: The Costs of and Response to COVID-19 Pandemic's Impact on the Education Sector in Latin America and the Caribbean." World Bank, Washington, DC.

World Bank. 2021i. *Middle East and North Africa: Macro Poverty Outlook.* Spring Meeting 2021. Washington, DC: World Bank.

World Bank. 2021j. *MENA Economic Update: Living with Debt: How Institutions can Chart a Path to Recovery for the Middle East and North Africa.* April. Washington, DC: World Bank.

World Bank. 2021k. *Commodity Markets Outlook: Causes and Consequences of Metal Price Shocks.* April. Washington, DC: World Bank.

World Bank. 2021l. *South Asia Economic Focus.* March. Washington, DC: World Bank.

World Bank. 2021m. *Africa's Pulse: COVID-19 and the Future of Work in Africa.* April. Washington, DC: World Bank.

World Bank. 2021n. "COVID-19 and Food Security." Brief, World Bank, Washington, DC. https://www.worldbank.org/en/topic/agriculture/brief/food-security-and-covid-19.

World Bank and German Development Cooperation. 2020. *Building for Peace. Reconstruction for Security, Equity, and Sustainable Peace in MENA.* Washington, DC: World Bank.

CHAPTER 3

HIGH TRADE COSTS

Causes and Remedies

As the global economy rebounds from the COVID-19-induced global recession, the accompanying strength in global trade offers an opportunity to jump-start the recovery in emerging market and developing economies (EMDEs). Lowering cross-border trade costs could help revive trade growth. Trade costs are high: on average, they double the cost of internationally traded goods in comparison to domestic goods. Tariffs account for only one-fourteenth of average trade costs; the bulk of trade costs are incurred in shipping and logistics, as well as cumbersome trade procedures and processes at and behind the border. Despite a decline since 1995, trade costs remain almost one-half higher in EMDEs than in advanced economies; about one-third of the gap may be accounted for by higher shipping and logistics costs and another one-third by trade policy. A comprehensive reform package to lower trade costs would include trade facilitation measures; deeper trade liberalization; efforts to streamline trade processes and clearance requirements; better transport infrastructure; more competition in domestic logistics, retail, and wholesale trade; and less corruption. Some of these measures could yield large dividends: among the worst-performing EMDEs, a hypothetical reform package to improve logistics performance, maritime connectivity, and border processes to those of the best-performing EMDEs is estimated to halve trade costs.

Introduction

Global trade collapsed by nearly 16 percent at the height of the COVID-19-induced global recession, in the second quarter of 2020, as pandemic-related policies disrupted shipping, international travel, and domestic economic activity. The subsequent rebound, however, was swift, especially for goods trade, and much faster than after the 2007-2009 global financial crisis. The recovery in global trade offers an opportunity for emerging market and developing economies (EMDEs) to jump-start their still-weak recovery from the pandemic. To seize this opportunity after a decade of slow trade growth, however, many countries may need to implement policies to lower the cost of trade.

Trade, powered by global value chain integration, has been an important engine of output and productivity growth over the past several decades. For example, a 1 percent increase in trade has been estimated to lift per capita income by 0.2 percent over the medium term (World Bank 2020a).[1] Global value chain participation, in

particular, has been associated with reduced vulnerability of trade activity to domestic shocks although it has come with increased sensitivity to external shocks (Espitia et al. 2021).

Yet, over the past decade, global trade growth has slowed as global value chains matured, investment weakness weighed on goods trade, and trade tensions emerged between major economies over the past three years (World Bank 2015, 2017). As a result, trade is no longer growing faster than output: instead of being twice as fast as global output growth, as it was during 1970-2008, trade growth is now likely to continue broadly in step with real GDP growth, in line with its behavior during the 2010s (figure 3.1; World Bank 2015). Absent a major policy effort, weaker prospects for global output growth in the 2020s than in the 2010s are likely to be mirrored in weaker trade growth, too (World Bank 2021a).

The recovery from the COVID-19-induced global recession offers an opportunity to revive trade growth as the global trade network is reshaped. The pandemic is likely to accelerate changes in supply-chains that had already begun, including by further regionalizing production networks and increasing digitalization. Multinational corporations operating in EMDEs have already increased the use of digital technologies and enhanced diversification of suppliers and production sites to increase their resilience to supply chain shocks (Saurav et al. 2020). As multinationals seek to diversify, EMDEs have a unique opportunity to

---

Note: This chapter was prepared by Franziska Ohnsorge, Lucia Quaglietti, and Cordula Rastogi.

[1] Trade has been associated with greater quality of products (Fieler, Eslava, and Xu 2018), technology transfers (Henry, Kneller, and Milner 2009), welfare gains from more varieties (Broda and Weinstein 2006), lower poverty (World Bank and WTO 2018), and distributional gains for lower-income households since they tend to spend more on tradable goods and services (Carroll and Hur 2020). At the same time, trade has been associated with a shift of income from labor to capital and, in some cases, environmental degradation (World Bank 2020a).

FIGURE 3.1 Global trade

Instead of being almost twice as fast as global output growth, as it was during 1970-2008, trade growth has expanded broadly in step with real GDP growth since 2011. Goods trade accounted for 75 percent of global trade during 2010-19.

A. Global trade and output growth

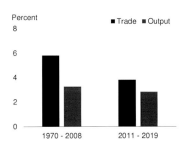

B. Composition of global trade, 2010-19

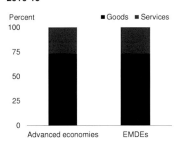

Source: World Bank.
Note: EMDEs = emerging market and developing economies.
A. Bars indicate annual average growth. World output is real GDP growth and it is aggregated using real U.S. dollar GDP weights at 2010-19 average prices and exchange rates as reported in the *Global Economic Prospects* report. Trade growth is average of import and exports data.
B. Shares of global goods and services trade in global trade, average of 2010-19.

integrate into global supply chains, provided they can offer a conducive business environment.[2]

Lower trade costs can help create a business environment conducive to global supply chain participation. Trade costs currently double the price of internationally traded goods over domestic ones, a phenomenon sometimes dubbed "thick borders" (World Bank 2009). In EMDEs, trade costs are almost one-half higher than in advanced economies. High trade costs raise the price of exports and imports, hinder competitiveness, limit participation in global value chains, and erode consumer welfare by reducing the availability of goods and services for consumption. Lowering trade costs could help boost trade flows and enhance welfare (World Economic Forum and World Bank 2013).

Trade costs capture the costs faced by countries when trading goods across borders, in excess of the costs that the same goods face when traded domestically (box 3.1). Implicitly, trade costs cover

the full range of costs associated with trading, including transportation and distribution costs, tariffs and nontariff barriers, costs of information and contract enforcement, legal and regulatory costs, as well as the cost of doing business across cultures, languages, and economic systems (Anderson and van Wincoop 2003).

This chapter will examine the following questions.

- What are trade prospects for the next decade?

- How large are trade costs?

- What are the correlates of trade costs?

- Which policies can help to lower trade costs?

Contribution to the literature. This chapter updates and confirms an earlier literature that estimates the magnitude of trade costs and its correlates (Arvis et al. 2016; Novy 2013). Like this literature, the analysis in this chapter confines itself largely to goods trade which accounts for about 75 percent of total world and EMDE trade (figure 3.1). Like the previous literature, this chapter uses goods trade costs estimates from the World Bank/UNESCAP database for 1995-2018, the latest year for which data are available.[3] The chapter adds a quantitative assessment of the costs of border and customs processes to factors considered elsewhere such as shipping, regulations, logistics, and governance and finds that such border and customs processes statistically significantly raise trade costs.[4] It builds upon the analytical findings to discuss policy options for lowering trade costs in support of the recovery from the COVID-19.

Main findings. This chapter offers the following findings.

First, the COVID-19-induced global recession of 2020 triggered a collapse in global trade, followed

---

[2] The supply chain response to the disruption caused by the 2011 earthquake in Japan may offer a guide to potential supply chain changes after the pandemic. After the 2011 earthquake, supply chain shifted away from the affected source but without any major near-shoring, reshoring or diversification (Freund et al. 2020).

[3] For 2018, trade costs data is available for 199 countries, including 150 EMDEs.

[4] For governance, see Hou, Wang, and Zhie (2021). For shipping and regulations, see Staboulis et al. (2020). For regional trade agreements, see Bergstrand, Larch, and Yotov (2015). For logistics, see Marti and Puertas (2019).

by a rapid rebound. Within six months, global goods trade had recovered to pre-pandemic levels and, by March 2021, global services trade was within 3 percent of pre-pandemic levels notwithstanding travel and tourism services still being just under 65 percent below. Looking ahead, absent a major policy effort, trade growth is likely to be weak over the next decade as output growth slows and as structural factors that supported the rapid trade expansion in the past have largely run their course. A reduction in trade costs may help accelerate trade growth.

Second, trade costs are high: on average, they are equivalent to a 100 percent tariff and, hence, they double the cost of internationally traded goods over domestic goods. Tariffs account for only one-fourteenth of average trade costs; the bulk are incurred in transport and logistics as well as cumbersome border and customs procedures. Despite a one-third decline since 1995, trade costs remain almost one-half higher in EMDEs than in advanced economies. About one-third of the explained difference in trade costs between EMDEs and advanced economies can be accounted for by higher shipping and logistics costs, and another one-third by trade policy (including trade policy uncertainty).

Third, services account for almost one-third of the value added of manufacturing exports. Services trade costs tend to be considerably higher than goods trade costs and, therefore, also spill over into higher goods trade costs. To a large extent, services trade costs have been attributed to regulatory restrictions.

Fourth, trade costs can be lowered effectively through comprehensive reforms packages that streamline trade processes and customs clearance requirements, enhance domestic trade-supporting infrastructure, increase competition in the domestic logistics, retail, and wholesale trade industries; lower tariffs; lower compliance costs with standards; and reduce corruption. Trade agreements that deepen integration beyond tariffs cuts can help lower nontariff barriers. Empirical analysis suggests that an EMDE in the quartile of EMDEs with the highest shipping and logistics costs and most unwieldy customs and border

processes could halve its trade costs if it improved these conditions to match the quartile of EMDEs with the lowest costs of shipping and logistics and the least cumbersome border and customs processes.

Prospects for trade growth

Trade growth slowdown over the past decade. Global trade growth slowed over the past decade, from 5.8 percent per year during 1970-2008 to just 3.8 percent per year during 2011-19. If global trade had continued to expand according to its historical trend, it would have been more than one-quarter above its actual level in 2019 (figure 3.2). With the exception of Europe and Central Asia (ECA), the slowdown in trade growth was broad-based, extending across all EMDE regions. In Sub-Saharan Africa (SSA), trade growth has been particularly weak, at about half the EMDE average after the global financial crisis. At the sectoral level, the slowdown was concentrated in goods trade. Services trade continued to outpace world GDP before the pandemic, rising 1.5 percentage point per year faster on average during 2011-2019.

Declining responsiveness of trade to economic activity. The slowdown in trade growth reflected weak economic growth in the decade following the global financial crisis but also a weakening responsiveness of trade to global economic growth (the income elasticity of trade). Estimates from an error correction model for 1970-2019 suggest that the long-run trade elasticity has declined from 2.2 during 1990-2011 to around 1 during 2011-19.[5] In EMDEs, the ratio of import growth to income growth declined from 1.7 during 1990-2008 to 0.9 during 2011-19. The slowdown in the global income elasticity of trade in the decade before the pandemic hit reflected several factors (World Bank 2015).

---

[5] The model allows both the long-run elasticity of trade with respect to income (which captures trend, or structural, factors) and the short-run elasticity (which is relevant to short run or cyclical developments). For further details on the model specification see Constantinescu et al. (2014)

FIGURE 3.2 Evolution of global trade

Global trade growth has slowed since 2011, in part as a result of slowing output growth. In addition, the elasticity of trade to global economic activity has fallen over the past decade amid slowing global investment, maturing global value chains, and mounting trade tensions. Global trade collapsed during the pandemic but rebounded quickly, with the exception of travel and tourism services, which remain depressed.

A. World trade, actual and trend

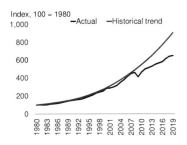

B. Trade elasticities

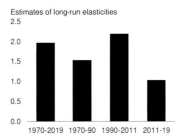

C. Aggregate demand components relative to historical trend, 2019

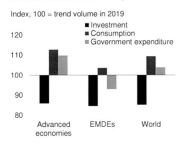

D. Import content of aggregate demand, 2014

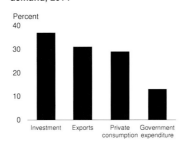

E. Share of global-value-chain-related trade in global trade

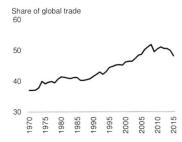

F. World trade

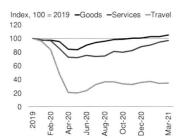

Sources: Auboin and Borino (2017); Constantinescu et al. (2014); CPB Netherlands Bureau for Economic Policy Analysis; World Bank; World Trade Organization.
Note: EMDEs = emerging market and developing economies; GVC = global value chain.
A. World trade refers to average imports and exports volumes. The historical trend is computed over the 1980-2019 period, using a Hodrick-Prescott filter.
B. Estimates from an error correction model estimated over the period 1970-2019. The model allows both the long-run elasticity of trade with respect to income (which captures trend, or structural, factors) and the short-run elasticity (which is relevant to short run or cyclical developments). For further details on the model specification see Constantinescu et al. (2014).
C. Trend levels in 2019 are obtained on the basis of the historical average trend growth computed over the period 1995-2008 and rebased to 100. Bars below 100 show deviations of actual 2019 levels from trends.
D. Data for 2014 as estimated in Auboin and Borino 2017.
E. Share of GVC trade in global trade as defined in *World Development Report* 2020. Latest available data is 2015.
F. Goods trade is the average of import and exports volumes, services trade is the average of imports and exports values. Goods trade data in 2021 relative to average of 2019, services and travel trade data relative to corresponding month in 2019. Total goods trade volumes for 38 advanced economies and 43 EMDEs, as reported in the CPB World Trade Monitor. Services trade and travel data from WTO statistics. Sample for services trade and travel includes 13 advanced economies and 16 EMDEs. Last observation is March 2021.

• *Changes in the composition of global demand.* The composition of global demand has shifted away from advanced economies towards EMDEs and towards less trade-intensive components of aggregate demand. EMDEs, which typically have a lower trade-intensity than advanced economies, accounted for just under two-fifths of global output during 2011-19, compared with just over one-quarter during 1980-2008 (Cabrillac et al. 2016; World Bank 2015). Investment, which tends to be more trade-intensive than other components of demand, has been weak over the past decade, especially in EMDEs (Bussière et al. 2013; Kose et al. 2017). In China, a policy-guided shift away from investment-led growth and, in commodity exporters, prolonged weakness of commodity prices slowed investment activity (World Bank 2017, 2019).

• *Maturing global value chains.* Over the past decade, the expansion of global value chains slowed (Antras and Chor 2021; World Bank 2015, 2020a). The overall share of global value chain-related trade in total world trade grew significantly in the 1990s and early 2000s but has stagnated or even declined since 2011. This has in part reflected rising labor costs in key emerging markets, a greater appreciation by firms of supply risks in the wake of some natural disasters, as well as mounting trade tensions over the past five years (Cabrillac et al. 2016; World Bank 2020a).

• *Trade tensions.* A slowing pace of trade liberalization may also have contributed to a declining trade elasticity (World Bank 2015). Tariff rates levelled off in both advanced economies and EMDEs in the early 2000s. At the same time, the use of regulatory measures and nontariff barriers such as export subsidies, restrictions on licensing or foreign direct investment, and domestic clauses in public procurement increased (Niu et al. 2018).

Trade collapse in early 2020. The global recession of 2020 was the deepest since the Second World War and was accompanied by a collapse in global trade of nearly 16 percent in the second quarter of

2020—6 percentage points steeper than in the first quarter of 2009, at the height of the global recession triggered by the global financial crisis. Unusually for global recessions, the collapse in global services trade was even larger than the collapse in global goods trade.

Goods trade rebound in late 2020. The recovery, however, was swifter than in the global financial crisis, particularly for goods trade. Goods trade had returned to pre-COVID-19 levels within six months of the trough of the trade collapse, 12 months earlier than after the global financial crisis. The recovery in goods trade was fairly broad-based, with global imports of cars, capital goods, consumer goods, and industrial supplies all back at or above pre-pandemic levels by January 2021 (IMF 2021). Global value chains have remained broadly resilient to the pandemic as companies increasingly turned to digital technologies and diversified suppliers and production sites (Saurav et al. 2020). Nevertheless, recently, some strains in supply chains have emerged. The strong recovery in global manufacturing has raised demand for containerized exports from Asia, pushing up freight rates. The week-long blockage of the Suez Canal temporarily stretched maritime supply chains further (World Bank 2021b).

Unusually pronounced drop in services trade during the pandemic. The decline in services trade was considerably more pronounced and the recovery more subdued than in the global financial crisis, reflecting to some extent a collapse in global tourism as countries closed their borders to stem the spread of the pandemic. In March 2021, global services trade was still 3 percent below pre-pandemic levels, whereas at a similar point after the global financial crisis, services trade had already recovered. While most components of services trade, including telecommunications and financial services, have fully recovered to pre-pandemic levels, travel services remain just under 65 percent below. The recovery in services trade was concentrated in East Asia and the Pacific (EAP) where China's services trade had already returned to pre-pandemic levels by December 2020. Service trade plays an increasingly important role in the global economy: Since 2000, global travel and tourism revenues have nearly

tripled, with the sector now accounting for 10 percent of global GDP and about 30 percent of global services trade, and providing one out of ten jobs worldwide (World Bank 2020b).

Weak prospects for global trade growth. Global trade is forecast to grow by 8.3 percent in 2021, reflecting the strength of global growth, but also the diminishing trade intensity of the global recovery. The structural factors that supported the rapid trade expansion in the two decades preceding the global financial crisis seem to have largely run their course, with the recent weakness in the relationship between global trade growth and global output growth likely to constitute a "new normal." Since global output growth itself is expected to slow going forward compared to the past decade, world trade growth would decline accordingly (World Bank 2021a). Over the 2020s, trade growth may slow by another 0.9 percentage point from the 2010s, broadly in line with global potential output growth, unless major policy efforts significantly increase the growth of trade (World Bank 2021a). The weakness may be more pronounced in goods trade, where new technologies may allow more localized and more centralized production (Coulibaly and Foda 2020; Zhan et al. 2020). In contrast, in services trade, rapidly growing data services promise a return to rapid expansion once the pandemic is brought under control (World Bank 2021c).

Patterns in trade costs

High, although declining, trade costs. Average trade costs are high, particularly in EMDEs where they double the price of goods traded domestically, and are far in excess of the average tariff of 7 percent.[6] Trade costs in EMDEs are almost one-half higher than those in advanced economies (figure 3.3). This is despite a sharp decline over the past two and a half decades (Bergstrand, Larch, and Yotov 2015). In 2018, average trade costs were about one-quarter lower

---

[6] This estimate of trade costs is of the same order of magnitude as other studies—such as Arvis et al. (2016) or Anderson and van Wincoop (2004) but is larger than others based on individual retail price data such as one for the United States and Canada (Gopinath et al. 2011).

FIGURE 3.3 Trade costs

Trade costs are roughly equivalent to a 100 percent tariff—far above actual average tariff rates. Despite a decline over the past two decades, trade costs remain high, especially for agricultural products and in EMDEs. Trade costs for agricultural goods are highest in South Asia and Sub-Saharan Africa, while trade costs in the manufacturing sector are the highest in Latin America and the Caribbean and Sub-Saharan Africa.

A. Average trade costs in 1995 and 2018

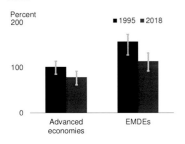

B. Average trade costs in EMDE regions

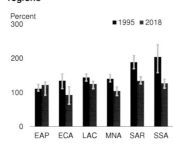

C. Average trade costs for agriculture in 1995 and 2018

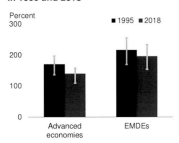

D. Average trade costs for agriculture for EMDE regions in 1995 and 2018

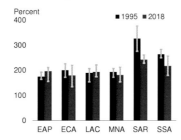

E. Average trade costs for manufacturing in 1995 and 2018

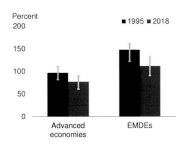

F. Average trade costs for EMDE regions for manufacturing in 1995 and 2018

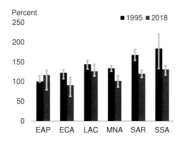

Sources: Comtrade (database); ESCAP-World Bank Trade Costs Database; World Bank; World Trade Organization.

Note: EMDEs = emerging market and developing economies; EAP = East Asia and Pacific, ECA = Europe and Central Asia, LAC = Latin America and the Caribbean, MNA = Middle East and North Africa, SAR = South Asia, SSA = Sub-Saharan Africa. Bilateral trade costs (as defined in the ESCAP database) measure the costs of a good traded internationally in excess of the same good traded domestically and are expressed as ad valorem (tariff) equivalent. Bilateral trade costs are aggregated into individual country measures using 2018 bilateral country exports shares from the Comtrade database. Regional and sectorial aggregates are averages of individual country measures. Bars show unweighted averages, whiskers show interquartile range. Sample in 1995 includes 33 advanced economies and 46 EMDEs, 5 in EAP, 7 in ECA, 4 in MNA, 15 in LAC, 2 in SAR, and 13 in SSA. Sample in 2018 includes 21 advanced economies and 58 EMDEs, 11 in EAP, 14 in ECA, 7 in MNA, 13 in LAC, 3 in SAR, and 10 in SSA.

in advanced economies and almost two-fifths lower in EMDEs than in 1995. Average trade costs fell in all sub-regions except East Asia and Pacific, with the fastest decline occurring in Sub-Saharan Africa (SSA). As discussed in the next section, both the decline in trade costs and the high trade costs in EMDEs reflect a wide range of factors.

Trade costs across EMDE regions. Among EMDE regions, average trade costs range from tariff equivalents of 93 percent in Europe and Central Asia (ECA) to 134 percent in South Asia (SAR), with wide heterogeneity within regions. This heterogeneity is particularly pronounced in East Asia and Pacific (EAP). Within Europe and Central Asia (ECA), countries that are members of the European Union or geographically close to it have two-thirds the average trade costs of other countries that are less integrated into EU global value chains.

Trade costs for agricultural goods. Trade costs for agricultural goods are about four-fifths higher than for manufacturing goods. Agricultural trade costs are particularly high in SAR and manufacturing trade costs are particularly high in SSA and Latin America and the Caribbean (LAC). Agricultural trade costs declined less than trade costs in manufacturing over the period 1995 to 2018, in part because of slower progress in tariff reductions and narrower coverage of trade agreements.

Trade costs for services. Goods and services trade are complementary. Tradable services are key links between stages of value chains and "enablers" of trade in goods, in particular communications, finance, business and logistics services. As a result, services account for almost one-third of the value added of manufacturing exports (OECD 2018). Comparable cross-country data on services trade costs and on policies affecting trade in services are however scant. The few attempts to quantify trade costs in services in the literature rely on observed trade and value-added flows-akin to the methodology embedded in the World Bank/ UNESCAP database for goods trade (Miroudot, Sauvage, and Shepherd 2010) or rely on an inventory of services trade restrictions (Benz 2017). Both types of studies suggest that trade costs for services are considerably higher than trade costs for goods and, in contrast to goods trade costs, have not fallen since the 1990s.

Correlates of trade costs

Methodology and data. A panel gravity equation with time fixed effects is used to quantify the correlates of trade costs (box 3.1). The regression uses bilateral data for 2007-2018 for 23 advanced economies and 63 EMDEs for which data on trade costs as well as its determinants is available from 2007. The sample is heavily constrained by data availability. For example, the *Doing Business* indicator for ease of trading is not available before 2006. Bilateral, sector-specific goods trade costs are regressed on geographical and cultural barriers (distance, common border or adjacency, and common language); trade policy (sector-specific bilateral tariffs, membership of a regional trade agreement and a proxy of trade policy uncertainty); logistics and connectivity (Logistics Performance Index LPI and the Liner Shipping Connectivity Index LSHI); and regulatory barriers (*Doing Business* score index for the time and costs it takes exporters to comply with documentary and border regulations).[7] The model is estimated in two versions: for all sectors of the economy and for manufacturing separately, and both specifications explain over half of the variation of trade costs in the sample (table 3.1).

Tariffs. Tariffs are associated with higher trade costs, both overall and for manufacturing more narrowly. While statistically significant, they have contributed less than other components to the reduction in trade costs over time or the difference between trade costs in EMDEs and advanced

economies. After steep reductions in the 1990s and early 2000s, manufacturing tariffs now average 6 percent in EMDEs—somewhat less than the average tariff of 7 percent across all sectors— and around 2 percent in advanced economies (figure 3.4). Agricultural tariffs remain two (EMDEs) and more than three (advanced economies) times higher than manufacturing tariffs.

Regional trade agreements. Membership of a regional trade agreement lowers bilateral trade costs statistically significantly by just under one-fifth.[8] All advanced economies are part of at least one regional trade agreement. The EU alone participates in 46 regional trade agreements, and other advanced economies are members of 75 regional trade agreements. Among EMDEs, membership of regional trade agreements is less common, although all but a handful of EMDEs are members of at least one agreement. Such agreements are most common in ECA, where parts of Central and Southern Europe are EU members and parts of Eastern Europe and Central Asia are members of the Free Trade Area between Members of the Commonwealth of Independent States, and in LAC where most countries are part of MERCOSUR and trade agreements with the United States, such as the U.S.-Mexico-Canada Agreement (USMCA) or the Dominican Republic-Central America Free Trade Agreement (CAFTA-DR).

Shipping and logistics costs. Transit delays have been identified as more important deterrents to trade flows than geography (Freund and Rocha 2011). Poor shipping connectivity, inadequate logistics infrastructure and services as well as underlying regulations are associated with significantly higher trade costs. The one-week blockage of the Suez Canal, through which 12 percent of global trade merchandize traffic passes,

---

[7] The World Bank's *Logistics Performance Index* (LPI) is based on a survey of global freight operators and express carriers about customs, logistics and transport infrastructure, international shipments, logistics competence, tracking and tracing, and timeliness. Logistic managers are asked questions related to the country of operation, including about the quality and transport infrastructure, the ability of the country to track and trace consignments, and the number of forms needed to be submitted to obtain clearance of imports and exports. The UNCTAD's Liner Shipping Connectivity Index is based on each country's number of ships, their container-carrying capacity, maximum vessel size, the number of services, and the number of companies that deploy container ships in a country's ports.

[8] This is somewhat lower than found by Bergstrand, Larch, and Yotov (2015) who estimate that an economic integration agreement lowers trade costs by 30 percent in a smaller and earlier sample (41 mostly advanced economies during 1996-2000). Qualitatively, it is consistent with Brenton, Portugal-Perez, and Regolo (2014) who find that trade agreements help to lower the price differential between domestic and traded foods.

BOX 3.1 Understanding the determinants of trade costs

Shipping and logistics, borders and customs processes, tariffs, and membership of regional trade agreements are statistically significant factors that influence trade costs.

Introduction

Elevated trade costs remain a significant impediment to cross-border trade. On average, trade costs double the cost of an internationally traded good over a similar domestic good. In EMDEs, trade costs are almost one-half higher than in advanced economies despite a decline since 1995.

This box considers the determinants of trade costs empirically by examining the following questions.

- How are trade costs measured in the literature?

- What are the main determinants of trade costs, empirically?

The results suggest that geographical distance and high bilateral tariff rates are positively associated with trade costs, including in the manufacturing sector. In contrast, common borders (adjacency), common language, and membership of a common regional trade agreement tend to reduce trade costs. Policies aimed at facilitating trade including maritime connectivity and stronger logistics performance are also associated with lower bilateral trade costs, as well as indicators related to the ease of doing trade.

Measures of trade costs

Conceptually, trade costs are the excess cost of an internationally traded good compared with a similar good traded domestically. By construction, trade costs can therefore move without any change in external costs of trading, simply as a result of changes in domestic trading costs. To measure trade costs, two main approaches have been developed in the literature: direct and indirect approaches.

Direct approaches rely on observable data that serve as a proxy for individual components. For instance, measures of costs faced at the border are often based on counting the average number of days that is needed for a good to cross the border, while transport costs are often inferred from the cost of ocean and air shipping (Hummels et al. 2007). Policy barriers such as tariffs and nontariff measures are directly available from a range of statistical sources. Direct approaches suffer from a series of limitations, including the fact the underlaying variables are only partially observable and can hardly be converted to plausible tariffs ad-valorem

equivalents, which makes it difficult to compare them but also to aggregate them into a summary measure of trade costs (Anderson and van Wincoop 2004). Therefore, trade cost estimates taken from such measures tend to be only partial.

Indirect approaches aim to circumvent these difficulties. These infer trade impediments top-down, from measures of trade flows and aggregate value added.[a] Under this approach, trade costs correspond to the difference between the trade flows that would be expected in a hypothetical "frictionless" world and what is observed in the data and are computed relative to domestic trade costs. Measures built through the indirect approach can be tracked over time and include all observed and unobserved factors that explain why trading with another country is more costly than trading domestically. Novy (2013) develop a micro-founded measure of aggregate bilateral trade costs by a theoretical gravity equation for the trade cost parameters that capture the barriers to international trade. The resulting solution expresses the trade cost parameters as a function of observable trade data, providing a micro-founded measure of bilateral trade costs. The measure is easy to implement empirically for a number of countries with readily available data. One drawback is that the contribution of the individual cost factors cannot be easily disentangled by simple inspection of the measure. A way proposed in the literature to overcome this is to combine indirect and direct measurements into a single regression (Arvis et al. 2013).

Determinants of trade costs

To estimate the contribution of different determinants of trade costs, a gravity model is estimated for a panel of 23 advanced economies and 63 EMDEs with annual data for both trade costs and all determinants of trade costs over 2007-2018.

Data

The estimation relies on bilateral trade costs from the UNESCAP-WB Trade Costs Database. Following Novy (2013), Arvis et al. (2013) derive measures of annual trade costs for the period 1995-2018. For any given country pair

---

a. Domestic trade flows are proxied by gross domestic output on a gross shipment basis or, if this is unavailable, gross value added.

BOX 3.1 Understanding the determinants of trade costs (*continued*)

i and j, trade costs are obtained as geometric averages of costs faced by country i when exporting to j and vice versa. They are computed according to the formula below:

$$(X_{ii} X_{jj})/(X_{ij} X_{ji})^{1/2(\sigma-1)}$$

where X_{ij} represents trade between countries i and j (goods produced and sold in i and goods produced and sold in j) and σ refers to the elasticity of substitution. This measure captures international trade costs relative to domestic trade costs. Intuitively, trade costs are higher when countries trade more with themselves than they do bilaterally, i.e., as the ratio $(X_{ii} X_{jj})/(X_{ij} X_{ji})$ increases. Intra-national (i.e., domestic) trade is proxied by the difference of gross output and total exports.

Trade costs thus computed, implicitly account for a wide range of frictions associated with international trade, including transport costs, tariffs and nontariff measures but also costs associated with differences in languages, currencies and import or export procedures. Trade costs are expressed as ad valorem (tariff) equivalent of the value of traded goods and can be computed as an aggregate referring to all sectors of the economy, but also specifically for the manufacturing and agriculture sectors.

Estimation

Gravity equations are widely used as a workhorse to analyze the determinants of bilateral trade flows. Chen and Novy (2011) and Arvis et al. (2013) employ a gravity specification also in the analysis of the determinants of bilateral trade costs in a cross-sectional set. In line also with Moïsé, Orliac, and Minor (2011), this study estimates determinants of trade costs in a panel specification

The regression equation takes the following form:

$$TC_{ijt} = \beta_1 \, RTA_{ijt} + \beta_2 \, tariff_{ijt} + \beta_3 \, LSHI_{ijt} + \beta_4 \, LPI_{ijt}$$

$$+ \, \beta_5 \, Ease \, of \, Trading_{ijt}$$

$$+ \, \beta_6 \, Trade \, Policy \, Uncertainty_{ijt}$$

$$+ \, \beta_7 \, Gravity_{ij} + \eta_t + \varepsilon_{ijt} \qquad (1)$$

where for any given country pair ij, bilateral trade costs TC observed at time t are regressed on a wide range of candidate drivers. These include standard gravity indicators such as distance, a common language and a common border (adjacency), but also trade policies such as bilateral tariff rates and belonging to a regional trade agreement. A

proxy for trade policy uncertainty is also included. In line with Osnago, Piermartini, and Rocha (2018), trade policy uncertainty is defined as the gap between binding tariff commitments and applied tariffs. To ascertain the role of policies aimed at facilitating trade, indexes of logistic performance (LPI) and maritime connectivity (LSHI) and an indicator of doing business related to compliance of documentary and border checks is included.

Specifically, the World Bank's *Logistics Performance Index* (LPI) is based on a survey of global freight operators and express carriers about customs, logistics and transport infrastructure, international shipments, logistics competence, tracking and tracing, and timeliness. UNCTAD's Liner Shipping Connectivity Index is derived from the number of ships, their container-carrying capacity, maximum vessel size, number of services, and number of companies that deploy container ships in a country's ports. The World Bank's *Doing Business* ease of trading across borders index is based on surveys of experts on regulations regarding customs documentation and time and costs of customs, clearance. The choice of variables in the panel is informed by Arvis et al. (2013), but also by findings from the stylized facts presented in the main text.[b] Full details of data and sources are presented in table 3.1.

Since trade costs data are obtained as bilateral geometric averages, trade facilitation indicators available at individual country level are transformed into bilateral measures by taking the geometric average of each country pair direction. Therefore, the unit of analysis is each individual country pair. Time fixed effects η_t are included in the estimation to control for country characteristics that might vary over time. As the measures of trade costs net out multilateral resistance components, in line with Novy (2013), the estimation does not include additional fixed effects.[c] Instead, to control for possible correlation of errors terms, clustered standard errors by country pairs are used.

---

b. Nontariff barriers or exchange rate volatility would ideally have been included in the regression estimation. However, these are difficult to measure and the available cross-country, over time-panel measures were too crude to yield statistically significant results. Ideally, the regression would also be applied to services; however, the database does not offer trade cost for services.

c. Outward multilateral resistance captures the fact that trade flows between i and j depend on trade costs across all potential markets for i's exports, while inward multilateral resistance captures the fact that bilateral trade depends on trade costs across all potential import markets. Therefore, the two indices summarize third-country effects that might affect bilateral trade flows between i and j. Novy (2013) shows that simple algebra makes it possible to eliminate the multilateral resistance terms from the gravity equations, and in so doing he derives an expression for trade costs.

BOX 3.1 Understanding the determinants of trade costs (*continued*)

FIGURE B3.1.1 Estimated contributions to trade costs

The panel estimation accounts for much of the difference in average trade costs between EMDEs and advanced economies and the difference between 2008 and 2018. About one-third of the predicted difference between average trade costs in EMDEs and advanced economies and two-thirds of the predicted difference between 2008 and 2018 is attributed to costs associated with shipping and logistics.

A. Actual and model-predicted differences in overall trade costs

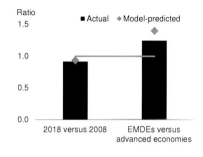

B. Model-based contributions to differences in overall trade costs

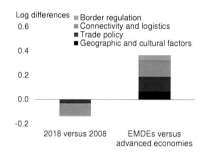

C. Model-based contributions to differences in manufacturing trade costs

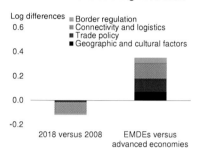

Sources: Comtrade (database); World Bank.

Note: EMDEs = emerging market and developing economies; RTA = regional trade agreement; LSCI = liner shipping connectivity index; LPI = logistics performance index.

Predicted ratios of overall trade costs between the two groups indicated on the x-axis (A) or the contributions (B, C) to differences in logarithms of trade costs. Computed using coefficient estimates for each variable and the following realizations for each indicator included in the regression: trade-weighted averages for all countries in the sample in 2018 minus trade-weighted average for all countries in the sample for 2008 for the comparison over time and trade-weighted averages for EMDEs minus trade-weighted average for advanced economies in 2018. Trade policy includes tariffs and membership in regional trade agreements; geographic and cultural factors includes distance, common border, and common language; border regulation includes the ease of trading; and connectivity and logistics include liner shipping connectivity index and logistics performance index. Gray horizontal line (A) indicates 1, that is, no difference in trade costs between the two groups indicated on the x-axis.

Two models are estimated: a general model for the determinants of trade costs in all sectors of the economy, and a sectoral model for the determinants of trade costs in the manufacturing sector. The two models follow the specification presented in equation 1, but trade costs and tariff rates are sector specific. Table 3.2 shows results from the estimations.

Results

All variables have the expected signs and magnitudes and are in line with the literature. Geographical distance and high bilateral tariff rates are positively associated with trade costs. In contrast, adjacency, common language and membership of a common regional trade agreement tend to reduce trade costs. Policies aimed at facilitating trade including maritime connectivity and stronger logistics performance are also associated with lower bilateral trade costs, both overall and in the manufacturing sector. Indicators related to the ease of doing trade are also statistically significant, with countries characterized by more cumbersome border processes facing higher trade

costs on average. Trade uncertainty is also positively associated with trade costs, including in the manufacturing sector.

The panel estimation explains most of the difference in trade costs between the average EMDE and the average advanced economy, and attributes about one-third of this gap to higher shipping and logistics costs in EMDEs and another one-third to trade policy (including trade policy uncertainty). The regression also explains most of the decline in average trade costs between 2008 and 2018 and attributes two-thirds of it to falling shipping and logistics costs.

Robustness

The estimations are robust to different specifications, lag structure, and estimators. An alternative estimation performed with the PPML estimator which is often employed in the literature on gravity models (Santos Silva and Tenreyro 2006) to control for heteroskedasticity produces similar results to the ones presented in table 3.2.

BOX 3.1 Understanding the determinants of trade costs (*continued*)

Adding further variables including the bilateral real exchange rate, GDP per capita income and a dummy characterizing landlocked country pairs does not alter the regression results, as the variables turn out to be statistically insignificant. Adding country fixed effects does not alter the stability of the model, with both the gravity and trade policy variables retaining the expected sign and statistically significant effects. Concerns about multicollinearity (including regarding the 0.5 correlations between the LPI with the LSHI and the *Ease of Trade* indicators) are mitigated by the results of a Variable Inflation Factor test, a standard diagnostic test conducted to detect the presence of multicollinearity among the regressors. They are also mitigated by the statistical insignificance of the difference between average bilateral tariffs in country pairs in a regional trade agreement and those outside it.

A few caveats apply to the analysis. One limitation relates to the interpretation of the effect of policies on trade costs. Changes in trade costs between two countries can be due to actions taken by one government or the other, or both together. The fact that the variables featuring in the regression (including the measure of trade costs) are computed as country pairs geometric averages doesn't allow us to disentangle the source of policy actions. In addition, due to lack of sufficiently long time-series data, the approach taken here does not take into account the possibility that the regression coefficients have changed over time, as has been found in other studies for the effect of distance (Yotov 2012) or trade agreements (de Sousa 2012).

Conclusion

The estimation results suggest that policies can have a statistically significant and economically sizable impact on trade costs. Better shipping connectivity, better logistics performance, less burdensome border and customs procedures, and less trade policy uncertainty are associated with statistically significantly lower trade costs. More challenging shipping and logistics account for about one-third, and trade policy for another one-third, of the predicted gap between trade costs in EMDEs and advanced economies. Improved shipping and logistics also account for about two-thirds of the predicted decline in trade costs since 2008.

after a container ship accident in March 2021 was a reminder of the critical role of shipping in global trade (World Bank 2021b). For advanced economies, poor logistics have been more important sources of trade costs than geographic distance (Marti and Puertas 2019; Staboulis et al. 2020). Global shipping connectivity and logistics remain considerably poorer in EMDEs than in advanced economies (figure 3.4) and trade costs remain higher in countries with poorer shipping connectivity and logistics (figure 3.5). The regression results suggest that a shift from the bottom quartile on these two indicators' scores to the highest quartile—equivalent to a comparison between Sierra Leone and Poland—is associated with about one-tenth to one-third lower trade costs (box 3.1).

Regulatory cost. Trade costs are significantly higher when compliance with trade and customs procedures and processes is more difficult (Staboulis et al. 2020).[9] Burdensome regulations have been associated with significantly lower trade—almost as much as the average tariff, for each additional signature to be collected for exports—especially for highly differentiated goods where price comparisons are more challenging (Hillberry and Zhang 2015; Sadikov 2007). The regression results suggest that a switch from the quartile furthest from the frontier in the *Doing Business* ease of trading to the closest quartile—equivalent to a comparison between Sierra Leone and Thailand—is associated with one-eight lower trade costs.

---

[9] This is consistent with studies that find that documentation requirements are an important deterrent for trade flows in OECD countries (Staboulis et al. 2020). For agricultural goods, regulations that cause border delays are particularly damaging to trade (Djankov, Freund, and Pham 2010). The Logistics Performance Index also captures in part regulatory compliance burdens.

FIGURE 3.4 Trade policy, border processes, and logistics

Tariffs declined sharply over the 1990s and early 2000s, in part because of regional and multilateral trade agreements, but began to tick upward again in 2017, especially in EMDEs. They are higher in EMDEs than in advanced economies and in agriculture than in manufacturing. Border processes and logistics tend to be easier, and shipping connectivity better, in advanced economies than in EMDEs.

A. Tariff rates in AEs and EMDEs

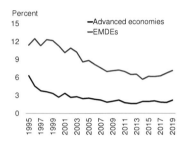

B. Tariff rates by different sectors

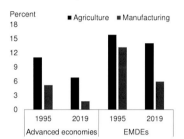

C. Trading across borders index

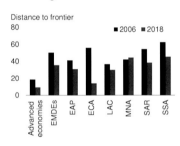

D. Logistics performance index

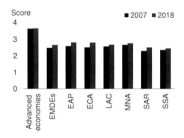

E. Liner shipping connectivity index

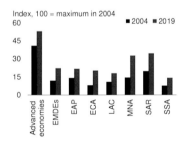

F. Regional trade agreement participation

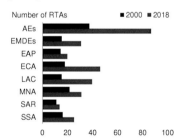

Sources: Gurevich and Herman (2018); World Bank; World Trade Organization.
Note: EMDEs = emerging market and developing economies; EAP = East Asia and Pacific, ECA = Europe and Central Asia, LAC = Latin America and the Caribbean, MNA = Middle East and North Africa, SAR = South Asia, SSA = Sub-Saharan Africa; RTAs = regional trade agreements.
A.B. Regional aggregates are computed as unweighted averages of country weighted tariff rates.
C. Doing Business index for "trading across borders" indicator on a range from 0 = lowest performance to 100 = best performance. Sample includes 82 EMDEs and 16 advanced economies for 2006 and 2018. Bars show distance to frontier in 2006 and 2018.
D. Logistics performance index (LPI) is a summary indicator of logistics sector performance, combining data on six core performance components into a single aggregate measure. The indicator is available for a sample of 160 countries. Sample includes 36 advanced economies and 123 EMDEs.
E. Liner shipping connectivity index (LSCI) is an average of five components and captures how well countries are connected to global shipping networks. The index value 100 refers to the country with the highest average index in 2004. Sample includes 30 advanced economies and 119 EMDEs.
F. Regional trade agreements are reciprocal trade agreements between two or more partners and include both free trade agreements and custom unions. The EU Treaty and the USMCA agreement are included. Regional aggregates are computed as averages of individual country participation in RTAs.

Regulatory costs in EMDE regions. Regulatory requirements for trading across borders have been streamlined significantly over the past decade, especially in ECA, SAR, and SSA. In ECA and SSA, the improvement appears to be linked to automation and digitalization of trade processes in a number of countries, which has reduced the time of compliance assessments at the location of customs clearance. In SAR, the improvement appears to be related to the upgrading of port infrastructure in India, coupled with the introduction of a new system of electronic submission of imports documents. In EAP, better governance and less burdensome customs procedures have been associated with somewhat lower trade costs.

Trade uncertainty. Uncertainty about, and high variability of, transit conditions, customs and border processes, tariffs, and other policies can impose significant costs. Uncertainty about trade policy may have lowered U.S. investment by more than 1 percent in 2018 (Caldara et al. 2020). Uncertainty also imposes significant costs by threatening on-time delivery. In Africa, for example, a single-day transit delay for an exporter is estimated to be equivalent to a 2 percent tariff in all importing partner countries (Freund and Rocha 2011). One dimension of trade uncertainty is the room for tariffs to be raised without violating WTO rules, that is, the difference between applied tariffs and bound tariffs, the "tariff water" (Osnago, Piermartini, and Rocha 2015). The regression results here suggest that a 10-percentage point narrower gap between the actual applied tariff and the maximum (bound) tariff is associated with one-seventh lower trade costs.

Differences between EMDEs and advanced economies. In 2018, trade costs for the average EMDE in the sample included in the regression were almost one-quarter higher than for the average advanced economy in the sample. The panel estimation can explain most of this gap and, in turn, attributes about one-third of it to poorer logistics and shipping connectivity in EMDEs, one-third to trade policy (including trade policy uncertainty), one-eighth to more cumbersome customs regulations and border processes, and just under one-fifth to the greater remoteness (geographically and culturally) of EMDEs.

Decline in goods trade costs over time. Between 2007 and 2018, trade costs have fallen by one-eighth, on average, in the countries in the sample, somewhat more than predicted by the regression. The regression attributes almost two-thirds of this decline to improved shipping connectivity and logistics, one-quarter to trade policy (tariff cuts, membership of regional trade agreements, and uncertainty related to trade policy) and one-tenth to easier customs and border processes.

Other factors. Other factors, beyond what can be captured in the empirical exercise used here, likely also contribute to cross-country difference in trade costs and their changes over time. Such factors include nontariff barriers, market structures, but also country-specific institutional and policy characteristics including information availability and automation of procedures and trade-supporting infrastructure beyond that included in the logistics surveys.

- *Nontariff barriers*—such as sanitary and phytosanitary standards, preshipment inspections, licensing requirements or quotas—have risen over time. In 2015, about 2,850 product lines were subject to at least one nontariff barrier, about double the 1,456 product lines in 1997 (Niu et al. 2018). The average nontariff barrier is equivalent to an 11.5 percent tariff (Kee and Nicita 2016). Nontariff barriers affect a higher share of imports—but a lower share of exports—in advanced economies than in EMDEs. Almost all agricultural imports face nontariff barriers, compared with about 40 percent on average across all sectors (World Bank and UNCTAD 2018). Low-income countries are particularly affected by nontariff barriers because of their more frequent use of nontariff barriers in the agricultural sector and the lower capacity of firms to comply with such requirements.

- *Export restrictions on sensitive sectors* have increased in the pandemic. Policy makers have adopted a wide range of measures to restrict exports and encourage imports of food and medical equipment, over concerns about food

FIGURE 3.5 Trade costs in EMDEs, by country characteristics

Trade costs are somewhat higher in EMDEs outside of regional trade agreements, with the poorest logistics performance, the least maritime connectivity, and the most challenging customs and border processes.

A. Trade costs, by regional trade agreements

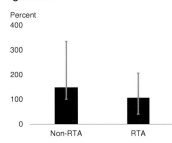

B. Trade costs, by quartile of logistics performance index

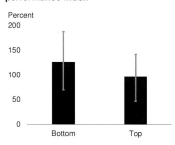

C. Trade costs, by quartile of liner shipping connectivity index

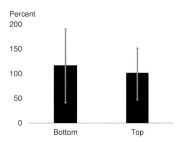

D. Trade costs, by quartile of trading across borders index

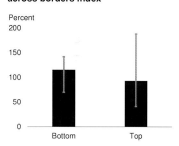

E. Trade costs, by median WGI control of corruption

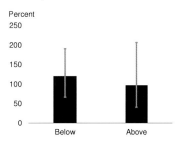

F. Trade costs, by median WGI regulatory quality

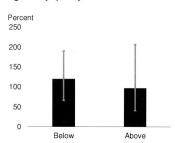

Sources: Comtrade (database); Gurevich and Herman (2018); ESCAP-World Bank Trade Costs Database; World Bank; World Trade Organization.

Note: EMDEs = emerging market and developing economies; RTA = regional trade agreements; LSCI = Liner Shipping Connectivity Index; LPI = Logistics Performance Index. Whiskers show minimum and maximum range. Orange wiskers indicate minimum and maximum range. Sample includes 59 EMDEs.

A. Average trade costs (unweighted) of countries based on their membership in regional trade agreements (RTAs) as defined in Gurevich and Herman (2018).

B. Average trade costs (unweighted) for countries ranked in the bottom and top quartile of the Logistics Performance Index.

C. Bars show the average trade costs (unweighted) for countries in the bottom and top quartiles of the liner shipping index

D. Average trade costs (unweighted) for countries ranked in the bottom and upper quartiles of the Doing Business "trading across borders" indicator.

E.F. Average trade costs (unweighted) for countries above and below median of the "Control of Corruption" and "Regulatory quality" of the World Governance Indicators (WGI). Control of corruption captures perceptions of the extent to which public power is exercised for private gain, including both petty and grand forms of corruption, as well as "capture" of the state by elites and private interests. Regulatory quality captures perceptions of the ability of the government to formulate and implement sound policies and regulations that permit and promote private sector development.

FIGURE 3.6 Services trade restriction policies

Services trade in EMDEs face more restrictions than those in advanced economies. Across regions, the most restrictive policies to services trade are applied in South Asia and in East Asia and Pacific.

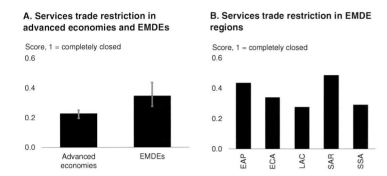

A. Services trade restriction in advanced economies and EMDEs

B. Services trade restriction in EMDE regions

Sources: Organisation for Economic Co-operation and Development; World Bank.

Note: EMDEs = emerging market and developing economies; EAP = East Asia and Pacific, ECA = Europe and Central Asia, LAC = Latin America and the Caribbean, SAR = South Asia, SSA = Sub-Saharan Africa.

Services trade restrictions index (STRI) helps identify which policy measures restrict trade. The STRI indices take the value from 0 to 1, where 0 is completely open and 1 is completely closed. They are calculated on the basis of information in the STRI database which reports regulation currently in force. Bars show denote the unweighted average and orange whiskers indicate the interquartile range. Sample includes 31 advanced economies and 17 EMDEs.

security and medical emergencies. In the first nine months of 2020 alone, 135 economies announced more than 600 such measures, of which 44 percent without a removal date (Evenett et al. 2020).

- *Better institutional quality and economic infrastructure*—including energy provision, transport and communication infrastructure and services, and greater transparency in policy decisions—have also been associated with lower trade costs (Cali and Te Velde 2011; Hou, Wang, and Xue 2021). In a large sample of countries in the early 2000s, the availability of trade-related information, the simplification and harmonization of documents, the streamlining of procedures and the use of automated processes were associated with more than 10 percent lower trade costs (Moïsé and Sorescu 2013). The impact of corruption has been more ambivalent: it may raise trade costs when corrupt officials extort bribes or it may lower trade costs when corrupt officials allow tariff evasion (Dutt and Traca 2010).

- *Noncompetitive market structures* can drive up trade costs. A lack of competition and the

existence of monopolies, including in transport industries, may raise high trade costs. In some countries in Sub-Saharan Africa, for example, the cost of moving goods domestically is up to five times higher than in the United States (Atkin and Donaldson 2015; Donaldson, Jinhage, and Verhoogen 2017). This difference has in part been attributed to a lack of competition (Teravaninthorn and Raballand 2008). Elsewhere, excessive competition can drive down the quality of transport services quality, with high road mortality, deteriorated roads, and poor vehicle quality.

- *Regulatory restrictions on services trade* can add to trade costs, even for goods trade. To a large extent, trade costs in the services sector reflect regulations which create entry barriers, such as licensing quotas. The OECD Service Trade Restrictions Index (STRI) measures *de jure* regulatory restrictions on services trade of different types in 44 countries for 2014-19 (figure 3.6). Like for goods trade, services trade remains more restricted in EMDEs than in advanced economies, especially with respect to the entry of foreign firms. Across regions, the most restrictive policies are applied by SAR and EAP, whereas countries in LAC tend to be more open.

Policies to lower trade costs

Menu of policy options. The literature suggests that high trade costs remain a considerable roadblock to trade. A menu of options is available to reduce trade costs at the border, between borders, and behind the border, as part of a broader package to return EMDEs to a green, resilient and inclusive development path (GRID; World Bank 2021d; OECD and WTO 2015). Some of these policies are under the sole control of country authorities (such as improving border and customs regulations and processes or facilitating shipping and logistics) while other policy changes require agreements with other country authorities (such as regional trade agreements). While some policies can be implemented quickly, others, such as increasing competition, can take years to pursue.

- Measures that lower trade costs at the border include trade facilitation (customs and border procedures) but also tariffs, and trade agreements.

- Measures that lower trade costs between borders include global road, port, air, communications and energy infrastructure and services networks.

- Measures that reduce trade costs behind the border include trade-related regulations and institutions; logistics and broader market governance; domestic transport infrastructure; market structure of domestic trucking and port operations; as well as nontariff barriers (e.g., standards and accreditation procedures for standards) and quotas.

Beyond policies to facilitate trade, complementary policies might also be needed to assure that the benefits are sustainable and widely shared.

At-the-border measures

Tariffs. Falling tariffs, often embedded in broader trade agreements, have contributed to rapid trade growth over the past three decades. However, tariffs have risen over the past five years as trade tensions mounted, raising concerns about a protectionist turn among some major economies (World Bank 2021a).

Trade agreements. The decline in trade costs over the past three decades has been supported by the introduction of regional trade agreements. In particular, the number of regional trade agreements more than quintupled between the early 1990s and the mid-2010s and these agreements have, over time, shifted focus from tariff cuts to lowering nontariff barriers (World Bank 2016). The largest trade agreement by the number of members, the African Continental Free Trade Area, for example, has been estimated to raise real incomes in its member countries mostly by lowering nontariff barriers to trade, rather than tariffs, and by implementing trade facilitation measures (World Bank 2020c). The two regional trade agreements in North America (USMCA) and Europe (European Union) alone cover more than 40 percent of global GDP (figure 3.7). Trade

FIGURE 3.7 Regional trade agreements

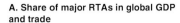

Countries engaged in regional trade agreements account for a large part of global GDP and, for some agreements, member countries' trade.

A. Share of major RTAs in global GDP and trade

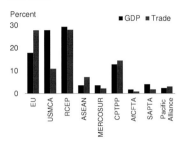

B. Intra-RTA trade

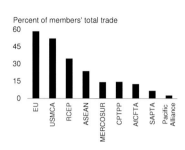

Sources: Comtrade (database); World Bank; World Trade Organization.
Note: RTAs are reciprocal trade agreements between two or more partners and include both free trade agreements and customs unions.
A.B. AfCFTA = African Continental Free Trade Area; ASEAN = Association of South East;
CPTPP = Comprehensive and Progressive Agreement for Trans-Pacific Partnership;
EU = European Union; MERCOSUR = Southern Common Market; RCEP = Regional Comprehensive Economic Partnership; SAPTA = South Asian Preferential Trading Arrangement; USMCA = United States–Mexico–Canada Agreement.

agreements have fostered domestic reforms in EMDEs and have generated their own momentum for greater liberalization and expansion (Baccini and Urpelainen 2014a, 2014b; Baldwin and Jaimovich 2010).

Border processes. In addition to the direct costs of tariffs, a multitude of indirect costs are imposed by administrative border and customs procedures (Moïsé and Le Bris 2013). In the average EMDE, it takes 56-67 hours to comply with border documentation for exports and imports and another 64-83 hours to comply with border processes more broadly—significantly longer than in the average advanced economy (figure 3.8). In the average EMDE, these compliance costs are two to four times those in the average advanced economy.

Trade facilitation. The WTO Agreement on Trade Facilitation (WTO TFA), which was adopted in 2014 and has been ratified by more than 90 percent of WTO members, provides a framework to streamline inefficient control and clearance procedures of border authorities, unnecessary border formalities, and opaque administrative cost. Seventy percent of commitments included in the agreement have been implemented to date. For example, in West

FIGURE 3.8 Customs and border procedures

Customs and borders procedures are considerably more burdensome in EMDEs than in advanced economies but have declined over time in both country groups.

A. Time to comply with import requirements

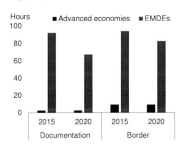

B. Trade facilitation index

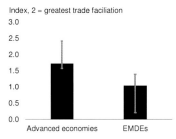

Sources: Organisation for Economic Co-operation and Development; World Bank.

Note: EMDEs = emerging market and developing economies.

A. Unweighted average for 39 advanced economies and 147 EMDEs.

B. Unweighted average for 36 advanced economies and 122 EMDEs. Trade facilitation index is an unweighted average of 11 subindices, all scored on a scale of 0-2. The indices score countries on information availability, trade consultations, advance rulings, appeals procedures for administrative decisions by border agencies, fees and charges on imports and exports, simplicity of trade document requirements, automation of border procedures and documentation, simplicity of border procedures, cooperation between domestic agencies, cooperation with neighboring agencies, and governance and impartiality. The data is collected from publicly available sources, country submissions, and private sector feedback. Orange wiskers indicate minimum and maximum range.

Africa, an initiative is underway to cut trade costs by electronically sharing customs transit data (World Bank 2021e). Guatemala and Honduras have reduced the time for traders to cross the border from 10 hours to 7 minutes by integrating their trade procedures and replacing duplicative processes with a single online instrument (de Moran 2018). Progress has been uneven, however, with less than 40 percent of commitments implemented in low-income countries.

Between-the-border measures

Global connectivity and market structure. High-quality and well-maintained transport infrastructure—at ports, airports, on land and in the hinterland—and efficient global shipping services lower logistics costs. Where bribes and transport monopolies are common, they also drive up trade costs. For example, in a pilot study of four African countries, responses from more than two-thirds of survey respondents suggest that bribery to accelerate transport services was common (Christie, Smith, and Conroy 2013). Efforts to

control corruption and to encourage competition can help lower transport costs. Policies that strengthen regional integration can also be beneficial, particularly in the case of small countries and these that are geographically isolated from trade hubs. Coupled with regional institutions that help thin borders, regional infrastructures can enable countries to exploit the benefits of regional and global trade networks (Deichmann and Gill 2008).

Lower search cost. That said, even in a competitive, well-governed environment, efforts to improve the match between trucking service providers and shippers can help reduce trade costs by reducing wait times and empty backhauls. Such efforts can, in particular, leverage information and communication infrastructure and services for timely information about shipping capacity and schedules that allows exporters and shippers with available capacity to be matched more efficiently. In addition, deeper regional trade agreements can also lower transport-related trade costs (Brenton, Portugal-Perez, and Regolo 2014).

Behind-the-border measures

Regulations and standards. Although not separately included in the empirical exercise above for lack of data, behind-the-border policies such as regulations, standards, inspection requirements, and labelling requirements, can impose considerable costs (Moïsé and Le Bris 2013). In Central America, sanitary and phytosanitary requirements, such as inspection requirements or labeling standards for meats and grains, have been estimated to raise import prices by about 30 percent on average (OECD and WTO 2015). Harmonization of standards can significantly increase trade, but (smaller) gains can also be achieved by mutual recognition of standards or conformity assessments (Chen and Mattoo 2008; World Bank 2016).

Taxation. Beyond standards, a shift in taxation away from trade-based taxation to income-based or consumption-based taxation can further lower barriers to trading. In middle- and high-income EMDEs, such a shift has not been associated with lasting revenue losses, but such losses have materialized in low-income countries (Baunsgaard and Keen 2010).

Global value chain participation. High transport costs, in part, reflect unbalanced trade flows since shipping at full capacity in both directions of a route is less costly than empty backhauls (Ishikawa and Tarui 2018). At any one time, two-fifths of ships have been estimated to carry no cargo (Brancaccio, Kalouptsidi, and Papageorgiou 2020). Over the longer term, and in a favorable business environment more broadly, increased global value chain participation can expand the volume of both exports and imports and thus help lower shipping costs.

Comprehensive reform packages

Country examples of reforms. Some of the most successful reform programs have covered a wide range of policies. In Cambodia, a combination of customs and border improvements, regulatory reform, and streamlined import and export procedures helped the country to leap 46 rankings on the Logistics Performance Indicators between 2010 and 2014 (World Bank 2018). In Africa's Great Lakes region, improved trade and commercial infrastructure in the border areas and simplified border crossing procedures have been credited with greater accountability of officials, declining rates of harassment at key borders (from 78 percent to 45 percent of survey respondents in South Kivu), extended border opening hours, increased trade flows, and a doubling of border crossings (World Bank 2021e).

Impact on trade cost of a hypothetical reform package. The empirical results above can be applied to a hypothetical comprehensive reform scenario. In particular, one can focus on those country pairs that average in the bottom quartile of the logistics performance index, the liner shipping connectivity index, and the *Doing Business* index for ease of trading. Three-quarters of these EMDEs are located in Sub-Saharan Africa. The coefficient estimated from the panel estimation suggest that an improvement in the average logistics performance, shipping connectivity, and border processes among these country pairs to the top quartile of the distribution of

FIGURE 3.9 Impact of policy improvements on trade costs

Better logistics, shipping connectivity, and border and customs processes could help lower trade costs by one-half in the quartile of EMDEs that score worst on these indicators.

A. Reduction in overall trade costs associated with policy improvements

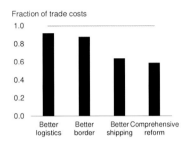

B. Reduction in manufacturing trade costs associated with policy improvements

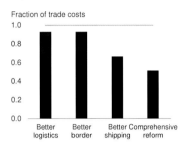

Source: World Bank.
Note: EMDEs = emerging market and developing economies.
A.B. Bars show the fraction of trade costs that would remain after policy improvements. Policy improvements assume that the average EMDE in the quartile of EMDEs with the poorest score for liner shipping connectivity index (LSCI), logistics performance index (LPI) or Doing Business "trading across borders" improves to match the score of the average EMDE in the quartile of EMDEs with the best score for liner shipping connectivity index (LSCI), logistics performance index (LPI) or Doing Business "trading across borders". The comprehensive package assumes that all three scores are improved simultaneously. Data refer to 2018. Gray line indicates 1 for unchanged trade costs in 2018 among the sample of EMDEs scoring in the poorest quartile on these indicators.

country pairs would halve their trade cost (figure 3.9).

Priority area for lowering trade costs: Medical equipment. At the current juncture, to ensure that the current global recovery broadens to EMDEs, one area in particular requires priority action to lower trade costs: medical equipment. Global vaccine production is concentrated in a small number of countries and these rely heavily on supply chains that span the globe. During 2017-19, vaccine producing nations sourced 88 percent of their key vaccine ingredients from other vaccine producing trading partners (Evenett et al. 2021). Export bans and other restrictions, such as those newly introduced on medical equipment in 2020-2021 in 80 countries and of which more than half are still in place, threaten to disrupt vaccine production globally (Global Trade Alert 2020; WTO 2020). To bring the pandemic under control, removing obstacles to trade in medical equipment is a priority.

Reforms to lower services trade costs. As manufacturers access services to produce and export goods, policies aimed at lowering trade costs in the services sector can help lower costs of trading goods. Opening services markets to more competition remains important for reducing trade costs, including in road and rail transport services and shipping. Liberal bilateral air services agreements can help lower trade costs for many goods that form part of global value chains or high value-added agricultural goods.

Reforms for improved agricultural trade. Due to their perishable nature, measures that accelerate the movement of agricultural traded goods are particularly important (USAID 2019). The WTO TFA includes several provisions aimed at making agricultural trade faster and more predictable, such as simplified and more efficient requirements regarding risk-based document verifications, physical inspections, and laboratory testing. In a Single Window, a single authority can reduce the amount of redundant and duplicated paperwork by processing all documents and coordinating with other relevant agencies to (UNESCAP 2011). Improved storage facilities can reduce spoilage and losses in perishable agricultural goods (UNESCAP 2017; Webber and Labaste 2010). Tracking and monitoring technologies can help accelerate paperwork and monitor environmental conditions (Beghin and Schweizer 2020). Such measures to lower agricultural trade costs can also help address prevent or reduce food insecurity.

Reforms to mitigate environmental and distributional impacts. A comprehensive package would also take into account the potential environmental degradation and distributional consequences that have been associated with trade.

- *Distributional impacts.* The failure of some firms participating in global value chains to pass costs reductions on to consumers and the declining share of labor income in countries integrated in global value chains have contributed to the perception of unequally shared gains from trade (World Bank 2020a). Conversely, growing services trade, global supply chains and digitalization have offered new economic opportunities to women (World Bank and WTO 2020). Going forward, labor market policies that can help share gains from global value chain participation more broadly include policies to

facilitate labor mobility with active labor market programs and wage insurance schemes (World Bank 2020b).

- *Environmental impacts.* In some countries, entry into global value chains in manufacturing has been accompanied by greater carbon dioxide emissions and global value chains have contributed to greater waste and increased shipping (World Bank 2020a). Shipping accounts for 7 percent of global carbon dioxide emissions and 15 percent of global sulfur dioxide and nitrogen oxides (World Bank 2020a). Being heavily concentrated in the electronics sector, global value chains have also contributed to e-waste which accounts for more than 70 percent of toxic waste in U.S. landfills (World Bank 2020a). Policies, such as eco-friendly industrial parks and community-based tourism, can encourage environmentally friendlier business practices (World Bank 2020b). Measures that price environmental degradation can help improve resource allocation while reducing CO_2 emissions (World Bank 2020b).

Leveraging digital technologies. Digital technologies may eventually lower trade costs behind the border, at the border, and between borders, including by improving transparency and price discovery as well as the information flow between exporters, shippers, and country authorities.[10] This may particularly support global supply chains. Robotics can help accelerate port procedures. Artificial intelligence can help lower logistics costs by optimizing route planning, storage and inventory, as well as improving tracking and monitoring; 3D printing can help shorten supply chains and localize supply chains, thus reducing the environmental footprint of trade; blockchain technology can help reduce time spent in customs, especially for time-sensitive goods, facilitate cross-border payments by increasing transparency and credibility, and enhance information sharing within supply chains (Fan, Weitz, and Lam 2019;

---

[10] Conversely, greater digitization in cross-border trade will create its own challenges, including to enforce value added tax payments if digitization makes ever smaller payment transactions profitable (World Bank 2021c).

WTO 2018). Such technologies may disproportionately benefit small and medium-sized enterprises that currently face larger trade costs than large enterprises.

Conclusion

Despite a decline over the past two decades, trade costs are high. In EMDEs, they amount to the equivalent of a 100 percent tariff, i.e., they double the price of a traded good over a similar domestic good. Trade costs are on average about four-fifths high on agricultural goods as on manufacturing goods and almost one-half higher in EMDEs than in advanced economies.

Trade costs have a wide range of sources. The bulk of these costs are caused by transport and domestic market conditions as well as regulatory and administrative practices; tariffs account for only about one-fourteenth of trade costs. In fact, about one-third of the difference in trade costs between EMDEs and advanced economies reflects the effects of impediments to logistics and shipping, and another one-third trade policy, incuding trade policy uncertainty.

Comprehensive packages of reforms have often been successful in reducing trade costs. Such a package can include trade facilitation measures as well as agreements for deeper trade integration and coordinated efforts to streamline trade procedures and processes at and behind the border, improved domestic infrastructure, increased competitiveness in shipping and logistics, reduced corruption, simplified trade-related procedures and regulations, and easier compliance with standards. Many of these reforms, especially those relating to the business climate and governance, would stimulate private, trade-intensive investment and output growth more broadly.

TABLE 3.1 Data employed in the panel regression

Data	Definition	Source
Trade costs	Logarithm of the geometric average of country i's and j's bilateral trade costs	UNESCAP-WB Trade Costs Database
Tariff rates	Logarithm of the geometric average of country i's and j's bilateral tariff rates	UNESCAP-WB Trade Costs Database
Regional trade agreement (RTA)	Dummy variable equal to unity if countries i and j share a common RTA	CEPII
Common border	Dummy variable equal to unity if countries i and j share a common land border (adjacency).	CEPII
Common language	Dummy variable equal to unity if countries i and j share a common language	CEPII
Distance	Logarithm	CEPII
Logistic Performance Index	Logarithm of the geometric average of country i's and j's scores	World Bank
Liner Shipping Connectivity Index	Logarithm of the geometric average of country i's and j's scores	World Bank
Ease of doing business. Trading across borders score	Logarithm of the geometric average of country i's and j's score indicators	WB Doing Business Database
Proxy of trade policy uncertainty	Logarithm of the geometric average of the country i's and j's gap between bounded and applied tariff rates	World Development Indicators Database

Source: World Bank.

TABLE 3.2 Panel regression results

	All sectors	Manufacturing sector
Liner Shipping Connectivity Index	-0.2329*** (0.007)	-0.2281** (0.007)
Logistics Performance Index	-0.3708*** (0.334)	-0.3849*** (0.036)
Ease of trading	-0.1993*** (0.014)	-0.1983*** (0.166)
Tariffs	0.2897*** (0.042)	
Manufacturing tariffs		0.3495*** (0.053)
Regional trade agreement membership	-0.0485*** (0.056)	-0.0535*** (0.007)
Trade policy uncertainty	0.0783 (0.048)	0.0748 (0.005)
Distance	0.2533*** (0.069)	0.2630*** (0.007)
Common border	-0.4197*** (0.034)	-0.4222*** (0.036)
Common language	-0.1660*** (0.013)	-0.1745*** (0.014)
Sample	50,370	49,754
R²	0.53656	0.5646

Source: World Bank.
Note: * p<0.05, ** p<0.01, ***p<0.001, robust standard errors are shown in parenthesis. The table shows estimated coefficients from a gravity panel regression estimated for 86 countries using annual data for 2007-2018 where the dependent variable is the log of bilateral trade costs. The regression includes time fixed effects. Standard errors are clustered by country pairs.

References

Anderson, J. E., and E. Van Wincoop. 2003. "Gravity with Gravitas: A Solution to the Border Puzzle." *American Economic Review* 93 (1): 170-192.

Anderson, J. E., and E. Van Wincoop. 2004. "Trade Costs." *Journal of Economic Literature* 42 (3): 691-751.

Antras, P., and D. Chor. 2021. "Global Value Chains." Discussion Paper 15908, Center for Economic Policy Research, London.

Arvis, J.-F., B. Shepherd, Y. Duval, and C. Utoktham. 2013. "Trade Costs and Development: A New Data Set." *Economic Premise* series 104: 1-4, World Bank, Washington, DC.

Arvis, J.-F., Y. Duval, B. Shepherd, C. Utoktham, and A. Raj. 2016. "Trade Costs in the Developing World: 1996-2010." *World Trade Review* 15 (3): 451-474.

Atkin, D., and D. Donaldson. 2015. "Who's Getting Globalized? The Size and Implications of Intra-National Trade Costs." NBER Working Paper 21439, National Bureau of Economic Research, Cambridge, MA.

Baccini, L., and J. Urpelainen. 2014a. "Before Ratification: Understanding the Timing of International Treaty Effects on Domestic Policies." *International Studies Quarterly* 58 (1): 29-43.

Baccini, L., and J. Urpelainen. 2014b. "International Institutions and Domestic Politics: Can Preferential Trading Agreements Help Leaders Promote Economic Reform?" *Journal of Politics* 76 (1): 195-214.

Baldwin, R., and D. Jaimovich. 2010. "Are Free Trade Agreements Contagious?" NBER Working Paper 16084, National Bureau of Economic Research, Cambridge, MA.

Baunsgaard, T., and M. Keen. 2010. "Tax Revenue and (or?) Trade Liberalization." *Journal of Public Economics* 94 (9-10): 563-577.

Beghin, J. C., and H. Schweizer. 2020. "Agricultural Trade Costs." *Applied Economic Perspectives and Policy* 43 (2): 500-530.

Benz, S. 2017. "Services Trade Costs: Tariff Equivalents of Services Trade Restrictions Using Gravity Estimation" OECD Trade Policy Paper 200, Organisation for Economic Co-operation and Development, Paris.

Bergstrand, J. H., M. Larch, and Y. V. Yotov. 2015. "Economic Integration Agreements, Border Effects, and Distance Elasticities in the Gravity Equation." *European Economic Review* 78 (C): 307-327.

Brancaccio, G., M. Kalouptsidi, and T. Papageorgiou. 2020. "Geography, Transportation, and Endogenous Trade Costs." *Econometrica* 88 (2): 657-691.

Brenton, P., A. Portugal-Perez, and J. Regolo. 2014. "Food Prices, Road Infrastructure, and Market Integration in Central and Eastern Africa." Policy Research Working Paper 7003, World Bank, Washington, DC.

Broda, C., and D. E. Weinstein. 2006. "Globalization and the Gains from Variety." *The Quarterly Journal of Economics* 121 (2): 541-585.

Bussière, M., C. Callegari, F. Ghironi, G. Sestieri, and N. Yamano. 2013. "Estimating Trade Elasticities: Demand Elasticities and the Trade Collapse of 2008-09." *American Economic Journal: Macroeconomics* 5 (3): 118-51.

Cabrillac, B., A. Al-Haschimi, O. Babecká Kucharčuková, A. Borin, M. Bussière, R. Cezar, A. Derviz, D. Dimitropoulou, L. Ferrara, and G. Gächter. 2016. "Understanding the Weakness in Global Trade—What is the New Normal?" Occasional Paper Series 178, European Central Bank, Frankfurt.

Caldara, D., M. Iacoviello, P. Molligo, A. Prestipino, and A. Raffo. 2020. "The Economic Effects of Trade Policy Uncertainty." *Journal of Monetary Economics* 110 (January): 38-59.

Cali, M., and D. W. Te Velde. 2011. "Does Aid for Trade Really Improve Trade Performance?" *World Development* 39 (5): 725-740.

Carroll, D. R., and S. Hur. 2020. "On the Heterogeneous Welfare Gains and Losses from Trade." *Journal of Monetary Economics* 109 (C): 1-16.

Chen, M. X., and A. Mattoo. 2008. "Regionalism in Standards: Good or Bad for Trade?" *Canadian Journal of Economics/Revue canadienne d'économique* 41 (3): 838-863.

Chen, N., and D. Novy. 2011. "Gravity, Trade Integration, and Heterogeneity across Industries." *Journal of International Economics* 85 (2): 206-221.

Christie, A., D. Smith, and K. Conroy. 2013. "Transport Governance Indicators in Sub-Saharan Africa." Sub-Saharan Africa Transport Policy Program Working Paper 95, World Bank, Washington, DC.

Comtrade (database). United Nations. Accessed May 25, 2021. https://comtrade.un.org.

Constantinescu, C., A. Mattoo, and M. Ruta. 2015. "The Global Trade Slowdown: Cyclical or Structural?" Policy Research Working Paper 7158, World Bank, Washington DC.

Coulibaly, B. S., and K. Foda. 2020. "The Future of Global Manufacturing." *Up Front* (blog), Brookings Institution, March 4, 2020. https://www.brookings.edu/blog/up-front/2020/03/04/the-future-of-global-manufacturing.

de Moran, M. A. 2018. "Customs Union Between Guatemala and Honduras, from 10 hours to 15 Minutes!" *Latin America and Caribbean* (blog), World Bank, April 2, 2018. https://blogs.worldbank.org/latinamerica/customs-union-between-guatemala-and-honduras-10-hours-15-minutes.

de Sousa, J. 2012. "The Currency Union Effect on Trade is Decreasing Over Time." *Economics Letters* 117 (3): 917-920.

Deichmann, U., and I. Gill. 2008. "The Economic Geography of Regional Integration." *Finance and Development* 45 (4): 45-47.

Doing Business (database). World Bank. Accessed May 25, 2021. https://www.doingbusiness.org.

Djankov, S., C. Freund, and C. S. Pham. 2010. "Trading on Time." *The Review of Economics and Statistics* 92 (1): 166-173.

Donaldson, D., A. Jinhage, and E. Verhoogen. 2017. "Beyond Borders: Making Transport Work for African Trade." IGC Growth Brief 009, International Growth Centre, London.

Dutt, P., and D. Traca. 2010. "Corruption and Bilateral Trade Flows: Extortion or Evasion?" *The Review of Economics and Statistics* 92 (4): 843-860.

Espitia, A., A. Mattoo, N. Rocha, M. Ruta, and D. Winkler. 2021. "Pandemic Trade: COVID-19, Remote Work and Global Value Chains." Policy Research Working Paper 9508, World Bank, Washington, DC.

Evenett, S., B. M. Hoeckman, N. Rocha, and M. Ruta. 2021. "The COVID-19 Vaccine Production Club: Will Value Chains Temper Nationalism?" Policy Research Working Paper 9565, World Bank, Washington DC.

Evenett, S., M. Fiorini, J. Fritz, B. Hoekman, P. Lukaszuk, N. Rocha, M. Ruta, F. Santi, Filippo, and A. Shingal. 2020. "Trade Policy Responses to the COVID-19 Pandemic Crisis: Evidence from a New Data Set." Policy Research Working Paper 9498, World Bank, Washington, DC.

Fan, C. F., A. Weitz, and Y. Lam. 2019. "Blockchain is Already Transforming Trade and Logistics—And That's Just the Beginning!" *Transport for Development* (blog), World Bank, June 6, 2019. https:// blogs.worldbank.org/transport/blockchain-already-trans forming-trade-and-logistics-and-thats-just-beginning.

Fieler, A. C., M. Eslava, and D. Y. Xu. 2018. "Trade, Quality Upgrading, and Input Linkages: Theory and Evidence from Colombia." *American Economic Review* 108 (1): 109-46.

Freund, C., A. Mattoo; A. Mulabdic; M. Ruta. 2020. "The Supply Chain Shock from COVID-19: Risks and Opportunities." In *COVID-19 in Developing Economies* 1 (1), edited by S. Djankov and U. Panizza, 303-315. London: Centre for Economic Policy Research.

Freund, C., and N. Rocha. 2011. "What Constrains Africa's Exports?" *World Bank Economic Review* 25 (3): 361-386.

Global Trade Alert. 2020. *21st Century Tracking of Pandemic-Era Trade and Investment Policies in Food and Medical Products.* Geneva: Global Trade Alert.

Gopinath, G., P.-O. Gourinchas, Ch.-T. Hsieh, and N. Li. 2011. "International Prices, Costs, and Markup Differences." *American Economic Review* 101 (6): 2450-86.

Gurevich T., and P. Herman. 2018. "The Dynamic Gravity Dataset: 1948-2016." USITC Working Paper 2018-02-A, U.S. International Trade Commission, Washington DC.

Henry, M., R. Kneller, and C. Milner. 2009. "Trade, Technology Transfer and National Efficiency in Developing Countries." *European Economic Review* 53 (2): 237-254.

Hillberry, R., and X. Zhang. 2015. "Policy and Performance in Customs: Evaluating the Trade Facilitation Agreement." Policy Research Working Paper 7211, World Bank, Washington, DC.

Hou, Y., Y. Wang, and W. Xue. 2021. "What Explains Trade costs? Institutional Quality and Other Determinants." *Review of Development Economics* 25 (1): 478-499.

Hummels, D., P. Minor, M. Reisman, and E. Endean. 2007. "Calculating Tariff Equivalents of Time in Trade." Nathan Associates Inc. for review by the United States Agency for International Development, Washington, DC.

IMF (International Monetary Fund). 2021. *World Economic Outlook: Managing Divergent Recoveries.* April. Washington, DC: International Monetary Fund.

Ishikawa, J., and N. Tarui. 2018. "Backfiring with Backhaul Problems: Trade and Industrial Policies with Endogenous Transport Costs." *Journal of International Economics* 111 (March): 81-98.

Kee, H. L., and A. Nicita. 2016. "Trade Frauds, Trade Elasticities, and Non-Tariff Measures." 5th IMF-World Bank-WTO Joint Trade Research Workshop, November 30, Washington, DC.

Kose, M. A., F. Ohnsorge, Y. Lei, and I. Ergys, 2017. "Weakness in Investment Growth: Causes, Implications and Policy Responses." Policy Research Working Paper 7990, World Bank, Washington, DC.

Marti, L., and R. Puertas. 2019. "Factors Determining the Trade Costs of Major European Exporters." *Maritime Economics and Logistics* 21 (3): 324-333.

Miroudot, S., J. Sauvage, and B. Shepherd. 2010. "Measuring the Cost of International Trade in Services." MPRA Paper 27655, University Library of Munich, Germany.

Moïsé, E., and F. Le Bris. 2013. "Trade Costs—What Have We Learned?: A Synthesis Report." OECD Trade Policy Papers 150, Organisation for Economic Co-operation and Development, Paris.

Moïsé, E., and S. Sorescu. 2013. "Trade Facilitation Indicators: The Potential Impact of Trade Facilitation on Developing Countries' Trade." OECD Trade Policy Paper 144, Organisation for Economic Co-operation and Development, Paris.

Moïsé, E., T. Orliac, and P. Minor. 2011. "Trade Facilitation Indicators: The Impact on Trade costs," Trade Policy Paper 118, Organisation for Economic Co-operation and Development, Paris.

Niu, Z., C. Liu, S. Gunessee, and C. Milner. 2018. "Non-Tariff and Overall Protection: Evidence Across Countries and Over Time." *Review of World Economics* 154 (4): 675-703.

Novy, D. 2010. "Trade Costs and the Open Macroeconomy." *Scandinavian Journal of Economics* 112 (3): 514-545.

Novy, D. 2013. "Gravity Redux: Measuring International Trade Costs with Panel Data." *Economic Inquiry* 51 (1): 101-121.

OECD (Organisation for Economic Co-operation and Development). 2018. *Trade in Value Added Database.* Paris: OECD Publishing.

OECD (Organisation for Economic Co-operation and Development) and WTO (World Trade Organization). 2015. "Why Trade Costs Matter for Inclusive, Sustainable Growth." In *Aid for Trade at a Glance 2015: Reducing Trade Costs for Inclusive, Sustainable Growth.* Paris: OECD Publishing.

Osnago, A., R. Piermartini, and N. Rocha. 2015. "Trade Policy Uncertainty as Barrier to Trade." WTO Staff Working Paper ERSD-2015-05, World Trade Organization, Geneva.

Osnago, A., R. Piermartini, and N. Rocha. 2018. "The Heterogeneous Effects of Trade Policy Uncertainty: How Much Do Trade Commitments Boost Trade?" Policy Research Working Paper 8567, World Bank, Washington, DC.

Sadikov, A. 2007. "Border and Behind-the-Border Trade Barriers and Country Exports." IMF Working Papers 2007/292, International Monetary Fund.

Santos Silva, J., and S. Tenreyro. 2006. "The Log of Gravity." *Review of Economics and Statistics* 88 (4): 641-658.

Saurav, A., P. Kusek, R. Kuo, and B. Viney. 2020. "The Impact of COVID-19 on Foreign Investors: Evidence from the Second Round of a Global Pulse Survey." World Bank, Washington, DC.

Staboulis, C., D. Natos, E. Tsakiridou, and K. Mattas. 2020. "International Trade Costs in OECD Countries." *Operational Research* 20 (3): 1177-1187.

Teravaninthorn, S., and G. Raballand. 2008. *Transport Prices and Costs in Africa: A Review of the International Corridors.* Washington, DC: World Bank.

UNESCAP (United Nations Economic and Social Commission for Asia and the Pacific). 2011. "Facilitating Agricultural Trade in Asia and the Pacific." *Studies in Trade and Investment* 74, United Nations, New York.

UNESCAP (United Nations Economic and Social Commission for Asia and the Pacific). 2017. "Tackling Agricultural Trade Costs in Asia and the Pacific." United Nations, New York.

USAID (United States Agency for International Development). 2019. *Assessing the Benefits of the Trade Facilitation Agreement for Agricultural Trade.* Washington, DC: USAID.

Webber, C. M., and P. Labaste. 2010. *Building Competitiveness in Africa's Agriculture.* Washington, DC: World Bank.

World Bank. 2009. *World Development Report: Reshaping Economic Geography.* Washington, DC: World Bank.

World Bank. 2015. *Global Economic Prospects: Having Fiscal Space and Using It.* January. Washington, DC: World Bank.

World Bank. 2016. *Global Economic Prospects: Spillovers amid Weak Growth.* January. Washington, DC: World Bank.

World Bank. 2017. *Global Economic Prospects: Weak Investment in Uncertain Times.* January. Washington, DC: World Bank.

World Bank. 2018. *Cambodia: Trade Facilitation and Competitiveness.* Washington, DC: World Bank.

World Bank. 2019. *Global Economic Prospects: Heightened Tensions, Subdued Investment.* June. Washington, DC: World Bank.

World Bank. 2020a. *World Development Report: Trading for Development in the Age of Global Value Chains.* Washington, DC: World Bank.

World Bank. 2020b. *Rebuilding Tourism Competitiveness. Tourism Response, Recovery and the Covid-19 Crisis.* Washington, DC: World Bank.

World Bank. 2020c. *The African Continental Free Trade Area: Economic and Distributional Effects.* Washington, DC: World Bank.

World Bank. 2021a. *Global Economic Prospects.* January. Washington, DC: World Bank.

World Bank. 2021b. "Sunny Skies Behind, Trouble Ahead." COVID-19 Trade Watch #11, World Bank, Washington.

World Bank. 2021c. "Creating Value in the Data Economy: The Role of Competition, Trade, and Tax Policy" In *World Development Report 2021.* Washington, DC: World Bank.

World Bank. 2021d. "From COVID-19 Crisis Response to Resilient Recovery: Saving Lives and Livelihoods while Supporting Green, Resilient and

Inclusive Development (GRID)." World Bank, Washington, DC.

World Bank. 2021e. *Implementation Status and Results Report: AFR RI-Great Lakes Trade Facilitation.* Washington, DC: World Bank.

World Bank. 2021f. *World Development Report: Data for Better Lives.* Washington, DC: World Bank.

World Bank and WTO (World Trade Organization). 2018. *Trade and Poverty Reduction: New Evidence of Impacts in Developing Countries.* Washington, DC: World Bank.

World Bank and WTO (World Trade Organization). 2020. *Women and Trade: The Role of Trade in Promoting Gender Equality.* Washington, DC: World Bank.

World Bank and UNCTAD (United Nations Conference on Trade and Development). 2018. *The Unseen Impact of Non-Tariff Measures: Evidence from a New Database.* Washington, DC: World Bank.

World Economic Forum and World Bank. 2013. *Enabling Trade: Valuing Growth Opportunities.* World Economic Forum, Geneva.

WTO (World Trade Organization). 2015. *World Trade Report: Speeding up Trade: Benefits and Challenges of Implementing the WTO Trade Facilitation Agreement.* Geneva: World Trade Organization.

WTO (World Trade Organization). 2018. *World Trade Report: The Future of World Trade: How Digital Technologies are Transforming Global Commerce,* Geneva: World Trade Organization.

WTO (World Trade Organization). 2020. *Export Prohibitions and Restrictions: Information Note.* April. Geneva: World Trade Organization.

Yotov, Y.V. 2012. "A Simple Solution to the Distance Puzzle in International Trade." *Economic Letters* 117 (3): 794-798.

Zhan, J., R. Balwijn, B. Casella, and A. S. Santos-Paulino. 2020. "Global Value Chain Transformation to 2030: Overall Direction and Policy Implications." VoxEU.org, CEPR Policy Portal, August 13, https://voxeu.org/article/global-value-chain-transformation-decade-ahead.

CHAPTER 4

EMERGING INFLATION PRESSURES

Cause for Alarm?

After declining in the first half of 2020, global inflation has rebounded quickly on recovering activity. While global inflation is likely to continue rising in the remainder of this year, inflation is expected to remain within target bands in most inflation-targeting countries. Among emerging market and developing economies (EMDEs) where recent price pressures may raise inflation above those economies' target ranges, such pressures may not warrant a monetary policy response—provided they are temporary and inflation expectations remain well-anchored. However, higher inflation may complicate the policy choices of EMDEs that are in danger of persistently breaching their inflation targets while also relying on expansionary policies to ensure a durable recovery. Measures to strengthen central bank credibility can help anchor inflation expectations in these economies. Unless risks from record-high debt are addressed, EMDEs remain vulnerable to financial market stress should investor risk sentiment deteriorate as a result of actual or perceived inflation pressures in advanced economies. Low-income countries are likely to experience rising aggregate and food price inflation in the remainder of this year, exacerbating food insecurity and threatening to increase poverty. Attempts to control food prices through price subsidies in many countries, or the re-emergence of protectionist policies could drive global prices higher and prove to be self-defeating.

Introduction

The COVID-19 pandemic plunged the global economy into its deepest recession since the Second World War (World Bank 2020a; 2021a). Amid a collapse in demand and plunging oil prices, global consumer price inflation declined by 0.9 percentage point between January and May 2020, and this decline was about one-third more pronounced in inflation in advanced economies than in EMDEs.

Since May 2020, however, inflation has gradually picked up. By April 2021, inflation had risen above pre-pandemic levels, in both advanced economies and EMDEs. The inflation pickup was broad-based and present in about four-fifths of countries, although the change in inflation varied widely, especially in EMDEs.

The 2020 global recession featured the most muted inflation decline and fastest subsequent inflation upturn of the five global recession episodes of the past 50 years (box 4.1). While this behavior partly reflects lower levels of inflation at the beginning of 2020, purchasing managers report growing pressures on input as well as output prices in 2021 (figure 4.1). Looking ahead, as the global economy gradually reopens, monetary and fiscal policies continue to be accommodative to support the global recovery, and pent-up demand may be about to be

FIGURE 4.1 Price trends

Firms report rising input as well as output prices.

A. Composite PMI: Output prices

Index, >50=Expansion
—Advanced economies —EMDEs

B. Composite PMI: Input prices

Index, >50=Expansion
—Advanced economies —EMDEs

Sources: Haver Analytics; World Bank.
Note: Subcomponent of composite purchasing managers index (PMI) for emerging markets ("EMDEs") and developed markets ("Advanced economies") for output prices and input prices. An index above 50 indicates price increases.

unleashed in advanced economies.[1] For major advanced economies, some have raised concerns that this confluence of factors may generate significant inflationary pressures (Blanchard and Pisani-Ferry 2020; Goodhart and Pradhan 2020; Landau 2021). Others, in contrast, see little reason for concern, at least for many advanced economies, because of the temporary nature of price pressures over the short-term as well as well-anchored inflation expectations and structural

---

Note: This chapter was prepared by Jongrim Ha, M. Ayhan Kose, and Franziska Ohnsorge.

---

[1] In the United States, CPI inflation has risen steadily since May 2020 to 4.2 percent in April 2021. In the euro area, inflation has risen since November 2020 and is now near the 2 percent target. Reflecting the recent inflation developments, short-term inflation expectations have also risen. In the United States, inflation expectations for 2021 are now at 2.8 percent, and in the euro area, they have risen to 1.7 percent with the inflation expectations above 2 percent in some economies (Czech Republic, Germany, and Norway). Medium-term inflation expectations, however, remain anchored around 2 percent.

factors still depressing inflation (Ball et al. 2021; Gopinath 2021).

If growing inflationary pressures cause financial market participants to become concerned about persistently higher inflation in advanced economies, they may reassess prospects for continued accommodative monetary policies by major central banks. This could trigger a significant rise in risk premia and borrowing costs. EMDEs are particularly vulnerable to such financial market disruptions because of their record high debt and a lagging economic recovery from the pandemic (chapter 1). In the event of financial market stress, sharp exchange rate depreciations and capital outflows may force them to abruptly tighten policies in a manner that could throttle their recoveries.

Even in the absence of dislocating financial market stress, EMDEs may face rising inflation as global price pressures feed into domestic inflation through input prices and exchange rate movements. A temporary increase in inflation may not warrant a monetary policy response. Again, if rapidly rising price pressures risk de-anchoring inflation expectations, EMDE central banks may be forced to tighten monetary policy before the recovery is fully entrenched.

Persistently higher inflation would erode discretionary incomes of the poorest households and may tip some back into poverty (Ha, Kose, and Ohnsorge 2019). This is a particularly serious risk for low-income countries (LICs; box 4.2). Since food accounts for a substantial share of consumption in these countries, recent increase in food prices have led to higher inflation and compounded the challenges confronting the poor during the pandemic.

Against this background, this chapter first briefly examines the evolution of global inflation over the past five decades and then asks the following questions:

- What have been the main drivers of recent developments in global inflation?

- How does the evolution of inflation during the 2020 global recession compare with that in earlier global recessions?

- What are prospects for global inflation?

- What are the policy implications of higher inflation for EMDEs?

The chapter contributes to the literature in four dimensions. First, it expands on existing studies by putting recent inflation developments into a historical context, drawing on a large inflation database that spans more than 80 countries and multiple inflation measures. It is the first study to compare the evolution of inflation during the 2020 global recession with those during previous global recessions. Second, it analyzes the driving forces of global inflation focusing on the 2020 global recession. To this end, it employs two approaches: a factor-augmented vector auto-regression (FAVAR) model of global variables with a novel identification strategy, and an event study of global inflation around global recessions. Third, based on the discussion of various factors that determine inflation dynamics, and model-based conditional forecast, it examines prospects for inflation. Fourth, it discusses the policy implications of potentially growing inflationary pressures for EMDEs, including LICs. For the purposes of this chapter, inflation refers to year-on-year percent changes in headline consumer price index (CPI) inflation, but other inflation measures are also examined.

The main findings of the chapter are the following (figure 4.2).

- *Shorter-lived decline but faster increase in inflation.* The decline in inflation during the 2020 global recession was the most muted and shortest-lived of any of the five global recessions over the past 50 years. Similarly, the increase in inflation since May 2020, amid a rebound in oil prices and global demand has been faster than after previous recessions, including after the 2009 global recession.

- *Dominant role of global demand in driving inflation.* The decline in global inflation from January-May 2020 was four-fifths driven by the collapse in global demand and another one-fifth driven by plunging oil prices, with some offsetting inflationary pressures from supply disruptions. This contrasts with the

2009 global recession in which the 13-month decline in global inflation that was three-fifths driven by plunging oil prices and only one-third driven by the contraction in global demand. In their rebounds, however, inflation developments after the end of two global recessions resembled each other: both were virtually entirely driven by sharp increases in global demand.

- *Higher inflation in 2021 but stable short-term inflation expectations.* Model-based forecasts and current inflation expectations point to an increase in global inflation for 2021 as a whole of just over 1 percentage point. For virtually all advanced economies and one-half of inflation-targeting EMDEs, an increase of this magnitude would leave inflation within target ranges. However, for another one-half of inflation-targeting EMDEs, it would raise inflation above target ranges. If this increase is temporary and inflation expectations remain well-anchored, this may not warrant a monetary policy response. If, however, inflation expectations risk becoming unanchored, EMDE central banks may be compelled to tighten monetary policy more than would be appropriate for their economies' recoveries.

- *Low and stable inflation over the long term.* For now, long-term expectations point to continued low and stable inflation. However, several structural forces (demographic changes, global supply chains) that have depressed inflation over the past five decades are beginning to fade amid trade tensions, population aging, and investment and productivity weakness. As they recede, increases in short-term inflation may become more persistent and, thus, threaten the anchoring of long-term inflation expectations.

- *More pronounced challenges in LICs.* Inflation challenges are larger for LICs, partly because of pressures on food prices. In contrast to other EMDEs, inflation in LICs increased with the outbreak of COVID-19, largely as a result of food price increases. In the near term, further rises in global agricultural prices are likely to add to inflationary pressures in

FIGURE 4.2 **Inflationary pressures**

Following a modest decline during January-May 2020, global inflation has rebounded quickly. The inflation decline in early 2020 was more muted than after the 2007-09 global financial crisis, and it was also shorter-lived in part because of a faster recovery in global demand. Global inflation has declined and been low for several decades. Model-based forecasts are consistent with an inflation uptick in 2021 by just over 1 percentage point but this uptick may be short-lived. Long-term inflation expectations remain broadly unchanged.

A. CPI headline inflation, monthly

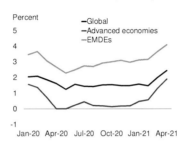

B. CPI headline inflation, annual

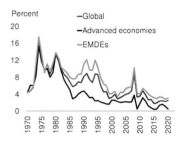

C. Contributions to monthly change in global headline CPI inflation: 2020-21

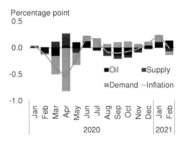

D. Global inflation in 2008-10 and 2020-21

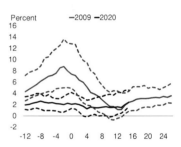

E. Model-based conditional forecast for global inflation

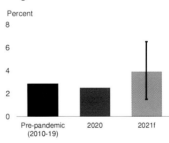

F. Inflation expectations: Five year ahead

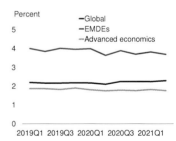

Sources: Haver Analytics; Consensus Economics; IMF World Economic Outlook; World Bank.
Note: Year-on-year inflation for 81 countries, of which 31 are advanced economies and 50 are EMDEs.
A. Median of year-on-year headline consumer price index (CPI) inflation in a sample of 81 countries.
B. Median of annual average headline CPI inflation in a sample of 155 countries.
C. Contributions to change in year-on-year headline consumer price inflation from the previous month for 81 countries, of which 31 are advanced economies and 50 are EMDEs, based on FAVAR estimation in annex 4.1. Monthly data. Unexplained residual is omitted from the graph.
D. Blue and red lines are medians, dotted lines are interquartile ranges. t=0 is September 2008 for 2009 and January 2020 for 2020.
E. Conditional forecast of global inflation based on quarterly FAVAR model of global inflation, global GDP growth, and oil price growth. Vertical line indicates 16-84 confidence bands. See annex 4.1 for details.
F. Median five-year-ahead consensus inflation expectations among 24 advanced economies and 23 EMDEs.

LICs. This, and potential pressures to finance large fiscal deficits can risk ingraining higher rates of inflation into expectations. Attempts to suppress food price inflation through price subsidies in many countries, or the re-emergence of protectionist policies, could drive global prices higher and prove to be self-defeating.

Global inflation before the pandemic

Inflation has been declining around the world over the past half century. Global inflation fell from 16.9 percent in 1974 to 2.3 percent in 2019, up from its lowest point on record of 1.8 percent in 2015 after a long slide in oil prices (figure 4.3).[2] In EMDEs, inflation declined from a peak of 17.5 percent in 1974 to 2.9 percent in 2019. In LICs, inflation fell from 25.2 percent in 1994 to 3.5 percent in 2019. The trend decline started earlier (in the mid-1980s) in advanced economies than in EMDEs and LICs (in the mid-1990s).

In EMDEs, this disinflation process cut across all regions, including those with a history of persistently high inflation, such as Latin America and the Caribbean and Sub-Saharan Africa. The downward trend was evident in all inflation measures, including headline CPI, core CPI, PPI, and GDP deflator inflation. By the early 2000s, the disinflation was largely completed, although it resumed after the global financial crisis at a milder pace.

The widely shared disinflation in advanced economies has been attributed partly to changes in monetary policy regimes, including the increased focus on price stability, which took hold during the early 1980s (Cecchetti et al. 2007; Levin and Piger 2004). Other factors may have included sounder fiscal policies, deregulation, globalization, growing global labor forces, and, in the 1990s, accelerating productivity growth in parts of the world (Goodhart and Pradhan 2020; Rogoff 2003).

In EMDEs, the introduction of inflation targeting, improvements in fiscal balances (prior to the 2007-09 financial crisis), greater exchange rate flexibility and macroeconomic stabilization programs helped lower inflation (Aizenman, Chinn, and Ito 2008; Mishkin and Schmidt-Hebbel 2007). Notwithstanding a pickup in the past 15 years, inflation expectations in EMDEs have become better-anchored and less responsive to inflation surprises (Kose et al. 2019).

Inflation during the pandemic

Between January and May 2020, amid a collapse in demand and plunging oil prices, global inflation ticked down by 0.9 percentage point, and EMDE and advanced-economy inflation by 1.2 and 1.6 percentage point, respectively (figure 4.4). A surge in global and EMDE food inflation during January-April 2020 was more than offset by a collapse in oil prices (Dunn, Hood, and Driessen 2020; Shapiro 2020).

Starting in May 2020, however, inflation began to pick up, although it has remained low by historical standards. By April 2021, inflation had risen 0.3-0.6 percentage point above pre-pandemic levels, in both advanced economies and EMDEs. The initial surge in global food prices, the plunge in global oil prices, and the decline in global core inflation have also been unwound since May 2020. The magnitudes of the inflation pickup, however, varied, especially in EMDEs where the interquartile range of inflation widened by 1 percentage point between May 2020 and March 2021 before narrowing again in April 2021 as the inflation pickup broadened.

The decline in inflation during January-May 2020 followed by a rebound that was broad-based across countries, EMDE regions, and inflation measures. In almost three-quarters of countries, inflation declined between January-May 2020 but rose thereafter.[3] Although EMDE core inflation re-

---

[2] Comparisons in this historical section are based on annual data of 155 countries.

[3] The pattern of inflation decline followed by a rebound to near pre-pandemic levels was seen in all EMDE regions except in East Asia and Pacific (EAP), although the decline was somewhat delayed in Middle East and North Africa (MNA) and Sub-Saharan Africa (SSA), in part because of rising food price inflation.

mained broadly stable, global core inflation declined by 0.6 percentage point during January-June 2020 before rising to within 0.2 percentage point of its pre-pandemic (January 2020) level.

Drivers of inflation during the pandemic

Plunges in aggregate demand, oil price declines, and supply disruptions contributed to global inflation developments in 2020. For EMDEs, global shocks were in part channeled into domestic inflation rates through exchange rate movements, compounding the effect of domestic supply shocks as lockdowns disrupted services activity and food supply chains.

- *Plunge in aggregate demand.* Lockdowns and weaker consumer confidence triggered a collapse in demand (Dunn, Hood, and Driessen 2020). Reflecting the sharp declines in aggregate demand, global trade also plunged. Uncertainty about the spread of the pandemic, future economic conditions, and policy responses deterred private consumption and investments (Caggiano, Castelnuovo, and Kima 2020; Leduc and Liu 2020a). Wages declined in response to higher unemployment: In the median country (among 44 countries), wages declined 5.4 percent (annualized) during the first half of 2020 and rebounded to pre-crisis levels in many countries in the second half. Global economic activity reached its trough in mid-2020 and subsequently recovered, supported by unprecedented policy measures. With the recovery in demand, accompanied by a shift from in-person to online purchases, retail sales bounced back, global trade rebounded, and demand for energy strengthened from mid-2020.

- *Oil price collapse.* Between late-January and mid-April 2020, amid the pandemic-induced global recession, oil prices plunged by more than 60 percent as lockdowns disrupted the transport and travel that accounts for two-thirds of global energy consumption (Kabundi and Ohnsorge 2020; Wheeler et al. 2020).

FIGURE 4.3 **Global inflation**

Since its peak in the mid-1970s, global inflation has been declining. The decline began in the mid-1980s among advanced economies before moving to EMDEs in the mid-1990s. This disinflation process cut across all EMDE regions and manifested in all inflation measures. During the COVID-19 pandemic, inflation in service and non-food goods sectors were subdued, while food inflation has increased.

A. Headline CPI inflation, by country group

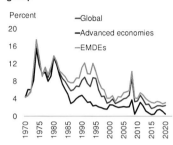

B. EMDE inflation, by region

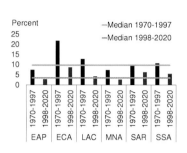

C. Core, food, and energy CPI inflation

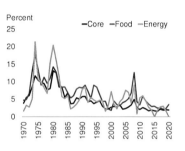

D. Sectoral contribution to headline CPI inflation: 2019-20

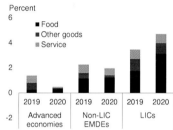

Sources: Havers Analytics; International Monetary Fund; World Bank.
Note: CPI = consumer price index; EMDEs = emerging market and developing economies.; LICs= low income countries. Cross-country medians unless otherwise specified.
A.-C. Based on a sample of 155 countries (30 advanced economies and 125 EMDEs). The values show headline CPI inflation or its sub-components.
B. EAP = East Asia and Pacific; ECA = Europe and Central Asia; LAC = Latin America and the Caribbean; MNA = Middle East and North Africa; SAR = South Asia; SSA = Sub-Saharan Africa.
D. Median headline CPI inflation (annual averages) in 12 sectors across 147 countries. Sectors are categorized following International Financial Statistics. Food indicates food and nonalcoholic beverages and alcoholic beverages, tobacco, and narcotics sectors. Other goods include clothing and footwear, housing, water, electricity, gas and other fuels, furnishings, household equipment and routine household maintenance sectors. Service sector includes health, transportation, communication, recreation, education, restaurants, and miscellaneous sectors.

For oil-importing countries and manufacturing, this lowered the cost of a critical input into economic activity. For oil-exporting countries, it reduced export and fiscal revenues and, in some, compelled authorities to curtail government spending. Oil prices recovered from May onwards and are now near their pre-pandemic level.

- *Supply disruptions.* Especially early in the pandemic, lockdowns disrupted economic activity. Services sector activity was sharply

FIGURE 4.4 Inflation during the pandemic

Global, advanced-economy and EMDE inflation slowed between January and May 2020 but then began to rebound. By April 2021, inflation had rebounded above pre-pandemic levels in both advanced economies and EMDEs, while inflation in the largest economies (the drivers of weighted average global inflation) was still somewhat below pre-pandemic levels.

A. Inflation, by country group

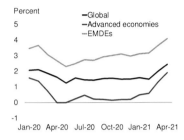

B. Global inflation, by measure

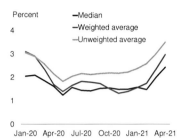

C. EMDE inflation, by measure

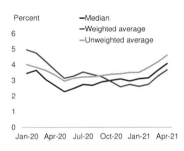

D. Global headline CPI, core CPI, and PPI inflation

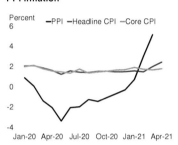

E. Global headline, food, and core inflation

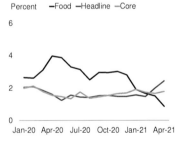

F. EMDE headline, food, and core inflation

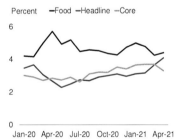

Sources: Haver Analytics; World Bank.
Note: CPI = consumer price index; PPI = producer price index. Year-on-year inflation for 81 countries, of which 31 are advanced economies and 50 are EMDEs.
A. Group medians.
B.C. Weighted average uses 2020 real GDP weights (at 2010 prices and exchange rates).
D.-.F. Year-on-year consumer price inflation for 81 countries, of which 31 are advanced economies and 50 are EMDEs. PPI inflation for 97 countries. Monthly data. Group medians.

curtailed as restrictions were imposed on transactions that required in-person inter-action. In some countries, restrictions on international travel complicated migration of agricultural workers and lockdowns of markets disrupted the sale of produce (World Bank 2020a, 2020c, 2021b).

- *Currency movements.* Larger depreciations during the pandemic, especially during the financial market stress and capital outflows of March and April 2020, were a key source of inflationary pressures in EMDEs (Banerjee et al. 2020). During the first half of 2020, currencies depreciated against the U.S. dollar by 10 percent or more in one-third of EMDEs before recouping some of their losses in the second half of 2020 (chapter 1). One-fifth of EMDEs ended 2020 with weaker exchange rates than at the start of the year. These depreciations fed into inflation: In EMDEs, a 10 percent depreciation has been estimated to raise consumer prices by about 1 percent over the following year (Ha, Stocker, and Yilmazkuday 2020). The strength of the exchange rate pass-through to inflation is particularly high in EMDEs when it is caused by global or domestic demand shocks or domestic supply shocks. Indeed, in EMDEs with 10 percent or higher currency depreciation, median inflation was 6.8 percent in 2020, about 3 percentage point higher than in other EMDEs.

- *Food price volatility.* In some countries, supply disruptions, such as market and trade res-trictions or curfews, appear to have affected domestic food supply chains, increasing wholesale and retail markups, and contributed to rising food price inflation (Husain et al. 2020; Swinnen and McDermott 2020).[4] Food price increases have been higher in countries with larger currency depreciations that raised prices of imported foods. Food supply instability during the pandemic has coincided with episodes of internal conflict in some EMDEs (Ide 2021). Food price increases have been particularly pronounced (2-3 percentage points above the median EMDE) in EMDEs with a history of higher food price inflation over the past decade (in particular in South Asia, and Sub-Saharan Africa) and in low-income countries (box 4.2).

---

[4] Using event studies, Ebrahimy, Igan, and Peria (2020) find that past epidemics, wars, and other disasters coincided with inflation increases, mainly driven by changes in food prices, although the increase was short-lived.

BOX 4.1 Inflation during global recessions

Some of the sharpest inflation movements over the past half century occurred around global recessions. During these episodes, inflation typically declined for several months, driven by the coincidence of several shocks, before recovering to a lower level than before the global recession. The 2020 global recession featured the most muted inflation decline and fastest subsequent inflation upturn among the five global recessions episodes over the past 50 years.

Introduction

Global inflation has steadily trended down since 1970. However, there were several notable departures from this downward trend associated with global recessions. During global recessions, global output collapsed, and oil prices plunged, thus lowering inflation (Baffes et al. 2015; Kose and Terrones 2015; Wheeler et al. 2020). Along the subsequent recovery path, some global recessions were followed by lasting supply weakness that compounded the inflationary pressures associated with the demand rebound. Against this backdrop, this box examines the following questions.

• How did inflation evolve during global recessions?

• What were the drivers of inflation during global recessions?

For the purposes of this box, global inflation is defined as the cross-country median of quarterly inflation rates of 25 advanced economies and 51 EMDEs during 1970-2020. To remove one-off factors, the four-quarter moving average of quarter-on-quarter annualized inflation is used as a proxy for trend inflation.[a] The analysis is restricted to CPI inflation for lack of a sufficiently large country sample for other inflation measures in the 1970s-1990s. Turning points of global business cycles before the outbreak of the COVID-19 pandemic are identified using global per capita gross domestic product (GDP) as in World Bank (2020b). Since 1970, there have been five global recessions with their troughs in 1975Q1, 1982Q4, 1991Q1, and 2009Q1, and 2020Q2. These recessions were associated with a wide range of adverse developments, including financial crises in advanced economies or EMDEs (Kose, Sugawara, and Terrones 2020).

Note: This box was prepared by Jongrim Ha, M. Ayhan Kose, and Franziska Ohnsorge.

a. The rolling average smooths out seasonal and short-term factors. Other studies often employed different measures of trend inflation that span somewhat longer horizons; Ball (1994) employed a nine-quarter centered rolling average to eliminate the irregular factors in inflation. If applied here, this would rule out a comparison with 2020 for lack of data. Therefore, the four-quarter trailing moving average of inflation is employed instead. The results are largely consistent using four-quarter centered rolling averages.

Evolution of inflation during global recessions

Global recessions set off a decline in global inflation that lasted several quarters beyond the trough of the recession and well into the recoveries (figure B4.1.1). Global inflation declined by a cumulative 6.2 percentage points, on average, between the trough of the global recession and the subsequent trough of global inflation. The global recession in 2009 was accompanied by a somewhat shallower (5.1 percentage point, peak to trough) and shorter-lived inflation decline, in part reflecting lower inflation at the start of the recession. Four quarters after the trough of the 2009 global recession, global inflation began to pick up. This pickup was delayed by another 1-2 years after the 1991 and 1975 global recessions and by five more years in the 1982 global recession. After all global recessions other than 1991, global inflation subsequently stabilized at a lower rate than before the global recession, returning to a path of long-term trend disinflation.

The disinflation around global recessions was broad-based across country groups (for both headline CPI and GDP deflator inflation) and inflation measures (figure B4.1.2). That said, in the 1970s through 1990s, the inflation decline was steeper in advanced economies than EMDEs, partly due to the delayed disinflation in EMDEs with high inflation in early 1990s. From 2000, the decline in inflation around global recessions was much more pronounced in EMDEs. Data for other inflation measures, such as core CPI and PPI inflation, is only available for the 2009 and 2020 recessions. In both the global recession of 2009 and of 2020, global inflation declined by all measures of inflation, but the inflation decline was larger and more prolonged in 2009 for all measures of inflation.

Drivers of inflation during global recessions

The inflation decline in the first five months of 2020 was predominantly demand-driven. With the exception of the 1991 global recession, disinflation in previous global recessions was driven by a broader range of factors (figure B4.1.3; Ha, Kose, and Ohnsorge 2019).

• The disinflation in the global recession of 1975 was predominantly driven by oil price shocks but also, in almost equal measures, by global supply and demand shocks. This was in part an unwinding of the surge in

BOX 4.1 Inflation during global recessions *(continued)*

FIGURE B4.1.1 Headline CPI inflation around global recessions

Global recessions (in 1975, 1982, 1991, 2009, and 2020) have typically been associated with slowing global inflation.

A. Global CPI inflation around global recessions

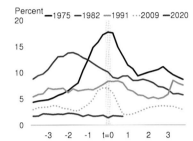

B. Advanced-economy CPI inflation around global recessions

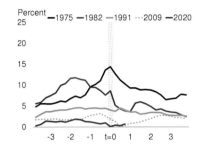

C. EMDE CPI inflation around global recessions

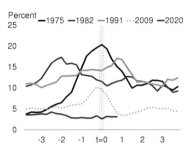

Sources: Kose, Sugawara, and Terrones (2020); World Bank (2020a, 2021a).
Note: Horizontal axes indicate years before and after the troughs of global recessions (shaded area, t = 0). Global inflation is defined as median trend inflation (4-quarter rolling average of quarterly annualized inflation) across 76 countries, consisting of 25 advanced economies and 51 EMDEs. Troughs of global recessions are identified using global per capita GDP and the algorithm in Harding and Pagan (2002) and are consistent with the results in Kose and Terrones (2015). Trough of global recession in 2020 is assumed to be at the second quarter of 2020. EMDEs = emerging market and developing economies.

FIGURE B4.1.2 Evolution of inflation during 2009 and 2020 global recessions

All measures of global and EMDE inflation tend to decline with the onset of global recessions before picking up again. By all measures, the movements of global and EMDE inflation through the global recession of 2020 were more muted and shorter-lived than those during the global recession of 2009.

A. Global PPI inflation

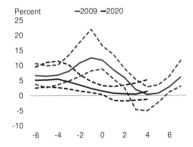

B. EMDE PPI inflation

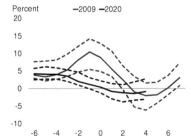

C. Global core CPI inflation

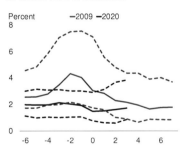

D. EMDE core CPI inflation

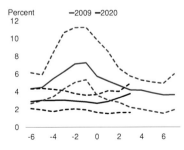

E. Global GDP deflator inflation

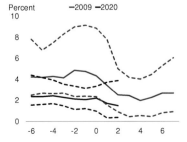

F. EMDE GDP deflator inflation

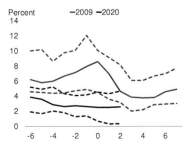

Sources: Kose, Sugawara, and Terrones (2020); World Bank (2020a, 2021a).
Note: Horizontal axes indicate quarters before and after the troughs of global recessions (t=0). Global inflation is defined as median trend inflation (four-quarter rolling average of quarterly inflation). Core inflation data are available for 51 countries, including 28 emerging market and developing economies (EMDEs), and producer price index (PPI) data are available for 85 countries, including 53 EMDEs, GDP deflator data are available for 81 countries, including 50 EMDEs. Troughs of global recessions are 2009Q1 and 2020Q2.

BOX 4.1 Inflation during global recessions *(continued)*

FIGURE B4.1.3 Drivers of disinflation in past global recessions

Inflation in global recessions has been driven by different types of factors. In 1991, demand largely explained the collapse in inflation movements. In 1975 and 2009, oil price movements were the main source of inflation variation.

A. Contribution to disinflation around global recessions: Headline CPI inflation

B. Contribution to disinflation around global recessions: PPI inflation

C. Contribution to disinflation around global recessions: Core CPI inflation

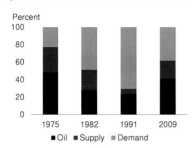

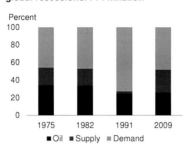

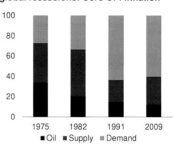

Sources: Ha, Kose, and Ohnsorge (2019); Kose, Sugawara, and Terrones (2020).
Note: Historical decompositions of global inflation measures are estimated by the global FAVAR model for the sample period 1970-2017. Troughs of global recessions are identified using global per capita GDP and the algorithm in Harding and Pagan (2002) and are consistent with the results in Kose and Terrones (2015). Charts show relative contribution of oil price, global demand, and global supply shocks to global disinflation from the trough of the global recession to the subsequent trough in global inflation.

inflation after the oil crisis in 1973-74 when oil prices quadrupled and an oil embargo disrupted transport and manufacturing.

- The disinflation in the 1982 global recession was driven by global demand shocks (one-half), global supply shocks (one-quarter) and global oil price shocks (one-quarter). This disinflation was in part the intended response to the monetary policy tightening in major advanced economies, after the oil price crisis of 1979 (following the Iranian revolution) led to a surge in inflation.

- The disinflation in the 1991 global recession was predominantly global demand driven as financial crises or credit crunches in several advanced economies culminated in a global recession.

- The disinflation at the height of the global recession of 2009 (2008Q4 and 2009Q1) was driven by both demand and oil price shocks in broadly equal measure. Despite coordinated global fiscal and monetary policy support, the global financial crisis caused a deep global recession that was accompanied by a two-thirds plunge in oil prices in the five months from July 2008.

Again, with the exception of the global recession of 1991, the predominance of demand shocks in driving down core

CPI and PPI inflation during the 2020 pandemic contrasts with the sources of disinflation in previous recessions.

- **In 1975**, oil price shocks and demand shocks were the main source of PPI disinflation and oil price shocks and supply shocks the main source of core CPI disinflation. Disinflation at that time mainly reflected an unwinding of earlier shocks—the oil price spike of 1974 and the inflationary impact of wage and consumer price controls being lifted, accompanied by the collapse of the Bretton Woods fixed exchange rate system in 1971. The large role of oil price shocks in core CPI inflation dynamics—notwithstanding the exclusion of energy from the core inflation aggregate—in the 1970s may also have reflected poorly anchored inflation expectations once the nominal anchor of the Bretton Woods fixed exchange rate regimes was lost (Ha et al. 2019b).

- **In 1982**, supply and demand shocks were the main source of core CPI disinflation and demand shocks the main source of PPI disinflation. Again, disinflation in part reflected a drawn-out unwinding of earlier shocks. By the late 1970s, inflation expectations had become unanchored in some advanced economies and inflation-wage spirals became entrenched in major advanced economies while output growth stagnated at a low level (Bryan 2021). The doubling of oil prices in 1979 added fuel

BOX 4.1 Inflation during global recessions *(continued)*

FIGURE B4.1.4 Inflation in 2008-10 and 2020-21

In the pandemic-induced global recession of 2020, inflation declined less and rebounded faster than in the financial-crisis-induced global recession of 2009.

A. Global inflation

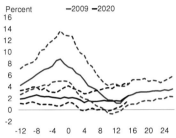

B. EMDE inflation

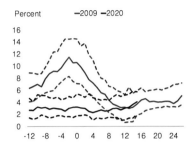

C. Share of countries with declining inflation

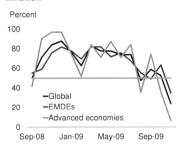

D. Global food price inflation

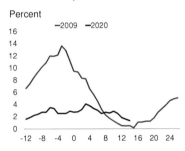

E. Oil price growth

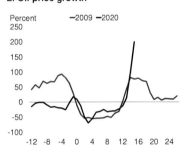

F. Inflation expectations for EMDEs

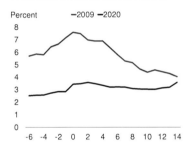

Sources: Consensus Economic; Haver Analytics; World Bank.

Note: Year-on-year monthly inflation for 81 countries, of which 31 are advanced economies and 50 are emerging market and developing economies (EMDEs). t=0 is September 2008 for 2009 and January 2020 for 2020.

A.B. Blue and red lines are medians, dotted lines are interquartile ranges.

C. Share of all countries, advanced economies and EMDEs in which year-on-year inflation slowed from one month to the next. Gray line shows 50 percent.

D. Median.

E. Year-on-year growth in the average of Brent, Dubai, and WTI oil prices.

F. Consensus inflation expectation for 2009 ("2009") and 2021 ("2020") for 48 EMDEs .

to inflation pressures. The monetary tightening across advanced economies in the early 1980s helped stabilize inflation expectations while also causing recessions.

- **In 2009,** negative oil price shocks and global demand shocks contributed, in almost equal measure, to declines in global PPI inflation while core CPI inflation remained broadly stable as negative demand shocks were offset by negative supply shocks. Well-anchored inflation expectations from the early 2000s helped stabilize inflation despite adverse demand shocks.

Inflation during the last two global recessions

A more granular comparison, using monthly data for 31 advanced economies and 50 EMDEs for 2001-2021, is

possible for the global recessions of 2009 and 2020. This exercise also shows that the global inflation decline during the global recession of 2020 has been more muted and shorter-lived than during the global recession of 2009 (figure B4.1.4). This may reflect the fact that the global recovery from the 2020 recession was swifter than that of any previous global recession in the past eight decades, despite the global recession being the most severe since the Second World War (box 1.1).

Inflation declined by 0.9 percentage point globally and 1.2 percentage point in EMDEs from January 2020 before reaching its trough in May 2020—five months after the beginning of the global pandemic. In contrast, inflation declined by 6.3 percentage points globally and 7.6 percentage points in EMDEs from September 2008 to its trough in October 2009—13 months after the bankruptcy

BOX 4.1 Inflation during global recessions *(continued)*

of Lehman Brothers that set off the global financial crisis. Whereas inflation started rising in the majority of countries five months after the onset of the pandemic, in May 2020, it only started rising in the majority of countries a year after the onset of the global financial crisis, in October 2009. The global recession of 2009 itself featured a shallower and shorter-lived inflation decline than previous global recessions.

The decline in global inflation from January-May 2020 was four-fifths driven by the collapse in global demand and another one-fifth driven by plunging oil prices, with some offsetting inflationary pressures from supply disruptions. This contrasts with the global financial crisis in which the 13-month decline in global as well as EMDE inflation was about one-half driven by plunging oil prices and only one-third driven by the contraction in global demand. The greater role of global demand in the inflation decline in 2020 than in previous global recessions may reflect the sheer severity of the recession of 2020 (World Bank 2021a). In their rebounds, however, global and EMDE inflation developments after the two global recessions of 2009 and 2020 resembled each other: both were virtually entirely driven by increases in global demand.

Short-term (one-year-ahead) inflation expectations inched down by 0.3 percentage point globally between March and

May 2020 before stabilizing again at 2.0 percent for the remainder of 2020. They only rose by 0.2 percentage point in March 2021 as it became apparent that the recovery was proceeding faster than anticipated and new policy support measures were approved (chapter 1). In EMDEs, inflation expectations declined by 0.5 percentage point throughout 2020 until a 0.4 percentage point uptick in March 2021. These minor movements of short-term inflation expectations stand in sharp contrast to the 2.1 percentage point decline globally and 2.6 percentage point decline in EMDEs in the 14 months following September 2008, through the global recession of 2009. Long-term inflation expectations also remained stable in 2020, both globally and in EMDEs—for EMDEs, in contrast to the 1.0 percentage point decline in the 18 months following September 2008. This in part reflected a view that the disruptions caused by the pandemic were temporary in nature and may have helped dampen fluctuations in global inflation.

Conclusion

Global recessions are associated with sharp movements in inflation. The 2020 global recession featured the most muted and least protracted inflation decline. This may have reflected lower initial inflation but, in 2020, also deployment of unprecedented policy support and a rapid economic recovery.

Relative importance of drivers of inflation

To disentangle the quantitative importance of some of these forces, a factor-augmented VAR (FAVAR) model with sign and narrative restrictions is estimated. The model is applied to three global variables—inflation, output growth, and oil price growth—all expressed in month-on-month growth rates. Global inflation and output growth are proxied by the common global factor estimated using a dynamic factor model of cross-country inflation and industrial production growth, respectively (annex 4.1). The dynamic factor model includes monthly data for 30 advanced economies and 51 EMDEs for 2001-2021. The global oil price is based on the average of Dubai, West Texas Intermediate, and Brent oil

prices, as reported in the World Bank's *Pink Sheet* of commodity prices. The exercise is repeated for advanced economies and EMDEs separately, and for headline CPI inflation, core CPI inflation, and PPI inflation. The PPI tends to have larger tradables content than the headline CPI, whereas the core CPI tends to have smaller tradables content than the headline CPI (Ha, Kose, and Ohnsorge 2019). The estimation results suggest a sequence of changing disinflationary forces in January-May 2020 that were subsequently unwound.

- *January-May 2020.* Between January and May, four-fifths of the decline in global inflation reflected the collapse in global demand as consumption and investment collapsed amid lockdowns and uncertainty about policies and growth prospects. Another

FIGURE 4.5 Drivers of inflation in 2020-21

In February and March 2020, an oil price plunge dampened global inflation; in March-May 2020, the demand collapse caused by a deep recession further lowered inflation, although supply disruptions offset some of the disinflationary pressures. These forces were unwound by mid-2020.

A. Contributions to monthly change in global headline CPI inflation in 2020-21

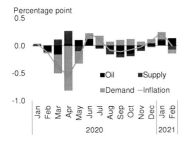

B. Contributions to monthly change in EMDE headline CPI inflation in 2020-21

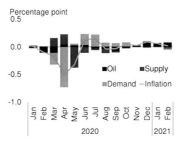

Source: World Bank.
Note: Contributions to changes in year-on-year headline consumer price inflation from the previous month for 81 countries, of which 31 are advanced economies and 50 are emerging market and developing economies (EMDEs), based on factor-augmented vector autoregression (FAVAR) estimation over the period of 2001-21 in annex 4.1. Monthly data. Unexplained residual is omitted from the graph. "Oil," "Supply," and "Demand" indicate oil price shocks, global supply shocks, and global demand shocks, respectively.

one-fifth reflected the plunge in oil prices. Both globally and for EMDEs, disinflationary effects from collapsing demand and oil prices were partly offset by the inflationary effect of supply disruptions such as disruptions to firm operations and global shipping caused by pandemic restrictions to domestic economic activity and international travel (figure 4.5). Within this five-month period, however, the forces affecting inflation shifted. In February and March 2020, the decline in global inflation was in almost equal measure due to the plunge in oil prices and a collapse in global demand, but the disinflationary impact of the collapse in global demand intensified in April.[5]

• *May 2020-February 2021.* The collapse in demand and oil prices as well as supply disruptions began to unwind as consumers,

---

[5] The predominant role of demand shocks and some offsetting role of supply shocks during the pandemic were also found in some recent studies; see, for instance, Bekaert, Engstrom, and Ermolov (2020) for the United States, and Baleer et al. (2020) and O'Brien, Dumoncel, and Gonçalves (2021) for the euro area.

firms, and investors began to adjust their behavior and operations. From May, as international trade and global manufacturing activity rebounded, supply factors began to lower inflation (figure 4.5). A sharp rebound in demand, however, raised inflation as consumption shifted from in-person to online transactions. For the period from May 2020 to February 2021, demand pressures account-ed for virtually all of the increase in global inflation and these were partially offset by improved supply conditions. For EMDEs, the recovery in oil prices from mid-2020 contributed one-third as much as the recovery in demand to the uptick in inflation.

Prospects for inflation

Short-term inflation prospects

The global recession of 2020 was unusually severe but short (chapter 1; box 1.1; box 4.1). This was also reflected in inflation developments. The accompanying inflation decline was unusually muted and short-lived. Looking ahead, some factors point to an increase in inflation over the near term but stable low inflation over the long term. However, shocks may interact with large-scale policy support to deliver higher inflation and inflation volatility over a 2-3-year horizon (Baldwin and di Mauro 2020; Blanchard 2020). Uncertainty about future inflation is also reflected in wide disagreement among survey respondents on future inflation prospects, which could be a sign of growing risk of inflation expectations becoming unanchored (Ebrahimy, Igan, and Peria 2020; Williamson 2021). A FAVAR model is used to project global, advanced-economy and EMDE inflation in coming months that would be consistent with the growth and oil price forecasts presented in chapter 1.

Global output growth is expected to exceed 5 percent in 2021 and oil prices are expected to rise over the year as a whole (Chapter 1). This suggests an increase in global inflation by 1.4 percentage points in 2021 (from 2.5 percent in 2020 to 3.9 percent in 2021; figure 4.6). The model-predicted global inflation of 3.9 percent in 2021 is comparable to average inflation during 2011-13 after the global financial crisis.

If a similar exercise has been conducted in January 2009, with the benefit of hindsight for output growth and oil price movements, it would have yielded a projected decline in global inflation of 3.3 percentage points for 2009—just below the actual decline of 4.5 percentage points. A similar exercise conducted in 2011 would have predicted an upturn in global inflation of 0.8 percentage point in 2011, which was just below actual inflation declined (1.3 percent), followed by an inflation decline of 0.5 percentage point in 2012, which was also just below actual declines (0.9 percentage point).

For advanced economies, growth and oil price forecasts are consistent with inflation rising to 1.8 percent in 2021 (from 0.5 percent in 2020)—still below the target rate of 2 percent in many advanced economies but a touch above the 1.4 percent average over the 2010s. For virtually all advanced economies, the model-predicted moderate inflation rise would bring inflation closer to inflation targets. A similar exercise conducted in January 2009 would have forecast a decline in advanced-economy inflation of 2.4 percentage point for 2009, again below the 3.4 percentage-point decline in inflation between 2008 and 2009 that actually materialized.

For EMDEs, growth and oil price forecasts would be consistent with inflation rising to 4.6 percent from 3.1 percent, well above the average over the 2010s of 3.8 percent. It would be just a touch above the mid-range (3.8 percent), but still below the 5.1 percent upper bound of the average inflation-targeting EMDE's target range. For the one-half of inflation-targeting EMDEs with inflation well below target, the model-predicted moderate inflation rise also would bring inflation closer to target. For another one-half of inflation-targeting EMDEs, however, a rise in inflation of this magnitude would put inflation above target. This may not warrant a policy response provided the inflation pickup is temporary. Should it, however, risk de-anchoring inflation expectations, it could become a monetary policy challenge that may hold back the recovery. In some EMDEs,

FIGURE 4.6 **Prospects for inflation**

Inflation has risen since the second half of 2020 in both advanced economies and EMDEs. Conditional forecasts of global inflation suggest that global inflation will increase by around 1.4 percentage point in 2021. Survey- and market-based inflation expectations also point to a moderate rise in global inflation in near future.

A. Model-based conditional forecast of global inflation

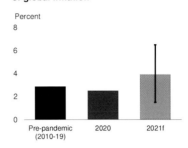

B. Model-based conditional forecast of EMDE inflation

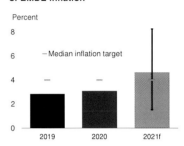

C. Survey-based inflation expectations: headline CPI inflation

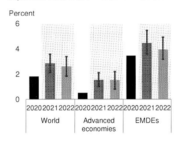

D. Inflation expectations by select central banks: headline CPI inflation

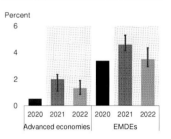

E. Market-based inflation expectations

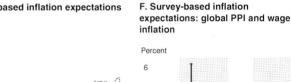

F. Survey-based inflation expectations: global PPI and wage inflation

Sources: Haver Analytics; Consensus Economics; World Bank.
Note: EMDEs = emerging market and developing economies; PPI = producer price index.
A. Conditional forecast of global inflation based on quarterly FAVAR model of global inflation, global GDP growth, and oil price growth. Vertical line indicates 16-84 confidence bands. See annex 4.1 for details.
B. Based on median inflation in 125 EMDEs and inflation target in 30 inflation-targeting EMDEs. 2021 inflation is based on the conditional forecast of EMDE inflation. Vertical line indicates 16-84 confidence bands.
C. Average headline CPI inflation expectations for 2021-22 based on surveys of May 2021 in 57 countries (31 advanced economies and 26 EMDEs). 2020 indicates actual inflation rates. Vertical lines indicate maximum and minimal responses.
D. Median headline CPI inflation expectations for 2021-22 based on surveys of G7 economies and seven large EMDEs (Brazil, China, Mexico, India, Indonesia, Russian Federation, Turkey).
E. Median implied breakeven inflation, measured as the spreads between nominal and real 5-year treasury bond yields in 7 advanced economies (Australia, Canada, Germany, the Republic of Korea, New Zealand, United Kingdom, and United States). Dotted lines indicate inter-quartile range.
F. Median Producer Prices Index (PPI) and wage inflation expectations for 2021-22 based on surveys of 9 and 23 economies, respectively. 2020 indicates actual inflation rates. Vertical lines indicate maximum and minimal responses.

BOX 4.2 Food price volatility and inflation in low-income countries

Inflation in low-income countries (LICs) increased in the run-up to, and following, the outbreak of COVID-19. The rise has been largely driven by increases in food prices and currency depreciations. Higher prices for food, which accounts for about half of consumption in LICs, threaten to increase poverty. In the near term, further rises in global agricultural prices are likely to add to inflationary pressures in LICs. Subsequently, an expected stabilization of commodity prices and moderate demand growth are likely to result in a gradual decline in consumer price inflation in these economies. A more persistent rise in agricultural commodity prices, or pressure to finance large fiscal deficits, could risk ingraining higher inflation into expectations and may warrant tighter monetary policy. In addition, attempts to lower food price inflation through price subsidies in a large number of countries, or the re-emergence of protectionist policies, could drive global prices higher and prove to be self-defeating.

Introduction

Inflation in low-income countries (LICs) has declined over the past three decades. The COVID-19 pandemic has been associated with a sharp growth slowdown in LICs, accompanied by rising consumer price inflation. The inflation pickup in 2020 predominantly reflected rising food price inflation. Rising inflation, particularly when driven by sharp increases in food prices, raises poverty, increases malnutrition, and curtails the consumption of essential services such as education and health care (IDA 2020; Laborde, Lakatos, and Martin 2019; World Bank 2011a). In addition, LICs face larger challenges in controlling inflation than other emerging market and developing economies (EMDEs) due to weaker policy frameworks and less developed financial systems; higher volatility of output and demand; and the larger influence of global commodity prices, particularly agricultural prices (Ha et al. 2019b).

The persistence of the recent rise in LIC inflation will depend upon the persistence of its drivers and the response of policy makers. The inflationary impact of one-off rises in commodity prices or currency depreciation may dissipate provided inflation expectations remain anchored and institutional credibility is sufficient. However, further upward momentum for commodity prices, or overly accommodative monetary policy, perhaps influenced by fiscal objectives, could lead to more persistent increases in inflation.

In light of these challenges, this box addresses the following questions:

• How has inflation evolved in LICs during the pandemic?

• What are the prospects for inflation in LICs?

• What are the implications of rising inflation for food security?

Recent inflation developments in LICs

Inflation before the pandemic. LICs have made large strides in price stabilization over the past three decades, lowering inflation from 25 percent in 1994 to 3.4 percent in 2019 as policy frameworks improved and demands for deficit financing on central banks were reigned in (Ha, Kose, and Ohnsorge 2019). Nevertheless, inflation has been persistently higher in LICs than in other EMDEs, at 4.4 percent since 2018, compared to just 2.7 percent in EMDEs (figure B4.2.1.A).[a] Historically, higher rates of inflation in LICs have been attributed to monetary financing of deficits and frequent negative supply shocks (Baldini and Poplawski-Ribeiro 2011; Weidmann 2013). More recently, inflation in LICs accelerated ahead of the outbreak of the pandemic as a result of a sharp increase in global food price inflation that started from the second half of 2019, rising from 3.5 percent in May 2019, to 3.9 percent in January 2020, before national lockdowns became widespread.

Rising inflation in 2020 in LICs. Whereas inflation in advanced economies and EMDEs fell after the widespread implementation of restrictions on movement across the world, median inflation in LICs rose from 3.9 percent in January 2020 to a new peak at 5.6 percent in April 2020 (figure B4.2.1.B). The pickup in inflation over this period affected the majority of LICs and ranged up to 5 percentage points. Since September 2020, inflation has somewhat moderated to approximately its level in 2019. As a result, LIC inflation for 2020 as a whole increased by 1.1 percentage points from the previous year, although remains about a percentage point below its average over 2015-2019.

a. See World Bank (2018) for the long-term trend of inflation in LICs over the last five decades.

BOX 4.2 Food price volatility and inflation in low-income countries (*continued*)

FIGURE B4.2.1 Inflation developments in LICs

Inflation has on average been higher in LICs relative to other EMDEs. In contrast to inflation in other EMDEs, inflation in LICs increased in both the months ahead of, and following, the announcement of widespread lockdown measures in March 2020. For 2020 as a whole, inflation in LICs rose by 1.1 percentage points as a result of rapid inflation of the price of food, which accounts for nearly half of consumption in LICs. A recent surge in agricultural commodity prices may add to inflationary pressures in LICs in the near term.

A. Median inflation in LICs and EMDEs: 2017-21

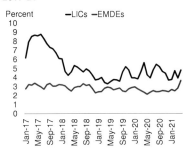

B. Inflation in LICs: 2020-21

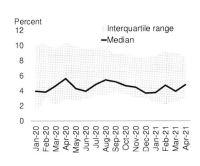

C. Contribution of food and energy prices to inflation

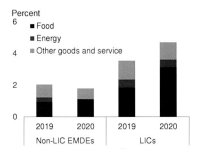

D. Agricultural commodity prices and food price inflation in LICs

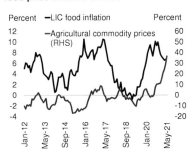

E. Share of food in goods imports and consumption

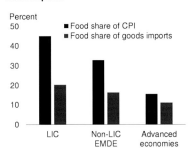

F. Exchange rate adjustment and inflation

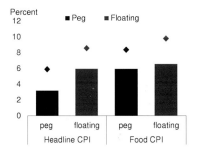

Sources: Havers Analytics; International Monetary Fund; National sources; World Bank.
Note: EMDEs = emerging market and developing economies; LICs = low-income countries.
A B. Based on headline consumer price inflation for up to 20 LICs and 80 EMDEs.
C. Sectoral headline consumer price index (CPI) inflation rates are based on median across 111 countries in 12 sectors. Sectors are categorized following International Financial Statistics. Food indicates food and nonalcoholic beverages and alcoholic beverages, tobacco, and narcotics sectors. Energy indicates housing, water, electricity, gas and other fuels. Other goods include clothing and footwear, furnishings, household equipment and routine household maintenance sectors. Service sector includes health, transportation, communication, recreation, education, restaurants, and miscellaneous sectors.
D. Average food and nonalcoholic beverage price inflation in up to 10 LICs and annual growth in the nominal agricultural commodity price (from the World Bank's Pink Sheet).
E. Weight of food and nonalcoholic beverages in the CPI and share of total merchandise imports.
F. Bars (diamonds) indicate headline and food CPI inflation in 19 LICs based on simple median (simple average) by de facto exchange rate regime as defined in Klein and Shambaugh (2010). Peg indicates LICs with fixed exchange rates.

Rising agricultural commodity prices. One of the primary drivers of the rise in consumer prices ahead of and following the COVID-19 pandemic was rising food prices.[b] In 2020, food prices contributed 1.3 percentage points to inflation in LICs, explaining most of the increase in headline inflation from 2019; this compares with an

increase in the contribution of just 0.2 percentage point in other EMDEs. In contrast, the contribution of the energy sector and other goods and services was little changed or declined in LICs in 2020 (figure B4.2.1.C).

Agricultural commodity prices rose sharply in 2020, driven largely by increasing prices of meals and oils (+16 percent) and grains (+5 percent) (figure B4.2.1.D). Strong demand, some weather-related supply disruptions, and the threat and enactment of export restrictions in some major

b. In April 2020, rice prices rose 32 percent above April 2019 levels. By November 2020, wheat prices were 11 percent higher, while soybean prices were 33 percent higher than in November 2019.

BOX 4.2 Food price volatility and inflation in low-income countries (*continued*)

FIGURE B4.2.2 Outlook for inflation in LICs

Following a sharp slowdown in growth in 2020, LICs are expected to experience a modest recovery in 2021-23. LIC inflation is expected to rise in 2021 as a result of the recent acceleration in food prices. The dispersion of forecasts remains large, however. Global agricultural prices are forecast to remain elevated in the coming years, amid continued high demand for staples, but the pace of growth will slow as COVID-related disruption, including trade restrictions, dissipates. Inflation is subsequently likely to moderate in 2022 owing to weak domestic demand.

A. GDP growth and inflation forecast

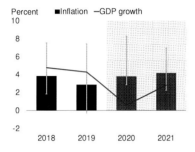

B. Commodity price forecasts

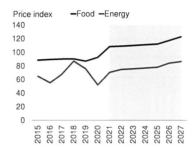

C. Food export restrictions in place

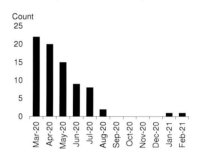

Sources: International Monetary Fund; Labord, Mamun, and Parent (2020); World Bank.
A. Median and interquartile range of consumer price growth forecasts among 19 LICs in the IMF's April 2021 *World Economic Outlook* and World Bank's June 2021 *Global Economic Prospects* forecast for GDP growth in LICs.
B. Nominal commodity price forecasts in the World Bank's April 2021 *Commodity Market Outlook*.
C. Number of restrictions on the export or import of food in place. Data on announcements available to end-November 2020.

grain producers added to price pressures. In LICs, food accounts for about half of consumption baskets and 20 percent of goods imports, a larger share than in other EMDEs (figure B4.2.1.E). There is therefore a strong relationship between globally determined agricultural commodity prices and LIC inflation; the correlation between agricultural prices and food price inflation in LICs is about 40 percent.

Exchange rate depreciation. Alongside rising agricultural commodity prices, exchange rates in some LICs depreciated at the start of the pandemic. Between December 2019 and April 2020, exchange rates in LICs depreciated by between 1 and 8 percent. The pass-through of depreciation into inflation tends to be stronger in LICs than in other EMDEs (Ha et al. 2019a). Indeed, inflation in LICs with floating exchange-rate regimes was two percentage points higher than in LICs with fixed exchange rate regimes in 2020 (figure B4.2.1.F).[c]

Price pressures due to conflict, and policy uncertainty. In fragile and conflict-affected LICs (including Chad and

Haiti) and those experiencing high levels of political uncertainty (Ethiopia), inflation was higher by two percentage points on average in 2020 than in other LICs. Food supply insecurity during the pandemic coincided with episodes of natural disasters and large-scale internal violence, including civil wars, in some LICs (FSIN and GNAFC 2021; WFP and FAO 2021).[d]

Inflation prospects in LICs

Inflation in LICs is likely to face offsetting pressures in the future. The recovery in LICs is expected to be subdued with growth returning only to its pre-COVID average and per capita incomes still below pre-pandemic levels in 2022. On the upside in the near term, the recent pickup in global agricultural and energy prices may pass more fully through to LIC inflation in the remainder of 2021. Overall, LICs are likely to face rising aggregate and food price inflation in 2021, which is expected to subsequently gradually decline. However, the outlook is highly

---

c. This is based on a de factor exchange regime as defined in Klein and Shambaugh (2010).

d. Conflict is estimated to be the main driver of food insecurity for over 120 million people in 2020 (FSIN and GNAFC 2021).

BOX 4.2 Food price volatility and inflation in low-income countries (*continued*)

uncertain and will depend on a range of factors, including the monetary policy response.[e]

Weak recovery in output. LICs are expected to experience a modest recovery in 2021-22. Until 2022, growth is expected to be weaker than average growth during 2010-19 (figure B4.2.2.A; box 1.3). In line with a weak recovery in demand, domestic price pressures are likely to remain subdued, such that inflation will decline as the effects of commodity price increases fade.

Recent rapid rise in agricultural prices. Agricultural commodity prices have grown rapidly; as of May 2021, agricultural commodity prices were 37 percent higher than a year ago, the fastest price increase since 2011. The historically rapid pass-through from commodity prices to domestic food price inflation, along with the prospect of a modest recovery in demand, and oil price increases suggests a further increase, albeit moderate, in LICs inflation in the remainder of 2021 (figure B4.2.2.B; chapter 1). Absent other shocks, a stabilization of agricultural prices later in 2021 may allow for a slowdown in LIC inflation in 2022 and beyond.

Food security: The implications of rising food prices during the pandemic

In the near term, rising food prices and accelerating aggregate inflation are likely to compound increasing food insecurity in LICs. In addition to rising food prices and inflation, lost income due to the pandemic, ongoing or intensifying conflicts or political instability has led to a surge in food insecurity in 2020 and 2021. The number of people experiencing a food shortage crisis increased from 135 million in 2019 to about 165 million people in 2020 (FSIN and GNAFC 2021; WFP and FAO 2021). Many cases of rising food insecurity are in LICs (table 4.1).

Food supply disruptions. Globally, food price inflation increased, from 2.4 percent in 2019 to 3.5 percent in 2020 reflecting higher commodity prices, domestic supply disruptions, outright hoarding, and depreciations that raised the price of imported foods. Pandemic-related restrictions on movement and labor supply damaged food production and distribution (IFPRI 2021). Export and import restrictions contributed to food supply disruptions, although most restrictions are no longer in force (figure

B4.2.2.C). Food price increases also followed previous pandemics and other natural disasters (Ebrahimy, Igan, and Peria 2020). LICs are particularly vulnerable to these disruptions, as poor transport links prevent the adaptation of supply chains, and food comprises a large share of household consumption (Bleaney and Francisco 2018; Cachia 2014; Ha, Kose, and Ohnsorge 2019). As a result, poorer households—which are more prevalent in LICs than in other EMDEs—may suffer greater welfare losses from food and other types of inflation than wealthier households. An erosion of their real incomes and assets through inflation could tip these households into extreme poverty.[f]

Potential spillovers of food prices to inflation in other sectors. Higher and more volatile inflation in LICs than in other EMDEs partly reflects the poorer anchoring of inflation expectations that allow fluctuations in food prices to spill over into inflation in other sectors.[g] In addition, exchange rates in LICs tend to be more volatile than those in other EMDEs, in part reflecting the greater frequency of supply shocks in LICs (World Bank 2020b). With inflation expectations poorly anchored, households in LICs are less able to protect the real value of their income and assets from the impact of persistent and elevated inflation (Ha et al. 2019b; World Bank 2020b).

Shocks to income. In addition to rising prices of staple foods, poorer households experienced a severe negative income shock due to COVID-19. The number of people living on less than $1.90 a day is estimated to have risen by 119-124 million in 2020 (Lakner et al. 2021). In some cases, the large concentration of production in agriculture in LICs can result in boosts to household income following rises in agricultural prices. However, the net impact of higher prices has been found to result in increasing poverty among LIC households, including during the last major rise in agricultural commodity prices in 2010-11 (Ivanic and Martin 2008; Ivanic, Martin, and Zaman 2012).[h]

---

e. This is consistent with the prospects for global and EMDE inflation based on survey-based inflation expectations and central-bank forecasts.

f. The literature provides empirical evidence that higher inflation is associated higher income inequality, or with a lower share of income held by the poor (Datt and Ravallion 1998; Siami-Namini and Hudson 2019).

g. The effectiveness of monetary policy in LICs remains limited--arising from higher economic volatility and pervasive use of administered pricing, conflicts among central bank policy objectives, and limited analytical capacity at central banks (Mishra and Monteil 2013; World Bank 2020b).

h. Longer term, rises in food prices have been found to boost wages and profits in food producers as output adjusts (Ivanic and Martin 2014).

BOX 4.2 Food price volatility and inflation in low-income countries (*continued*)

Policy options

High inflation in LICs, driven by rising food prices, COVID-related supply disruptions, and to some extent, currency depreciation, is likely to increase poverty in LICs. A key objective for policy makers could be to ensure that rising inflation rates do not lead to a de-anchoring of inflation expectations and the further erosion of real household income. Subsidies or price controls to reduce the burden of rising food prices may appear attractive but carry the risk of increased strains on the fiscal balance of highly indebted governments, and also risk adding further upward pressure on global agricultural prices.

Response to more persistent or broad-based price rises. While many LICs responded to the pandemic by cutting policy rates in 2020, some LICs (Mozambique, Tajikistan) started to raise interest rates in 2021. In LICs with large economic slack and below-target inflation, continued monetary easing and fiscal support can help the recovery gain traction and raise inflation towards the target. Furthermore, in LICs where inflation rises above target due to temporary commodity price rises but noncommodity goods and services inflation remains weak, there may be continued scope for accommodative monetary policy. In 2020, there was little evidence of a broad-based increase in non-commodity inflation in LICs, although this could rapidly change (figure B4.2.1.C). In LICs where the economic recovery from the pandemic is further advanced, or where there appears to be a broad-based or persistent increase in commodity prices, authorities could consider monetary policy tightening.

Monetary policy independence and credibility. Inflation in LICs has fallen substantially in recent decades, mirroring a broader decline in inflation in EMDEs more generally. Nevertheless, monetary policy transmission in LICs remains limited (Mishra and Montiel 2013). LICs could continue to improve monetary policy frameworks to prevent rises in inflation from becoming ingrained and persistent. By stabilizing output fluctuations that disproportionally hurt the poor, the adoption of a credible monetary policy regime that maintains low and stable inflation may help reduce poverty and inequality (Romer and Romer 1999).

In part, historical falls in inflation in LICs were achieved through reduced demand for deficit monetization as debt burdens and deficits in LICs declined after the 1980s (Ha, Kose, and Ohnsorge 2019). Rising debt burdens and fiscal deficits in LICs in the run-up to, and following, the COVID-19 pandemic may increase risks that moneti-

zation is pursued to a greater degree once again, in particular in an environment of rising global and domestic interest rates. Average debt-to-GDP ratios in LICs increased by 6 percentage points in 2020, while average debt-to-GDP ratios currently stand at nearly 70 percent. While they are expected to gradually decline from 2021 onwards, further adverse shocks could result in rising deficit financing requirements (World Bank 2021a).

Risks of food price subsidies and export restrictions. Previous food price spikes led to large increases in poverty, with the 2010-11 price spike estimated to have increased the global number of those in poverty by 8.3 million (Laborde, Lakatos, and Martin 2019). The recent increase in agricultural commodity prices, a 37 percent annual increase, is the largest since 2011 when inflation peaked at 39 percent. Even before the COVID-19 crisis, many LICs imposed price controls on food products, although the share of food subjected to controls in consumption baskets is small (Guénette 2020). Many governments have turned to subsidies and export restrictions to lower domestic food prices in previous food price spikes; however, these insulating policies can often exacerbate global price spikes, increasing the demand for food (subsidies) or reducing their supply (export restrictions). In 2011, insulating policies were estimated to have contributed 25-40 percent of the increase in global maize and wheat prices (Laborde, Lakotos, and Martin 2019). Export restrictions imposed in 2020 in South Asia contributed to logistical bottlenecks and resulted in rising prices for key food staples for the region as a whole (World Bank 2021c). Countercyclical purchases of nonperishable agricultural commodities when prices are low, and targeted, rather than blanket subsidies, are less likely to contribute to higher global food prices.

Measures to reduce food insecurity. To reduce the impact of rising food prices and the repercussion of COVID-19 for food security, a range of measures can be taken, including scaling up social safety net programs and ensuring the distribution of, and access to, food. Targeted social protection measures, such as cash and food transfers, may mitigate the impacts of the pandemic on food security with fewer adverse impacts on global food prices than price and export controls. Such measures have been substantially increased since the start of the pandemic in EMDEs and some LICs (Gentilini et al. 2020). However, LICs may face larger challenges than other EMDEs in delivering and developing sources of revenue for these transfers, requiring technical and financial assistance. International support for improved logistical capabilities and to ensure the climate resilience of local food supply can contribute to both near- and longer-term food security in LICs (IDA 2020).

inflation may rise even further if they are subject to above-average depreciation pressures or food price increases.[6]

Consistent with the model-based inflation forecasts, survey-based consumer price inflation expectations suggest that global inflation is expected to rise by about 1 percentage point in 2021, from its low rate in 2020 (figure 4.6). The expected inflation rise is broad-based, in both advanced economies and EMDEs. It is also anticipated for PPI inflation, although not for wage inflation: Consensus forecasts point to an increase in global PPI inflation (defined as median across 9 countries) to about 4 percent in 2021 (from -1 percent in 2020; figure 4.6).[7] Forecasts of headline CPI inflation by major central banks also suggest a moderate increase in inflation in 2021 (by 1.5 percentage points in G7 economies and 1.2 percentage points in seven large EMDEs). Finally, although the data are limited to a few advanced economies, market-based inflation expectations point to a similar conclusion: break-even implied inflation (measured as the spreads between nominal and real 5-year bond yields) has risen moderately since April 2020 and recovered to pre-pandemic level by January 2021.

Longer-term inflation prospects

The pandemic-induced global recession was preceded by a decade of extremely low global inflation (2 percent) as well as low advanced-economy and EMDE inflation. This stands in contrast to previous global recessions when pre-recession global inflation ranged from 6 percent (2008) to 16 percent (1975). This may account for the more muted inflation response in the 2020 global recession than in earlier ones.

This points to longer-term structural factors in depressing global inflation. Provided they continue to exert their influence, these factors may also dampen any post-pandemic uptick in inflation. Well-anchored inflation expectations, greater price transparency, and growing automation may continue to dampen inflation. In contrast, turning demographic trends, stabilizing global value chains, potential demand pressures, and weaker fiscal positions may increase inflation pressures.

- *Well-anchored inflation expectations.* In contrast to short-term inflation expectations, long-term inflation expectations have been broadly stable trough the pandemic and continue to forecast global, advanced-economy, and EMDE inflation at 2.3, 1.8, and 3.7 percent, respectively, half a decade from now (figure 4.7). Such robust anchoring of inflation expectations in part reflected the introduction of more resilient macroeconomic policy frameworks such as inflation targeting, fiscal rules, and greater exchange rate flexibility in EMDEs (Ha, Kose, and Ohnsorge 2019). The median EMDE inflation target has remained steady at around 4 percent since the mid-2010s but the number of EMDEs meeting their targets has risen (Ha et al. 2019b). If, however, inflation expectations start de-anchoring from central banks' targets, inflation can rise in unexpected ways in the medium-term (Armantier et al. 2021).

- *Greater price transparency.* During the pandemic, consumers have switched to online shopping from in-store shopping. To the extent that e-retail helps increase price transparency and competition, this may extend the downward pressure on prices (Charbonneau et al. 2017). If this price adjustment stretches over several years, it may appear to be disinflation. Conversely, growing market power of online retailers may increase profit margins and may mute any disinflation effects from greater transparency (Charbonneau et al. 2017).

- *Automation.* The pandemic may induce a move by firms to increase automation to lift productivity and reduce their need to fill

---

[6] A similar exercise conducted in January 2009 would have yielded a forecast of a decline in EMDE inflation by 6.9 percentage point for 2009, above the actual decline of 5.2 percentage points in 2009. In some EMDEs, inflation may rise even further if they are subject to above-average depreciation pressures or food price pressures. A similar exercise conducted in January 2009 based on January forecasts for output and oil prices would have yielded a forecast of a decline in EMDE inflation by 3.7 percentage point for 2009, also less than the actual decline of 5.2 percentage points in 2009.

[7] In contrast, global wage inflation (defined as median across 23 economies) is expected to remain broadly stable in 2020-22.

FIGURE 4.7 Inflation expectations in 2008-10 and 2020-21

Inflation expectations during 2020-21 fell less than during the global financial crisis. Five-year-ahead inflation expectations have remained stable throughout 2020-21.

A. Advanced-economy inflation expectations: one year ahead

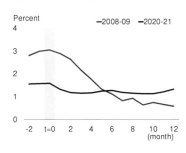

B. EMDE inflation expectations: one year ahead

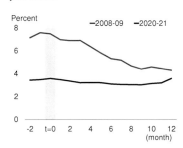

C. Advanced-economy inflation expectations: five year ahead

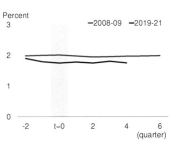

D. EMDE inflation expectations: five year ahead

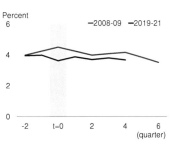

Sources: Consensus Economics; World Bank.
Note: Median short-term (A, B) or long-term (C, D) inflation expectations among 33 advanced economies (A, C) and 51 EMDEs (B, D). Shaded areas (t = 0) indicate the outbreak of COVID-19 pandemic (March 2020) and the Global Financial Crisis (September 2008).

vacancies as job markets tighten in the recovery (Ding and Molina 2020; Leduc and Liu 2020b). This may continue and deepen a long-term trend in advanced economies, where increased automation and labor market flexibility may have held down wage growth over the past decade (Haldane 2018, 2021).

- *Global value chains.* Global value chains have contributed to lower inflation through greater competition (Andrews, Gal, and Witheridge 2018; de Soyres and Franco 2019). Over the past decade, maturing global value chains appear to have contributed to slowing trade growth (chapter 3; World Bank 2020d). If global value chains were to outright reshore rather than relocate to other countries, this could reverse some of the disinflationary pressures over the past several decades.

- *Demographics.* Over the past five decades, deflationary pressures demographic trends have begun to wane; this could result in inflationary pressures in the next few years. Over the past three decades, the entry of China and Eastern Europe into the world's trading system combined with rapid population growth to limit input cost increases and lower inflation (Goodhart and Pradhan 2020). The disinflationary benefits reaped from this process may, however, now be at an inflection point as the share of the working-age population stabilizes even in EMDEs (World Bank 2018).

- *Unprecedented policy support.* During the pandemic, many central banks in advanced economies resumed or expanded large-scale asset purchases, and central banks in about two dozen EMDEs launched asset purchase programs (Rebucci, Hartley, and iménez 2020; World Bank 2021a). The literature generally suggests that monetary easing, both conventional and unconventional, typically boosts aggregate demand and inflation with a lag of 1-3 years, with somewhat clearer evidence for advanced economies than for EMDEs (Ha, Kose, and Ohnsorge 2019; World Bank 2021a).[8] In addition, many countries have put in place unprecedented fiscal support programs (chapter 1; Miles and Scott 2020). If these unprecedented policy measures are not unwound before demand runs well ahead of potential output, inflation could pick up. This inflation pickup could be temporary once excess demand pressures recede, provided that inflation expectations remain well-anchored.

- *Weak fiscal positions.* Government fiscal positions have deteriorated markedly since the start of the pandemic and are unlikely to

---

[8] While the design of unconventional monetary policy after the global financial crisis and global recession of 2009 meant that most of the injections remained within the banking system in the form of excess reserves and did not filter through to the broader money aggregates that matter for inflation, in the COVID-induced recession, measures have instead taken the form of injecting support that raised the broader measures of money (Goodhart and Pradhan 2020).

return to pre-pandemic levels in the next two years (chapter 1). The average EMDE will continue to run a fiscal deficit in excess of 3 percent of GDP in 2022 and 2023; EMDE government debt has risen to a record high of 66 percent of GDP in 2020. Several EMDEs have implemented asset purchases that may further tighten links between fiscal and monetary policy. Where such purchases continue to grow and fiscal positions are weak, central banks may be subject to political pressure to ease government financing conditions, deepening perceptions of monetary financing of fiscal deficits and further skewing secondary markets (Mandelman 2020[1]; World Bank 2021a). These developments could further increase price pressures and de-anchor long-run inflation expectations.

Policy implications

Inflation has rebounded quickly from an unusually muted decline during the global recession of 2020, despite this recession being the deepest since the Second World War. This has reflected the rapid rebound in aggregate demand, supported by unprecedented macroeconomic policy measures.

Model-based forecasts and inflation expectations point to a short-term increase in inflation of just over 1 percentage point. For virtually all advanced economies and about one-half of EMDEs, an increase of this magnitude would leave inflation within target ranges but, for another one-half of EMDEs, it would raise inflation above target ranges. Over the longer-term, however, well-anchored long-term inflation expectations point to continued low and stable inflation. As long as expectations remain well-anchored and any inflation increase—even above target ranges—is temporary, there may not be a need for a monetary policy response.

The short-term increase in inflation might extend over the longer term if policy makers are unable to keep inflation expectations anchored. Structural forces—such as demographics, growing globalization, and improvements in policy frameworks—

supported disinflation over the past decade. However, if the recovery from the pandemic coincides with a turning point in some of these forces, the expected inflation pickup in 2021 may extend and, in EMDEs, could risk de-anchoring inflation expectations. Concerns over poorly anchored inflation expectations and the possibility of permanently higher inflation may compel EMDE central banks to tighten monetary policy earlier, or more strongly, than warranted by their cyclical positions.

Similar policy responses may also become necessary in some EMDEs if concerns about advanced-economy inflation prospects causes investors to reassess inflation risks and result in a sudden increase in global borrowing costs. In EMDEs with flexible exchange rates and limited financial vulnerabilities to exchange rate movements, currency depreciation may help buffer some of the impact of tightening financial conditions on activity (Gourinchas 2018). In other EMDEs, however, financial stability concerns may force central banks to tighten monetary policy more than warranted by the strength of their economies' recovery. In part due to concerns about financial stability, a number of EMDE central banks that had implemented expansionary monetary policy in 2020 have begun to tighten policy in 2021.

Anchoring inflation expectations will be critical in preserving central banks' room to maneuver even during periods of financial stress. To achieve this, several policy options are available.

- *Monetary, fiscal, and macroprudential policies.* In inflation-targeting EMDEs with large economic slack and below-target inflation, monetary easing and fiscal support can help the recovery gain traction and raise inflation towards the target. In EMDEs where the economic recovery from the pandemic is further advanced, a more nuanced design of monetary policy will be necessary. While it may be premature to withdraw monetary and fiscal support, it would be prudent to prepare now for the possibility of future inflation risks materializing, especially those related to exchange market disruptions. Central banks can embark on an opportunistic buildup of foreign exchange reserves, heighten foreign currency risk monitoring, and strengthen macroprudential policies in anticipation of possible capital outflows once advanced economies begin to withdraw accommodative policies.

- *Central bank transparency.* Better-anchored inflation expectations will help stabilize inflation over the next few years. To minimize the extent to which fluctuations in energy and food prices will spill over to headline inflation and affect household and corporate inflation expectations, central banks will need to clearly communicate their inflation target and improve policy transparency (box 4.2; Baldwin and di Mauro 2020). Enhancing central bank transparency help anchor inflation expectations (Gelos, Rawat, and Ye 2020; Kose et al. 2019). In EMDEs that employ unconventional policies, including asset purchase programs, forward guidance, transparent objectives and operational details can help maintain investor confidence (World Bank 2021a).

- *Ensure accurate measurement of inflation.* Sharp changes in the composition of consumer spending, such as that took place during the pandemic, may distort inflation estimates (Cavallo 2020).[9] Many prices have become unobservable, either because the shops are closed or because field collection is not possible during the lockdown. Supply disruptions may create perceptions of scarcity, even if not accompanied by actual price increases (Baker et al. 2020; Coibion, Gorodnichenko, and Weber 2020). A new challenge is the collection of prices for an increasing number of services that are offered digitally or remotely. Central banks may need

---

[9] Using data from credit and debit transactions in the United States to update the official basket weights and estimate the impact on the CPI, Cavallo (2020) finds that the "COVID inflation," which reflected changes in consumption baskets after the pandemic, could have been higher than the official CPI for both headline and core indices in 2020. In addition, by applying the methodology to 17 other countries, the study also finds that, official CPI inflation after the pandemic could have been underestimated by 0.4 percentage point on average in 13 economies, while, in five countries, the official inflation could have been overestimated by 0.3 percentage point.

to consider the possibility that actual inflation is considerably higher or lower than official estimates and avoid policy overshoots that might result (Lane 2020; Tenreyro 2020). Statistical agencies could develop a supplementary index whose weights reflect new spending patterns emerging as a result of the pandemic to give policy makers a more accurate picture of the prices that consumers are currently paying (Reinsdorf 2020).

ANNEX 4.1 Methodology and database

This annex presents a novel factor-augmented vector autoregression (FAVAR) model. The empirical framework is based on recent studies that employ standard sign-restricted VAR models to explore the drivers of global inflation (Charnavoki and Dolado 2014; Ha et al. 2019c), or more generally, the Philips-curve framework (Forbes 2019). However, it deviates from these approaches in three ways to accommodate the circumstances of the 2020 pandemic.

First, the model employs higher frequency (monthly) data rather than quarterly or annual data, to minimize the concerns over the endogeneity among variables. The use of monthly data is particularly important when the pace of recessions and recoveries differs. That said, monthly data is available only for a smaller set of countries for services activity. Therefore, the exercise with monthly data relies on industrial production series, which rebounded faster than services from the global recession of 2020 (box 1.4). For the historical comparison with global recessions before 2001, when sufficiently comprehensive monthly data is unavailable, the model employs quarterly GDP data. The main findings for the comparison between the global recession of 2020 and earlier ones are consistent, regardless of the choice of monthly or quarterly data.

Second, on top of the standard sign restrictions, an additional set of narrative restrictions is imposed for the periods of large oil price fluctuations. The sign restrictions are not sufficient to identify the structural shocks, in particular in the presence of multiple large shocks. Third, the model allows for time-varying volatility in the global variables.

Model specification

The model consists of three global variables: global inflation, global output growth, and oil price growth. All variables are detrended such that, effectively global output proxies the output gap. Global output growth and global inflation are proxied by the global industrial production growth and global inflation factors estimated separately using the following dynamic factor models:

$$Y_t^i = \beta_{global} f_t^{Y,global} + e_t^{Y,i}$$

$$\pi_t^i = \beta_{global} f_t^{\pi,global} + e_t^{\pi,i}$$

where Y_t^i and π_t^i are output growth and inflation in country i in month t, respectively, while $f_t^{\pi,global}$ and $f_t^{Y,global}$ are the global factors for inflation and output growth in month t, respectively. In its structural form, the FAVAR model is represented by:

$$B_o Z_t = \alpha + \sum_{i=1}^{L} B_i Z_{t-i} + \varepsilon_t$$

where ε_t is a vector of orthogonal structural innovations, and Z_t consists of global inflation, global output growth, and oil price growth. The vector ε_t consists of a shock to the global supply of goods and services ("*global supply shock*"), a shock to the global demand for goods and services ("*global demand shock*"), and a shock to oil prices ("*oil price shock*").

While the traditional VAR model assumes that the variance-covariance matrix of residuals are constant over time, this assumption could be problematic in this analysis, given the exceptionally large macroeconomic volatility induced by the COVID-19 pandemic (Lenza and Primiceri 2020; Primiceri and Tambalotti 2020). To resolve the issue, the model assumes stochastic volatility of structural shocks—the residuals are independently but not identically distributed across time. Their variance-covariance is allowed to be period-specific, hence rendering volatility stochastic and

introducing heteroskedasticity (Carriero et al. 2019).[10]

Identification of shocks

Sign restrictions. The chapter follows the methodology in Charnavoki and Dolado (2014) and Ha et al. (2019c) in using sign restrictions to identify the global shocks.[11] Postulating that B_0^{-1} as a recursive structure such that the reduced form errors (u_t) can be decomposed according to $u_t = B_0^{-1} \varepsilon_t$, as follows:

$$\begin{bmatrix} u_t^{Y,global} \\ u_t^{OilPrice} \\ u_t^{\pi,global} \end{bmatrix} = \begin{bmatrix} + & - & + \\ + & + & + \\ + & + & - \end{bmatrix} \begin{bmatrix} \varepsilon_t^{GlobalDemand} \\ \varepsilon_t^{OilPrice} \\ \varepsilon_t^{GlobalSupply} \end{bmatrix}$$

- A positive *global demand shock* is assumed to increase global output growth, global inflation, and oil price growth.

- A positive *global non-oil supply shock* (hereafter "*global supply shock*") is assumed to raise global output and oil price growth but reduce global inflation.

- A positive *oil price shock* is defined as raising oil prices and global inflation but depressing global output growth.

Narrative restrictions. Since oil price shocks are the main drivers of variations in global inflation, the identification of oil price shocks deserves further robustness checks. In particular, similar to Antolín-Díaz Rubio-Ramírez (2018), these identified oil price shocks (or historical decompositions of the shocks) can further be constrained to ensure that they agree with the established narrative account of historical episodes. The narrative sign restrictions are imposed by considering the subset of successful draws in Bayesian estimation that result in negative oil price shocks (or negative historical contributions

---

[10] As a robustness check, the conventional model with fixed shock variances is estimated.

[11] See also Melolinna (2015) and Gambetti, Pappa, and Canova (2005) for the identification. Note that Kilian and Murphy (2012) argue that sign restrictions may not in all instances correctly identify shocks. The narrative restrictions used here help the identification.

to oil prices) during key historical episodes since 2000 identified in Baffes et al. (2015) and Wheeler et al. (2020):

- Structural oil price shocks are negative in January 2015 and March 2020.

- Historical contributions of oil price shocks to oil prices are negative in January 2015 and March 2020.

- Historical contributions of oil price shocks to oil prices are more sizeable (in absolute values) than other global shocks in January 2015.

Bayesian estimation

The model is estimated by using monthly data with four lags, as is standard in the literature. In the Bayesian estimation, the estimation first searches for 10,000 successful draws from at least 15,000 iterations with 5,000 burn-ins; the results reported are based on the median of these 10,000 successful draws, along with 16-84 percent confidence intervals. The estimation process is standard Gibbs sampling except that the volatility of residuals is endogenously determined.

To reflect a sudden change in the volatility in variables around global recessions and oil price shocks, stochastic volatility is assumed to have random inertia—this introduces an extension of the standard stochastic volatility model by turning it into an endogenous variable integrated to the Bayesian estimation process.[12] In the model, the inertia of stochastic volatility is endogenously estimated, allowing for variable-specific inertia (Cogley and Sargent 2005).

Database

The sample for the monthly estimation includes data for up to 30 advanced economies and 55 EMDEs for 2001-2021. Global output growth is

the global common factor of month-on-month, seasonally adjusted industrial production growth. Global inflation is defined as the global common factor of month-on-month headline CPI inflation. The estimation is repeated using core inflation and producer price index inflation, similarly defined. Oil price growth is the month-on-month growth rate of nominal oil prices (average of Dubai, West Texas Intermediate, and Brent).

The sample for the quarterly estimation includes data for up to 35 advanced economies and 52 EMDEs for 1970-2020. Inflation is defined as the common factor of quarter-on-quarter detrended CPI inflation; oil price growth is defined as quarter-on-quarter nominal oil price changes; output growth is defined as the common factor of quarter-on-quarter real GDP growth.

Robustness exercises

Since the FAVAR estimation in this chapter rests on various assumptions about the relationships among endogenous variables, several robustness checks on the assumptions are performed. The main results are robust to the following changes:

- Alternative frequency of data (quarterly instead of monthly) and output growth (GDP instead of industrial production);

- Alternative measures of global inflation and global output in the estimation: (i) global inflation and output factors estimated with an identical group of countries and (ii) median output growth and inflation rates among countries;

- Alternative measures of oil prices: real oil prices and nominal energy prices;

- A standard VAR model specification as an alternative to the stochastic volatility model.

Conditional forecast of global inflation

Global inflation in 2021 is forecast conditional on the FAVAR estimates over 2001-20 and the baseline forecast scenario of chapter 1. In the estimation, quarterly data are employed to directly reflect GDP growth (instead of industrial

---

[12] The standard stochastic volatility components model can have two limitations. First, the value of the autoregressive coefficient has to be predetermined. For instance, volatility in GDP growth may increase during a period of crisis, but it will clearly return to a lower, long-run value once the crisis is over. Second, the inertia in volatility is assumed to be common to all the variables included in the model.

production) and to reduce the degree of uncertainty in the forecasting. Median draws and 16-84 percentile are reported. The exercise suggests that global inflation may rise by 1.4 percentage points in 2021 globally, 1.5 percentage points in EMDEs and 1.3 percentage points in advanced economies.

Had a similar exercise been conducted in January 2009, based on forecasts developed in the January 2009 edition of the *Global Economic Prospects* report, it would have yielded a forecast of a decline in global inflation by 1.7 percentage points for 2009—considerably less than the actual decline in global inflation of 4.5 percentage points in 2009. The steeper-than-forecast actual inflation decline in part reflected a more severe-than-forecast global recession, in which global growth was -1.8 percent instead of the anticipated 0.9 percent, and lower-

than-expected oil prices, which declined to $61.8 per barrel in 2009 instead of the anticipated $74.5 per barrel (World Bank 2009).

A forecast exercise conducted in 2011 based on the baseline scenario presented in the January 2011 edition of the *Global Economic Prospects* report, would have yielded a predicted upturn in global inflation by 1.3 percentage points in 2011, that was broadly in line with actual inflation outturns, followed by an inflation decline of 1.4 percentage point in 2012 that was also broadly in line with actual outturns (World Bank 2011b). The exercise would have yielded a forecast of a decline in advanced-economy inflation by 0.7 percentage point for 2009, again considerably less than the 3.4 percentage point decline in inflation between 2008 and 2009 that actually materialized.

TABLE 4.1 LICs with highest food insecure populations

Country	Population with high food insecurity	Drivers (additional to high global food prices)
Congo, Dem. Rep.	21.8M	Conflict and violence; economic shocks and COVID-19 disruption; weather extremes; agricultural pests and diseases.
Republic of Yemen	13.5M	Conflict and violence; economic shocks and COVID-19 disruption; Weather extremes.
Afghanistan	13.2M	Conflict and violence; economic shocks and COVID-19 disruption; Weather extremes.
Syrian Arab Republic	12.4M	Conflict and violence; economic shocks and COVID-19 disruption; weather extremes.
Sudan	9.6M	Conflict and violence; economic shocks and COVID-19 disruption; weather extremes.
Ethiopia	8.6M	Conflict and violence; economic shocks and COVID-19 disruption; weather extremes; agricultural pests and diseases.
South Sudan	6.5M	Conflict and violence; economic crisis; economic shocks and COVID-19 disruption; weather extremes.
Zimbabwe	4.3M	Economic shocks and COVID-19 disruption; weather extremes; agricultural pests and diseases.
Haiti	4.1M	Conflict and violence; economic crisis; economic shocks and COVID-19 disruption; weather extremes.

Source: FSIN and GNAFC (2021).
Note: Number of people in Integrated Food Security Phase Classification (IPC) and Cadre Harmonise (CH) Phase 3 or above in 2020.

References

Aizenman, J., M. D. Chinn, and H. Ito. 2008. "Assessing the Emerging Global Financial Architecture: Measuring the Trilemma's Configurations over Time." NBER Working Paper 14533, National Bureau of Economic Research, Cambridge, MA.

Andrews, D., P. Gal, and W. Witheridge. 2018. "A Genie in a Bottle? Globalisation, Competition, and Inflation." OECD Economics Department Working Paper 1462, Organisation for Economic Co-operation and Development, Paris.

Antolín-Díaz, J., and F. Rubio-Ramírez. 2018. "Narrative Sign Restrictions for SVARs." *American Economic Review* 108 (10): 2802-29.

Armantier, O., G. Koşar, R. Pomerantz, D. Skandalis, K. Smith, G. Topa, and W. Van der Klaauw. 2020. "Inflation Expectations in Times of COVID-19." *Liberty Street Economics* (blog), May 13, 2020. Federal Reserve Bank of New York.

Baffes, J., M. A. Kose, F. Ohnsorge, and M. Stocker. 2015. "The Great Plunge in Oil Prices—Causes, Consequences, and Policy Responses." Policy Research Note 1, World Bank, Washington, DC.

Baker, S. R., R. A. Farrokhnia, S. Meyer, M. Pagel, and C. Yannelis. 2020. "How Does Household Spending Respond to an Epidemic? Consumption During the 2020 COVID-19 Pandemic." NBER Working Paper 26949, National Bureau of Economic Research, Cambridge, MA.

Baldini, A., and M. Poplawski-Ribeiro. 2011. "Fiscal and Monetary Determinants of Inflation in Low-Income Countries: Theory and Evidence from Sub-Saharan Africa." *Journal of African Economies* 20 (3): 419-62.

Baldwin, R. 2020. "The Supply Side Matters: Guns versus Butter, COVID-style." VoxEU.org, CEPR Policy Portal, March 22, https://voxeu.org/article/supply-side-matters-guns-versus-butter-covid-style.

Baldwin, R., and B. W. di Mauro, eds. 2020. *Mitigating the COVID Economic Crisis: Act Fast and Do Whatever It Takes.* London: CERP Press.

Ball, L. 1994. "What Determines the Sacrifice Ratio?" In *Monetary Policy,* edited by G. Mankiw. Chicago: Chicago University Press.

Ball, L., G. Gopinath, D. Leig, P. Mitra, and A. Spilimbergo. 2021. "U.S. Inflation: Set for Take-off?" VoxEU.org, CEPR Policy Portal, May 7, https://voxeu.org/article/us-inflation-set-take.

Banerjee, A., M. Alsan, E. Breza, A. G. Chandrasekhar, A. Chowdhury, E. Duflo, P. Goldsmith-Pinkham, and B. A. Olken. 2020. "Messages on COVID-19 Prevention in India Increased Symptoms Reporting and Adherence to Preventive Behaviors Among 25 Million Recipients with Similar Effects on Non-recipient Members of Their Communities." NBER Working Paper 27496, National Bureau of Economic Research, Cambridge, MA.

Bekaert, G., E. Engstrom, and A. Ermolov. 2020. "Aggregate Demand and Aggregate Supply Effects of COVID-19: A Real-time Analysis." Finance and Economics Discussion Series 2020-049, Board of Governors of the Federal Reserve System, Washington, DC.

Blanchard, O. 2020. "Is there Deflation or Inflation in Our Future?" VoxEU.org, CEPR Policy Portal, April 24, https://voxeu.org/article/there-deflation-or-inflation-our-future.

Blanchard, O., and J. Pisani-Ferry. 2020. "Monetisation: Do Not Panic." VoxEU.org, CEPR Policy Portal, April 10, https://voxeu.org/article/monetisation-do-not-panic.

Bleaney, M., and M. Francisco. 2018. "Is the Phillips Curve Different in Poor Countries?" *Bulletin of Economic Research* 70 (1): E17-E28.

Bryan, M. F. 2021. "The Great Inflation." Federal Reserve History Series, Federal Reserve Bank of Atlanta, Atlanta, GA.

Cachia, F. 2014. "Regional Food Price Inflation Transmission." FAO Working Paper ESS/14-01, Food and Agriculture Organization of the United Nations, Rome.

Caggiano, G., E. Castelnuovo and R. Kima. 2020. "The Global Effects of Covid-19-induced Uncertainty." Research Discussion Papers 11/2020, Bank of Finland.

Carriero, A., T. E. Clark, and M. Marcellino, 2019. "Large Vector Autoregressions with Stochastic Volatility and Non-Conjugate Priors." *Journal of Econometrics* 212 (1): 137-154.

Cavallo, A. 2020. "Inflation with COVID Consumption Baskets." NBER Working Paper 27352, National Bureau of Economic Research, Cambridge, MA.

Cecchetti, S. G., P. Hooper, B. C. Kasman, K. L. Schoenholtz, and M. Watson. 2007. "Understanding the Evolving Inflation Process." U.S. Monetary Policy Forum 2007, Washington, DC.

Charbonneau, K. B., A. Evans, S. Sarker, and L. Suchanek. 2017. "Digitalization and Inflation: A Review of the Literature." Staff Analytical Note 17-20, Bank of Canada.

Charnavoki, V., and J. Dolado. 2014. "The Effects of Global Shocks on Small Commodity-Exporting Economies: Lessons from Canada." *American Economic Journal: Macroeconomics* 6 (2): 207-237.

Cogley, T. and T. J. Sargent. 2005. "Drift and Volatilities: Monetary Policies and Outcomes in the Post WWII U.S." *Review of Economic Dynamics* 8 (2): 262-302.

Coibion, O., Y. Gorodnichenko, and M. Weber. 2020. "The Cost of the Covid-19 Crisis: Lockdowns, Macroeconomic Expectations, and Consumer Spending." NBER Working Paper 27141, National Bureau of Economic Research, Cambridge, MA.

Datt, G., and M. Ravallion. 1998. "Why Have Some Indian States Done Better Than Others at Reducing Rural Poverty?" *Economica* 65 (257): 17-38.

de Soyres, F., and S. Franco. 2019. "Inflation Synchronization through GVCs." Unpublished working paper, World Bank, Washington, DC.

Ding, L., and J. S. Molina. 2020. "'Forced Automation' by COVID-19? Early Trends from Current Population Survey Data." Discussion Paper 88713, Federal Reserve Bank of Philadelphia, PA.

Dunn, A. C., K. K. Hood, and A. Driessen. 2020. "Measuring the Effects of the COVID-19 Pandemic on Consumer Spending Using Card Transaction Data." Bureau of Economic Analysis Working Paper 2020–5, U.S. Department of Commerce.

Ebrahimy, E., D. Igan, and S. M. Peria. 2020. "The Impact of COVID-19 on Inflation: Potential Drivers and Dynamics." Special Notes Series on COVID-19, International Monetary Fund, Washington, DC.

Forbes, K. 2019. "Has Globalization Changed the Inflation Process?" BIS Working Paper 791, Bank for International Settlements, Basel.

FSIN (Food Security Information Network) and GNAFC (Global Network Against Food Crises). 2021. "Global Report on Food Crises." Global Network Against Food Crises, Rome.

Gambetti, L., E. Pappa, and F. Canova. 2005. "The Structural Dynamics of US Output and Inflation: What Explains the Changes?" Economics Working Papers 921, Universitat Pompeu Fabra, Barcelona.

Gelos, G., U. Rawat, H. Ye. 2020. "COVID-19 in Emerging Markets: Escaping the Monetary Policy Procyclicality Trap." VoxEU.org, CEPR Policy Portal, August 20, https://voxeu.org/article/covid-19-emerging -markets-escaping-monetary-policy-procyclicality-trap.

Gentilini, U., M. Almenfi, I. Orton, and P. Dale. 2020. "Social Protection and Jobs Responses to COVID-19: A Real-Time Review of Country Measures." World Bank, Washington, DC.

Goodhart, C., and M. Pradhan. 2020. "Future Imperfect After Coronavirus." VoxEU.org, CEPR Policy Portal, March 27, https://voxeu.org/article/ future-imperfect-after-coronavirus.

Gopinath, G. 2021. "Structural Factors and Central Bank Credibility Limit Inflation Risks." *IMF Blog*, February 19, 2021. https://blogs.imf.org/2021/02/19/ structural-factors-and-central-bank-credibility-limit-inflation-risks.

Gourinchas, P.-O. 2018. "Monetary Policy Transmission in Emerging Markets: An Application to Chile." Central Banking Analysis and Economic Policies 25, Central Bank of Chile, Santiago.

Guénette, J. D. 2020. "Price Controls: Good Intentions, Bad Outcomes." Policy Research Working Paper 9212, World Bank, Washington, DC.

Ha, J., A. Ivanova, P. Montiel, and P. Pedroni. 2019a. "Inflation in Low-Income Countries." Policy Research Working Paper 8934, World Bank, Washington, DC.

Ha, J., A. Ivanova, F. Ohnsorge, and F. Unsal. 2019b. "Inflation: Concepts, Evolution, and Correlates." Policy Research Working Paper 8738, World Bank, Washington, DC.

Ha, J., M. A. Kose, and F. Ohnsorge, and H. Yilmazkuday. 2019c. "Sources of Inflation: Global and Domestic Drivers." In *Inflation in Emerging and Developing Economies: Evolution, Drivers, and Policies*, edited by J. Ha, M. A. Kose, and F. Ohnsorge, 143-204. Washington, DC: World Bank.

Ha, J., M. A. Kose, and F. Ohnsorge, eds. 2019. *Inflation in Emerging and Developing Economies: Evolution, Drivers, and Policies*. Washington, DC: World Bank.

Ha, J., M. Stocker, and H. Yilmazkuday. 2020. "Inflation and Exchange Rate Pass-through." *Journal of International Money and Finance* 105 (July): 102187.

Haldane, A. 2018. "Pay Power." Speech at ACAS Future of Work Conference, Bank of England, October 10.

Haldane, A. 2021. "Inflation: A Tiger by the Tail?" Online speech, Bank of England, February 26.

Harding, D., and A. Pagan. 2002. "Dissecting the Cycle: A methodological Investigation." *Journal of Monetary Economics* 49 (2): 365-81.

Husain, A. S., Sandström, F. Greb, J. Groder, C. Pallanch, and P. Agamile. 2020. "Economic and Food Security Implications of the COVID-19 Outbreak." World Food Programme, Washington, DC.

IDA (International Development Association). 2020. "Responding to the Emerging Food Security Crisis." International Development Association, World Bank, Washington, DC.

Ide, T. 2021. "COVID-19 and Armed Conflict." *World Development* 140 (C). https://doi:10.1016/j.worlddev.2020.105355.

IFPRI (International Food Policy Research Institute). 2021. *2021 Global Food Policy Report: Transforming Food Systems after COVID-19.* Washington, DC: International Food Policy Research Institute.

Ivanic, M., and W. Martin. 2008. "Implications of Higher Global Food Prices for Poverty in Low-Income Countries." Policy Research Working Paper 4594, World Bank, Washington, DC.

Ivanic, M., and W. Martin. 2014. "Short- and Long-Run Impacts of food Price Changes on Poverty" Policy Research Working Paper 7011, World Bank, Washington, DC.

Ivanic, M., W. Martin, and H. Zaman. 2012. "Estimating the Short-Run Poverty Impacts of the 2010-11 Surge in Food Prices." *World Development* 40 (11): 2302-17.

Kabundi, A., and F. Ohnsorge. 2020. "Implications of Cheap Oil for Emerging Markets." Policy Research Working Paper 9403, World Bank, Washington, DC.

Kilian, L., and D. P. Murphy. 2012. "Why Agnostic Sign Restrictions Are Not Enough: Understanding the Dynamics of Oil Market VAR Models." *Journal of the European Economic Association* 10 (5): 1166-1188.

Klein, M. W., and J. Shambaugh. 2010. *Exchange Rate Regimes in the Modern Era.* Cambridge, MA: MIT Press.

Kose, M. A., H. Matsuoka, U. Panizza, and D. Vorisek. 2019. "Inflation Expectations: Review and Evidence." Policy Research Working Paper 8785, World Bank, Washington, DC.

Kose, M. A., N. Sugawara, and M. E. Terrones. 2020. "Global Recessions." Policy Research Working Paper 9172, World Bank, Washington, DC.

Kose, M. A., and M. E. Terrones. 2015. *Collapse and Revival: Understanding Global Recessions and Recoveries.* Washington, DC: International Monetary Fund.

Laborde, D., C. Lakatos, and W. Martin. 2019. Poverty Impacts of Food Price Shocks and Policies. In *Inflation in Emerging and Developing Economies: Evolution, Drivers, and Policies,* edited by J. Ha, M. A. Kose, and F. Ohnsorge. Washington, DC: World Bank.

Laborde, D., A. Mamun, and M. Parent. 2020. "COVID-19 Food Trade Policy Tracker." International Food Policy Research Institute, Washington, DC. https://www.ifpri.org/project/covid-19-food-trade-policy-tracker.

Lakner, C., N. Yonzan, D. G. Mahler, R. A. Castaneda Aguilar, and H. Wu. 2021. "Updated Estimates of the Impact of COVID-19 on Global Poverty: Looking Back at 2020 and the Outlook for 2021." *Data Blog,* January 11, 2021. https://blogs.worldbank.org/opendata/updated-estimates-impact-covid-19-global-poverty-looking-back-2020-and-outlook-2021.

Landau, J. 2021. "Inflation and the Biden Stimulus." VoxEU.org, CEPR Policy Portal, February 8, https://voxeu.org/article/inflation-and-biden-stimulus.

Lane, T. 2020. "Policies for the Great Global Shutdown and Beyond." Online speech to CFA Society Winnipeg and Manitoba Association for Business Economics, May 20. https://www.bankofcanada.ca/2020/05/policies-great-global-shutdown-and-beyond/.

Leduc S., and Z. Liu, 2020a. "The Uncertainty Channel of the Coronavirus." FRBSF Economic Letter 2020-07, Federal Reserve Bank of San Francisco.

Leduc, S., and Z. Liu. 2020b. "Can Pandemic-Induced Job Uncertainty Stimulate Automation?" Working Paper 2020-19, Federal Reserve Bank of San Francisco, CA.

Lenza, M., and G. E. Primiceri. 2020. "How to Estimate a VAR after March 2020." NBER Working Paper 27771, National Bureau of Economic Research, Cambridge, MA.

Levin, A. T., and J. M. Piger. 2004. "Is inflation persistence intrinsic in industrial economies?" Working Paper Series 334, European Central Bank.

Mandelman, F. S. 2021. "Money Aggregates, Debt, Pent-Up Demand, and Inflation: Evidence from WWII." Policy Hub Papers 4-2021, Federal Reserve Bank of Atlanta .

Melolinna, M. 2015. "What has Driven Inflation Dynamics in the Euro Area, the United Kingdom and the United States. Working Paper Series 1802, European Central Bank, Frankfurt.

Miles, D., and A. Scott. 2020. "Will Inflation Make a Comeback after the Crisis Ends?" VoxEU.org, CEPR Policy Portal, April 4, https://voxeu.org/article/will-inflation-make-comeback-after-crisis-ends.

Mishkin, F. S., and K. Schmidt-Hebbel. 2007. "Does Inflation Targeting Make a Difference?" NBER Working Paper 12876, National Bureau of Economic Research, Cambridge, MA.

Mishra, P., and P. Montiel. 2013. "How Effective is Monetary Transmission in Low-Income Countries? A Survey of the Empirical Evidence." *Economic Systems* 37 (2): 187-216.

O'Brien, D., C. Dumoncel, and E. Gonçalves. 2021. "The Role of Demand and Supply Factors in HICP Inflation during the COVID-19 Pandemic—A Disaggregated Perspective." ECB Economic Bulletin 1/2021, European Central Bank, Frankfurt.

Primiceri, G. E., and A. Tambalotti. 2020. "Macroeconomic Forecasting in the Time of COVID-19." Unpublished paper.

Rebucci, A., J. S. Hartley, and D. Jiménez. 2020. "An Event Study of COVID-19 Central Bank Quantitative Easing in Advanced and Emerging Economies." NBER Working Paper 27339, National Bureau of Economic Research, Cambridge, MA.

Reinsdorf, M. B. 2020. "COVID-19 and the CPI: Is Inflation Underestimated?" IMF Working Paper 2020/224, International Monetary Fund, Washington, DC.

Rogoff, B, 2003. *The Cultural Nature of Human Development.* Oxford, U.K.: Oxford University Press.

Romer, C., and D. Romer. 1999. "Monetary Policy and the Well-being of the Poor." *Federal Reserve Bank of Kansas City Economic Review* 84 (Q I): 21-49.

Shapiro, A. H. 2020. "A Simple Framework to Monitor Inflation." Working Paper 2020-29, Federal Reserve Bank of San Francisco.

Siami-Namini, S., and D. Hudson. 2019, "Inflation and Income Inequality in Developed and Developing Countries." *Journal of Economic Studies* 46 (3): 611-632.

Swinnen, J., and J. McDermott, eds. 2020. *COVID-19 and Global Food Security.* Washington, DC: International Food Policy Research Institute.

Tenreyro, S. 2020. "Monetary Policy During Pandemics: Inflation Before, During, and After Covid-19." Online presentation, Bank of England, April 16.

Weidmann, J. 2013. "Who Calls the Shots? The Problem of Fiscal Dominance." Speech at the 4th Bank of France-Deutsche Bundesbank Macroeconomics and Finance Conference, Paris, May 24.

Wheeler, C. M., J. Baffes, A. Kabundi, G. Kindberg-Hanlon, P. S. Nagle, and F. Ohnsorge. 2020. "Adding Fuel to the Fire: Cheap Oil during the COVID-19 Pandemic." Policy Research Working Paper 9320, World Bank, Washington, DC.

Williamson, S. 2021. "The Mysteries of Inflation" (blog). https://stevewilliamson.substack.com/p/the-mysteries-of-inflation.

World Bank. 2009. *Global Economic Prospects: Commodities at the Crossroads.* January. Washington, DC: World Bank.

World Bank. 2011a. "Responding to Global Food Price Volatility and Its Impact on Food Security." World Bank, Washington, DC.

World Bank. 2011b. *Global Economic Prospects: Maintaining Progress Amid Turmoil.* June. Washington, DC: World Bank.

World Bank. 2018. *Global Economic Prospects: Broad-Based Upturn, but for How Long?* January. Washington, DC: World Bank.

World Bank. 2020a. *Global Economic Prospects,* June. Washington, DC: World Bank.

World Bank. 2020b. *Global Economic Prospects.* January. Washington, DC: World Bank.

World Bank. 2020c. *Commodity Markets Outlook: Implications of COVID-19 for Commodities.* April. Washington, DC: World Bank.

World Bank. 2020d. *World Development Report: Trading for Development in an Age of Global Value Chains.* Washington, DC: World Bank.

World Bank. 2021a. *Global Economic Prospects.* January. Washington, DC: World Bank.

World Bank. 2021b. *Commodity Markets Outlook: Causes and Consequences of Metals Price Shocks.* April. Washington, DC: World Bank.

World Bank. 2021c. *South Asia Economic Focus: South Asia Vaccinates.* Washington, DC: World Bank.

WFP (World Food Program) and FAO (Food and Agriculture Organization of the United Nations). 2021. "Hunger Hotspots. FAO-WFP Early Warnings on Acute Food Insecurity." March to July 2021 outlook. Rome: WFP and FAO.

STATISTICAL APPENDIX

Real GDP growth

	Annual estimates and forecasts [1] (Percent change)						Quarterly estimates [2] (Percent change, year-on-year)					
	2018	2019	2020e	2021f	2022f	2023f	19Q4	20Q1	20Q2	20Q3	20Q4	21Q1e
World	3.2	2.5	-3.5	5.6	4.3	3.1	2.4	-1.6	-9.1	..	..	..
Advanced economies	2.3	1.6	-4.7	5.4	4.0	2.2	1.4	-1.1	-11.0	-3.7	-3.0	..
United States	3.0	2.2	-3.5	6.8	4.2	2.3	2.3	0.3	-9.0	-2.8	-2.4	0.4
Euro area	1.9	1.3	-6.6	4.2	4.4	2.4	1.0	-3.3	-14.6	-4.1	-4.9	-1.8
Japan	0.6	0.0	-4.7	2.9	2.6	1.0	-1.3	-2.2	-10.2	-5.5	-1.0	-1.8
Emerging market and developing economies	4.6	3.8	-1.7	6.0	4.7	4.4	3.9	-2.4	-6.1	..	..	..
East Asia and Pacific	6.5	5.8	1.2	7.7	5.3	5.2	5.6	-5.5	1.1	3.4	4.9	15.3
Cambodia	7.5	7.1	-3.1	4.0	5.2	6.0	..	..	..	..	..	..
China	6.8	6.0	2.3	8.5	5.4	5.3	5.8	-6.8	3.2	4.9	6.5	18.3
Fiji	3.5	-0.4	-19.0	2.6	8.2	6.9	..	..	..	..	..	..
Indonesia	5.2	5.0	-2.1	4.4	5.0	5.1	5.0	3.0	-5.3	-3.5	-2.2	-0.7
Kiribati	3.8	3.9	-1.9	3.0	2.6	2.5	..	..	..	..	..	..
Lao PDR	6.3	5.5	0.4	4.0	4.6	4.7	..	..	..	..	..	..
Malaysia	4.8	4.3	-5.6	6.0	4.2	4.4	3.7	0.7	-17.2	-2.7	-3.4	-0.5
Marshall Islands [3]	3.3	6.6	-4.5	-1.0	3.0	2.0	..	..	..	..	..	..
Micronesia, Fed. Sts. [3]	0.2	1.2	-1.5	-3.5	2.5	1.0	..	..	..	..	..	..
Mongolia	7.0	5.0	-5.4	5.9	6.1	7.0	-0.7	-10.9	-8.8	-2.7	-0.9	15.5
Myanmar [3 6]	6.4	6.8	1.7	-10.0	..	..	..	..	..	..	..	..
Nauru [3]	5.7	1.0	0.7	1.3	0.9	1.0	..	..	..	..	..	..
Palau [3]	4.1	-4.2	-10.0	-4.0	12.0	6.0	..	..	..	..	..	..
Papua New Guinea	-0.3	5.9	-3.9	3.5	4.2	2.4	..	..	..	..	..	..
Philippines	6.3	6.0	-9.6	4.7	5.9	6.0	6.6	-0.7	-17.0	-11.6	-8.3	-4.2
Samoa [3]	-2.2	3.5	-3.5	-7.7	5.6	4.9	..	..	..	..	..	..
Solomon Islands	3.9	1.2	-5.0	2.0	4.5	4.3	..	..	..	..	..	..
Thailand	4.2	2.3	-6.1	2.2	5.1	4.3	1.3	-2.1	-12.1	-6.4	-4.2	-2.6
Timor-Leste	-1.1	1.8	-7.3	1.8	3.7	4.3	..	..	..	..	..	..
Tonga [3]	0.3	0.7	-1.5	-3.0	2.3	2.8	..	..	..	..	..	..
Tuvalu	4.3	4.1	-0.5	3.0	4.0	3.0	..	..	..	..	..	..
Vanuatu	2.8	3.0	-10.0	4.0	3.9	3.3	..	..	..	..	..	..
Vietnam	7.1	7.0	2.9	6.6	6.5	6.5	7.0	3.7	0.4	2.6	4.5	4.5
Europe and Central Asia	3.5	2.7	-2.1	3.9	3.9	3.5	4.0	2.2	-8.8	-1.4	-0.4	..
Albania	4.1	2.2	-3.3	4.4	3.7	3.7	0.0	-2.3	-10.6	-2.8	3.0	..
Armenia	5.2	7.6	-7.6	3.4	4.3	5.3	7.6	4.2	-13.5	-8.7	-8.7	-3.3
Azerbaijan	1.5	2.2	-4.3	2.8	3.9	3.4	..	..	..	..	..	..
Belarus	3.1	1.4	-0.9	-2.2	1.9	1.2	2.2	-0.2	-3.3	-0.2	-0.2	..
Bosnia and Herzegovina [2]	3.7	2.8	-4.3	2.8	3.5	3.7	1.9	2.3	-9.0	-6.3	-3.8	..
Bulgaria	3.1	3.7	-4.2	2.6	3.3	3.4	3.2	1.8	-8.5	-4.2	-4.7	..
Croatia	2.8	2.9	-8.0	5.5	6.2	5.7	2.3	0.9	-14.4	-10.1	-7.2	-0.7
Georgia	4.9	5.0	-6.1	6.0	5.0	5.0	4.6	2.3	-13.2	-5.6	-6.8	..
Hungary	5.4	4.6	-5.0	6.0	4.7	4.3	4.3	2.1	-13.3	-4.6	-3.5	-2.1
Kazakhstan	4.1	4.5	-2.6	3.2	3.7	4.8	5.0	2.7	-6.0	-4.7	-2.1	..
Kosovo	3.8	4.9	-6.9	4.0	4.5	4.1	..	..	..	..	..	..
Kyrgyz Republic	3.8	4.6	-8.6	3.8	4.3	4.5	..	..	..	..	..	..
Moldova	4.3	3.6	-7.0	3.8	3.7	3.8	0.2	0.9	-14.0	-9.8	-3.3	..
Montenegro [5]	5.1	4.1	-15.2	7.1	4.5	3.5	..	..	..	..	..	..
North Macedonia	2.9	3.2	-4.5	3.6	3.5	3.4	3.3	0.9	-14.9	-3.3	-0.7	..
Poland	5.4	4.7	-2.7	3.8	4.5	3.9	4.0	2.0	-7.9	-2.0	-2.7	-1.4
Romania	4.5	4.1	-3.9	6.0	4.5	3.9	4.3	2.4	-10.0	-5.6	-1.4	-0.2
Russian Federation	2.8	2.0	-3.0	3.2	3.2	2.3	2.9	1.4	-7.8	-3.5	-1.8	-1.0
Serbia	4.4	4.2	-1.0	5.0	3.7	3.9	6.3	5.2	-6.3	-1.4	-1.0	1.7
Tajikistan	7.6	7.4	4.5	5.3	5.6	6.0	..	..	..	..	..	..
Turkey	3.0	0.9	1.8	5.0	4.5	4.5	6.4	4.5	-10.3	6.3	5.9	7.0
Ukraine	3.4	3.2	-4.0	3.8	3.1	3.1	1.4	-1.2	-11.2	-3.5	-0.5	-2.0
Uzbekistan	5.4	5.8	1.6	4.8	5.5	5.8	..	..	..	..	..	..

Real GDP growth *(continued)*

	Annual estimates and forecasts [1] (Percent change)						Quarterly estimates [2] (Percent change, year-on-year)					
	2018	2019	2020e	2021f	2022f	2023f	19Q4	20Q1	20Q2	20Q3	20Q4	21Q1e
Latin America and the Caribbean	**1.8**	**0.9**	**-6.5**	**5.2**	**2.9**	**2.5**	**0.8**	**-1.0**	**-15.4**	**..**	**..**	**..**
Argentina	-2.6	-2.1	-9.9	6.4	1.7	1.9	-1.1	-5.2	-19.0	-10.1	-4.3	..
Bahamas, The	3.0	1.2	-16.2	2.0	8.5	4.0	..	..	..	..	..	..
Barbados	-0.6	-0.1	-18.0	3.3	8.5	4.8	..	..	..	..	..	..
Belize	2.9	1.8	-14.1	1.9	6.4	4.2	-2.2	-6.3	-23.8	-12.8	-13.0	..
Bolivia	4.2	2.2	-8.8	4.7	3.5	3.0	1.1	0.6	-21.7	..	..	..
Brazil	1.8	1.4	-4.1	4.5	2.5	2.3	1.6	-0.3	-10.9	-3.9	-1.1	1.0
Chile	3.7	0.9	-5.8	6.1	3.0	2.5	-2.0	0.2	-14.2	-9.0	0.0	0.3
Colombia	2.6	3.3	-6.8	5.9	4.1	4.0	3.3	0.6	-15.7	-8.4	-3.6	1.1
Costa Rica	2.1	2.2	-4.1	2.7	3.4	3.1	4.1	1.0	-8.4	-6.4	-2.7	..
Dominica	2.3	3.6	-10.0	1.0	3.0	2.5	..	..	..	..	..	..
Dominican Republic	7.0	5.1	-6.7	5.5	4.8	4.8	5.8	0.0	-16.9	-7.2	-2.9	..
Ecuador	1.3	0.1	-7.8	3.4	1.4	1.8	-1.4	-1.9	-12.8	-9.1	-7.2	..
El Salvador	2.4	2.6	-7.9	4.1	3.1	2.4	3.0	0.1	-19.8	-10.0	-2.1	..
Grenada	4.1	1.9	-12.6	3.5	5.0	4.9	..	..	..	..	..	..
Guatemala	3.3	3.9	-1.5	3.6	4.0	3.8	4.1	1.2	-8.9	-1.4	3.0	..
Guyana	4.4	5.4	43.5	20.9	26.0	23.0	..	..	..	..	..	..
Haiti [3]	1.7	-1.7	-3.3	-0.5	1.5	2.0	..	..	..	..	..	..
Honduras	3.8	2.7	-9.0	4.5	3.9	3.8	2.6	-1.3	-19.2	-7.9	-7.7	..
Jamaica [2]	1.9	0.9	-10.0	3.0	3.8	3.2	0.0	-2.4	-18.4	-10.6	-8.3	..
Mexico	2.2	-0.2	-8.3	5.0	3.0	2.0	-0.7	-1.3	-18.7	-8.7	-4.5	-3.6
Nicaragua	-3.4	-3.7	-2.0	0.9	1.2	1.4	1.2	1.1	-6.3	-1.0	-1.9	..
Panama	3.6	3.0	-17.9	9.9	7.8	4.9	3.4	0.4	-38.2	-23.6	-10.9	..
Paraguay	3.2	-0.4	-0.6	3.5	4.0	3.8	3.2	4.3	-6.7	-1.3	1.0	..
Peru	4.0	2.2	-11.1	10.3	3.9	3.5	1.9	-3.7	-30.0	-9.0	-1.7	3.8
St. Lucia	2.6	1.7	-20.4	2.6	11.5	8.1	..	..	..	..	..	..
St. Vincent and the Grenadines	2.2	0.5	-3.8	-6.1	8.3	6.1	..	..	..	..	..	..
Suriname	2.6	0.3	-14.5	-1.9	0.1	1.3	..	..	..	..	..	..
Uruguay	0.5	0.4	-5.9	3.4	3.1	2.5	-0.5	-1.9	-12.9	-5.8	-2.9	..
Middle East and North Africa	**0.6**	**0.6**	**-3.9**	**2.4**	**3.5**	**3.2**	**1.2**	**-1.0**	**-6.6**	**..**	**..**	**..**
Algeria	1.2	0.8	-5.5	3.6	2.3	1.6	0.2	-3.9	..	..	..	..
Bahrain	2.0	1.9	-5.4	3.3	3.2	3.2	-0.3	-1.7	-9.0	-6.9	-5.5	..
Djibouti	8.4	7.8	0.5	5.5	6.0	6.2	..	..	..	..	..	..
Egypt, Arab Rep. [3]	5.3	5.6	3.6	2.3	4.5	5.5	5.6	5.0	-1.7	0.7	2.0	..
Iran, Islamic Rep. [3]	-6.0	-6.8	1.7	2.1	2.2	2.3	1.8	-6.8	-2.9	4.9	3.4	..
Iraq	-1.2	4.4	-10.4	1.9	8.4	4.2	..	..	..	..	..	..
Jordan	1.9	2.0	-1.6	1.4	2.2	2.3	2.1	1.3	-3.6	-2.2	-1.6	..
Kuwait	1.2	0.4	-5.4	2.4	3.6	2.8	-1.1	-1.0	-13.4	-11.5	..	..
Lebanon [6]	-1.9	-6.7	-20.3	-9.5	..	..	..	..	..	..	..	..
Libya [6]	15.1	2.5	-31.3	66.7	..	..	..	..	..	..	..	..
Morocco	3.1	2.5	-7.1	4.6	3.4	3.7	2.3	-0.1	-15.1	-7.2	-6.0	..
Oman	0.9	-0.8	-6.3	2.5	6.5	4.2	..	..	..	..	..	..
Qatar	1.2	0.8	-3.7	3.0	4.1	4.5	0.2	0.0	-6.1	-4.6	-3.9	..
Saudi Arabia	2.4	0.3	-4.1	2.4	3.3	3.2	-0.3	-1.0	-7.0	-4.6	-3.9	-3.3
Tunisia	2.9	0.9	-8.8	4.0	2.6	2.2	0.9	-2.1	-21.3	-5.7	-6.1	-3.0
United Arab Emirates	1.7	4.8	-6.1	1.2	2.5	2.5	0.8	-0.3	-7.4	..	..	..
West Bank and Gaza	1.2	1.4	-11.5	3.5	3.6	3.7	-1.4	-3.5	-19.5	-10.8	-12.2	..

Real GDP growth *(continued)*

	Annual estimates and forecasts [1] (Percent change)						Quarterly estimates [2] (Percent change, year-on-year)					
	2018	2019	2020e	2021f	2022f	2023f	19Q4	20Q1	20Q2	20Q3	20Q4	21Q1e
South Asia	**6.4**	**4.4**	**-5.4**	**6.8**	**6.8**	**5.2**	**3.3**	**2.8**	**-23.9**	**-7.1**	**0.3**	..
Afghanistan	1.2	3.9	-1.9	1.0	2.6	3.0	..	..	..	..	..	..
Bangladesh [3 4]	7.9	8.2	2.4	3.6	5.1	6.2	..	..	..	..	..	..
Bhutan [3 4]	3.8	4.3	-0.8	-1.8	5.0	5.6	..	..	..	..	..	..
India [3 4]	6.5	4.0	-7.3	8.3	7.5	6.5	3.3	3.0	-24.4	-7.4	0.5	1.6
Maldives	8.1	7.0	-28.0	17.1	11.5	8.3	9.3	-4.2	-51.8	-44.2	-30.5	..
Nepal [3 4]	7.6	6.7	-2.1	2.7	3.9	5.1	4.7	2.7	4.4	1.1	-15.3	-4.6
Pakistan [3 4]	5.5	2.1	-0.5	1.3	2.0	3.4	..	..	..	..	..	..
Sri Lanka	3.3	2.3	-3.6	3.4	2.0	2.1	1.6	-1.8	-16.4	1.3	1.3	..
Sub-Saharan Africa	**2.7**	**2.5**	**-2.4**	**2.8**	**3.3**	**3.8**	**2.1**	**1.8**	**-10.2**	**-4.0**	..	..
Angola	-2.0	-0.6	-5.2	0.5	3.3	3.5	..	..	..	..	..	..
Benin	6.7	6.9	2.0	5.0	6.0	6.5	..	..	..	..	..	..
Botswana	4.5	3.0	-7.9	6.9	4.3	4.1	1.7	2.7	-24.0	-6.0	-4.1	..
Burkina Faso	6.7	5.7	0.6	3.1	5.0	5.7	..	..	..	..	..	..
Burundi	1.6	1.8	0.3	2.0	2.5	3.0	..	..	..	..	..	..
Cabo Verde	4.5	5.7	-14.0	3.9	5.2	6.1	..	..	..	..	..	..
Cameroon	4.1	3.7	-2.1	2.1	2.7	3.8	..	..	..	..	..	..
Central African Republic	3.7	3.1	0.0	0.7	2.8	4.4	..	..	..	..	..	..
Chad	2.4	3.2	-0.9	1.0	2.5	2.9	..	..	..	..	..	..
Comoros	3.4	2.0	-0.5	0.2	2.2	4.2	..	..	..	..	..	..
Congo, Dem. Rep.	5.8	4.4	0.8	2.5	3.0	4.1	..	..	..	..	..	..
Congo, Rep.	-6.2	-3.5	-7.9	-0.1	2.3	3.1	..	..	..	..	..	..
Côte d'Ivoire	6.9	6.2	1.8	5.7	6.0	6.5	..	..	..	..	..	..
Equatorial Guinea	-6.4	-5.6	-4.9	2.4	-5.6	-2.3	..	..	..	..	..	..
Eritrea	13.0	3.7	-0.6	2.0	4.9	3.8	..	..	..	..	..	..
Eswatini	2.4	2.2	-3.1	1.3	1.1	1.5	..	..	..	..	..	..
Ethiopia [3]	6.8	8.4	6.1	2.3	6.0	7.5	..	..	..	..	..	..
Gabon	0.8	3.9	-1.9	1.5	2.5	3.6	..	..	..	..	..	..
Gambia, The	7.2	6.1	0.0	3.5	5.5	7.0	..	..	..	..	..	..
Ghana	6.3	6.5	1.1	1.4	2.4	3.6	6.0	7.0	-5.7	-3.2	3.3	..
Guinea	6.2	5.6	4.7	5.5	5.2	5.2	..	..	..	..	..	..
Guinea-Bissau	3.8	4.6	-2.4	3.0	4.0	5.0	..	..	..	..	..	..
Kenya	6.3	5.4	-0.3	4.5	4.7	5.8	5.4	5.2	-5.5	-1.1	..	..
Lesotho	1.5	1.4	-5.8	2.9	3.1	3.2	-4.5	2.6	-21.5	-9.9	-15.3	..
Liberia	1.2	-2.3	-2.9	3.3	4.2	4.7	..	..	..	..	..	..
Madagascar	4.6	4.9	-4.2	2.0	5.8	5.4	..	..	..	..	..	..
Malawi	4.4	5.4	0.8	2.8	3.0	4.5	..	..	..	..	..	..
Mali	4.7	4.8	-2.0	2.5	5.2	5.0	..	..	..	..	..	..
Mauritania	2.1	5.9	-1.5	2.7	3.7	6.0	..	..	..	..	..	..
Mauritius	3.8	3.0	-15.6	3.6	5.9	4.3	..	..	..	..	..	..
Mozambique	3.4	2.3	-1.3	1.7	4.1	6.3	1.2	1.7	-3.5	-1.2	-1.8	0.1
Namibia	1.1	-1.6	-7.3	1.8	1.8	1.5	5.1	-2.7	-11.2	-11.8	-6.0	..
Niger	7.2	5.9	0.8	4.7	8.9	12.1	..	..	..	..	..	..
Nigeria	1.9	2.2	-1.8	1.8	2.1	2.4	2.5	2.0	-6.0	-3.1	0.0	0.4
Rwanda	8.6	9.4	-3.3	4.9	6.4	7.5	8.5	3.6	-12.4	-3.6	-0.7	..
São Tomé and Príncipe	2.9	1.3	3.1	2.7	3.5	4.0	..	..	..	..	..	..
Senegal	6.4	5.3	-0.7	3.1	4.9	8.9	..	..	..	..	..	..
Seychelles	3.8	5.3	-13.3	1.8	4.3	4.2	..	..	..	..	..	..
Sierra Leone	3.4	5.5	-2.2	3.0	3.7	4.0	..	..	..	..	..	..

Real GDP growth *(continued)*

	Annual estimates and forecasts[1] (Percent change)						Quarterly estimates[2] (Percent change, year-on-year)					
	2018	2019	2020e	2021f	2022f	2023f	19Q4	20Q1	20Q2	20Q3	20Q4	21Q1e
Sub-Saharan Africa (continued)												
South Africa	0.8	0.2	-7.0	3.5	2.1	1.5	-0.5	0.4	-17.8	-6.2	-4.1	..
South Sudan [3]	-3.5	-0.3	9.5	-3.4	1.5	3.0	..	..	..	..	..	..
Sudan	-2.3	-2.5	-3.6	0.4	1.1	2.6	..	..	..	..	..	..
Tanzania	5.4	5.8	2.0	4.5	5.5	6.0	..	..	..	..	..	..
Togo [7]	4.9	5.3	0.7	3.4	4.6	5.0	..	..	..	..	..	..
Uganda [3]	6.3	6.4	3.0	3.3	4.7	6.4	9.0	0.0	-6.1	-0.1	1.6	..
Zambia	3.5	1.4	-3.0	1.8	2.9	3.8	0.2	-0.3	-5.9	-3.1	-2.7	..
Zimbabwe	4.8	-8.1	-8.0	3.9	5.1	5.0	..	..	..	..	..	..

Sources: World Bank; Haver Analytics.

Note: e = estimate; f = forecast.

1. Aggregate growth rates calculated using GDP weights at average 2010-19 prices and market exchange rates.

2. Quarterly estimates are based on non-seasonally-adjusted real GDP, except for advanced economies, as well as Algeria, Ecuador, Morocco, Poland and Tunisia. Data for Bosnia and Herzegovina are from the production approach. Data for Timor-Leste represent non-oil GDP. Quarterly data for Jamaica are gross value added.

Regional averages are calculated based on data from the following economies.

East Asia and Pacific: China, Indonesia, Malaysia, Mongolia, the Philippines, Thailand, and Vietnam.

Europe and Central Asia: Albania, Armenia, Belarus, Bosnia and Herzegovina, Bulgaria, Croatia, Georgia, Hungary, Kazakhstan, Moldova, North Macedonia, Poland, Romania, the Russian Federation, Serbia, Turkey, and Ukraine.

Latin America and the Caribbean: Argentina, Belize, Bolivia, Brazil, Chile, Colombia, Costa Rica, the Dominican Republic, Ecuador, El Salvador, Guatemala, Honduras, Jamaica, Mexico, Nicaragua, Panama, Paraguay, Peru, and Uruguay.

Middle East and North Africa: Bahrain, the Arab Republic of Egypt, the Islamic Republic of Iran, Jordan, Kuwait, Morocco, Qatar, Saudi Arabia, Tunisia, the United Arab Emirates, and West Bank and Gaza.

South Asia: India, Maldives, Nepal and Sri Lanka.

Sub-Saharan Africa: Botswana, Ghana, Kenya, Lesotho, Mozambique, Namibia, Nigeria, Rwanda, South Africa, Tanzania, Uganda, and Zambia.

3. Annual GDP is on fiscal year basis, as per reporting practice in the country.

4. GDP data for Pakistan are based on factor cost. For Bangladesh, Bhutan, Nepal, and Pakistan, the column labeled 2019 refers to FY2018/19. For India, the column labeled 2018 refers to FY2018/19.

5. Quarterly data are preliminary.

6. Forecasts beyond 2021 are excluded due to a high degree of uncertainty.

7. For Togo, growth figures in 2018 and 2019 are based on pre-2020 rebasing GDP estimates.

To download the data in this table, please visit www.worldbank.org/gep.

Data and Forecast Conventions

The macroeconomic forecasts presented in this report are prepared by staff of the Prospects Group of the Equitable Growth, Finance and Institutions Vice-Presidency, in coordination with staff from the Macroeconomics, Trade, and Investment Global Practice and from regional and country offices, and with input from regional Chief Economist offices. They are the result of an iterative process that incorporates data, macro-econometric models, and judgment.

Data. Data used to prepare country forecasts come from a variety of sources. National Income Accounts (NIA), Balance of Payments (BOP), and fiscal data are from Haver Analytics; the World Development Indicators by the World Bank; the World Economic Outlook, Balance of Payments Statistics, and International Financial Statistics by the International Monetary Fund. Population data and forecasts are from the United Nations World Population Prospects. Country- and lending-group classifications are from the World Bank. The Prospects Group's internal databases include high-frequency indicators such as indus-trial production, consumer price indexes, emerging market bond indexes (EMBI), exchange rates, exports, imports, policy rates, and stock market indexes, based on data from Bloomberg, Haver Analytics, IMF Balance of Payments Statistics, IMF International Financial Statistics, and J. P. Morgan.

Aggregations. Aggregate growth for the world and all sub-groups of countries (such as regions and income groups) is calculated using GDP weights at average 2010-19 prices and market exchange rates of country-specific growth rates. Income groups are defined as in the World Bank's classification of country groups.

Forecast process. The process starts with initial assumptions about advanced-economy growth and commodity price forecasts. These are used as conditioning assumptions for the first set of growth forecasts for EMDEs, which are produced using macroeconometric models, accounting frameworks to ensure national account identities and global consistency, estimates of spillovers from major economies, and high-frequency indicators. These forecasts are then evaluated to ensure consistency of treatment across similar EMDEs. This is followed by extensive discussions with World Bank country teams, who conduct continuous macroeconomic monitoring and dialogue with country authorities and finalize growth forecasts for EMDEs. The Prospects Group prepares advanced-economy and commo-dity price forecasts. Throughout the forecasting process, staff use macro-econometric models that allow the combination of judgement and consist-ency with model-based insights.

Global Economic Prospects: Selected Topics, 2015-21

Growth and Business Cycles		
Economics of Pandemics		
	Regional macroeconomic implications of COVID-19	June 2020, Special Focus
	Lasting Scars of the COVID-19 Pandemic	June 2020, chapter 3
	Adding fuel to the fire: Cheap oil during the pandemic	June 2020, chapter 4
	How deep will the COVID-19 recession be?	June 2020, box 1.1
	Scenarios of possible global growth outcomes	June 2020, box 1.3
	How does informality aggravate the impact of COVID-19?	June 2020, box 1.4
	The impact of COVID-19 on global value chains	June 2020, box SF1
	How do deep recessions affect potential output?	June 2020, box 3.1
	How do disasters affect productivity?	June 2020, box 3.2
	Reforms after the 2014-16 oil price plunge	June 2020, box 4.1
	The macroeconomic effects of pandemics and epidemics: A literature review	June 2020, annex 3.1
Informality		
	How does informality aggravate the impact of COVID-19?	June 2020, box 1.4
	Growing in the shadow: Challenges of informality	January 2019, chapter 3
	Linkages between formal and informal sectors	January 2019, box 3.1
	Regional dimensions of informality: An overview	January 2019, box 3.2
	Casting a shadow: Productivity in formal and informal firms	January 2019, box 3.3
	Under the magnifying glass: How do policies affect informality?	January 2019, box 3.4
	East Asia and Pacific	January 2019, box 2.1.1
	Europe and Central Asia	January 2019, box 2.2.1
	Latin America and the Caribbean	January 2019, box 2.3.1
	Middle East and North Africa	January 2019, box 2.4.1
	South Asia	January 2019, box 2.5.1
	Sub-Saharan Africa	January 2019, box 2.6.1
Inflation		
	Emerging inflation pressures: Cause for alarm?	June 2021, chapter 4
	Low for how much longer? Inflation in low-income countries	January 2020, Special Focus 2
	Currency depreciation, inflation, and central bank independence	June 2019, Special Focus 1.2
	The great disinflation	January 2019, box 1.1
Growth prospects		
	Global growth scenarios	January 2021, box 1.4
	The macroeconomic effects of pandemics and epidemics: A literature review	June 2020, annex 3.1
	How deep will the COVID-19 recession be?	June 2020, box 1.1
	Lasting Scars of the COVID-19 Pandemic	June 2020, chapter 3
	Regional macroeconomic implications of COVID-19	June 2020, Special Focus
	Growth in low-income countries: Evolution, prospects, and policies	June 2019, Special Focus 2.1
	Long-term growth prospects: Downgraded no more?	June 2018, box 1.1
Global output gap		
	Is the global economy turning the corner?	January 2018, box 1.1
Potential growth		
	Global economy: Heading into a decade of disappointments?	January 2021, chapter 3
	How do deep recessions affect potential output in EMDEs?	June 2020, box 3.1
	Building solid foundations: How to promote potential growth	January 2018, chapter 3
	What is potential growth?	January 2018, box 3.1
	Understanding the recent productivity slowdown: Facts and explanations	January 2018, box 3.2
	Moving together? Investment and potential output	January 2018, box 3.3
	The long shadow of contractions over potential output	January 2018, box 3.4
	Productivity and investment growth during reforms	January 2018, box 3.5
	East Asia and Pacific	January 2018, box 2.1.1
	Europe and Central Asia	January 2018, box 2.2.1
	Latin America and the Caribbean	January 2018, box 2.3.1
	Middle East and North Africa	January 2018, box 2.4.1
	South Asia	January 2018, box 2.5.1
	Sub-Saharan Africa	January 2018, box 2.6.1

Global Economic Prospects: Selected Topics, 2015-21

Growth and Business Cycles

Cross-border spillovers

Who catches a cold when emerging markets sneeze?	January 2016, chapter 3
Sources of the growth slowdown in BRICS	January 2016, box 3.1
Understanding cross-border growth spillovers	January 2016, box 3.2
Within-region spillovers	January 2016, box 3.3
East Asia and Pacific	January 2016, box 2.1.1
Europe and Central Asia	January 2016, box 2.2.1
Latin America and the Caribbean	January 2016, box 2.3.1
Middle East and North Africa	January 2016, box 2.4.1
South Asia	January 2016, box 2.5.1
Sub-Saharan Africa	January 2016, box 2.6.1

Productivity

How do disasters affect productivity?	June 2020, box 3.2
Fading promise: How to rekindle productivity growth	January 2020, chapter 3
EMDE regional productivity trends and bottlenecks	January 2020, box 3.1
Sectoral sources of productivity growth	January 2020, box 3.2
Patterns of total factor productivity: A firm perspective	January 2020, box 3.3
Debt, financial crises, and productivity	January 2020, box 3.4
Labor productivity in East Asia and Pacific: Trends and drivers	January 2020, box 2.1.1
Labor productivity in Europe and Central Asia: Trends and drivers	January 2020, box 2.2.1
Labor productivity in Latin America and the Caribbean: Trends and drivers	January 2020, box 2.3.1
Labor productivity in Middle East and North Africa: Trends and drivers	January 2020, box 2.4.1
Labor productivity in South Asia: Trends and drivers	January 2020, box 2.5.1
Labor productivity in Sub-Saharan Africa: Trends and drivers	January 2020, box 2.6.1

Investment slowdown

Investment: Subdued prospects, strong needs	June 2019, Special Focus 11
Weak investment in uncertain times: Causes, implications, and policy responses	January 2017, chapter 3
Investment-less credit booms	January 2017, box 3.1
Implications of rising uncertainty for investment in EMDEs	January 2017, box 3.2
Investment slowdown in China	January 2017, box 3.3
Interactions between public and private investment	January 2017, box 3.4
East Asia and Pacific	January 2017, box 2.1.1
Europe and Central Asia	January 2017, box 2.2.1
Latin America and the Caribbean	January 2017, box 2.3.1
Middle East and North Africa	January 2017, box 2.4.1
South Asia	January 2016, box 2.5.1
Sub-Saharan Africa	January 2016, box 2.6.1

Forecast uncertainty

Scenarios of possible global growth outcomes	June 2020, box 1.3
Quantifying uncertainties in global growth forecasts	June 2016, Special Focus 2

Fiscal space

Having space and using it: Fiscal policy challenges and developing economies	January 2015, chapter 3
Fiscal policy in low-income countries	January 2015, box 3.1
What affects the size of fiscal multipliers?	January 2015, box 3.2
Chile's fiscal rule—an example of success	January 2015, box 3.3
Narrow fiscal space and the risk of a debt crisis	January 2015, box 3.4
Revenue mobilization in South Asia: Policy challenges and recommendations	January 2015, box 2.3

Other topics

Education demographics and global inequality	January 2018, Special Focus 2
Recent developments in emerging and developing country labor markets	June 2015, box 1.3
Linkages between China and Sub-Saharan Africa	June 2015, box 2.1
What does weak growth mean for poverty in the future?	January 2015, box 1.1
What does a slowdown in China mean for Latin America and the Caribbean?	January 2015, box 2.2

Global Economic Prospects: Selected Topics, 2015-21

Prospects Group:
Selected Other Publications on the Global Economy, 2015-21

Commodity Markets Outlook	
Causes and consequences of metal price shocks	April 2021
Persistence of commodity shocks	October 2020
Food price shocks: Channels and implications	April 2019
The implications of tariffs for commodity markets	October 2018, box
The changing of the guard: Shifts in industrial commodity demand	October 2018
Oil exporters: Policies and challenges	April 2018
Investment weakness in commodity exporters	January 2017
OPEC in historical context: Commodity agreements and market fundamentals	October 2016
From energy prices to food prices: Moving in tandem?	July 2016
Resource development in an era of cheap commodities	April 2016
Weak growth in emerging market economies: What does it imply for commodity markets?	January 2016
Understanding El Niño: What does it mean for commodity markets?	October 2015
How important are China and India in global commodity consumption?	July 2015
Anatomy of the last four oil price crashes	April 2015
Putting the recent plunge in oil prices in perspective	January 2015

Inflation in Emerging and Developing Economies: Evolution, Drivers, and Policies	
Inflation: Concepts, evolution, and correlates	Chapter 1
Understanding global inflation synchronization	Chapter 2
Sources of inflation: Global and domestic drivers	Chapter 3
Inflation expectations: Review and evidence	Chapter 4
Inflation and exchange rate pass-through	Chapter 5
Inflation in low-income countries	Chapter 6
Poverty impact of food price shocks and policies	Chapter 7

A Decade After the Global Recession: Lessons and Challenges for Emerging and Developing Economies	
A decade after the global recession: Lessons and challenges	Chapter 1
What happens during global recessions?	Chapter 2
Macroeconomic developments	Chapter 3
Financial market developments	Chapter 4
Macroeconomic and financial sector policies	Chapter 5
Prospects, risks, and vulnerabilities	Chapter 6
Policy challenges	Chapter 7
The role of the World Bank Group	Chapter 8

Global Waves of Debt: Causes and Consequences	
Debt: Evolution, causes, and consequences	Chapter 1
Benefits and costs of debt: The dose makes the poison	Chapter 2
Global waves of debt: What goes up must come down?	Chapter 3
The fourth wave: Ripple or tsunami?	Chapter 4
Debt and financial crises: From euphoria to distress	Chapter 5
Policies: Turning mistakes into experience	Chapter 6

Prospects Group:
Selected Other Publications on the Global Economy, 2015-21

Global Productivity: Trends, Drivers, and Policies	
Global productivity trends	Chapter 1
What explains productivity growth	Chapter 2
What happens to productivity during major adverse events?	Chapter 3
Productivity convergence: Is anyone catching up?	Chapter 4
Regional dimensions of productivity: Trends, explanations, and policies	Chapter 5
Productivity: Technology, demand, and employment trade-offs	Chapter 6
Sectoral sources of productivity growth	Chapter 7

The Long Shadow of Informality: Challenges and Policies	
Overview	Chapter 1
Understanding the informal economy: Concepts and trends	Chapter 2
Growing apart or moving together? Synchronization of informal- and formal-economy business cycles	Chapter 3
Lagging behind: informality and development	Chapter 4
Informality in emerging market and developing economies: Regional dimensions	Chapter 5
Tackling informality: Policy options	Chapter 6

High-Frequency Monitoring	
Global Monthly newsletter	

ECO-AUDIT
Environmental Benefits Statement

The World Bank Group is committed to reducing its environmental footprint. In support of this commitment, we leverage electronic publishing options and print-on-demand technology, which is located in regional hubs worldwide. Together, these initiatives enable print runs to be lowered and shipping distances decreased, resulting in reduced paper consumption, chemical use, greenhouse gas emissions, and waste.

We follow the recommended standards for paper use set by the Green Press Initiative. The majority of our books are printed on Forest Stewardship Council (FSC)-certified paper, with nearly all containing 50-100 percent recycled content. The recycled fiber in our book paper is either unbleached or bleached using totally chlorine-free (TCF), processed chlorine-free (PCF), or enhanced elemental chlorine-free (EECF) processes.

More information about the Bank's environmental philosophy can be found at http://www.worldbank.org/corporateresponsibility.